Polycrisis and Economic Development in the Global South

Global polycrisis refers to the simultaneous occurrence of multiple interconnected crises. It is marked by the convergence and interaction of combined events, such as geopolitical tensions, economic instability, environmental degradation, public health emergencies, and social disturbance. In this context, this book explores the challenges and opportunities encountered by the Global South amid political instability, climate change, humanitarian crises, technological advancements, and regional cooperation.

The book adopts a multidisciplinary framework, integrating theoretical studies with empirical cases from various southern regions in Africa, Asia, and Latin America. This approach helps to foster an in-depth understanding of the complex challenges associated with development in these regions. The book emphasizes the perspectives and experiences of Global South countries, providing a platform for their voices to be heard. This allows readers to gain a more nuanced understanding of the unique contexts, perspectives, and successful experiences of countries in Africa, Asia, and Latin America. Furthermore, it investigates issues such as governance, security, migration, development, and emergent technologies, illuminates the role of regional organizations in fostering regional integration, peace, and stability and ultimately, provides a comprehensive and refined analysis of the Global South that challenges prevalent stereotypes and offers new perspectives on the world's complex realities today. It includes case studies that enhance the practical relevance of the book, offering real-world examples that illustrate the theoretical concepts and highlighting successful approaches to addressing development challenges.

The book will appeal to scholars, researchers, and students interested in comprehending and addressing the challenges encountered by the Global South in a time of global polycrisis.

Hebatallah Adam is a professor of Economics, founder and director of Jindal Centre for the Global South (JCGS) at Jindal School of International Affairs (JSIA), O.P. Jindal Global University, Haryana, India.

Ravinder Rena is a professor of Economics in the Faculty of Management Sciences, Durban University of Technology, Durban, South Africa.

Routledge Studies in Development Economics

Special Economic Zones in South Asia
Structural Change, Competitiveness and Growth
Aradhna Aggarwal

Infrastructure Policy and Inequality
Michael A. Cohen

Responsible Business and Sustainable Development
The Use of Data and Metrics in the Global South
Edited by David Mhlanga and Mufaro Dzingirai

Unlocking Economic Development
The Unlearning Process of Nations
Ahmed Tahiri Jouti

Economic Shocks and Globalisation
Between Deglobalisation and Slowbalisation
Edited by Elsabé Loots

The Economics of Financial Inclusion
Edited by Firdous Ahmad Malik and Tarika Singh Sikarwar

Financial Sustainability of Local Governments in Southern Africa
In Pursuit of Sustainable Cities and Communities
Edited by Nirmala Dorasamy and Tonderai Kapesa

The Political Economy of Underdevelopment in Sub-Saharan Africa
Christopher E. S. Warburton

Polycrisis and Economic Development in the Global South
Edited by Hebatallah Adam and Ravinder Rena

For more information about this series, please visit: www.routledge.com/Routledge-Studies-in-Development-Economics/book-series/SE0266

Polycrisis and Economic Development in the Global South

Edited by Hebatallah Adam and
Ravinder Rena

Routledge
Taylor & Francis Group
LONDON AND NEW YORK

First published 2025
by Routledge
4 Park Square, Milton Park, Abingdon, Oxon OX14 4RN

and by Routledge
605 Third Avenue, New York, NY 10158

Routledge is an imprint of the Taylor & Francis Group, an informa business

British Library Cataloguing-in-Publication Data
A catalogue record for this book is available from the British Library

Library of Congress Cataloging-in-Publication Data
Names: Adam, Hebatallah, editor. | Rena, Ravinder, editor.
Title: Polycrisis and economic development in the Global South / edited by Hebatallah Adam and Ravinder Rena.
Description: Abingdon, Oxon ; New York, NY : Routledge, 2025. | Series: Routledge studies in development economics | Includes bibliographical references and index.
Identifiers: LCCN 2024032368 (print) | LCCN 2024032369 (ebook) | ISBN 9781032694320 (hardback) | ISBN 9781032694313 (paperback) | ISBN 9781032694337 (ebook)
Subjects: LCSH: Economic development--Developing countries. | Crises--Economic aspects--Developing countries.
Classification: LCC HC59.7 .P585 2025 (print) | LCC HC59.7 (ebook) | DDC 338.9009172/4--dc23/eng/20240808
LC record available at https://lccn.loc.gov/2024032368
LC ebook record available at https://lccn.loc.gov/2024032369

ISBN: 978-1-032-69432-0 (hbk)
ISBN: 978-1-032-69431-3 (pbk)
ISBN: 978-1-032-69433-7 (ebk)

DOI: 10.4324/9781032694337

Typeset in Times New Roman
by SPi Technologies India Pvt Ltd (Straive)

Contents

Figures

Tables

Contributors' and Editors' Biographies

Abakporo, Princewill Chukwuma holds a faculty position in Theatre Arts Programme, Bowen University, Iwo, Osun State, Nigeria. The beacon of his research interests is culture, indigenous epistemologies, decolonization, and aesthetics. He has a master of arts degree in Theatre Arts and is currently a doctoral candidate at the Imo State University, Owerri, Nigeria.

Adam, Hebatallah is an academician, editor, and scholar with over two decades of teaching and research experience in International Economic Development. She works as a professor of Economics, assistant dean for Academic Affairs (master's program) at Jindal School of International Affairs (JSIA), founder and director of Jindal Centre for the Global South and associate director at Jindal India Institute – O.P. Jindal Global University, Haryana – India. Before this, she was affiliated with the Department of Economics, Faculty of Business, Ain Shams University, Cairo-Egypt. In addition to her teaching experience, she had also worked at the German University in Cairo and the Arab Academy for Science, Technology, and Maritime Transport.

Dr. Adam is the visionary behind establishing the Jindal Centre for the Global South, a distinguished research center affiliated with Jindal Global University's (JGU) School of International Affairs. The primary mission of the Centre is to promote cutting-edge global research in fields such as Global South studies, South-South Cooperation, and Sustainable Development. Beyond that, it aspires to become an intellectual hub that fosters inventive solutions to the problems encountered by the Global South.

Dr. Adam has founded the Africa Dialogue Forum (ADF), an initiative to bring together a coalition of organizations and intellectuals committed to advancing the Better Africa Cause. The ADF is a forum for substantive conversations with internationally renowned experts, academicians, and influential African thought leaders. These dialogues are centered on extensive research and promoting innovative ideas and solutions to achieve measurable and sustainable transformations across Africa.

Dr. Adam has earned her BA, MA, and PhD degrees from universities in Egypt and France, including the Department de Gestion et de Commerce International (D.G.C.I.) at Faculty of Business Ain Shams University, Poitiers University in France, and I.A.E. de Paris – Sorbonne University, France. She has numerous publications in poverty, financial inclusion, fintech, Global South, international development, and development finance. Additionally, she has supervised master's and PhD students from both India and Egypt.

Dr. Adam's research interests relate to Global South Studies, Political Economy of Development, International Trade, Green Economics, and International Development Economics.

Agarwal, Arth is a research intern at the Centre for Security Studies, Jindal School of International Affairs, O.P. Jindal Global University, India. He is a recipient of the Emile Boutmy Scholarship (Issued by Sciences Po, Paris). He has been published on various issues, such as Leadership Dynamics in the Global South and the meteoric rise of the Chinese Geopolitical/Geo Economic Apparatus. He has worked as a researcher with the Center for Policy Research and Governance, Jindal Centre for the Global South, and Centre for a New South Asia.

Agarwal, Priti is an assistant professor at the Jindal School of Government and Public Policy, O.P. Jindal Global University. She completed her PhD in Economics in 2021 from the Centre for International Trade and Development, Jawaharlal Nehru University, New Delhi. She is particularly interested in empirical work pertaining to Sustainable Development, Environmental and Natural Resource Economics. Her research work is published in peer-reviewed international journals. She has over ten years of teaching experience in several reputed colleges of the University of Delhi before joining O.P. Jindal Global University.

Agha, Ambreen is an associate professor at O.P. Jindal Global University. Before joining the University, she worked as a research fellow at the Indian Council of World Affairs (ICWA) in New Delhi. At the Council, she was engaged in research on religion and conflict, particularly conflict in Afghanistan. Dr. Ambreen Agha's research focuses on comparative studies of Muslim societies, emphasizing the interplay of identity politics, gender, and religion. In her research, she explores and understands women's role in religious revivalist movements and how gender is mobilized in nationalist politics.

Agha, Aqsa specializes in medieval Indian history and has worked on gender, state, and political transition in eighteenth-century India. Besides her interest in history, she has been associated with organizations in the field of human rights, social justice, and participatory research engaging with grassroots communities. She holds her PhD from Jawaharlal Nehru University,

India, and presently serves as a faculty member in the Department of History at SRM University, Andhra Pradesh, India.

Bhutia, Ugen's academic pursuits are centered on exploring the multifaceted discourses that arise from the intersection of media, culture, nationalism, and urbanism. Holding MPhil in Mass Communication and Journalism and a PhD in History from Sikkim University, he presently serves as a faculty member in the Department of Liberal Arts at SRM University, Andhra Pradesh.

Bikku's academic pursuits center on exploring the Human-Animal Interface, Nomadic Pastoralism and Conservation, Religion and Ecology Climate Change. Currently, he is working in the areas of Tribes in Colonial and Modern India, Sustainable Cities and Religious Deities, Changing Geographic Belongingness among the Tribes of South India. He holds PhD in Anthropology from the University of Hyderabad, India. Dr. Bikku was postdoctoral research fellow at the Department of Anthropology, University College London (UCL) London, United Kingdom. He presently serves as a faculty member in the Department of Liberal Arts at SRM University, Andhra Pradesh, India.

Deka, Chandna's research focuses on Socio-political Philosophy, Philosophy of Religion, and Ethics. She has a PhD in Philosophy from the Department of Humanities and Social Sciences, IIT Guwahati. She presently serves as a faculty member in the Department of Liberal Arts at SRM University, Andhra Pradesh.

Ferraz dos Santos, Rafael holds a bachelor's degree in Production Engineering with a specialization in Oil and Gas Engineering, graduated from the Alberto Luiz Coimbra Institute for Graduate Studies and Research in Engineering at the Federal University of Rio de Janeiro (COPPE/UFRJ). Currently pursuing a master's degree in Transportation Engineering at the same institution (PET/COPPE/UFRJ), focusing on research in Transportation Sustainability. Serving as an engineer at the Exploration and Production Logistics Center (EP), in the maritime fleet analysis and allocation sector, located at the Leopoldo Américo Miguez de Mello Research and Development Center (CENPES).

Homer, Stephen T Homer, a seasoned academic and researcher, specializes in business management, CSR, and sustainable development. Since joining Sunway University in 2017, initially as a PhD student, he has progressed to senior lecturer, significantly contributing to academia. His doctoral research on Perceived Corporate Citizenship from 2017 to 2020 resulted in seminal publications, establishing a foundation for his ongoing scholarly work. Dr. Homer excels in teaching courses like CSR, Business Ethics, and Principles of Management, consistently receiving positive feedback. He has also presented his research at international conferences, earning accolades such as the Best Presentation Award at the International El Ruha Congress of Social Science in 2020. Beyond academia, Dr. Homer actively engages in research projects focusing on sustainable business education post-pandemic and developing CSR evaluative tools. His interdisciplinary research includes innovative projects like "Artistically Exploring Future Cities with AI," showcasing his collaborative spirit. In 2022, he enhanced his teaching skills with a postgraduate diploma in teaching from Open University Malaysia. Currently, as director of the Yunus Social Business Centre at Sunway University, Dr. Homer spearheads entrepreneurship and responsible management education initiatives, overseeing operations, strategizing long-term goals, and fostering external collaborations. His work advances CSR, sustainable development, and management education, inspiring students and colleagues alike.

Hussain, Irfan is a dedicated economist and academic, with a PhD in Economics and a passion for teaching and research. With over 14 years of professional experience, he has held various positions, including visiting lecturer of Economics at Bahauddin Zakariya University, Bahadur Layyah Campus (since 2014), NCBA Multan Campus (2019–2023), and GC University Faisalabad (2015–2018). He has also taught at Govt Degree College Choubara (2008–2009) and Prime College of Commerce (2009–2010). Irfan's expertise lies in economics, and he has taught various courses, including MPhil economics classes. He is committed to inspiring and educating future generations of economists and leaders.

Iorbo, Rita is an assistant professor at the Jindal School of International Affairs, O.P. Jindal Global University in Sonipat, Haryana, India. She holds a doctorate and BSc in Sociology focusing on social inclusion and psychosocial issues of forcibly displaced persons and a master of arts degree in international peace studies from the United Nations – mandated University for Peace, Costa Rica. Her research interests include Peace and Conflict Studies, human security, forced displacement and Humanitarian Crisis. She is an Affiliate of the Refugee Law Initiative at the University of London.

Issac, Anushka Lydia brings a unique perspective with a background in Engineering [Hons.] and an MBA. She holds prestigious credentials such as an FHEA and a Lead IQA Certificate; she has the skills and knowledge to design, deliver, and assess high-quality learning experiences in higher education. Her passion for understanding people and their personalities has propelled her to excel in communications and public speaking at an international level. As a lecturer and program manager at Westford University College, she actively contributes to the development of students. Her PhD research from the University of Plymouth, UK, focuses on flexible work arrangements.

Kasatkin, Petr I. is a professor at the Department of World Political Processes at Moscow State Institute of International Relations (MGIMO University). His research interests are concentrated in the study and evaluation of political problems of international relations and non-state actors in the world politics. The most valuable scientific results were obtained in assessing the development of modern scientific and educational policy and the philosophy and axiology of education.

Kolesnikova, Tatiana V. is a professor at the Department of International Business at Saint-Petersburg State University of Aerospace Instrumentation. Her current research interests focus on protectionism in government economic policies, international economic relations, and economic growth in developed and developing countries. The priority areas of research are related to determining the optimal economic strategy, which is aimed at ensuring economic security and international competitiveness simultaneously.

Kovalchuk, Julia is a professor at Asset Management Department at Moscow State Institute of International Relations (MGIMO University). Choosing strategic aspects of industrial development as a scientific priority, she has long specialized in industrial modernization. She has accumulated a wealth of experience in strategic research of the high-tech industry, including competition and cooperation factors. Her current research interests include the digital transformation of companies and value creation in the digital arena, considering the understanding of resource constraints.

Kumari, Mamta is working as an assistant professor of Economics at Alliance University, Bengaluru. She teaches subjects like microeconomics, macroeconomics, international economics, law and economics, research methodology, and international business. She holds a doctoral degree in Economics from the Indian Institute of Technology Patna on "Trade Facilitation: South Asia and Beyond." Her work contributes to assessing the benefits of trade facilitation (TF) from the global and regional perspectives.

She has published several research papers in international peer-reviewed journals, such as *Maritime Economics & Logistics*, *South Asia Economic Journal*, *Millennial Asia*, and *International Trade Journal*. She has presented papers at renowned conferences and attended workshops related to her interests. Her research interests include macroeconomics, international trade, political economy, economic integration, sustainable development, and the structural gravity model.

Malik, Avisha is a research scholar in School of Humanities and Social Sciences, Thapar Institute of Engineering and Technology, Patiala, Punjab. Her scholarly pursuits are concentrated in international economics, reflecting her commitment to advancing theoretical and empirical insights into the intricacies of global economic phenomena. She has published research papers in the ABDC category and Scopus-indexed journals and has presented her work at various national and international conferences.

Nirola, Nupur is an applied macroeconomist with research interests in growth models, institutional economics, and fiscal federalism. She has presented her research work in various international and national educational organizations such as Illinois State University, USA; University of Cambridge; University of Seville, Spain; University of Ljubljana, IIM Bangalore; IIT Kharagpur; National Institute of Public Finance and Policy; Gujarat National Law University. She has works published in international journals like *Annals of Regional Science*, *Heliyon*, *Economic Change and Restructuring*, and *Regional Studies Association*. She also referees for journals: *Nature*, *Public Administration and Development*, *Cogent Economics & Finance*, and *Journal of Infrastructure, Policy and Development*.

Nwodo, Ikenna Paulinus is an alumnus of Enugu State University of Science and Technology and University of Nigeria, Nsukka, where he obtained bachelor's and master's degrees in economics. He also holds a master's in business administration – MBA (Business Analytics). He is a Central Bank of Nigeria (CBN) scholar. He is also a research expert and data analyst with comprehensive publications in high-impact factor journals (Scopus and Web of Science indexed). His research interests include microeconometrics, macroeconometrics, advanced timeseries analysis, panel data modeling, environmental and health economics, and applied econometrics.

Oda, Sandra holds a bachelor's degree in Civil Engineering from the Federal University of São Carlos (1992), a master's degree in Transportation Engineering with a focus on unpaved road management from the University of São Paulo (1995), and a PhD in Transportation Engineering from the University of São Paulo (2000), where she defended her thesis titled "Analysis of the Technical Feasibility of Using Asphalt-Rubber Binder in Paving Works." She is an associate professor in the Department of Transportation Engineering at the Polytechnic School of the Federal University of Rio de Janeiro, where she has been a faculty member since 2012. Currently, she serves as the academic coordinator of the Transport Engineering Program (PET/COPPE), PET's representative on the CPGP, and a member of the PIBIC-UFRJ Institutional Committee. Her research interests include the use of tailings, waste, and fibers in paving materials, the application of life cycle assessment (LCA) in the selection of paving materials, sidewalk management systems, and the conversion of asphalt sidewalk heat into electrical energy.

Ohenhen, Stanley Timeyin is an associate professor of Theatre Management Arts Administration, Advocacy, and Entrepreneurship. He has a bachelor of arts degree in Theatre Arts of the University of Benin, Benin City, Nigeria, an MA and a PhD, both of the University of Ibadan, Nigeria, specializing in Theatre Management and Arts Administration. His areas of study have been the management and economics of the performing arts and culture; Indigenous epistemologies and practices of the Global South and cultural renaissance; colonialism and the Global South region's agenda for decolonization; eco-criticism; and the relationship between theatre and society, specifically how African theatre and cultural practice, as well as other Indigenous performative activities contribute to the fight against the sustained colonization and neo-colonization of the Global South, and the degradation of the environment and global climate. He is a faculty of the Theatre Arts Programme and is currently the Provost of the College of Liberal Studies at Bowen University, Iwo, Osun State, Nigeria.

Omeje, Ambrose Nnaemeka is currently a lecturer in the Department of Economics, University of Nigeria, Nsukka. Dr. A.N. Omeje has published many papers in both international and local peer-reviewed journals, and several conference papers. He has also published some chapters in edited books. He has also undertaken research and consultancy for SAVI-DFID, UNICEF and was an assistant facilitator for Central Bank of Nigeria – South-East Entrepreneurship Development Centre (SEEDC) Training on Entrepreneurship and Development, Nigeria. He is a member of the Nigerian Economic Society (NES). His research interests span across development economics, financial economics, econometrics, environmental economics, entrepreneurships, micro- and macro- economic/econometrics.

Panigrahi, Manoj Kumar is an assistant professor and co-director of the Centre for Northeast Asia Studies at the Jindal School of International Affairs at O.P. Jindal Global University. He is also a non-residential research fellow at Taiwan NextGen Foundation, Taipei.

He teaches courses on Taiwanese History and Politics, Cross-strait relations between Taiwan and China, East Asian Politics, and Peace-making in Ethnic Conflicts.

His recent publication includes a monograph published, titled *Taiwan-China Conundrum: What Can be India's Policy Trajectories?* (October 2023), and a co-edited book titled *Drifts and Dynamics: Russia's Ukraine War and Northeast Asia* (August 2022).

Rena, Ravinder is a profound academician and distinguished scholar in economics with over 31 years of teaching and research experience. Dr. Rena is a professor of Economics at the DUT Business School, Faculty of Management Sciences, Durban University of Technology, South Africa. He is also an adjunct professor of Economics at Monarch Business School, Monarch University, Switzerland. He published widely in development economics, especially on African issues. He published over 150 peer-reviewed articles in reputed journals and 50 chapters in edited books across the globe. He is the founding editor-in-chief of the *International Journal of Education,*

Economics and Development. He supervised over 60 PhDs, MPhils, and masters' theses and dissertations across the globe. As a chairman and panel member, he served on many academic and professional committees. He has also been an external examiner/moderator for master's and PhD at different Universities in Africa, Europe, Asia, America, and Australia.

Sah, Ash Narayan is currently working as an associate professor specializing in Economics, Econometrics, and Finance in School of Humanities and Social Sciences, Thapar Institute of Engineering and Technology in Patiala, Punjab. He earned his doctoral degree in Finance from the University of Hyderabad, India. With over 20 research publications in Web of Science and Scopus indexed journals, Dr. Sah's academic contributions have been recognized internationally, with two of his papers being selected for prestigious conferences at IIM Kozhikode and IIM Kolkata. He has authored two books – *Data Analysis Using Microsoft Excel* and *Statistics Management using Microsoft Excel*, showcasing his expertise in the field. His research interests include Financial Markets and Macroeconomics, reflecting his diverse academic pursuits. Notably, he has also undertaken a research project for the National Stock Exchange (NSE) on Stock Market Seasonality, adding to his credentials as a researcher and academician.

Sahu, Debendra is an assistant professor and assistant dean for online programs at Jindal School of International Affairs (JSIA), O.P. Jindal Global University. Dr. Sahu is also an assistant director at the Jindal India Institute, a strategic initiative that promotes the positive aspects and achievements of India and spreads global awareness about India's extraordinary potential in the twenty-first century. Dr. Sahu holds a PhD in Japanese Studies from the School of International Studies, Jawaharlal Nehru University. Dr. Sahu was a recipient of the Monbukagakusho fellowship and pursued research at the University of Tokyo. Dr. Sahu has interviewed various high-profile dignitaries, including Mr. Shinzo Abe, former prime minister of Japan, for his research. He was chosen from India in the prestigious Program for Human Resource Development in Asia for Peacebuilding commissioned by the Ministry of Foreign Affairs of Japan. Dr. Sahu contributed to the Japan-South Asia and Japan-Korean Peninsula segment of an illustrious database, "The World and Japan," funded by grants-in-aid from the Ministry of Education, Japan, and Japan Society for Promotion of Science. Dr. Sahu previously worked at the University Grants Commission, the apex regulator of higher education in India and focused on the internationalization of higher education and implementation of the National Education Policy, 2020.

Santos, Andrea Souza is a Brazilian professor, member of the "Women in Green Hydrogen Network." Andrea has 18 years of significant experience in the environmental area. She has been working with sustainability and climate change issues, including public policy on climate change, and the development of studies and projects for national and international institutions. Biologist, PhD in Transportation Engineering, PhD from COPPE – Alberto Luiz Coimbra Institute of Graduate Studies and Engineering Research of the Federal University of Rio de Janeiro – UFRJ (2014); Master in Sustainable Development from the Center for Sustainable Development of the University of Brasília – UnB (2008); Bachelor in Biological Sciences from the Catholic University of Salvador (2001). She was the coordinator of Climate Change and Sustainability for the Ministry of Environment, Brazil (2008–2009). She is the executive secretary of the Brazilian Panel on Climate Change (2009–currently). She acts as a senior consultant in the areas of environment, climate change policies; climate change (mitigation; vulnerabilities, impacts, adaptation; and resilience of cities); smart cities; transportation; and sustainability. Currently, she is an adjunct professor at COPPE/UFRJ, researcher and coordinator of the Sustainable Transport Lab (LabTS), and vice coordinator of the Transportation Engineering Program – PET/COPPE/ Universidade Federal do Rio de Janeiro (UFRJ) in the research lines on Technology and Sustainability in Transportation; cities and mobility; and works in the area of impacts, vulnerabilities, and adaptation in the transportation sector. Andrea was Contributing Author of the Sixth Report (AR6) of the Intergovernmental Panel on Climate Change (IPCC) and Contributing Author of the Third Assessment Report (ARC3.3) of the Urban Climate Change Research Network (UCCRN) of Columbia University.

Sheikh, Muhammad Ramzan is a renowned economist and academic leader, currently a professor at the School of Economics, Bahauddin Zakariya University (BZU), Multan, Pakistan. He has held various administrative positions, including editor of the *Pakistan Journal of Social Sciences* (PJSS), managing editor of PJSS, program coordinator for BS Economics and Finance, and director of the Sub-Campus Vehari, BZU. With a distinguished academic background, including a post-doctorate in Economics from the London School of Economics and Political Science (LSE), UK, and a PhD in Economics from BZU, Dr. Sheikh has received numerous awards and honours for his teaching, research, and contributions to the field of economics. His research focuses on various aspects of economics, and he has published extensively in reputable journals. He is a sought-after speaker and has presented his research at international conferences. Dr. Sheikh's dedication to academia and his passion for economics have made him a respected figure, inspiring generations of economists and researchers.

Singh, Maanvender's academic pursuits are centered on exploring the area of caste and modernity, interrogating the judicial and constitutional epistemology of caste. He is currently working on the area of global urbanism in India. Holding a PhD in History from Sikkim University, he presently serves as a faculty member in the Department of History at SRM University, Andhra Pradesh.

Souza de Abreu, Victor Hugo is pursuing a post-doctorate in Transportation Engineering focusing on Resilient Infrastructure. He holds a PhD in Transport Infrastructure, specializing in Climate Risk Analysis, and a master's degree in Transport Planning and Infrastructure. Both degrees are from the Transport Engineering Program of the Alberto Luiz Coimbra Institute for Graduate Studies and Engineering Research of the Federal University of Rio de Janeiro (PET/COPPE/UFRJ). Additionally, he has postgraduate degrees in Environment and Oil and Gas from COPPE/UFRJ and a degree in Civil Engineering with an emphasis on Transport Engineering from POLI/UFRJ. He is a professor of Scientific Methodology for Executive Postgraduate Courses in Environment, Oil and Gas, and Energy at COPPE/UFRJ. He also teaches Transportation and Environment and Transportation and Energy in the Executive Postgraduate Courses in Environment and Energy at COPPE/UFRJ. As a researcher for the Brazilian Panel on Climate Change (PBMC), he focuses on Critical Infrastructure and Climate Resilience. He is also a Human Resources Fixation Fellow (Level C) for the National Council for Scientific and Technological Development (CNPq), concentrating on biofuel production. Furthermore, he serves as a consultant for the H2 Green Brazil Project of the Deutsche Gesellschaft für Internationale Zusammenarbeit (GIZ) and the Specialized Technical Advisory Project in Transport Engineering for the Oswaldo Cruz Foundation (Fiocruz).

Stepnov, Igor M. is the head of Asset Management Department and professor at Moscow State Institute of International Relations (MGIMO University). With more than 30 years of experience in researching the dynamics of production and economic systems and businesses consulting to innovative development, he formed the theory of organizational platform of interaction, which includes an original model of strategic development of companies. His current research interests are focused on the dynamics of digital ecosystems and their elements, such as pricing and profit control in business models, investment attractiveness of digital business and digital asset management, digital business models design, modern technological competition between countries and companies.

Sultan, Sana a distinguished academic and economist, hails from the vibrant city of Multan. She earned her BS in Economics from Bahauddin Zakariya University (BZU) in 2018 and completed her MPhil in Economics from the same esteemed institution in 2020, where she was honoured with a prestigious gold medal for her outstanding academic achievements. Currently, Sana is a visiting lecturer at BZU, sharing her expertise and inspiring students with her passion for economics. Her research interests and teaching focus on various aspects of economics, aiming to make a meaningful impact in the field and nurture the next generation of economists and leaders.

Tripathi, Smita is a lecturer in Leadership and Human Resource Studies. Her undergraduate and postgraduate programs teaching focuses on approaches to managing and developing people and critical issues in leadership, governance, human resource management, organizational change, and performance. Her most recent research in collaboration with the Faculty of Health aimed to investigate "the perceived role of AHP leaders and future leaders around more sustainable healthcare practices". She has previously collaborated on research projects exploring partnership working and the leadership and governance of higher education delivery in Further Education Colleges. She is equally committed to teaching and research. She strongly believes in the synergies between the two and how that can contribute to education's transformative impact on learners and society through research that makes a difference. This drives her priorities of research-informed teaching and enhancing the student experience. She has an MBA (distinction) from the University of Plymouth (2002–2003) and an MPhil (Merit) from Jawahar Lal Nehru University, Delhi, India, in Sociology (1992–1994). She describes herself as a lapsed practitioner in academia and is passionate about academic teaching and learning and its broader relevance to the workplace. This drives her agenda of research-informed teaching and enhancing the student experience.

Introduction

Polycrisis and Economic Development in the Global South

Global South countries are facing an unparalleled period of interconnected and compounded crises known as a "polycrisis." This book provides a thorough and multidisciplinary examination of the opportunities and challenges these regions face regarding development.

The book explores several facets of the polycrisis and its effects on economic development. It is organized into six parts.

Part I: The Development Paradox: Models of Development in the Global South Amidst a World of Polycrisis

The book's first part challenges conventional development models during polycrisis. It examines how underdevelopment is sustained after colonialism and cultural eroding (Chapter 1). The "resource curse" is also reviewed, exploring how the current commodity boom offers chances and challenges for avoiding this problem (Chapter 2). In Chapter 3, the intricate topic of migration and brain drain is finally discussed, emphasizing how it affects human capital in the Global South.

Part II: Political Instability, Conflict, and the Global South

Beyond the economic perspective, Part II illuminates the political factors impeding progress. Chapter 4 delves into topics such as internally displaced persons (IDPs) and their economic vulnerability, providing valuable policy ideas for developing nations. The catastrophic impacts of intercommunal conflict on displacement, humanitarian crises, and development are demonstrated using the example of Nigeria (Chapter 5). Chapter 6 delves into the intricacies of "just war" and the predicament of Afghanistan, characterized by its divided sovereignties. Chapter 7 analyses the effects of cross-strait tensions between China and Taiwan on the Global South.

DOI: 10.4324/9781032694337-1

Part III: Climate Change and Environmental Sustainability in the Global South

In Part III, climate change's constant threat is in the spotlight. In Chapter 8, the book examines the vital connection between gender justice and green growth in Africa. The effects of the climate catastrophe on developing countries are illustrated in the case studies of Brazil and India (Chapter 9). Chapter 10 delves into the intricate connection between environmental policy, economic complexity, and carbon footprint, as explored by the authors. Lastly, the book uses dynamic panel data to examine how climate change affects living standards in the Global South (Chapter 11).

Part IV: Technological Advancements and Digital Divides in the Global South

Technological developments present new challenges as well as possible answers. The digital divide—the glaring difference in the Global North and South's access to technology—is examined in this part (Chapter 12). Using a new model, it also looks at how trade and technology interact in developing nations (Chapter 13).

Part V: Cooperation and Integration among Regions of the Global South

Part V focuses on regional cooperation and integration as the key to finding solutions. In Chapter 14, the book examines how China may use international alliances to support Latin America's energy transition. Chapter 15 analyses the dynamics of foreign direct investment and its effects on economic development in the Global South.

Part VI: Global South Countries' Perspectives and Experiences

The last part explores the experiences of Global South countries as case studies. Chapter 16 provides a bibliometric review of Malaysia's post-pandemic polycrises. In Chapter 17, India's ambitions to lead the Global South are also discussed. Ultimately, Chapter 18 of the book offers a case study of postcolonial urbanism in India, exploring the challenges of building a "world-class city."

Our book *Polycrisis and Economic Development in the Global South* is an invaluable resource for scholars, decision-makers, and readers interested in comprehending the complex opportunities and challenges that developing nations face in our interconnected world because it offers interdisciplinary and cross-regional perspectives.

Prof. (Dr.) Hebatallah Adam
Professor of Economics
Jindal School of International Affairs (JSIA)
O.P. Jindal Global University (JGU)
Haryana-131001 (NCR of Delhi), India
E-mail: dhadam@jgu.edu.in
Website: https://jgu.edu.in/jsia/dr-hebatallah-adam/
ORCID: https://orcid.org/0000-0002-3038-7037

Prof. (Dr.) Ravinder Rena
Professor of Economics
DUT Business School
Faculty of Management Sciences (FMS)
Durban University of Technology
ML Sultan Campus, Po Box 1334
Durban 4001, Republic of South Africa
Email: ravinder.rena@gmail.com
ORCID: https://orcid.org/0000-0002-4156-8693

Part I

The Development Paradox

Models of Development in the Global South Amidst a World of Polycrisis

1 Interrogating the Role of Colonialism and Deculturation in the Sustained Underdevelopment of the Global South

Stanley Timeyin Ohenhen and Princewill Chukwuma Abakporo

1.1 Introduction

A major concern in the Global South is its sustained underdevelopment. These areas, including Africa, Asia, and Latin America, struggle with ongoing socio-economic issues that impede their development and keep them from realising their full potential despite having abundant natural resources and substantial human capital (Bhambra 2021). Without considering the enduring consequences of colonialism and deculturation as well as their historical legacies, it is impossible to comprehend the conditions that continue to contribute to the underdevelopment of the Global South. The continent of Africa – a key part of these areas, is renowned for its diverse and rich cultural history, as well as for being the home of several cultural institutions that are vital for fostering social cohesion, identity formation, and economic growth (Abakporo & Ohenhen, 2024). Yet, the continent has continued to grovel under the umbrella of underdevelopment.

According to Grewal (2022), colonialism is the political and economic hegemony of one society over another, usually involving outside manipulation and exploitation. During the era of European colonial expansion from the 15th to the 20th centuries, colonial powers imposed their influence on vast territories of the Global South. They frequently had little concern for the welfare and right to self-determination of the indigenous communities as they tried to exploit the resources of these areas (Dunbar-Ortiz, R., 2021). As reported by Smith (2024), the interwoven processes of deculturation and underdevelopment in the Global South have also been the subject of current studies. In his analysis, Smith examines how colonial education institutions marginalised indigenous languages and customs while advancing Western notions of modernity and development. He contends that in many post-colonial societies, the process of deculturation has contributed to the breakdown of social cohesiveness and the continuation of social inequality.

Rodríguez (2023) interrogated how neocolonial power dynamics sustain underdevelopment, showing how Western organisations and multinational businesses continue to take advantage of the labour and resources of the Global South for their gain. This chapter examines how colonialism and consequent

DOI: 10.4324/9781032694337-3

deculturation contribute to the persistent underdevelopment of the Global South, aiming to deconstruct the interactions and impacts of colonialism that feed the persistent underdevelopment in these areas. It examines how colonial powers destroyed indigenous cultural frameworks as well as upset unique socioeconomic and political structures in these spaces.

The chapter aims to shed light on how colonial institutions influenced the political and economic issues that the Global South faces today. It offers insights into local struggles and suggests development options while shedding light on the effects of colonialism and deculturation. It advances post-colonial discourse by using a comparative method to support conversations and changes in policy aimed at redressing past injustices and promoting sustainable development (Gruber et al., 2023). The investigation of the devastating effects of deculturation on indigenous communities and their identities is the core of the study.

1.2 Literature Review

A remarkable period in human history was colonialism, which is widely described as the political, economic, and social dominance of one nation over another. The crucial part it played in creating the persistent underdevelopment of the Global South has been highlighted by several recent studies. In his analysis of how colonialism affected economic systems, Chibber (2021) makes the case that colonial powers purposefully destroyed native agricultural and industrial systems, resulting in a persistent reliance on extractive economies. Expanding upon this economic examination, Mbembe (2022) delves into the cultural aspects of colonialism, stressing the methodical elimination of native knowledge systems and enforcing Western principles and customs, which persistently impede regional self-governance and growth initiatives. Similar to this, Escobar (2023) looks into the ecological effects of colonialism, showing how land appropriation and extractive industries have worsened vulnerabilities in the Global South and contributed to environmental deterioration.

In her analysis of the colonial roots of comparative development, Bhambra (2021) argue that the institutional framework established during colonialism, such as legal systems, property rights, and extractive economic practices, has had a long-lasting impact on subsequent development outcome in colonised spaces. Ohenhen et al. (2024) dig deeper into colonialism's cultural effects. Their research explores how colonial forces created and controlled images of the colonised populace through systems of knowledge production and control. They claim that to maintain the superiority of the colonisers and the subjection of the colonised, Eurocentric ideals and epistemologies were highly utilised.

The social and cultural fabrics of colonised nations were severely impacted by colonialism, in addition to its effects on the economic and political spheres. In their study of the impact of colonial rule on indigenous epistemologies, racial and gender dynamics, Ohenhen and Abakporo (2024) emphasise on how colonial rule was carried out through close relationships. They reveal the interconnections of colonial control and personal relationships inside the colonial framework by investigating the intersections of power and racial hierarchies, as dramatised through indigenous performative arts. Colonisation had a significant impact on indigenous peoples' rights. Chatterjee (2021) compares early 1970s advances to current times to critically assess the development of human rights for indigenous populations. She emphasises the significance of decolonising institutions and legal frameworks to remedy historical wrongs and protect the rights of indigenous communities.

Examining colonialism's impact on the economy and systems of global power relations is crucial to comprehend its global dimension. A historical explanation of capitalism and underdevelopment in Latin America is given by Al-Belushi (2022), who contends that the underdevelopment and exploitation of peripheral countries through colonial and neocolonial practices were closely related to the development of capitalism in core states. The impacts of colonialism were not limited to economic exploitation; it also had profound implications on the psyche and identity of colonised peoples. Abakporo and Ohenhen (2023) explore the psychological consequences of colonial domination on the colonised, including their eco-systems, emphasising the process of "decolonising the mind" as crucial to reclaiming agency and sovereignty.

Colonialism stands as the core of deculturation and underdevelopment in the Global South. Deculturation is the loss or weakening of cultural practices, identities, and traditions due to outside forces, including colonisation, globalisation, and quick sociocultural shifts. According to Dunbar-Ortiz, (2021), colonialism is inextricably related to deculturation since it pushes colonised peoples to adopt the cultural norms and values of the conquerors. According to Ohenhen and Abakporo (2024), deculturation can potentially be a side effect of modernity and globalisation. They contend that as consumerism, technology, and Western cultural influences proliferate, traditional cultural activities are frequently marginalised and devalued, leading to cultural diversity and identity loss. Deculturation has multiple negative effects on underdevelopment, including negative effects on social cohesiveness, health, education, and economic possibilities.

Deculturation can damage educational systems by imposing Western curriculum and disregarding indigenous knowledge systems, which results in a lack of relevance and efficacy in education and perpetuates underdevelopment (Maringe, 2023). Sadowsky and Greene (2023) emphasise the detrimental effects of deculturation on indigenous cultures concerning health, particularly healthcare practices and health outcomes. Deculturation can make it more difficult for underdeveloped communities to engage in markets and other economic activity on their terms. According to Shilliam (2022), adopting Western development models has caused local economies and traditional livelihoods to deteriorate, favouring global economic systems that uphold disparities and overuse natural resources without providing enough value to nearby populations. Deculturation can also make it harder for people to create strong identities and social bonds. Camara (2023) emphasises how consumer culture and global media have contributed to the homogenisation of global identities and the erasure of regional identities. Underdevelopment may be exacerbated by causing a cultural identity crisis and a break with traditional values and social systems.

The investigation of deculturation and its relationship to underdevelopment demonstrates the variety of ways that external forces can destroy cultural practices, values, and identities, detrimental to developmental outcomes. Shilliam (2022), Al-bulushi (2022), Sadowsky and Greene (2023), Chatterjee (2021), Maringe, (2023), and Camara (2023) are only a few of the academic works highlighted that offer insights into the concept of deculturation and its consequences for underdevelopment. History, sociology, and post-colonial studies are just a few fields that have examined and theorised extensively on colonialism. Colonialism establishes and maintains political, economic, and cultural dominance by one civilisation over another (Veracini, 2021). It entails the establishment of unequal power relations, the imposing of foreign rule, and the exploitation of resources (Mignolo, 2022). To further their agendas, colonial powers sought to enslave indigenous populations, undermine their cultural identities, and alter social systems (Kumar, 2021). On the other hand, deculturation describes the process through which indigenous cultures in colonised communities are lost, eroded, or suppressed as a direct effect of colonial rule (Rios & Arzubiaga, 2021). It involves the deliberate erasure or marginalisation of local customs, traditions, languages, belief systems, and practices, often through the forced adoption of the colonisers' way of life (Grewal, 2022).

Deculturation has profound implications for the development trajectories of the Global South, as it disrupts social cohesion, inhibits the transfer of traditional knowledge, and weakens collective identities (Ricatti & Dutto, 2023). The legacy of colonialism on the Global South is significant and enduring. The economic exploitation and resource extraction for the gain of the colonial powers is a crucial component (Bialostocka, 2022). For instance, European conquerors developed extractive industries that drained enormous amounts of natural resources, upsetting indigenous economies, and fostering dependency (Antić,2022). By impeding industrialisation and limiting chances for self-sustaining economic growth, this resource extraction contributed to the underdevelopment of the Global South (Wilfred & Wilfred, 2021). Additionally, social institutions were altered by colonialism in ways that fuelled underdevelopment. According to Aguirre-Rodriguez et al. (2023), European powers frequently pursued policies that upended indigenous societies' traditional social structures, created hierarchies, and altered power relationships.

The creation of cohesive societies and other efforts towards development has been hampered by this sociocultural fabric disintegration. (Davis, 2023). The deculturation brought on by colonialism has had a negative impact on the development of the Global South. The imposition of foreign cultural values and norms undermined sustainable local practices by eroding indigenous knowledge systems. (Ohenhen & Abakporo, 2024; Muñoz Martínez, 2022).

Due to this disruption of traditional agricultural practices, resource management, and community collaboration, the environment was harmed, and there was a rise in food insecurity (O'Connor, 2021). Deculturation has also contributed to the marginalisation of indigenous populations and the worsening of socioeconomic disparities. Indigenous languages and cultural manifestations were suppressed due to forced acculturation, resulting in the loss and alienation of cultural legacy (Bingemer, 2023). The resulting loss of identity and cultural consciousness hindered social cohesion and perpetuated disparities in political representation, access to resources, and development opportunities (Ferdous, 2024).

1.3 Theoretical Framework and Methodology

Two frameworks were adopted for this work: post-colonial and critical race theories. The post-colonial and critical race frameworks provide unique perspectives on resistance, power, and identity. Said pioneered post-colonial theory, which elucidates the effects of colonialism on identities, languages, literature, and knowledge in the Global South (1978). On the other hand, Derrick Bell's critical race theory sheds light on the power disparities and racial hierarchies that colonialism maintained in the distribution of resources, improving our comprehension of structural racism in this setting (1992).

Engaging historical document analysis, comparative case studies, focused group discussions and ethnographic fieldwork, the study interrogated colonialism, deculturation, and underdevelopment in the Global South, focusing on Nigeria and Indonesia. The methods foster in-depth discussion to understand underdevelopment and cultural loss through interactions with activists, scholars, policymakers, and community members.

Purposive sampling was employed to select participants for the focused group discussions, ensuring representation from diverse stakeholder groups, including community members, activists, scholars, and policymakers. Data obtained were subjected to thematic and content analysis. Participants were provided with information about the study objectives, procedures, and potential risks, and their informed consent was obtained before participating in interviews and discussions. Also, the confidentiality of participants' responses was maintained, while respect and sensitivity for their perspectives and experiences were ensured.

1.4 Colonialism and Deculturation Cases in the Global South

1.4.1 Nigeria

Nigeria, home to more than 250 ethnic groupings, was ruled by the British from the late 1800s until 1960. British colonial policy significantly impacted Nigeria's political, social, and economic systems, which led to the country's underdevelopment. The British established a mono-economy by concentrating on producing raw materials for export, such as oil, cocoa, and palm oil. Following independence, Nigeria's economy continued to depend on the export of basic commodities, leaving it open to changes in world prices. Underdevelopment and economic instability resulted from prioritising cash crops and oil extraction over environmentally friendly industrial and agricultural methods.

Nigeria's colonial infrastructure development prioritised resource exploitation over all-encompassing national development. Regional imbalances resulted from the roads and railways that connected resource-rich areas to ports. Due to oil exploitation, the Niger Delta and adjacent areas experience environmental deterioration and a shortage of social services and basic infrastructure. The Niger Delta's environment has severely degraded because of the extraction of resources, with gas flaring and oil spills destroying livelihoods and ecosystems. Health problems, the loss of fertile land, and contaminated water make poverty worse in communities. Indirect rule by the British colonial administration gave self-serving local leaders more authority, leaving a legacy of corrupt and ineffective government.

Colonial policies suppressed indigenous cultures, imposing English in administration, education, and commerce. This deculturation alienated Nigerians from their heritage and undermined local languages and traditions. The British education system prioritised Western knowledge, marginalising indigenous knowledge systems and causing a loss of cultural identity and self-esteem. This system also created an elite class educated in British schools, entrenching social inequalities, and perpetuating the colonial legacy of exploitation and underdevelopment. Many Nigerians felt disconnected from their roots, exacerbating social and cultural fragmentation. The British divide-and-rule strategy worsened ethnic tensions, favouring certain groups and sowing discord. This legacy of ethnic and religious conflicts persists, hindering Nigeria's national unity and development. Nigeria's underdevelopment is a result of the legacies of colonialism and deculturation, which led to the exploitation of natural resources, eviction of native communities, and the imposition of foreign languages and cultural norms, weakened social cohesion, and exposed communities to external pressures.

1.4.2 Indonesia

Indonesia's history has been shaped by centuries of colonial rule, resulting in cultural assimilation and exploitation from the Dutch East India Company's arrival in the 17th century to establishing the Dutch East Indies colony. This history of colonialism has influenced Indonesia's socioeconomic dynamics and development prospects, with economic exploitation being a major factor in its underdevelopment. The Dutch East India Company's search for natural resources and spices led to a system of extraction that prioritised colonial interests over the welfare of the native population. The Dutch colonial government imposed a farming system that forced Indonesian peasants to grow cash crops for export, like coffee, sugar, and indigo, which resulted in land confiscation and community deprivation. Throughout the colonial era, this pattern of exploitation was maintained, aggravating inequality and impeding the development of indigenous industries and economic self-sufficiency.

Colonialism in Indonesia led to economic exploitation and deculturation, eradicating indigenous cultures and customs. The Dutch language, legislation, and educational system imposed on indigenous populations disempowered them, destroying their knowledge systems and cultural sovereignty. The divide-and-rule policies further splintered Indonesian society, undermining organised resistance to colonial control. Today, as oppressed people fight to reclaim and preserve their cultural history amidst globalisation and standardisation, the residue of cultural erasure remains evident in modern Indonesia.

Indonesia's political evolution was significantly influenced by colonialism, which established authoritarian regimes that persist today. The Dutch administration disenfranchised indigenous leaders and concentrated power in colonial officials. After gaining independence in 1945, Indonesia's post-colonial history is marked by military incursions, elite dominance, and political instability, resulting in corruption and authoritarianism that hinders democratic governance and sustainable development. In summary, the Indonesian case study provides insightful information about the long-lasting effects of colonialism and deculturation on the underdeveloped Global South. Examining the various effects of political oppression, cultural erasure, and colonial exploitation, the study sheds light on the intricate processes influencing Indonesia's socioeconomic environment and future course.

1.5 Key Findings and Discussion

Several critical insights emerged through the purposive sampling of key informants consisting of policymakers, historians, activists, scholars, and community leaders for the in-depth group discussions held variously in Nigeria and Indonesia, representing the Global South region. Participants consistently highlighted how colonial powers extensively exploited both natural and human resources, leaving behind a legacy characterised by depleted resources and economic structures tailored to benefit the colonisers rather than local populations. This exploitation established patterns of economic dependency that continue to this day, with many former colonies relying heavily on exporting raw materials while importing finished goods from their former colonisers.

A key recurring theme from the discussions was the loss of indigenous knowledge and cultural practices because of colonial policies that suppressed regional customs and created cultural alienation. Stakeholders observed that education systems imposed by colonial powers marginalised local languages and knowledge systems in favour of the languages and worldviews of the colonists. In post-colonial cultures, this has had a lasting impact on the relevance and quality of education. Effective learning and participation in the global economy have been hampered by the requirement that foreign languages be taught in schools.

The discussions revealed colonial administrative structures prioritised control over development, leading to weak post-colonial governance. The divide-and-rule legacy fuels political instability and corruption, hindering development. Colonial economic policies still disadvantage the Global South, perpetuating poverty. Stakeholders criticised post-colonial policies influenced by former colonial powers and financial institutions, as structural adjustment programs have worsened economic hardships.

The significant social and psychological ramifications of colonisation and deculturation were also revealed in the discussions. A recurring theme in post-colonial nations was an identity crisis as people and groups battled to restore their cultural identities. It was determined that the psychological effects, including feelings of helplessness and inferiority, constituted a serious obstacle to social and economic advancement. These results highlight the complex and long-lasting effects of colonisation and deculturation on the Global South. They emphasise the need for all-encompassing, culturally aware methods of development that rectify past injustices and encourage local empowerment.

1.6 Recommendations

Colonialism left behind structural disparities that must be addressed to alleviate underdevelopment in the Global South. Policies that support economic diversity make investments in regional businesses and allow marginalised people to participate in decision-making processes are necessary to achieve this. Because deculturation has a lasting effect, efforts to encourage the resuscitation of indigenous languages, cultural practices, and knowledge systems are necessary. Education systems must be changed to include a range of viewpoints and encourage cultural diversity as an asset rather than a hindrance to advancement.

Strategies for sustainable development must prioritise environmental conservation and indigenous peoples' rights to land and resources, considering the ecological effects of colonialism. This means encouraging renewable energy sources, bolstering community-based conservation efforts, and tightening environmental rules. To combat underdevelopment, it is necessary to question the neocolonial power structures that support dependency and exploitation in the Global South.

This entails supporting initiatives to improve local governance and accountability systems, promoting fair trade policies, and reforming international financial institutions. To provide a thorough understanding of the intricate dynamics underlying underdevelopment in the Global South, future research should employ interdisciplinary approaches that integrate insights from economics, sociology, anthropology, cultural studies, and environmental science.

1.7 Conclusion

This study has shed light on the complex effects of past injustices on the current socioeconomic environments of the Global South. It is evident from a detailed examination of archival records, a nuanced analysis of cultural dynamics, and a thorough investigation of socioeconomic indicators that the legacy of colonial rule continues to have lasting impacts on the developmental paths of formerly colonised regions. Moreover, the sneaky deculturation process, deeply entwined with colonial dominance, has deeply wounded indigenous identities and knowledge systems, making sustainable development even more difficult.

It is critical to acknowledge the enormous effects of colonialism in the Global South, highlighting the need to protect cultural heritage, give marginalised populations more authority, and ensure that resources are distributed fairly. For a sustainable and equitable future, addressing colonial legacies necessitates aggressive international initiatives, fighting structural inequalities, and accepting multiple cultural viewpoints. To summarise, redressing historical injustices, empowering marginalised communities, and promoting inclusivity are essential measures for reducing the long-term effects of deculturation and colonisation.

1.8 Further Research

Subsequent studies could investigate the long-lasting effects of colonial legacies on post-colonial cultures, including how these effects affect indigenous knowledge, cultural practices, and institutions. Multidisciplinary approaches combining historical, cultural, economic, social, and anthropological viewpoints are required. Studying extractive economies, neocolonial processes, and contemporary globalisation is essential to comprehending the marginalisation of the Global South.

Bibliography

Abakporo, P. C. & Ohenhen, S.T. Decolonizing tropical environments: Awakening Nigeria's indigenous dance theatre. Anita Lundberg. (Ed.) *Decolonizing the Tropics* (Special Issue), eTropic: *Electronic Journal of Studies in the Tropics*, 22(1). https://doi.org/10.25120/etropic.22.1.2023.3958. (2023).

Abakporo, P.C. & Ohenhen, S.T. Indigenous environmentalism through dance: The Ohaji-Egbema experiment. *Rupkatha Journal on Interdisciplinary Studies in Humanities*, 16(1). https://doi.org/10.21659/rupkatha.v16n1.06. (2024)

Aguirre-Rodriguez, A., Luna, D., Alvarez, C. M., & Montoya, D. Ethnic identity-based motivation: A model emergent from US Hispanic consumers. *Journal of Consumer Psychology*, 33(2), 303–327. (2023).

Al-Bulushi, Y. Thinking racial capitalism and black radicalism from Africa: An intellectual geography of Cedric Robinson's world-system. *Geoforum*, 132, 252–262. (2022).
Anaya, S. J. *Indigenous Peoples in International Law*. Oxford University Press, United Kingdom. (2004).
Antić, A. Global Imaginations and Non-alignment: Waging War Against Backwardness. In A. Antić *Non-Aligned Psychiatry in the Cold War: Revolution, Emancipation and Re-Imagining the Human Psyche* (pp. 155–197). Springer International Publishing, Cham. (2022).
Bell, D. *Faces at the Bottom of the Well: The Permanence of Racism*. Basic Books, New York. (1992).
Bhambra, Gurminder K. *Decolonizing the University*. Pluto Pres, United Kingdom. (2021).
Bialostocka, O. Transmodern heritage as radical delinking from modernity. *Curator: The Museum Journal*, *65*(3), 509–522. (2022).
Bibi, S., van der Weide, R., Yoshida, N., Samji, S., & Koettl, J. Protecting all citizens? Exploring the accessibility and adequacy of social protection programs in developing countries. *World Development*, 139, 105309. (2021).
Billig, M. Europe and the third world: From colonialism to dependency? *World Development*, 11(6), 523–527. (1983).
Bingemer, M. C. 'Theology in Latin America'. *St Andrews Encyclopaedia of Theology*. Brendan N. Wolfe et al. (ed). https://www.saet.ac.uk/Christianity/TheologyinLatinAmerica (2023).
Blackstock, C., Ogden, E., Weenie, E., Williams, L., & Loppie, C. Healing the wounds of the past: How indigenous peoples experience and understand healing. *International Journal of Indigenous Health*, 14(2), 115–139. (2019).
Camara, M.S. African Cultures and Representations in the Digital Era. In Akpan, U.S. (Eds.), *African Media Space and Globalization*. Palgrave Macmillan, Cham. https://doi.org/10.1007/978-3-031-35060-3_16. (2023).
Castagno, A. E. The paradox of Native American acculturation in rural schools: A review of the literature. *Review of Educational Research*, 83(3), 387–425. (2013).
Chambers, R., Potts, D., & Grieco, A. Transforming power relations to improve development outcomes. *World Development*, 129, 104868. (2020).
Chatterjee, P. *Nationalist Thought and the Colonial World: A Derivative Discourse?*. Zed Books, United Kingdom. (1986).
Chatterjee, Piya. A time for intolerable interculturalism: On decolonization, deculturation, and the black lives matter movement. *Comparative Literature* 73(4): 404–423. (2021)
Chibber, V. Colonialism and economic underdevelopment: A historical perspective. *Journal of Global Economic Development*, 7(2), 45–62. (2021).
Davis, M. H. Race and decolonization in North Africa. In *Oxford Research Encyclopedia of African History*. https://doi.org/10.1093/acrefore/9780190277734.013.1054 (22 February 2023). Retrieved false9 Aug. 2024
Dubow, S. *Apartheid, 1948-1994*. Oxford University Press, United Kingdom. (2014).
Dunbar-Ortiz, R. *Not "a nation of immigrants": Settler colonialism, white supremacy, and a history of erasure and exclusion*. Beacon Press. (2021).
Economic Commission for Latin America and the Caribbean. Financial mechanisms for infrastructure development: Towards more inclusive and sustainable financing in Latin America and the Caribbean. Retrieved from https://www.cepal.org/en/publications/46549-financial-mechanisms-infrastructure-development-towards-more-inclusive (2021).
Escobar, A. Ecological consequences of colonialism in the Global South. *Environmental Sociology Review*, 15(1), 78–94. (2023).

Falola, T., & Heaton, M. M. *A history of Nigeria*. Cambridge University Press, United Kingdom. (2008).
Fanon, F. *The Wretched of the Earth*, Grove Press, New York. (1961).
Feinstein, C. *An Economic History of South Africa: Conquest, Discrimination, and Development*. Cambridge University Press, United Kingdom. (2005).
Ferdous, J. Transformative Approaches to Gender, Migration, and Development. In J. Ferdous (Ed.) *Gendered Migrations: Navigating Challenges and Opportunities for Development* (pp. 1–27). https://doi.org/10.1007/978-981-97-0444-6_1 Springer Nature Singapore, Singapore. (2024).
Grewal, Inderpal. Transnational Feminist Cultural Studies: Beyond the Marxism/Poststructuralism/Feminism Divides. Transnational Feminist Cultural Studies: Beyond the Marxism/Poststructuralism/Feminism Divides. (2022).
Grieco, M., Scandurra, R., & Ronghi, M. Socio-economic empowerment in indigenous communities: An analysis of four successful cases. *World Development Perspectives*, 5, 16–20. (2017).
Grosfoguel, R. The epistemic decolonial turn. *Cultural Studies*, 21(2–3), 211–223. (2007).
Gruber, V. V., Ndi, G. S., & Banguero Velasco, R. Towards Transcultural Self-Writing: Mapping the Struggles of Minoritised Cultures in Colombia. In Montecinos, J.B., Grunfelder, T., & Wieland, J. (Eds). *A Relational View on Cultural Complexity: Implications for Theory and Practice* (pp. 173–189). Springer International Publishing, Cham. (2023).
Gupta, R., & Chandna, A. Inclusive growth and development in India: Issues and challenges. *Global Business Review*, 19(6), 1540–1552. (2018).
Havemann, P. Documenting cultural change as a response to pressure on cultural diversity. *Australian Journal of Indigenous Education*, 34(S1), 132–140. (2005).
Horrell, S., & Swart, H. Class, Race, and Inequality in South Africa: Economic History of South Africa. In Peil, J. & Staveren, I.V. (Eds.) *Handbook of Economics and Ethics* (pp. 1–26). Edward Elgar Publishing, United Kingdom. (2019).
Hudson, R., & England, P. Justice and the reparation of indigenous land rights in settler states: Making claims in Canadian political contexts. *Political Studies*, 60(2), 397–415. (2012).
Huggins, C. Land restitution to indigenous peoples in practice: The case of Australia. *Australian Journal of Political Science*, 46(2), 385–401. (2011).
Janes, C. R., Downey, L., Fiske, J., Kowal, E., Mosby, I., Rist, M.,… Watene, K. Theorizing indigenous-settler relations: An introduction. *Settler Colonial Studies*, 7(1), 1–8. (2017).
Jones, H. L.. Indigenous peoples and collaborative governance: Comparative analysis. *Forum for Development Studies*, 44(3), 333–355. (2017).
Kabeer, N. Gender equality and women's empowerment: A critical analysis of the third millennium development goal. *Gender & Development*, 20(3), 427–435. (2012).
Khan, M. H. Governance, Economic growth and development since the 1960s. *World Development*, 38(5), 645–653. (2010).
Kirsch, S. Rights in translation: An indigenous model of rights discourse. *Law & Society Review*, 48(1), 5–37. (2014).
Kumar, S. Decolonization, Deculturation and Development. In A.K. Fosu (Ed.) *Achieving Development Success: Strategies and Lessons from the Developing World*. Oxford: Oxford University Press. https://www.wider.unu.edu/sites/default/files/RP2009-31.pdf (2021)
Kuokkanen, R. *Reshaping the University: Responsibility, Indigenous Epistemes, and the Logic of the Gift*. UBC Press, British Columbia. (2007).
Lynn, H., Sloane, J. A., Fernald, L., & Brown, E. "I Am My Language": Khmer language revitalization in a New England community. *Harvard Educational Review*, 88(1), 33–57. (2018).

Maringe, F. The Conceptual 'Jungle' of the Decolonisation of Higher Education: Contestations, Contradictions, and Opportunities. In Maringe, F. (Ed.) *Colonization and Epistemic Injustice in Higher Education Precursors to Decolonization* (pp. 1–22), Routledge, London. (2023).
Mbembe, A. Culture and colonialism: Revisiting the Legacy of European Expansion. *Postcolonial Studies Quarterly*, 9(3), 211–230. (2022).
McCarty, T. L., & Nicholls, G. Language Planning and Policy in Native America. In S. May & N. H. Hornberger (Eds.), *Encyclopedia of Language and Education*, 2nd Ed., Volume 1: Language Policy and Political Issues in Education (pp. 367–384). Springer. (2007).
Mignolo, W. Delinking: The rhetoric of modernity, the logic of coloniality and the grammar of de-coloniality. *Cultural Studies*, 21(2–3), 449–514. (2007).
Mignolo, Walter D. *Local Histories/Global Designs: Coloniality, Subaltern Knowledges, and Border Thinking*. Princeton University Press, New Jersey. (2022).
Moser, C. *Gender planning and development: Theory, practice, and training*. Routledge, London. (2020).
Niezen, R. The truth and reconciliation commission: Review and prospects. *Indigenous Law Journal*, 11(1), 43–70. (2012).
O'Connor, B. *Blood Red Lines: How Nativism Fuels the Right*. Haymarket Books, Chicago. (2021).
Ohenhen, S.T. & Abakporo, P.C. Resisting eco-colonial ideologies through indigenous epistemologies and performances. *Rupkatha Journal on Interdisciplinary Studies in Humanities*, 16(1), 2024. https://doi.org/10.21659/rupkatha.v16n1.02. (2024).
Ohenhen, S. T., Nnawulezi, U, Abakporo, P.C., Adenikiju, O., Ibironke, S., Ajay, I. M., Olawale, K., Faniyi, O. Managing Africa's cultural institutions for global impact and sustainable development. *Journal of Infrastructure, Policy and Development*, 8(2): 3168. https://doi.org/10.24294/jipd.v8i2.3168. (2024).
Oromia Support Group. Political participation, representation and decision making in Ethiopia. Retrieved from https://www.oromiamedia.org/pubs/1601/PoliticalParticipationReport_vol6.pdf. (2015).
Quijano, A. Coloniality of power and Eurocentrism in Latin America. *International Sociology*, 15(2), 215–232. (2000).
Ricatti, F., & Dutto, M. First Nations Sovereignty: Towards a Decolonial Approach to Italy–Australia Relations. In G. Abbondanza, & S. Battiston (Eds.) *Italy and Australia: Redefining bilateral relations for the twenty-first century* (pp. 113–136). Springer Nature Singapore, Singapore. (2023).
Rios, Orlando J., & Arzubiaga, Angela E.. Coloniality of power and schooling: How education marginalizes and silences immigrant students. *Review of Research in Education*, 45(1), 417–449. (2021).
Rodríguez, L. Neocolonial power dynamics and underdevelopment in the Global South. *Development Studies Quarterly*, 17(2), 145–163. (2023).
Said, E. W. *Orientalism*. Vintage Books, New York. (1978).
Sadowsky, J., & Greene, J. A. The Colonial and Postcolonial Roots of Global Mental Health Efforts. In B. Acharya, & A. E. Becker (Eds.) *Global Mental Health Training and Practice* (pp. 21–34). Routledge, London. (2023).
Shilliam, Robbie. *The Black Pacific: Anticolonial Struggles and Oceanic Connections*. NYU Press, New York. (2022)
Simpson, L. R. *Land as pedagogy: Nishnaabeg intelligence and rebellious transformation*. Decolonization: Indigeneity, Education & Society, 3(3), 1–25. (2014).
Smith, J. Deculturation and development: The legacy of colonial education systems in the Global South. *Cultural Studies Journal*, 12(4), 301–318. (2024).
Tsosie, R. Indigenous Peoples and Human Rights: International and Regional Jurisprudence. In D. A. Clausen & W. Sterk (Eds.), *Routledge Handbook of Religion and Social Justice* (pp. 286–303). Routledge, London. (2015).

UNCTAD. The Least Developed Countries Report 2020: Productive capacities for the new decade. United Nations Conference on Trade and Development. Retrieved from https://unctad.org/system/files/official-document/ldcr2020_en.pdf. (2020).

UN DESA. *World Economic and Social Survey 2018: Frontier issues in economic thought*. United Nations Department of Economic and Social Affairs. (2018).

UNDP. *Empowering People and Ensuring Inclusiveness and Equality: UNDP Strategic Plan, 2018–2021*. United Nations Development Programme. (2016).

UNDP. *Human Development Report 2020*. United Nations Development Programme. (2020).

United Nations. United Nations Declaration on the Rights of Indigenous Peoples. Retrieved from https://www.un.org/development/desa/indigenouspeoples/declaration-on-the-rights-of-indigenous-peoples.html. (2007).

United Nations. UN Declaration on the Rights of Indigenous Peoples. Retrieved from https://www.un.org/development/desa/indigenouspeoples/declaration-on-the-rights-of-indigenous-peoples.html. (2018).

Veracini, Lorenzo. *Settler Colonialism: A Theoretical Overview*. Springer, New York. (2021).

Warren, K., Phibbs, A., Hamburg, S., Kastelic, V., & Richardson, F. Facilitating collaboration between indigenous and western knowledge systems: A review of the literature. *Environmental Science & Policy*, 51, 251–263. (2015).

Watson, I. Can the nation-state accommodate national diversity? American Indian Tribal Nationalism and the Democratic Project. *Ethnicities*, 13(2), 239–259. (2013).

Watts, M. Blood Oil: The Anatomy of a Petro-insurgency in Niger Delta. *Focaal: Journal of Global and Historical Anthropology*, (52), 18–38. https://doi.org/10.3167/fcl.2008.520102. (2008).

Wilfred, F., & Wilfred, F. Religious identities: From the colonial to the global. F. Wilfred (Ed.) *Religious Identities and the Global South: New Approaches to Religion and Power*. 41–63. Palgrave Macmillan, https://doi.org/10.1007/978-3-030-60738-8_3. (2021).

2 The Resource Curse and the World Commodity Boom

Modern Chances to Overcome and Traps in the Global South Countries

Julia Kovalchuk and Petr I. Kasatkin

2.1 Introduction

The modern period of world history and economy is connected not only with digitalization, which has engulfed countries, companies, and an absolute multitude of people but also with the growing demand for raw materials. Initially, when the first computers appeared, it was more inspiring and gave hope for rapid changes. Still, we are witnessing the global complex impact of infocommunication and digital technologies, which is backed by an increase in technical means and equipment. This increase in production should be provided with raw materials, metals, and fuel – considering the prospects for further development of the digital economy, the need for them will increase more and more. So, we will witness a commodity boom (super-cycle) that will affect gold and silver mining, the oil and gas industry and copper, which are the most capital-deficient sectors of the economy in the world, due to the expected strong economic recovery after the COVID pandemic.

We should not forget about energy development – the next energy transition requires a significant increase in ore and metal production. Achieving zero emissions by 2050 and generating 82% of the world's energy from alternative sources (now it is 17%) will be achieved by increasing demand for tangible assets, namely, according to estimates by the International Energy Agency [8], 37 of the most important metals and minerals needed for the transition for environmentally friendly energy, including lithium, nickel, cobalt, graphite, copper, aluminium, and rare earth elements. Thus, this, in turn, will require an increase in their extraction, but there are the countries of the Global South, representing the continents of Africa and Latin America, that are rich in these resources.

At the same time, the resource curse phenomenon, especially for developing countries, becomes the basis for understanding their role and development trajectories in increasing resource demand and its political and technological dependence on economically successful countries with great influence.

Therefore, the research's purpose is to assess the contribution of economic influence on decisions in the use of natural resources of countries, as well as the influence of the resource curse philosophy in explaining the phenomenon

DOI: 10.4324/9781032694337-4

of development of developing countries, which in most cases choose the path of catching up or dependent development.

Currently, there is a political confrontation in the world for technological leadership, the consequence of which will inevitably be the destruction of trade relations and further price increases for the most important minerals for developing the economy, industry, and energy. Therefore, the research question about the role of countries' resource wealth is relevant today.

2.1.1 The Philosophy of the Resource Curse: Literature Review

There is no unequivocal recognition in science of the negative impact of resource wealth on the country. Still, the relationship between the abundance of natural resources of a country and its economic growth is being debated. Moreover, the basis of this discussion is always the economic, social, and political consequences, and the historical justification is usually the relationship between the oil boom and the resource curse. At the same time, sceptics of the resource curse phenomenon do not forget Smith's thesis about the importance of natural resources for the economy's well-being.

The term "the natural resource curse" appeared in the works of R.A. Auty in 1993 [4] to emphasize the lack of power to use resource wealth for the prosperity of the country, and then scientific evidence began to appear of a negative relationship between resource wealth and the economic well-being of the country. Thus, it was found that an increase in exports of metals and mineral resources mined in the country in the short term can give a significant boost to economic development, but in the long term, an increase in exports by 25% on average leads to a slowdown in economic growth per capita by 0.5–1% per year.

History gives us examples of the absence of the "resource curse" [22], which becomes a source of protection for the trajectories of raw material development of countries [7] – the main point is that it only takes time for economic growth, which will surely come.

Thus, many rich and developed countries (USA, Australia, Norway, etc.) have used natural resources, which they are generously endowed with, to increase their economic power. A study from 2007 to 2020 about developing fuel-exporting countries clearly showed that the impact of dependence on natural resources on well-being is negative and significant [12], which confirmed the thesis of the resource curse about this group of countries [1].

Turkish researchers have found an inverse U-shaped relationship between dependence on resources and economic growth [6]. They concluded that resource dependence is not an obstacle to economic growth in 17 out of 28 countries (such as Botswana, Jordan, Canada, Cyprus, Mexico, Morocco, Senegal, Tunisia). Still, it is an obstacle to sustainable development in 9 out of 17 countries (Australia, Bahrain, Bolivia, Cameroon, Colombia, Indonesia, Niger, Norway, Peru, etc.), as well as in 11 other countries. In addition, it is concluded that increased trade openness contributes to economic growth, harming sustainable development.

Another thesis the authors are considering relates to philosophy – supposedly, countries endowed with resource wealth are just lucky [21]. Natural resources become assets, which are then transformed into benefits of economic development – government revenues, corporate income and taxes, schools and hospitals, sports facilities, and tourist facilities. However, there is a significant disadvantage in this interpretation – the mining process itself, which can be very difficult and dirty, with a negative impact on nature and people who continue to extract minerals literally with their hands, which is harmful to health.

The researchers note that countries rich in minerals are cursed only if they have low-quality institutions, and the curse is lifted if the institutions are good enough. We can draw an unambiguous conclusion that corruption, business conflicts, and the influence of transnational corporations become a source for the formation of a resource curse, which, as production volumes increase, leads to negative consequences for the country's socio-economic development. Researchers from Cameroon note the importance of strengthening property rights in reducing the effects of the resource curse [3]. Researchers from countries that have suffered greatly from their resource wealth, which has caused wars and economic disaster [19], note that if the quality of institutions were better and investments in human capital were a priority, countries would certainly be able to achieve economic sustainability in the long term. Modern researchers [13] also note the influence of institutions on the fiscal development of the country and the formation of natural resource rent.

In addition to the institutional factor, there is a factor in the economic and technological policies of countries rich in natural resources [11]. Thus, countries with initially strong economic and political positions use the development of their technologies to increase production efficiency and export development, so they implement breakthrough development strategies using new technologies that may be uncertain in their future advantages [17]. At the same time, investments are also being made in related sectors of the economy [15], including the development of science and technology at universities [10] and green technologies [20], which confirms investments in human capital at the same time with increasing protectionism in economic policy [18].

Other countries adhere to either catch-up or dependent development. In general, dependent development is confirmed for the countries of the Global South [5], manifested itself most vividly in the history of Latin American countries, and was only then extended to the entire "third world". Dependent development is not a stage on the way to industrialization, but an inevitable consequence of capitalism. Therefore, external factors are important for these countries (first of all, the possibility of exporting raw materials), while internal factors are denied or considered insignificant. At the same time, there is one big trap – "flawed growth" for commodity economies, when countries increase exports to compensate for lower prices. However, as a result, the terms of trade deteriorate further. In this regard, accelerated industrialization is necessary with the mandatory development of heavy industry, and economic diversification is also important [14] – as a transition from one source of income to multiple sources of income due to the development of different sectors of the economy to export not only raw materials but also goods.

Thus, it is important to understand that resource wealth is a source of development. Still, dependence on it triggers a resource curse when rents from natural resources are not transformed into investments in industry and human capital.

2.2 Methodology

The authors rely on a critical understanding of the phenomenon of "resource curse" and the contextual and essential disclosure of the phenomenon of "resource blessing". Most examples of countries with resource abundance over a long period show a negative effect. However, the authors consider the dilemma of the country's development precisely during the expected confirmed commodity boom in the world, which is objectively justified and inevitable.

The trend towards exceeding the total GDP of developing countries (especially the Asian region) in comparison with the GDP of developed countries has been going on for more than two decades. The most current forecasts by the IMF [9] indicate that fast-growing economies should be considered among developing countries, which are mainly represented by the poorest countries and, nevertheless, possess significant reserves of metals, minerals, and rare earth elements that are currently in demand.

The factor of political influence and sometimes confrontation is very important for countries with resource wealth. In this study, we will not delve into the oil wars that have arisen since the 1970s but note the continued importance of oil even now, when everyone is discussing the "green" agenda. Still, they understand that the path to using alternative energy sources is long globally. From the systematized data from Table 2.1, there are countries of the Global South for almost all commodity positions in the top three countries that lead in world production. Thus, Chile and Peru are the leaders in copper mining. Congo provides 67% of all cobalt mined in the world [2], mainly used in producing heat-resistant, magnetic, superhard, and corrosion-resistant

Table 2.1 Share of top three countries in world production, percentage of global volume.

Commodities / Raw material	*Top one*		*Top two*		*Top three*	
Lithium	50,62	Australia	23,57	Chili	12,36	China
Cobalt	67,07	Congo	5,76	Russia	4,90	Cuba
Nickel	42,82	Indonesia	13,36	Russia	9,22	Philippines
Copper	28,14	Chili	11,94	Peru	8,19	China
Silicon	70,00	China	7,00	Russia	5,40	Norway
Rare earth elements	69,8	China	11,30	Myanmar	8,10	Australia

Source: Compiled by the authors based on [2, 9].

alloys and coatings. Cobalt compounds are used to produce resistant enamels and paints, ceramics, and glass.

The research uses data from macroeconomic statistics of countries included in the Global South groups and reports and reviews from the International Monetary Fund and the International Energy Agency, which disclose data on the extraction and export of metals, minerals, and rare earth elements.

2.3 The Resource Wealth of the Global South

2.3.1 Oil

Oil remains one of the world's most demanded raw fuel commodities despite the declared "green" agenda. In the fuel and energy balance of any country in the world, there are either exports or imports of oil, emphasising its importance as an energy resource.

Latin American countries are permanent players in the black gold market. Still, their positions have been significantly weakened over the past 20 years: countries are constantly facing political pressure and economic crises, and despite similar problems, they are trying to find ways to overcome the crisis.

Now, Brazil is expanding the exploitation of huge subsalt oil reserves on the continental shelf on the principles of implementing production-sharing agreements. Argentina has concentrated on developing a large shale oil field, "Vaca Muerta". Venezuela, the richest oil country in Latin America, seeks to reduce dependence on the American market and diversify its exports. Now, it is a country with significant financial problems and a lack of opportunities to attract investment. Still, at the same time, the oil wealth is huge, but it cannot be used for the economy and society – oil has turned out to be a trap for Venezuela. Mexico encourages the participation of foreign companies in its refining industry. Now the country sells crude fuel abroad and imports expensive petroleum products (gasoline and diesel) after processing. Therefore, a strategy is being considered to reduce oil exports to zero, independently refine oil, and meet their fuel needs.

It can be concluded that the Latin American oil industry is undergoing structural transformations caused by both internal problems (inflation, social sphere, lack of investment, lack of ability of state-owned companies to ensure the development of the oil industry) and the design of solutions for the development of international relations.

The countries of sub-Saharan Africa, rich in oil fields, unlike the countries of Latin America, are more concerned about the initial parameters of production as countries with a new development strategy due to the discovered oil resource and do not want to repeat the mistakes of Nigeria.

Oil was discovered in Nigeria at the beginning of the 20th century, but development began only 55 years later. Oil export revenues for the entire period of Nigeria's foreign trade since 1956 amounted to at least $600 billion, which was facilitated by the oil booms in the 1970s, but which created efficiency problems due to the shadow economy, corruption, poverty and human rights violations, oil theft, ageing infrastructure, and reduced investment. The most significant failure was the construction of a steel mill on export revenues, which had not started its activities. The country depends on international companies and foreign contractors for 95% of its oil activities. Most of the hydrocarbons – more than 50% – belong to Shell and the local Nigerian National Petroleum Company. It was only in 2021 that the Oil Industry Law was passed, but this did not stop the departure of international oil companies that sell their assets to Nigerian companies.

In Uganda, the government is focused on a comprehensive assessment of the consequences of the development of the oil industry. It aims to reach the level of a middle-income country by 2040 through the development of production of a recently discovered large field. At the same time, oil revenues are planned to improve infrastructure and stimulate industrial development, with a full understanding of the potential resource curse if this goal is not fulfilled and institutions do not function effectively. To avoid this, under the 2013 oil law, an oil fund was established in Uganda under the Ministry of Finance, Planning and Economic Development. The funds will be collected by the Uganda Revenue Authority and deposited in the Oil Fund of the Bank of Uganda.

2.3.2 Diamonds

Diamonds are the most valuable and expensive stones on earth. The discovery of a diamond deposit on the territory of the state is a guarantee of economic growth and development. Today, 70% of global diamond production is accounted for by three corporations: the international De Beers Corporation, the Russian diamond mining company Alrosa, and the Australian-British concern Rio Tinto Group. However, the territories where the deposits are located and where diamond mining occurs are also important in diamond mining. According to the British Geological Survey, the main diamond-producing countries include Russia, Botswana, Canada, the Democratic Republic of the Congo, Australia, and South Africa.

Diamond mining in Botswana began five years after independence in 1966. In 1969, the De Beers Botswana Mining Company was founded as a joint venture between De Beers and Botswana Development Corporation to develop the only operating mine at that time, the Orapa mine. This company was renamed the Debswana Diamond Company with a 50:50 share ratio. The sale of diamonds on the world market allowed Botswana to obtain the status of an "African miracle" and accumulate foreign exchange reserves (now about 75% of the country's GDP), which, during the difficult period of falling diamond prices in the 1980s, allowed to stabilize domestic government spending and implement a relatively balanced growth model. In general, revenues from the diamond industry were invested in foreign capital markets, and a limited amount was spent domestically on constructing roads, hospitals, and schools to significantly increase citizens' incomes.

From the example of Botswana, many researchers conclude that the resource curse has been abandoned. However, sceptics argue that it is still ahead since the country has not managed to diversify its economy despite the attempts made. The possibilities for developing the cutting and polishing industry have not been confirmed due to the strong competition from other processing centres in India and China. The idea of creating a shopping centre inside the country and competing with other centres, such as Antwerp or Dubai, has not yet been implemented. The country recognized that its reserves would eventually be depleted and needed to make efforts to maintain the positive impact of diamonds on its economy.

The most difficult situation in diamond mining is that, despite the UN initiative and the organization of the Kimberlite Process, the supply of smuggled diamonds from African countries is still ongoing. Funds from the sale of stones are used to support military conflicts in the region.

2.3.3 Copper and Cobalt

Analysts at Bank of America and Morgan Stanley have been recording a shortage in the copper market for several years in a row.

Chile is a world leader in copper mining and has 24% of the world's copper reserves. Initially, Chile's copper industry was owned by foreign companies. Still, in 1971 the government nationalized the three largest copper companies of American origin and created the state coordinating company Codelco, responsible for the exploration, development, extraction, production, and commercialization of copper. Despite this, foreign companies are still interested in developing the Chilean copper industry, which is manifested at a new level – through introducing new technologies and innovations. The state policy aims to convert natural resources into competitive advantages of the country, therefore, the system of knowledge generation and innovation activity based on the interaction of companies, universities, and the state is actively used. Codelco periodically updates and expands production facilities and considers projects to transfer some enterprises to an underground mining method to increase their operational life and copper production. Certain difficulties can be called the current decline in copper production in 2023, which has become the most significant in the last ten years, caused by decreased ore quality and accidents.

Zambia is the fourth largest copper producer in the world and the second largest in Africa, accounting for about 6% of the world's copper reserves. It is significant that copper accounts for 60% of the country's total exports and generates 45% of government revenues. Zambia's copper industry is highly privatized, which has allowed foreign investors to come to the country.

Zambia actively supports the activities of multinational corporations that provide cleaner technologies and better management practices and create employment opportunities – copper mining companies are the largest employers in Zambia, employing at least 60,000 people and creating about 220,000 indirect jobs. However, despite the economic results, copper mining companies are often blamed for poor waste management and pollution of nearby settlements and water supply.

Congo is considered one of the most resource-rich countries. Significant reserves of copper, diamonds, gold and silver, oil, uranium, and cobalt are mined from Congo. However, Congo is one of the poorest countries on the planet, where 63% of the population is below the poverty line, and mismanagement and a combination of historical circumstances have caused this. Historically, during the colonial period, the Belgians mainly extracted natural resources in this territory. After the declaration of independence in 1960, the country had constant uprisings and coups, leading to a protracted economic crisis. The reforms carried out by the government in conjunction with the IMF and other countries, such as Canada and Ireland, to modernize the country's mining sector did not lead to the planned results. However, the most striking decision due to the closure of state-owned mining companies was to allow citizens to extract minerals independently, which led to uncontrolled mining and the development of illegal activities.

Cobalt, whose reserves in Congo account for half of the world's proven reserves, is mainly used in producing batteries and accumulators. The lack of regulated cobalt mining in Congo has become a source of significant traps that prevent the country and its citizens from receiving a fair income from resource wealth.

The lack of government regulation in the mining industry has led to the fact that cobalt is mined almost manually with picks and chisels, without special clothing and protection from toxic doses of cobalt, which leads to serious diseases, which are practically impossible to get treatment for in this country with undeveloped medicine. More than 250,000 people are employed in such cobalt mining in Congo, of which at least 35,000 are children. Therefore, cobalt mining in this country is an example of "unethical exploitation".

At the same time, the population and economy of Congo receive practically nothing from this extraction, because almost all the extracted ore is taken by concession by Chinese companies, which receive trillions of dollars from the sale of refined cobalt. However, there are also deposits of this metal in China. Cobalt ore is of interest to foreign companies because of their compact localization in one region and high concentration in cobalt ores, unlike similar deposits, for example, in Zambia.

Notably, in the context of the trade wars between China and the United States, cobalt is a kind of object of economic blackmail in the face of growing global demand for cobalt and batteries. An indirect justification for China's active role in using Congo's resources is that, according to an agreement signed with the government, Chinese companies must build public infrastructure facilities (highways and railways, hospitals, airports).

Of course, the expectations of resource-rich countries from partnerships with economically and technologically stronger countries are overestimated in practice, although there are exceptions. On the other hand, using already mastered technologies allows production at lower costs but increases dependence on foreign technologies and partner companies. Understanding the effect of the resource curse at any moment in the functioning of a resource-rich economy should be embedded in the strategic decisions of the countries' governments. To do this, resource extraction must be properly organized, and revenues from resource exports must not only cover current needs but also become the basis for investments in economic development, the welfare of citizens and human capital.

2.4 Are Sovereign Wealth Funds Way Out for Resource-rich Countries / the Global South?

Natural rent is the result of owning resource wealth. When countries sell their resources, they consider export revenues as a source of their economic development, which will contribute to improving the quality of life of the population, universal prosperity, and be evidence of the correctness of the decision to sell the country's resources, which God or nature endowed it with.

We can confidently talk about the forms of capitalization of income from resource exports in the form of sovereign wealth funds that have shown their effectiveness.

As a rule, sovereign wealth funds are created in those states whose budget strongly depends on world commodity prices. The first national welfare fund created was the Kuwait Investment Authority in 1952, formed from profits from the sale of Kuwaiti oil. Some countries accumulate funds in such funds for the period when the subsoil is depleted – the funds can be used to cover the state budget deficit during unfavourable market conditions. Nevertheless, the main goal of the sovereign wealth fund is to use the income from resources to finance economic growth in the long term. In this way, there should be a counteraction to the resource curse.

Currently, the total assets of the 100 largest funds in the world amount to about $11.8 trillion [16], most of them in the regions of developing countries (Table 2.2).

Table 2.2 Sovereign wealth funds in the world

Regions of the world	*Quantity*
Africa	30
Asia	32
The Middle East	30
Australia and the Pacific	9
Latin America	19
Europe	26
North America	21

Source: Compiled by the authors based on [16].

The largest, most well-known, and effective fund is the Norway Government Pension Fund Global, which has become the standard for oil countries. It aims to achieve responsible and long-term revenue management from Norway's oil and gas resources. The fund receives stable income from investing in stocks and real estate and lending to countries and companies.

There are examples among developing countries, such as Social Funds in Brazil, whose goal is to ensure that future generations benefit from exploiting commodities. In Chile, the fund is named following the purpose of creation – the Social and Economic Stabilization Fund.

Today, sovereign wealth funds are not just a fund to collect part of export revenues from the sale of a country's natural resources – they are a source of development, a source of overcoming social problems (from poverty to the digital divide), and a source of prosperity in the future.

2.5 Conclusion

Thus, understanding the importance of growing global demand for raw materials forms a particularly sensitive development agenda for the countries of the Global South, taking into account their resource wealth, which not only determines their economic growth trajectory but also becomes an arena of political and technological contradictions, when methods of extracting minerals and foreign trade volumes have become an instrument of diplomacy for strong influence from the economically and politically stronger countries, which are represented by the Global North.

Resource wealth is not only a source for generating income from exports but also an arena of political and technological contradictions in the choice of ways to extract minerals and foreign trade, especially at present, when the historically fourth commodity boom in the world continues and the cost of metals and mineral resources is constantly growing.

Each country's resource curse and resource dependence are unique and depend on its conditions and experience. Legislation and public policy should ensure the conversion of natural resources into the country's competitive advantages.

To somewhat smooth out the confrontation between sceptics and followers of the phenomenon of the resource curse, it should be noted that research continues. The authors found it extremely interesting that the potential formation of a resource curse or a resource blessing should be considered for various minerals. So, suppose countries are rich in diamonds and precious metals. In that case, the positive and negative effects of using raw materials for development are manifested to a greater extent than in countries with other minerals.

Understanding the effect of the resource curse should be embedded in the strategic decisions of the governments of resource-rich but economically not-rich countries. This requires a certain policy of state regulation of the extraction of resources and their sale, and revenues from the export of resources should contribute to the development of the economy, society, and the citizens' welfare. The modest current results of the sovereign wealth funds of developing countries, however, should be assessed as the foundation for the sustainability of the future. When implementing government programmes to promote industry and exports and reduce corruption, there are good chances not to replenish the lists of cases about the resource curse.

References

1. Alssadek, M., Benhin, J.: Natural resource curse: A literature survey and comparative assessment of regional groupings of oil-rich countries. *Resources Policy* 84, 103741 (2023).
2. Alvarez, J., et al: Geoeconomic Fragmentation and Commodity Markets. WPIEA2023201. IMF (2023).
3. Awoa Awoa, P., et al: Africa's resource curse: The key role of property rights. *Resources Policy* 91, 104929 (2024).
4. Auty, R.M.: *Resource Abundance and Economic Development*. U Press, Oxford: (2002).
5. Bastos, P., Bottan, N.: Resource rents, coercion, and local development: Evidence from post-apartheid South Africa. *World Development* 169, 106289 (2023).
6. Destek, M.A., Aydın, S., Destek, G.: Investigating an optimal resource dependency to prevent natural resource curse: Evidence from countries with the curse risk. *Resources Policy* 79, 102981 (2022).
7. Destek, G., Hossain, M.R., Aydın, S., Destek, M.A.: Can the resource curse be reversed through financialization, human capital, and institutional quality? Evidence from Sustainable Development Index. *Resources Policy* 86, 104245 (2023).
8. IEA: Critical Minerals Data Explorer, https://www.iea.org/data-and-statistics/data-tools/critical-minerals-data-explorer, last accessed 2024/03/24.
9. IMF: World Economic Outlook. Navigating Global Divergences. October, 2023, https://www.imf.org/en/Publications/WEO/Issues/2023/10/10/world-economic-outlook-october-2023, last accessed 2024/03/24.
10. Kasatkin, P.I., et al: The modern universities role in the formation of the digital wave of Kondratiev's long cycles. *Voprosy Ekonomiki* 12, 123–140 (2019).
11. Li, H., et al: Does natural resource cause equitable development or resource curse? An analysis of macroeconomic policies for reducing environmental degradation. *Resources Policy* 87, 104311 (2023).
12. Lotfalipour, M.R., Sargolzaie, A., Salehnia, N.: Natural resources: A curse on welfare? *Resources Policy* 79, 103056 (2022).
13. Masi, T., Savoia, A., Sen, K.: Is there a fiscal resource curse? Resource rents, fiscal capacity and political institutions in developing economies. *World Development* 177, 106532 (2024).
14. Oyelaran-Oyeyinka, B., Lal, K.: *Industrialization and Economic Diversification: Post-Crisis Development Agenda in Asia and Africa*. pp. 206. Routledge, London (2022).
15. Shelomentsev, A.G., et al: Strategic Innovation as a Factor of Adaptation of National Economies to the Development of Global Value Chains. *Sustainability* 13, 9765 (2021).
16. Sovereign Wealth Fund Institute: List of 170 Sovereign Wealth Fund Profiles by Region, https://www.swfinstitute.org/profiles/sovereign-wealth-fund, last accessed 2024/03/24.
17. Stepnov, I.: The Uncertainty of the Technological Future. In: Stepnov, I. (eds) *Technology and Business Strategy*. pp. 19–37. Palgrave Macmillan, Cham (2021).

18. Stepnov, I.M., Kovalchuk, J.A., Kolesnikova, T.V.: Protectionism and Technological Development: The Green Agenda. In: Popkova, E.G. (eds) *Smart Green Innovations in Industry 4.0 for Climate Change Risk Management*. Environmental Footprints and Eco-design of Products and Processes. pp. 85–94. Springer, Cham (2023).
19. Syed, Q.R., et al: Testing natural resource curse hypothesis amidst geopolitical risk: Global evidence using novel Fourier augmented ARDL approach. *Resources Policy* 88, 104317 (2024).
20. Yadav, S., et al: Nexus between fintech, green finance and natural resources management. *Resources Policy* 91, 104903 (2024).
21. Yan, H.: Financial development, violence, and resource curse: How mineral resources are contributing towards growth of resource-rich countries. *Resources Policy* 89, 104546 (2024).
22. Yanıkkaya, H., Turan, T.: Curse or Blessing? An Empirical Re-examination of Natural Resource-Growth Nexus. *Journal of International Development* 30, 1455–1473 (2018).

3 Migration and Brain Drain

Balancing Human Capital Gains and Losses in the Global South

Anushka Lydia Issac and Smita Tripathi

3.1 Introduction

3.1.1 Overview of the Significance of Brain Drain in the Global South

Brain drain, a phenomenon where highly skilled individuals emigrate from their home countries to seek opportunities abroad, holds profound implications for the Global South. This mass exodus of intellectual capital has far-reaching effects on the socio-economic landscapes of these nations (Saxenian, 2005). The Global South, comprising regions in Asia, Africa, Latin America, and the Middle East, often grapples with the loss of its brightest minds to more developed countries. This phenomenon is particularly significant due to its interconnectedness with migration, human capital, and economic growth (Ansah, 2002).

Migration, a pivotal aspect of the brain drain narrative, acts as the vessel through which human capital flows across borders. Skilled individuals seeking enhanced prospects in advanced economies contribute to a substantial outflow of talent from the Global South. This migration of highly skilled individuals, including doctors, engineers, scientists, and professionals in various fields, significantly impacts the regions they leave behind (Ansah, 2002; Saxenian, 2005). Human capital, a critical driver of economic development, encompasses the knowledge, skills, and expertise that individuals possess. The departure of these skilled professionals adversely impacts the human capital base of their home countries, thereby hindering their growth potential (Sager, 2014). This loss of skilled workforce leads to a shortage of expertise in key sectors, such as healthcare, technology, and education. Consequently, the capacity for innovation and development is curtailed, leaving the Global South at a disadvantage in the global knowledge economy.

Moreover, this depletion of human capital exerts a downward pressure on economic growth, impeding the Global South's progress toward sustainable development. Brain drain is a complex and pressing issue for the Global South (Raghuram, 2009). It represents not only a loss of valuable human capital but also a hindrance to the region's overall socio-economic advancement. Addressing

DOI: 10.4324/9781032694337-5

this challenge requires strategic policies that aim to retain and attract skilled professionals, while also creating an environment conducive to innovation, research, and development.

3.1.2 Aim and Objectives

In the Global South, where human capital development is pivotal for economic growth, the dynamics of skilled migration present both challenges and opportunities. This section examines the aim and objectives of this analysis, focusing on the intricate relationship between migration, human capital, and economic growth. The goals are to identify significant patterns and impacts, explore sector-specific effects, examine innovative policies, and assess the contributions of skilled migrants to both their home and host countries. Through this comprehensive approach, the chapter aims to provide valuable insights and strategies for policymakers, economists, and development practitioners dedicated to fostering sustainable economic growth in the Global South amidst the realities of brain drain.

3.2 Literature Review

3.2.1 Defining Brain Drain in the Global South

Brain drain, at its core, is the process in which highly skilled and educated individuals choose to leave their home country in search of opportunities in foreign lands. These individuals encompass a wide range of professionals, from scientists and engineers to doctors and other experts in various fields (Kuehn, 2007). Their emigration is propelled by a desire for improved prospects, which can encompass factors such as higher wages, enhanced working conditions, and access to innovative research facilities. This phenomenon stems from the inherent human drive for self-improvement and a better quality of life. In many cases, individuals who pursue extensive education and training seek environments that not only recognize their skills and expertise but also provide an ecosystem conducive to their continued growth and development (Raghuram, 2009). Advanced economies often present such environments, offering attractive career prospects, robust research infrastructure, and the promise of a higher standard of living. The departure of these highly skilled professionals, however, carries significant implications for their country of origin. It results in a tangible loss of intellectual and creative potential within the source nation (Kofman & Raghuram, 2012). This is particularly impactful when considering the potential contributions these individuals could have made to critical sectors such as healthcare, technology, and education. Their absence can lead to skill shortages, reduced capacity for innovation, and even hinder the advancement of key industries (Raghuram, 2009).

Furthermore, brain drain is not solely a one-way process. It is part of a broader phenomenon that encompasses both the outflow of skilled individuals from the source country and the inflow of talent into destination countries. This intricate interplay shapes the global distribution of human capital and has implications for economies and societies on a global scale (Kuehn, 2007). Overall, understanding brain drain is crucial for policymakers and stakeholders seeking to foster environments that retain and nurture skilled professionals. It calls for strategic initiatives that not only address the pull factors that attract individuals to foreign destinations but also create conditions that incentivize them to stay and contribute to the growth and development of their home country (Sager, 2014).

3.2.2 Contextualizing Brain Drain within the Global South

In the context of the Global South, the phenomenon of brain drain takes on distinct and pronounced characteristics. These regions, comprising countries in Asia, Africa, Latin America, and the Middle East, face a set of unique structural challenges that compound the impacts of skilled emigration (Raghuram, 2009). One of the foremost challenges is the limited access to quality education. Many nations in the Global South struggle to provide educational opportunities that are on par with those in more developed regions. This is often due to a combination of factors, including inadequate infrastructure, a shortage of qualified educators, and a lack of resources for educational institutions (Stock et al., 2019). As a result, individuals who aspire to attain advanced degrees or specialized training may face significant hurdles in their home countries, prompting them to seek education abroad. Insufficient research funding further exacerbates this issue. Research and development are crucial drivers of innovation, technological progress, and economic growth (Nawyn, 2016a). Inadequate funding for research initiatives limits the capacity of institutions in the Global South to conduct innovative research and compete on the global stage. This lack of resources can be a significant deterrent for highly skilled professionals who are seeking an environment that fosters intellectual growth and innovation (Adamson & Tsourapas, 2020).

Moreover, constrained career advancement opportunities are a prevalent concern in the Global South. In many cases, individuals who have acquired specialized skills and knowledge find themselves in environments where there are limited prospects for professional growth and recognition (Adamson & Tsourapas, 2020). This lack of upward mobility can be a significant factor motivating skilled professionals to seek opportunities in more developed countries. The emigration of skilled professionals exacerbates these existing disparities. When individuals with advanced skills and knowledge leave their home countries, they take with them not only their expertise but also the potential to contribute to the development and progress of their nations

(Nawyn, 2016b). This creates a cycle of underdevelopment, where the departure of skilled individuals perpetuates the very challenges that drove them to leave in the first place (Awad & Natarajan, 2018). To truly understand and address brain drain in the Global South, it is imperative to undertake a nuanced exploration of its underlying causes. This involves recognizing and tackling the structural challenges that hinder education, research, and career advancement. Additionally, it requires a comprehensive understanding of the intricate web of socio-economic factors that contribute to this phenomenon (Adamson & Tsourapas, 2020).

3.3 Theoretical Frameworks Shaping Our Understanding of Skilled Migration and Brain Drain

3.3.1 Pull and Push Model

The Pull and Push model provides a comprehensive framework for comprehending the dynamics of skilled migration. It recognizes that individuals make the decision to migrate based on a combination of factors, both pushing them away from their home country and pulling them toward a new destination. The pull factors are the enticing elements that attract skilled professionals to a destination country. They often include higher wages, superior working conditions, advanced research facilities, and a conducive environment for career growth. The promise of better opportunities and a higher standard of living acts as a powerful magnet for skilled individuals. The push factors are the conditions or limitations in the source country that prompt individuals to seek opportunities elsewhere. Common push factors include limited career prospects, inadequate educational resources, political instability, and socio-economic constraints. These challenges compel individuals to look beyond their home country for a brighter future (Beine et al., 2001).

3.3.2 Drain or Gain Model

The Drain or Gain model provides a nuanced assessment of the impact of emigration on a source country's development. It recognizes that brain drain represents a loss of valuable human capital, but also considers potential gains from emigration-related activities. Brain Drain is the aspect that acknowledges the depletion of skilled professionals from the source country. Their departure can lead to skill shortages and a reduction in the capacity for innovation and development. This can have significant implications, particularly in critical sectors like healthcare, education, and technology. The Potential Gains model also highlights potential benefits that can arise from emigration. This includes remittances sent back to the source country, which can provide a vital source of income for families and stimulate local economies. Additionally, knowledge transfer and contributions from the diaspora can lead to positive effects on development (Portes & Celaya, 2013).

3.3.3 Economic Models

Various economic models, such as the Solow-Swan model and endogenous growth models, delve into the intricate relationship between human capital, technological progress, and economic growth. The Solow-Swan model focuses on the role of capital accumulation and technological progress in economic growth. It demonstrates how investments in human capital, including education and skills, contribute to long-term economic development. The endogenous Growth models expand on the Solow-Swan framework by emphasizing the role of innovation, research, and development in driving economic growth. They highlight how investments in human capital and technology lead to sustained economic advancement (Berger, 2022; Bhardwaj & Sharma, 2023).

Brain drain introduces complexities into these economic models. It involves the migration of skilled individuals, potentially resulting in a loss of productivity in the source country. However, it also acknowledges the potential gains from remittances and knowledge transfer. These models collectively provide a comprehensive framework for understanding the intricate dynamics of skilled migration, its impact on source countries, and the broader implications for economic development. They underscore the need for strategic policies and interventions to effectively manage brain drain and maximize the benefits of skilled migration for all parties involved.

3.4 The Interplay between Migration, Human Capital, and Economic Growth

3.4.1 Examination of the Intricate Relationship

The interplay between migration, human capital, and economic growth is a dynamic phenomenon that shapes the socio-economic landscapes of both source and destination countries (Nawyn, 2016b). As individuals embark on this migration, they carry with them a wealth of knowledge, innovation, and expertise. This knowledge transfer has far-reaching effects on both the source and destination countries. Source countries experience a depletion of their human capital base. This is particularly significant in sectors such as healthcare, technology, and education, where skilled professionals play a pivotal role in driving innovation and progress. The loss of these experts can result in skill shortages, reduced capacity for innovation, and even hinder the advancement of key industries (Bhandari, 2019). On the other side, destination countries reap the benefits of this influx of skilled professionals. They enrich the local workforce with diverse perspectives and expertise, contributing significantly to research, development, and innovation efforts. This influx bolsters the competitiveness of industries that rely on specialized skills, such as healthcare, engineering, and technology (Bhandari, 2019; Crush, 2002). It also fosters a culture of diversity and cross-cultural understanding, which can lead to new avenues of growth and collaboration on a global scale.

However, it is important to recognize that this interplay is not a one-way street. It is part of a broader phenomenon that encompasses both the outflow of skilled individuals from the source country and the inflow of talent into destination countries. This intricate dance of human capital influences the global distribution of knowledge and expertise, impacting economies and societies on a global scale (Chakraborty, 2006). Ultimately, understanding and managing this interplay is crucial for policymakers and stakeholders seeking to navigate the challenges and opportunities presented by skilled migration. It calls for strategic initiatives that not only address the pull factors attracting individuals to foreign destinations but also create conditions that incentivize them to stay and contribute to the growth and development of their home country (Papapicco et al., 2021). Achieving this balance is key to maximizing the benefits of skilled migration for both source and destination countries.

3.4.2 Discussion of Their Mutual Influence and Impact

The relationship between migration, human capital, and economic growth is indeed symbiotic, yet intricately complex. It encompasses a dynamic exchange of skills, knowledge, and expertise that shapes the socio-economic landscapes of both source and destination countries. In the context of brain drain from the Global South, the emigration of highly skilled individuals has significant repercussions (Gueye, 2002). The departure of these professionals creates a substantial shortage of expertise in critical sectors, including healthcare, technology, and education. This dearth of skilled personnel hampers the source countries' capacity to foster innovation and sustain economic growth (Gibson & McKenzie, 2011). Without a robust pool of skilled professionals, these nations face challenges in advancing their industries, conducting innovative research, and providing high-quality services to their populations (Portes, 1976).

Furthermore, the absence of skilled professionals can perpetuate a cycle of underdevelopment. The sectors most affected by brain drain are often those that play a central role in the development and well-being of a nation. For instance, a shortage of healthcare professionals can result in inadequate medical services and compromised public health outcomes. Similarly, a lack of skilled educators and researchers in the education sector can hinder the quality of education provided to the next generation, impacting their prospects and potential contributions to society (Gibson & McKenzie, 2011; Mason, 1973; Portes, 1976). On the other hand, destination countries stand to gain from an injection of skilled talent. These professionals contribute to knowledge-based industries, driving innovation and economic prosperity. They bolster research efforts, advance technological capabilities, and enhance the competitiveness of industries that rely on specialized skills. This influx of talent fuels the growth of key sectors and contributes to the overall economic dynamism of destination countries (Mason, 1973; Portes, 1976).

However, it is important to note that destination countries also face challenges in harnessing the full potential of skilled migrants. Issues such as brain waste, where foreign-trained professionals face barriers to practice their professions, can result in the underutilization of their skills. Additionally, integration challenges related to language, cultural adaptation, and recognition of foreign qualifications can pose hurdles to their full participation in the workforce (Papapicco et al., 2021). Navigating this complex relationship requires a nuanced and multifaceted approach. Policymakers and stakeholders must strive to create environments that not only retain skilled professionals in their home countries but also provide them with the opportunities and resources they need to thrive. This includes investing in education, research infrastructure, and creating conducive environments for innovation and entrepreneurship (Awad & Natarajan, 2018; Bhandari, 2019). Balancing the needs and aspirations of individuals with the imperatives of national and global development is key to maximizing the benefits of skilled migration for all parties involved.

3.5 Methodology

The adoption of a multifaceted case study design is a methodological decision centered in the search of comprehensive insights and nuanced knowledge within the context of the Global South (Hollweck & Robert K. Yin, 2015). The employing of a case study design indicates an attention to context-specific analysis, allowing the research to delve deeply into the distinctive aspects of migration, human capital development, and economic growth in the Global South. The case studies drawn from various sources, including academic literature, government reports, and institutional analyses are included to ensure a comprehensive and balanced representation of the patterns and impacts of skilled emigration on both countries of origin and destination. Specific attention is paid to the differential effects of brain drain on key sectors such as healthcare, education, and technology, with each case study providing insights into sector-specific dynamics and challenges. The use of case studies as a methodological approach allows for a comprehensive and in-depth exploration of migration and brain drain in the Global South, facilitating informed policy formulation and strategic decision-making aimed at promoting sustainable economic growth and human capital development (Baxter & Jack, 2008; Tellis, 1997) (See Table 3.1 and 3.2).

3.5.1 Case Studies in Global South Nations – South Asian Countries

Case Study 1: India

India, with its burgeoning population and diverse economy, grapples with the complex issue of brain drain. Despite being a hub of technological innovation and a significant contributor to the global IT sector, India faces challenges in retaining its skilled workforce. Factors such as limited research funding, bureaucratic hurdles, and uneven access to quality education contribute to this phenomenon (Cervantes & Guellec, 2002; Oommen, 1989; Reza Iravani Assistant Professor, 2011). A significant proportion of skilled Indian professionals seek opportunities abroad, with North America and Europe being favored destinations. The IT and healthcare sectors witness substantial emigration, as professionals in these fields seek higher wages, better working conditions, and access to advanced facilities abroad (Chadha et al., 2016; Hawkes et al., 2009). The impact of brain drain on India is twofold. On the one hand, it has led to a loss of critical human capital, particularly in sectors like healthcare and technology. This results in a shortage of skilled professionals, hindering the country's capacity for innovation and development (Cervantes & Guellec, 2002). On the other hand, the Indian diaspora abroad contributes significantly to remittances, knowledge exchange, and even investment in their home country (Docquier & Rapoport, 2012; Krishna & Khadria, 1997; Rizvi, 2005).

Case Study 2: Pakistan

Pakistan, while endowed with a youthful population and immense potential, faces challenges in retaining its skilled workforce. Political instability, security concerns, and limited access to quality education contribute to brain drain in the country (Farooq & Ahmad, 2017). Skilled professionals from Pakistan often seek opportunities in North America, the Middle East, and Europe. The fields of medicine, engineering, and information technology witness significant emigration (Kalsoom & Ali, 2015; Sajjad & Scholar, 2015). The departure of skilled professionals poses a significant challenge to Pakistan's development efforts. Critical sectors like healthcare and technology face shortages of skilled personnel, impacting the country's ability to innovate and grow (Tahir et al., 2011; Ume Laila & Farhan Fiaz, 2018).

Case Study 3: Bangladesh

Bangladesh, a densely populated country in South Asia, faces challenges in retaining its skilled workforce. Factors such as limited access to quality education, political instability, and inadequate research funding contribute to brain drain (Abdullah, 2014). Skilled professionals from Bangladesh often seek opportunities in North America, Europe, and the Middle East. The fields of healthcare, engineering, and information technology witness significant emigration (Rahman, 2013). The departure of skilled professionals poses a significant challenge to Bangladesh's development efforts. Critical sectors like healthcare and technology face shortages of skilled personnel, impacting the country's ability to innovate and grow (Chowdhury, 2018; Levy, 2003).

Case Study 4: Sri Lanka

Sri Lanka, an island nation in South Asia, grapples with brain drain driven by various factors. These include limited career opportunities, political uncertainty, and concerns about safety and security (Anas & Wickremasinghe, 2010). Skilled professionals from Sri Lanka often seek opportunities in countries like the United States, Canada, and Australia. The fields of healthcare, engineering, and finance witness significant emigration (Dodani & LaPorte, 2005). The departure of skilled professionals poses a challenge to Sri Lanka's development efforts. Critical sectors face shortages of skilled personnel, impacting the country's ability to innovate and grow (Carrington. & Detragiache, 1998).

3.5.2 Case Studies in Global South Nations Middle East and African Countries

Case Study 1: Nigeria

Nigeria, as one of the most populous countries in Africa, grapples with a unique set of challenges. Despite being a resource-rich nation, political instability, corruption, and limited access to quality education have fueled brain drain. Additionally, the oil and gas sector, a critical component of the Nigerian economy, faces significant skill shortages (Anetoh & Onwudinjo, 2020). Nigeria experiences emigration primarily in the fields of healthcare, engineering, and information technology. Skilled professionals often seek opportunities in Western countries, particularly the

United States, Canada, and the United Kingdom, drawn by the promise of better working conditions and higher wages (Mba & Ekeopara, 2012). The impact of brain drain on Nigeria is profound. The loss of skilled professionals in critical sectors exacerbates the country's struggle to provide quality healthcare and infrastructure. Moreover, the departure of expertise hampers technological advancements and economic diversification efforts. Nigeria seeks to address this challenge through initiatives aimed at improving education and creating a conducive environment for skilled professionals to thrive (Omonijo Dare Ojo, 2011).

Case Study 2: South Africa

South Africa, with its diverse economy and well-established institutions, grapples with brain drain driven by various factors. These include political uncertainty, limited career opportunities, and concerns about safety and security (Martineau et al., 2004). Skilled professionals from South Africa often seek opportunities in countries like the United Kingdom, Australia, and Canada. The fields of healthcare, engineering, and finance witness significant emigration (Kaplan & Höppli, 2017). The departure of skilled professionals poses a challenge to South Africa's development efforts. Critical sectors face shortages of skilled personnel, impacting the country's ability to innovate and grow (Dovlo, 2004).

Case Study 3: Egypt

Egypt, with its rich history and strategic location in North Africa, grapples with brain drain driven by factors such as limited access to quality education, political instability, and concerns about economic opportunities (Loza & Sorour, 2016). Skilled professionals from Egypt often seek opportunities in the Gulf countries, North America, and Europe. The fields of healthcare, engineering, and information technology witness significant emigration (Russell, 1992). The departure of skilled professionals poses a significant challenge to Egypt's development efforts. Critical sectors like healthcare and technology face shortages of skilled personnel, impacting the country's ability to innovate and grow (Ayubi, 1983; Jenkins, 2016).

Case Study 4: Kenya

Kenya, a prominent East African nation, grapples with brain drain driven by factors such as limited access to quality education, political instability, and concerns about safety and security (Kirigia et al., 2006; Misau et al., 2010). Skilled professionals from Kenya often seek opportunities in countries like the United States, Canada, and the United Kingdom. The fields of healthcare, engineering, and finance witness significant emigration (Odhiambo, 2013). The departure of skilled professionals poses a challenge to Kenya's development efforts. Critical sectors face shortages of skilled personnel, impacting the country's ability to innovate and grow (Oyelere, 2008).

Table 3.1 Comparative overview of the challenges leading to brain drain, major emigration destinations, and the impact on development across countries in South Asia, the Middle East, and Africa (Mishra, 2006b; Policy Centre for the New South, 2021; Tanner, 2005).

Country	*Challenges Leading to Brain Drain*	*Major Emigration Destinations*	*Impact on Development*
India	Limited research funding, bureaucratic hurdles, uneven education access	North America, Europe	Loss of critical human capital, hindering innovation, and growth
Pakistan	Political instability, security concerns, limited education access	North America, Middle East, Europe	Shortages in critical sectors, hindering innovation, and growth
Bangladesh	Limited education access, political instability, inadequate funding	North America, Europe, Middle East	Shortages in critical sectors, hindering innovation, and growth
Sri Lanka	Limited career opportunities, political uncertainty, safety concerns	United States, Canada, Australia	Shortages in critical sectors, hindering innovation, and growth
Nigeria	Political instability, corruption, limited education access	United States, Canada, United Kingdom	Struggle to provide quality services, hampering development
South Africa	Political uncertainty, limited career opportunities, safety concerns	United Kingdom, Australia, Canada	Shortages in critical sectors, hindering innovation, and growth
Egypt	Limited education access, political instability, economic concerns	Gulf countries, North America, Europe	Shortages in critical sectors, hindering innovation, and growth
Kenya	Limited education access, political instability, safety concerns	United States, Canada, United Kingdom	Shortages in critical sectors, hindering innovation, and growth

Table 3.2 The impacts of brain drain on human capital development in the healthcare, education, and technology sectors, detailing the effects on source and destination countries (Dodani, 2005; Mishra, 2006a, 2006b).

Sector	*Impacts of Brain Drain*	*Source Countries*	*Destination Countries*
Healthcare	Shortages of doctors, nurses, and specialists lead to inadequate healthcare services (Hooper, 2008; Serour, 2009).	Experiences decreased productivity	May face challenges due to competition for talent, healthcare disparities may worsen, domestic medical education system may weaken.
	Exacerbates health disparities and hinders efforts to combat diseases (Akinwale & George, 2023; List, 2009).	Increased healthcare costs	May experience brain waste if foreign-trained professionals face barriers to practice, domestic educational institutions may be discouraged (Bassey Eno Offiong et al., 2023; Najib et al., 2019).
	Diminishes capacity to respond to health emergencies	Overall quality of life for citizens may suffer	
Education	Loss of experienced educators affects the quality of education provided	Hinders development of skilled workforce	Benefit from influx of highly educated individuals contributing to research, innovation, and the knowledge economy
	Impedes efforts to improve educational outcomes (Miyagiwa, 1991).	Hampers economic growth and innovation	Address issues of diversity and inclusion to ensure equal opportunities for immigrants in the sector (Wong & Yip, 1999).
	Limits access to quality education for future generations	Perpetuates cycle of limited educational access	Must address brain waste and invest in domestic educational institutions to prevent reliance on foreign-educated individuals (Burke & Gaughran, 2006).
Technology	Limits capacity of source countries to develop and compete in the digital economy (Davenport, 2004).	Hampers ability to harness technology for development and growth	Benefit from skilled technology professionals contributing to innovative ecosystems (Chacko, 2007).
	Missed opportunities for job creation and economic empowerment	Leads to missed opportunities for job creation and economic empowerment	Must ensure diversity and inclusion to provide equal opportunities for all individuals, including immigrants, in the sector (Dodani & LaPorte, 2005).

3.6 Strategies for Mitigating Brain Drain

India has actively implemented a range of policies to mitigate brain drain, acknowledging the importance of retaining skilled professionals. Initiatives include fostering research collaborations, providing incentives for professionals returning to the country, and creating conducive environments for innovation in key sectors. Additionally, the government emphasizes skill development programs aimed at retaining and attracting talent. The multifaceted approach reflects India's commitment to managing the outflow of skilled individuals (Anetoh & Onwudinjo, 2020; Dovlo, 2004; Kaplan & Höppli, 2017). Similarly, Nigeria has undertaken strategic initiatives to counteract brain drain. These efforts encompass creating opportunities for professional development, improving working conditions, and investing in research and innovation. The government's focus extends beyond professional aspects to address political and economic challenges that contribute to the departure of skilled professionals (Abdullah, 2014; Anas & Wickremasinghe, 2010; Levy, 2003). In Egypt, concerted strategies have been put in place to combat brain drain. These include initiatives to enhance education and research infrastructure, provide financial incentives for researchers, and promote knowledge exchange with the diaspora. Concurrently, efforts are underway to foster a supportive environment for start-ups and innovation, reflecting an integrated approach to retaining skilled individuals (Cervantes & Guellec, 2002; Farooq & Ahmad, 2017; Kalsoom & Ali, 2015). South Africa employs a diverse set of measures to mitigate brain drain, recognizing the multifaceted nature of the challenge. These include targeted recruitment and retention strategies, substantial investments in education and skills development, and the creation of a conducive business environment for highly skilled professionals. Moreover, the government is actively addressing socio-political challenges that contribute to the emigration of skilled individuals. The comprehensive approach reflects South Africa's commitment to balancing human capital gains and losses (Anas & Wickremasinghe, 2010, Carrington. & Detragiache, 1998; Chadha et al., 2016; Ume Laila & Farhan Fiaz, 2018). From these strategies, several key lessons and best practices emerge. Notably, fostering a supportive environment for research and innovation is crucial, along with providing incentives for skilled professionals to stay.

3.7 Leveraging Skilled Diaspora Communities

Establishing knowledge exchange programs facilitates the transfer of expertise between skilled diaspora communities and their home countries. These programs can take the form of collaborative research projects, mentorship initiatives, or skills-building workshops (Chowdhury, 2018; Levy, 2003; Rahman, 2013). Initiatives such as venture capital funds, start-up incubators, and business development grants can encourage diaspora members to contribute to their country's economy (Cervantes & Guellec, 2002; Farooq & Ahmad, 2017;

Kalsoom & Ali, 2015). Creating platforms for skilled migrants to connect and collaborate with professionals and institutions in their home countries can lead to meaningful partnerships. These networks can be virtual or physical, providing opportunities for knowledge sharing and joint projects (Chadha et al., 2016; Gueye, 2002). Investing in education and research institutions is crucial for building a strong human capital base. This includes enhancing infrastructure, providing quality education, and supporting research initiatives in key sectors (Awad & Natarajan, 2018; Bhandari, 2019). Creating an environment that encourages innovation and entrepreneurship empowers skilled individuals to contribute to economic growth. This involves policies that support start-ups, provide access to funding, and promote a culture of creativity and risk-taking (Adamson & Tsourapas, 2020; Nawyn, 2016b).

3.7.1 Migration and Economic Growth in Destination Countries

Skilled migrants bring diverse perspectives, expertise, and innovation to destination countries. They contribute significantly to research and development efforts, driving technological advancements and bolstering the competitiveness of industries (Ansah, 2002; Sager, 2014). Highly skilled migrants often fill critical roles in sectors where there may be a shortage of qualified professionals. This leads to increased productivity and competitiveness in industries such as healthcare, technology, and finance, contributing to the overall economic growth of destination countries (Sager, 2014; Saxenian, 2005). Skilled migrants enrich the cultural fabric of destination countries, fostering diversity and cross-cultural understanding. Additionally, they bring with them valuable international networks, which can facilitate trade, investment, and collaboration on a global scale (Kuehn, 2007; Raghuram, 2009). While skilled migrants bring significant expertise, there can be instances of "brain waste" where their skills are underutilized or unrecognized in the destination country. Implementing policies to recognize foreign qualifications and facilitate professional integration is crucial for maximizing the benefits of skilled migration (Nawyn, 2016a; Stock et al., 2019). Ensuring that skilled migrants have equal opportunities for advancement and success is essential for realizing the full potential of their contributions. Policies promoting diversity and inclusion in the workplace and society at large are vital for a mutually beneficial relationship (Awad & Natarajan, 2018; Bhandari, 2019). Encouraging knowledge exchange and collaboration between skilled migrants and local professionals can lead to synergies that drive innovation and economic growth. Establishing platforms for meaningful collaboration and partnership-building is key (Chakraborty, 2006; Gueye, 2002).

3.8 Conclusion

The phenomenon of brain drains, particularly in the Global South, is a multifaceted challenge with profound implications for both source and destination countries. This outline has conducted a comprehensive exploration, from defining and contextualizing brain drain to scrutinizing its impacts on critical sectors and proposing potential strategies for mitigation. By examining case studies from diverse South Asian and African nations, we have gained valuable insights into the unique economic, social, and political contexts that shape emigration patterns (Tahir et al., 2011; Ume Laila & Farhan Fiaz, 2018). These cases serve as powerful exemplars of the far-reaching significance of brain drain on human capital development. Skilled migrants make substantial contributions to advanced economies, yet their departure creates a crucial void in their home nations, especially in pivotal sectors like healthcare, education, and technology (Farooq & Ahmad, 2017; Kalsoom & Ali, 2015). Strategies for mitigating brain drain provide a beacon of hope for retaining and attracting skilled professionals. Furthermore, harnessing the potential of skilled diaspora communities emerges as a potent force for bolstering human capital development (Docquier & Rapoport, 2012; Krishna & Khadria, 1997). The reciprocal relationship between skilled migration and economic growth in destination countries spotlights the need for inclusive policies that address issues like brain waste and promote diversity and inclusion (Hawkes et al., 2009; Oommen, 1989). It is crucial to conduct thorough policy impact assessments to better understand the effectiveness of existing measures that help mitigate brain drain. Fostering collaboration among governments, international organizations, academia, and the private sector, countries can impact and drive positive change on a global scale.

3.8.1 Future Directions and Research Agenda

Conducting comprehensive assessments of the effectiveness of policies aimed at mitigating brain drain is essential. This involves evaluating the outcomes of specific interventions to refine and optimize strategies (Chakraborty, 2006; Papapicco et al., 2021). Exploring the long-term effects of brain drain on source countries is crucial for understanding the sustained impacts on economic development, social services, and overall well-being of their populations (Chakraborty, 2006; Papapicco et al., 2021). Studying different models of diaspora engagement and their impact on source countries can provide valuable insights into the most effective strategies for harnessing the potential of skilled migrants (Bhandari, 2019; Crush, 2002).

References

Abdullah, A. M. (2014). Brain drain: Economic and social sufferings for Bangladesh. *Asian Journal of Humanity, Art and Literature*, *1*(1), 9–17. https://doi.org/10.18034/ajhal.v1i1.278

Adamson, F. B., & Tsourapas, G. (2020). The migration state in the Global South: Nationalizing, developmental, and neoliberal models of migration management. *International Migration Review*, *54*(3), 853–882. https://doi.org/10.1177/0197918319879057

Akinwale, O. E., & George, O. J. (2023). Personnel brain-drain syndrome and quality healthcare delivery among public healthcare workforce in Nigeria. *Arab Gulf Journal of Scientific Research*, *41*(1), 18–39. https://doi.org/10.1108/AGJSR-04-2022-0022

Anas, M. U. M., & Wickremasinghe, S. I. (2010). Brain drains of the scientific community of developing countries: The case of Sri Lanka. *Science and Public Policy*, *37*(5), 381–388. https://doi.org/10.3152/030234210X501199

Anetoh, B. C., & Onwudinjo, V. G. (2020). Association for the promotion of African studies 86 emigration and the problem of brain drain in Nigeria: A philosophical evaluation. *Journal of African Studies and Sustainable Development*, *3*(1), 2630–7073. https://doi.org/10.13140/RG.2.2.15954.71365

Ansah, E. E. (2002). Theorizing the brain drain. *African Issues*, *30*(1), 21. https://doi.org/10.2307/1167085

Awad, I., & Natarajan, U. (2018). *The Dominant Discourse on International Migration Privileges a Northern Agenda and Obfuscates the Real Causes and Consequences of Human Mobility*.

Ayubi, N. (1983). The Egyptian "brain drain": A multidimensional problem. *International Journal of Middle East Studies*, *15*(4), 431–450. https://doi.org/10.1017/S0020743800051370

Bassey Eno Offiong, G. Salibi, & Nikolaos Tzenios. (2023). *Medical Brain Drain Scourge in Africa: Focusing on Nigeria*.

Baxter, P., & Jack, S. (2008). Qualitative Case Study Methodology: Study Design and Implementation for Novice Researchers. In *The Qualitative Report* (Vol. 13). http://www.nova.edu/ssss/QR/QR13-4/baxter.pdf

Beine, M., Docquier, F., & Rapoport, H. (2001). *Brain Drains and Economic Growth: Theory and Evidence* (Vol. 64). www.elsevier.comrlocatereconbase

Berger, S. (2022). *Brain Drain, Brain Gain, and Its Net Effect*. www.KNOMAD.org.

Bhandari, R. (2019). Global student and talent flows: Re-examining the brain drain equation. *International Higher Education*, *99*, 6–7. https://doi.org/10.6017/ihe.2019.99.11643

Bhardwaj, B., & Sharma, D. (2023). Migration of skilled professionals across the border: Brain drains or brain gain? *European Management Journal*. https://doi.org/10.1016/j.emj.2022.12.011

Burke, S., & Gaughran, W. F. (2006). Intelligent environmental management for SMEs in manufacturing. *Robotics and Computer-Integrated Manufacturing*, *22*(5–6), 566–575. https://doi.org/10.1016/j.rcim.2005.11.008

Carrington, J. W., & Detragiache, E. (1998). How Big is the Brain Drain? In *IMF Working Paper No. 98/102* (98/102; https://Ssrn.Com/Abstract=882624)

Cervantes, M., & Guellec, D. (2002). The brain drains: Old myths, new realities. *Organization for Economic Cooperation and Development*, *230*, 40–42.

Chacko, E. (2007). From brain drain to brain gain: reverse migration to Bangalore and Hyderabad, India's globalizing high tech cities. *GeoJournal*, *68*(2–3), 131–140. https://doi.org/10.1007/s10708-007-9078-8

Chadha, B., Rai, R. S., & Dugar, A. (2016). Globalizing higher education in India: Brain drain in reverse – A Review. *Prabandhan: Indian Journal of Management*, *9*(10), 23. https://doi.org/10.17010/pijom/2016/v9i10/103071

Chakraborty, B. S. (2006). Brain drain: An alternative theorization. *The Journal of International Trade & Economic Development*, *15*(3), 293–309. https://doi.org/10.1080/09638190600871602

Chowdhury, F. (2018). *Brain Drain: Factors Affecting Student Migration from Bangladesh*.

Crush, J. (2002). The global raiders: Nationalism, globalization, and the South African brain drain. *Journal of International Affairs*, *56*(1), 147–172. http://www.jstor.org/stable/24357887

Davenport, S. (2004). Panic and panacea: brain drain and science and technology human capital policy. *Research Policy*, *33*(4), 617–630. https://doi.org/10.1016/j.respol.2004.01.006

Docquier, F., & Rapoport, H. (2012). Globalization, brain drain, and development. *Journal of Economic Literature*, *50*(3), 681–730. https://doi.org/10.1257/jel.50.3.681
Dodani, S., & LaPorte, R. E. (2005). Brain drain from developing countries: How can brain drain be converted into wisdom gain? *Journal of the Royal Society of Medicine*, *98*(11), 487–491. https://doi.org/10.1177/014107680509801107
Dovlo, D. (2004). The brain drain in Africa: An emerging challenge to health professionals' education. *Journal of Higher Education in Africa / Revue de l'enseignement Supérieur En Afrique*, *2*(3), 1–18. http://www.jstor.org/stable/24486291
Farooq, S., & Ahmad, E. (2017). Brain drain from Pakistan: An empirical analysis. *Forman Journal of Economic Studies*, *00*, 55–81. https://doi.org/10.32368/fjes.20170003
Gibson, J., & McKenzie, D. (2011). Eight questions about brain drain. *Journal of Economic Perspectives*, *25*(3), 107–128. https://doi.org/10.1257/jep.25.3.107
Gueye, A. (2002). Dark side of the African brain drain: Experiences of Africans holding doctoral degrees in social sciences and humanities living in France. *African Issues*, *30*(1), 62. https://doi.org/10.2307/1167093
Hawkes, M., Kolenko, M., Shockness, M., & Diwaker, K. (2009). Nursing brain drain from India. *Human Resources for Health*, *7*(1), 5. https://doi.org/10.1186/1478-4491-7-5
Hollweck, T., & Robert K. Yin. (2015). Case study research design and methods. *Canadian Journal of Program Evaluation*, *30*(1), 108–110. https://doi.org/10.3138/cjpe.30.1.108
Hooper, C. R. (2008). Adding insult to injury: The healthcare brain drains. *Journal of Medical Ethics*, *34*(9), 684–687. https://doi.org/10.1136/jme.2007.023143
Jenkins, R. (2016). Brain drain. *BJPsych. International*, *13*(3), 53–55. https://doi.org/10.1192/S2056474000001215
Kalsoom, A., & Ali, H. (2015). Two-fold aspect of brain drain in Pakistan: An empirical investigation. *Global Journal of Science*, *3*(3). https://www.researchgate.net/publication/288344523
Kaplan, D., & Höppli, T. (2017). The South African brain drain: An empirical assessment. *Development Southern Africa*, *34*(5), 497–514. https://doi.org/10.1080/0376835X.2017.1351870
Kirigia, J. M., Gbary, A. R., Muthuri, L. K., Nyoni, J., & Seddoh, A. (2006). The cost of health professionals' brain drains in Kenya. *BMC Health Services Research*, *6*(1), 89. https://doi.org/10.1186/1472-6963-6-89
Kofman, E., & Raghuram, P. (2012). Women, migration, and care: Explorations of diversity and dynamism in the global south. *Social Politics: International Studies in Gender, State & Society*, *19*(3), 408–432. https://doi.org/10.1093/sp/jxs012
Krishna, V. V., & Khadria, B. (1997). Phasing scientific migration in the context of brain gain and brain drain in India. *Science, Technology and Society*, *2*(2), 347–385. https://doi.org/10.1177/097172189700200207
Kuehn, B. M. (2007). Global shortage of health workers, brain drain stress developing countries. *JAMA*, *298*(16), 1853. https://doi.org/10.1001/jama.298.16.1853
Levy, L. F. (2003). The first world's role in the third world brain drains. *BMJ*, *327*(7407), 170. https://doi.org/10.1136/bmj.327.7407.170
List, J. M. (2009). Justice and the Reversal of the Healthcare Worker 'Brain-Drain.' *The American Journal of Bioethics*, *9*(3), 10–12. https://doi.org/10.1080/15265160802654186
Loza, N., & Sorour, E. (2016). Brain drain: the issues raised for Egypt by the emigration of psychiatrists. *BJPsych. International*, *13*(3), 59–61. https://doi.org/10.1192/S2056474000001239
Martineau, T., Decker, K., & Bundred, P. (2004). "Brain drain" of health professionals: From rhetoric to responsible action. *Health Policy*, *70*(1), 1–10. https://doi.org/10.1016/j.healthpol.2004.01.006

Mason, H. R. (1973). "Physician migration: Brain drain or overflow?" *JAMA: The Journal of the American Medical Association*, *226*(4), 463. https://doi.org/10.1001/jama.1973.03230040037010

Mba, P. N., & Ekeopara, C. (2012). "BRAIN DRAIN": Implication for economic growth in Nigeria. In *American Journal of Social Issues & Humanities* (Vol. 2, Issue 2).

Misau, Y. A., Al-Sadat, N., & Bakari Gerei, A. (2010). Brain-drain and health care delivery in developing countries. *Journal of Public Health in Africa*, *1*(1). https://doi.org/10.4081/jphia.2010.e6

Miyagiwa, K. (1991). Scale economies in education and the brain drain problem. *International Economic Review*, *32*(3), 743. https://doi.org/10.2307/2527117

Najib, M., Juni, M. H., & Salloum, A. (2019). Brain-drain phenomenon among health-care workers. *International Journal of Public Health and Clinical Sciences*, *6*, 90–103. https://doi.org/10.32827/ijphcs.6.3.90

Nawyn, S. J. (2016a). Migration in the global south: Exploring new theoretical territory. *International Journal of Sociology*, *46*(2), 81–84. https://doi.org/10.1080/00207659.2016.1163991

Nawyn, S. J. (2016b). New directions for research on migration in the global south. *International Journal of Sociology*, *46*(3), 163–168. https://doi.org/10.1080/00207659.2016.1197719

Odhiambo, G. O. (2013). Academic brain drain: Impact and implications for public higher education quality in Kenya. *Research in Comparative and International Education*, *8*(4), 510–523. https://doi.org/10.2304/rcie.2013.8.4.510

Ojo, Omonijo Dare. (2011). Understanding the escalation of brain drain in Nigeria from poor leadership point of view. *Mediterranean Journal of Social Sciences*. https://doi.org/10.5901/mjss.2011.v2n3p434

Oommen, T. K. (1989). India: 'Brain Drain' or the migration of talent? *International Migration*, *27*(3), 411–425. https://doi.org/10.1111/j.1468-2435.1989.tb00355.x

Oyelere, R. U. (2008). Brain drain, waste or gain? What we know about the Kenyan case. *Journal of Global Initiatives: Policy, Pedagogy, Perspective*, *2*(2), 113–139.

Papapicco, C., D'Errico, F., & Mininni, G. (2021). Affective detection of 'brain drain' through video-narrative interview. *World Futures*, *77*(4), 266–284. https://doi.org/10.1080/02604027.2021.1914486

Portes, A. (1976). Determinants of the brain drain. *International Migration Review*, *10*(4), 489–508. https://doi.org/10.1177/019791837601000402

Portes, A., & Celaya, A. (2013). Modernization for emigration: Determinants & consequences of the brain drain. *Daedalus*, *142*(3), 170–184. https://doi.org/10.1162/DAED_a_00226

Raghuram, P. (2009). Caring about 'brain drain' migration in a postcolonial world. *Geoforum*, *40*(1), 25–33. https://doi.org/10.1016/j.geoforum.2008.03.005

Rahman, T. (2013). From Brain Drain to Brain Gain: Leveraging the Academic Diaspora for Development in Bangladesh. In *Diaspora Engagement and Development in South Asia* (pp. 124–144). Palgrave Macmillan UK. https://doi.org/10.1057/9781137334459_7

Reza Iravani, M. (2011). Brain drains Problem: A Review. In *International Journal of Business and Social Science* (Vol. 2, Issue 15). www.ijbssnet.com

Rizvi, F. (2005). Rethinking "brain drain" in the era of globalisation. *Asia Pacific Journal of Education*, *25*(2), 175–192. https://doi.org/10.1080/02188790500337965

Russell, M. L. (1992). The Female Brain Drain, the State, and Development in Egypt. In *Women and Development in the Middle East and North Africa* (pp. 122–143). BRILL. https://doi.org/10.1163/9789004474130_011

Sager, A. (2014). Reframing the brain drain. *Critical Review of International Social and Political Philosophy*, *17*(5), 560–579. https://doi.org/10.1080/13698230.2014.919061

Sajjad, N., & Scholar, M. (2015). *Causes and Solutions to Intellectual Brain Drain in Pakistan*.

Saxenian, A. (2005). From brain drain to brain circulation: Transnational communities and regional upgrading in india and China. *Studies in Comparative International Development*, *40*(2), 35–61. https://doi.org/10.1007/BF02686293
Serour, G. I. (2009). Healthcare workers and the brain drain. *International Journal of Gynecology & Obstetrics*, *106*(2), 175–178. https://doi.org/10.1016/j.ijgo.2009.03.035
Stock, I., Üstübici, A., & Schultz, S. U. (2019). Externalization at work: Responses to migration policies from the Global South. *Comparative Migration Studies*, *7*(1), 48. https://doi.org/10.1186/s40878-019-0157-z
Tahir, W., Kauser, R., & Ali Tahir, M. (2011). *Brain drains of doctors; causes and consequences in Pakistan*. https://www.researchgate.net/publication/287480268
Tellis, W. M. (1997). Application of a Case Study Methodology. In *The Qualitative Report* (Vol. 3, Issue 3). http://nsuworks.nova.edu/tqr/vol3/iss3/1
Ume Laila, S., & Farhan Fiaz, M. (2018). Impact of Brain Drain on Economic Growth in Pakistan. In *The Business and Management Review* (Vol. 9).
Wong, K., & Yip, C. K. (1999). Education, economic growth, and brain drain. *Journal of Economic Dynamics and Control*, *23*(5–6), 699–726. https://doi.org/10.1016/S0165-1889(98)00040-2

Part II

Political Instability, Conflict, and the Global South

4 Internally Displaced Persons and Economic Vulnerability in Developing Countries

Some Policy Implications

Muhammad Ramzan Sheikh, Sana Sultan, and Irfan Hussain

4.1 Introduction

Internal displacement is a global issue that has drawn worldwide scrutiny. Internal displacement refers to the forceful movement of people from one region of a country to another as a result of violence, conflict, or calamity. Because the same process has been growing in strength and inflating global IDP numbers, developing countries are most affected. Internal displacement has negative consequences on people's lives and livelihoods, affecting the economy. The process of relocation, which generally means losing one's job, home, and social network, makes the affected populations more vulnerable. It is essential to comprehend the economic areas of internally displaced persons to create protean intervention strategies that address the long-term requirements of IDPs while also promoting their durable integration into the life of society.

Thus, IDPs immediately impact economies in a number of interconnected ways. These effects can be further classified according to two dimensions: direct material, and short term; and indirect intangible, and long term. The primal ones include the costs of providing food, shelter, medical treatment, and the outlays associated with the rehabilitation of the displaced. The second category, indirectly short, also referred to as the opportunity cost of settlement of the IDPs, considers the use of resources to bring the IDPs to an idyllic state. It can manifest itself in the forms of lower productivity, misallocated development investments, and worsening social cohesion and increasing conflicts (IDMC, 2018). There are many ways through which IDPs may influence the economy as various pieces of research have pointed out that IDPs may affect social and cultural life, housing and infrastructure, education, health, environment, security, and livelihoods (IDMC, 2018).

The research work related to IDPs is mostly confined to analysis of the socio-economic conditions of internally displaced people rather than their effect on the various dimensions of the economy and particularly on the economic vulnerability (see, for example, Chambers, 1989; Platt, 1991; Moser, 1996; May & Norton, 1997; Ollenburger & Tobin, 1998; Holzmann & Jorgensen, 1999; Leus et al., 2001; Vogel, 2004; Barrientos & Hulme, 2009; O'Brien et al., 2009; Chan & Stevens, 2001).

DOI: 10.4324/9781032694337-7

Displacement can result from different causes: environmental degradation, civil unrest, persecution as well as economic collapse. These unplanned population movements have strong and far-reaching implications for economies all over the world (UNCT Ukraine, 2019). Displacement impacts the labor markets, leading to a loss of human capital in both the hosting and sending countries. In the host countries where displacement enhances the diversity and skill set of the workforce, while it presents challenges for social services, housing, and employment opportunities (UNHCR, 2023a, 2023b). For homelands, the loss of a heady portion of productive individuals and the disruption of economic processes can aggravate even more the prevailing economic hardships. The long-term nature of displacement is another factor that halts the development prospects for displaced people as they often face barriers that block their access to education, health, and economic opportunities, thus they fail to contribute to their economy as much as they can (UNHCR, 2015). Displacement is, in most cases, a complex challenge with far-reaching economic consequences requiring comprehensive approaches for mitigation and response at national and international levels.

The present study is a valuable addition to the existing literature on IDPs because none of the earlier studies have attempted such type of analysis. The analysis represents a wider viewpoint of the overall economic exposure caused by displacement, and it expresses the implications of displacement in terms of multiple sectors. This whole systemic view is the key for the formulation of comprehensive policy frameworks which will consider the whole economy and its implications to displacement guiding the efforts to build resilience and mitigate the vulnerabilities at both the individual and societal levels. This, in turn, allows policymakers to achieve a clear and balanced view of the intricate changes in processes, hence the effectiveness of policy interventions on economic vulnerability among the IDP population in developing countries. Secondly, the major contribution of this study is also to trace out the impacts of IDPS on the developing economy that has been and still passing through the crises of IDPs. Thirdly, it is the credit of this study that an economic vulnerability index has been designed specifically to magnify the impact of IDPs on the economy of developing countries.

4.2 Objective and Research Question of the Study

The present study is an attempt to thrash out the ways and means through which IDPs affect the economy which has been the victim of IDPs since the war against terrorism. The link between the economic variables creates ripple effects when IDPs are taken underhand. Many studies have attempted to explore the association in multiple ways but it is the contribution of this study to analyze the impact through economic vulnerability. The specific objective of the study is to examine the impact of internal displacement on economy's vulnerability.

4.3 Literature Review

Internally Displaced Persons, or IDPs, constitute a significant aspect of economic vulnerability, as they refer to the group of people who are forcibly displaced within their homelands as a result of conflicts, natural disasters, or human-made crises. These people experience substantial losses of their livelihoods, assets, and access to social services, contributing to deepening poverty and inequality. The primary sources of economic vulnerability of IDPs include the lack of employment opportunities, the reduced access to educational and healthcare facilities, and the increased risks of exploitation and violence. This section discusses the studies on internally displacement persons and macroeconomic variables (See Table 4.1).

The lack of previous studies explicitly looking at the combined and disaggregated effects of internally displaced people (IDPs) on developing economies through economic vulnerability is the source of the research gap in this study. The chapter makes the unusual claim that it employs MMQR methodology, but it does not cite any related studies.

4.4 Model Specification, Data Sources, and Methodology

We have specified a-theoretic model. In this model, we have examined the impact of IDPs on economic vulnerability index. To estimate the results, we have used the Method of Moment Quantile Regression (MMQR) developed by Machado and Silva (2019). This method provides a flexible framework to capture the coefficient at various quantile levels. The use of quantiles in MM-QR is essential because it provides a broad perspective of the association between variables throughout the distribution. An extensive examination of the quantiles may reveal how the association differs depending on which location in the data foil; this is easier to comprehend in comparison to traditional regression methods. There are a total of 134 countries in the world, but we dropped 64 countries and have taken the data of only 70 developing countries over the period 2009–2022 due to the unavailability of the internally displaced persons data. (see Figure 4.1).

4.4.1 Model: Economic Vulnerability and IDP$_S$

$$\mathrm{EVI} = f\left(\mathrm{IDPs}, \mathrm{GDPPC}, \mathrm{POV}, \mathrm{UR}\right)$$

This model explains the impact of IDPs on economic vulnerability of nations. In this model, the control variables are GDP per capita, poverty, and unemployment rate. The econometric form is given as:

$$\mathrm{EVI}_{it} = \beta_0 + \beta_1 \mathrm{IDPs}_{it} + \beta_2 \mathrm{GDPPC}_{it} + \beta_3 \mathrm{POV}_{it} + \beta_4 UR_{it} + \varepsilon_{it}$$

Table 4.1 Literature Review of the Related Studies

Author(s)	*Time Period*	*Countries*	*Methodology*	*Main Results*
Roberts et al. (2022)	2010–2019	Low Middle-Income Countries (LMICs)	Nonlinear least-squared regression analysis	IDP population size (+), National per capita GDP (+), National government health expenditure (+), Universal health coverage indicator (+), National life expectancy (+), Maternal mortality, ratio (+), Infant mortality ratio (+)
Nguyen and Thanh (2022)	2002–2015	73 low- and middle-income economies	panel Granger causality two-step system generalized method	EV shows negative impact on Energy Price, industry and positive impact on Financial Development, income and Human Capital
Lu et al. (2021)	2017–2020	Chifeng City, China	difference-in-differences method	Health Poverty Alleviation Project (HPAP) reduce catastrophic health expenditure. It reduces economic Vulnerability.
Sheikh (2021)	October 2019–January 2020	Northern Syria 268 camps	OLS Regression Analysis	Poverty (−), Health Condition (+), Education (−)
Johnson et al. (2021)	July 22, 2017	Ukraine	Logistic regression models	Mental Health (+), Conflict (+)
Canh and Thanh (2020)	2002–2017	79 countries	the two-step GMM	EVI is dependent variable which show positive relation with economic growth, trade openness, Inflation and negative relation to institutional quality, industrialization, and domestic tourism.
Owoaje et al., 2016	2000–2016	Africa	Literature Review	The study found that people in the camps face health problems.
Singh et al., 2015	267 men in IDP camps	Kenya	Frequency and percentage analysis	According to the results, men's mean BMI was 20.3 kg/m2, and roughly 23.9% of the participants were underweight. Moreover, there was significant food insecurity in 75% of the homes that were tested.

Guerrier et al., 2009	30 cluster of households from IDPs camp in Ouaddai	Chad	Preliminary Analysis	The daily rate of child death was 1.8 per 10,000 in the IDP settlements and 0.3 per 10,000 in the non-IDP settlements. The rate of acute malnutrition among children who were internally displaced (IDP) was around 20.6%, whereas the rate in non-IDP children was roughly 16.4%.
Olwedo et al., (2008)	672 Children	Uganda	Qualitative	The findings of the study indicated that children in the IDP camps most frequently experienced fever, coughing, and diarrhea. Fever and being a male child between the ages of three and twenty-four months were strongly correlated with malnutrition.
Kim et al., 2007	1293 household	South Darfur.	Frequency and percentage analysis	In IDP camps, a household study found that 31% of respondents had depression. In the preceding year, 2% of families disclosed that one of their members had taken their own life.
Turnip and Hauff (2007)	460	Indonesia	Frequency and percentage analysis	The findings of the study indicated that 47% of people reported having psychological distress overall. Regardless of their roles in the home, women had the highest prevalence (55%), while males had the lowest (37%).

Source: Authors' compilation.

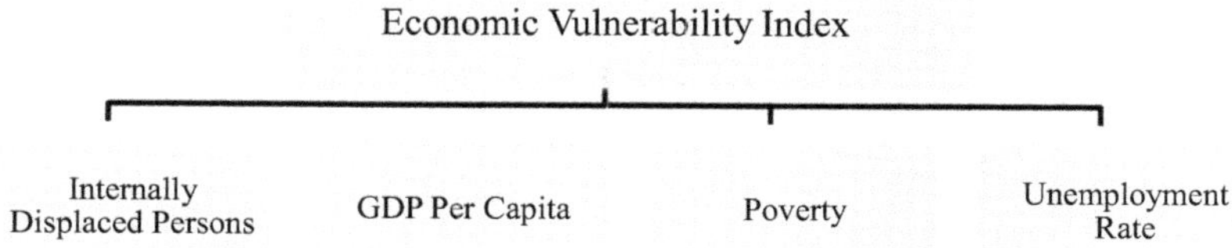

Figure 4.1 Model Structure.

Source: Authors' elaboration.

The general quantile conditional function for quantile τ is given as:

$$Q_{\mathrm{EVI}_{it}}(\tau \mid \gamma_i, \delta_t, X_{i,t}) = \gamma_i + \delta_t + \lambda_{1,\tau}\mathrm{IDPs}_{i,t} + \lambda_{2,\tau}\mathrm{GDPPC}_{i,t} + \lambda_{3,\tau}\mathrm{POV}_{i,t} + \lambda_{4,\tau}\mathrm{UR}_{i,t} + \varepsilon_{\tau,i,t}$$

where t is the time period beginning at $t = 1$, and τ represents quantiles such as the 10th, 25th, 50th, 75th, and 90th $i = 1,\ldots..N$ is for cross-sections.

IDPs = Internally Displacement Persons
GDPPC = GDP per capita growth (annual %)
POV = Poverty headcount ratio at national poverty lines (% of population)
UR = Unemployment Rate (annual %)
EVI = Economic Vulnerability Index
The Economic Vulnerability Index (EVI) is derived from the UNCDP 2009 review and is computed as the simple arithmetic mean of the exposure and shock indices.
EVI = 0.5 × Exposure + 0.5 × Shock

4.5 Results and Discussions

The study's findings are explained in this section.

4.6 Summary Statistics and Correlation Analysis

The correlation analysis and summary statistics for the variable under consideration are explained in this section. Table 4.2 shows the descriptive and correlation analysis of the key variables. The variable "IDPS," representing internally displaced persons, exhibits a mean of 597,945, with a median of 125,000, indicating a substantial difference between the average and middle values. The range spans from a minimum of 362 to a maximum of 7,246,000, reflecting considerable variability. The standard deviation of 1,417,174 underscores the wide dispersion of values. The skewness of 3.214 suggests a highly positively skewed distribution, indicating a long tail on the right side. The kurtosis value of 12.232 points to a

Table 4.2 Descriptive and Correlation Analysis

	IDPS	*GDPPC*	*POV*	*UR*	*EVI*
Mean	597945	2.508	40.026	6.338	29.139
Median	125000	2.709	39.000	4.390	27.000
Maximum	7246000	14.440	59.500	20.710	72.000
Minimum	362	−13.546	25.100	0.250	8.000
Std. Dev.	1417174	3.785	6.933	4.803	10.690
Skewness	3.214	−0.798	0.441	1.058	1.141
Kurtosis	12.232	6.032	2.719	3.518	5.332
Jarque-Bera	1059.819	98.344	7.167	39.710	89.118
Probability	0.000	0.000	0.028	0.000	0.000
IDPS	1.000				
GDPPC	−0.013	1.000			
POV	0.420	−0.077	1.000		
UR	0.229	0.048	0.018	1.000	
EVI	−0.226	−0.105	−0.187	−0.002	1.000

Source: Authors' calculations.

distribution with extreme outliers and heavy tails. The Jarque-Bera statistic of 1059.819, coupled with a probability of 0.000, indicates a significant departure from normality, emphasizing distinctive characteristics in the distribution of internally displaced persons. The variable "GDPPC" represents the annual growth percentage of gross domestic product per capita. The mean growth rate is 2.508%, with a median of 2.709%, indicating a relatively stable distribution. The range spans from a minimum contraction of −13.546% to a maximum growth of 14.440%, highlighting a considerable variability in economic performance across the observed units. A considerable degree of dispersion is shown by the standard deviation of 3.785%.

The skewness of −0.798 implies a slight leftward asymmetry, while a kurtosis of 6.032 indicates a distribution with heavier tails and more extreme values than a normal distribution. The Jarque-Bera statistic of 98.344, along with a probability of 0.000, indicates a departure from a normal distribution, emphasizing the non-normative characteristics in the annual growth percentage of gross domestic product per capita. The low probability suggests that the observed distribution is significantly different from what would be expected under normality assumptions.

The variable "POV," representing the poverty headcount ratio at national poverty lines (% of the population), exhibits a mean value of 40.026 and a median of 39.000, indicating a central tendency around these values. The range spans from 25.100 to 59.500, showcasing variability in the poverty ratio across the dataset. The data appear to be somewhat dispersed, based on the 6.933 standard deviation. A distribution that is somewhat positively skewed, with a larger tail on the right side, is indicated by the skewness of 0.441.

The kurtosis value of 2.719 suggests a distribution with a moderate peak, while the Jarque-Bera test statistic of 7.167 with a probability of 0.028 indicates departure from a normal distribution. The non-zero probability suggests that the distribution of poverty ratios may deviate from normality, reflecting potential asymmetry or outliers in the data.

The variable "UR," representing the Unemployment Rate (annual %), features a mean of 6.338, reflecting a moderate average unemployment rate. The median, at 4.390, indicates a distribution less affected by extreme values. With a range from 0.250 to 20.710, there is noticeable variation in unemployment rates. The standard deviation of 4.803 highlights dispersion around the mean. The slightly positively skewed distribution (skewness: 1.058) suggests a tendency for moderate to high unemployment rates. A kurtosis value of 3.518 indicates tails that are less heavy than a normal distribution. The Jarque-Bera test, with a statistic of 39.710 and a probability of 0.000, strongly points to non-normality, emphasizing distinctive features in the distribution of unemployment rates. The low probability value implies that the observed distribution is unlikely under normality assumptions. The variable "EVI," representing the Economic Vulnerability Index, shows an average index value of 29.139, offering insights into the economic susceptibility of a given region. The median, standing at 27.000, suggests a central tendency less swayed by extreme values. With a range extending from a minimum of 8.000 to a maximum of 72.000, there is notable diversity in economic vulnerability among different regions. The standard deviation of 10.690 indicates significant variability around the mean. The positively skewed distribution (skewness: 1.141) implies a tail on the right side, pointing to a higher prevalence of regions with heightened economic vulnerability. Compared to a normal distribution, the kurtosis value of 5.332 indicates a distribution with considerably more prominent tails. The Jarque-Bera test, with a statistic of 89.118 and a probability of 0.000, strongly suggests non-normality, underscoring distinctive features in the distribution of the Economic Vulnerability Index. The low probability value indicates that the observed distribution is unlikely under the assumption of normality.[1]

Table 4.2 also shows the correlation analysis of the key variables. IDPS shows a moderate positive correlation with POV (0.420) and weak positive correlations with UR (0.229), while having a weak negative correlation with EVI (−0.226). GDPPC has almost no correlation with the other variables, indicated by values close to zero, such as −0.013 with IDPS and −0.077 with POV. POV has a weak negative correlation with EVI (−0.187) but almost no correlation with UR (0.018). UR itself has almost no correlation with EVI (−0.002).

4.7 Cross-Section Dependence and Slope Heterogeneity Results

Table 4.3 provides the results of Pesaran's Cross-Sectional Dependence (CD) test for a set of variables. The CD test is used to assess whether there is cross-sectional dependence among the variables in a dataset. The table shows the

Table 4.3 Results of CD Test

Variable	*CD-test*	P-*Value*
IDPs	54.710	0.000
GDPPC	39.267	0.000
POV	17.072	0.000
UR	−1.812	0.070
EVI	11.097	0.000

Source: Authors' calculations.

Table 4.4 Slope Homogeneity Test

Model	*(Pesaran and Yamagata, 2008)*		*(Blomquist and Westerlund, 2013)*	
	Delta Test	P-*Value*	*HAC Robust Adjusted Delta Test*	P-*Value*
1	17.903	0.0000	−16.890	0.0000

Source: Authors' calculations.

variables being tested and their corresponding CD-test statistic values and *p*-values. The null hypothesis of CD test is there is no cross-sectional dependence among the observations in the dataset. These results indicate that for most of the variables, there is evidence of cross-sectional dependence, implying that the observations of these variables are not independent and may be influenced by common factors or shared characteristics.

However, UR shows weaker or no evidence of cross-sectional dependence. The *p*-values being very close to zero for all variables indicate that the evidence against the null hypothesis of no cross-sectional dependence is strong.

Table 4.4 presents results from slope homogeneity tests for the proposed model, indicating a statistically significant rejection of the null hypothesis of homogeneity for both Pesaran and Yamagata (2008) and Blomquist and Westerlund (2013) methods, as evidenced by low *p*-values (0.0000).

4.7.1 Unit Root Test Results

The Second-Generation Panel Unit Root Test findings, with and without trends, are shown in Table 4.5 for a variety of socio-economic factors using the Cross-Section-Dependence based Im-Pesaran-Shin (CSDIPS) approach.

In the "Without Trend" column, GDPPC, UR, and EVI exhibit stationary behavior without trend, as indicated by statistically significant Zt Statistics and *p*-values of 0.000. Conversely, variables such as IDPs and POV show non-stationary behavior without trend. In the "With Trend" column, GDPPC, UR, and EVI remain stationary with trends, while IDPs and POV continue to exhibit non-stationary behavior with trends.

Table 4.5 Unit Root Test

	CSDIPS Unit Root Test					
Variables	*Without Trend*			*With Trend*		
	Lags	*Zt Statistics*	P-*Value*	*Lags*	*Zt Statistics*	P-*Value*
IDPs	1	−5.156	0.021	1	3.990	0.991
GDPPC	0	−4.460	0.000	0	−7.330	0.000
POV	1	−3.617	0.001	0	−1.756	0.003
UR	0	−2.753	0.000	0	−3.315	0.000
EVI	1	0.653	0.000	0	0.978	0.000

Source: Authors' calculations.

4.7.2 Panel Cointegration Tests

Table 4.6 presents the results of various cointegration tests, including the Kao Test, Pedroni Test, and Westerlund Test, for different models involving socio-economic variables.

Cointegration is a crucial concept in Panel date analysis, indicating the presence of long-term relationships among variables. The Economic Vulnerability Index (EVI) model demonstrates cointegration.

4.7.3 MMQR-Based Results

Table 4.7 shows the MMQR estimates of economic vulnerability index with the dependent variables IDPs, GDPPC, POV, and UR. The coefficient of first variable IDPs is positive indicates that IDPs is negatively linked with the economic vulnerability. First of all, GDPPC is positively statistically related to the factor of population displacement. The theory behind this is that such a large proportion of the population transplanted will strain the receiving location's infrastructure and services to their breaking point, increasing demand for basic commodities. Such demand may exacerbate economic vulnerabilities by depleting the minimal resources already available to the affected region, further reducing its ability to meet the basic needs of hosting and displaced populations (Dershem et al., 2002). Another reason why this factor may increase GDPPC is the fact that people are being moved against their will, which may disrupt their way of life and entire economic activity, reducing output and income, and increasing GDPPC. Finally, the existence of IDPs may place an extra financial strain on the nation's governments because regular funding to jumpstart economic development will be diverted to social services, and humanitarian assistance (Guillaumont, 2004). The second factor is GDPPC and it is negatively statistically significant with GDPPC. There are several reasons why an increase in gross domestic product per capita might decrease GDPPC. First, an increased GDPPC typically indicates more general

Table 4.6 Cointegration Tests Results

Cointegration Tests											
Kao Test					*Pedroni Test*			*Westerlund Test*			
Modified Dickey-Fuller	*Dickey-Fuller*	*Augmented Dickey-Fuller*	*Unadjusted modified Dickey*	*Unadjusted Dickey-Fuller*	*Modified Phillips-Perron*	*Phillips-Perron*	*Augmented Dickey-Fuller*	*Gt*	*Ga*	*Pt*	*Pa*
Model: EVI/ IDPs, GDPPC, POV, UR											
−0.46 0.00	0.35 0.00	−0.69 0.02	0.55 0.01	−0.34 0.01	−1.65 0.00	−2.76 0.00	−6.78 0.00	−0.57 0.80	−0.87 0.00	12.69 0.00	12.86 0.00

Source: Authors' calculations.

Table 4.7 MMQR Estimates of Economic Vulnerability

DV: Economic Vulnerability Index (EVI)							
Variables	*Location*	*Scale*	$Q_{0.10}$	$Q_{0.25}$	$Q_{0.50}$	$Q_{0.75}$	$Q_{0.90}$
IDPs	0.171**	0.459***	0.573***	0.801	0.866***	0.632**	0.639***
	(0.012)	(0.000)	(0.000)	(0.276)	(0.009)	(0.020)	(0.000)
GDPPC	−0.337***	−0.247*	−0.017**	−0.459*	−1.442***	−0.615***	−0.087***
	(0.000)	(0.097)	(0.034)	(0.098)	(0.000)	(0.000)	(0.000)
POV	0.524	0.798**	0.450*	0.257***	0.171***	0.065***	0.312***
	(0.290)	(0.016)	(0.065)	(0.003)	(0.000)	(0.000)	(0.000)
UR	0.965**	0.333	0.819	0.213***	2.805	0.518	0.975
	(0.012)	(0.310)	(0.970)	(0.000)	(0.000)	(0.876)	(0.755)
Constant	0.307***	0.975***	0.273***	1.270	1.963***	0.784***	0.196***
	(0.000)	(0.000)	(0.000)	(0.000)	(0.000)	(0.000)	(0.000)

Source: Authors' calculations.

Note: P-Values in parentheses *** $p < 0.01$, ** $p < 0.05$, * $p < 0.1$.

economic development, which results in better social services, infrastructure, and shock resilience. A higher GDPPC may signal a more robust economy with a diversified range of businesses, less reliant on a single industry, or a few others. Second, increased GDPPC usually means lower poverty rates and improved living standards and social stability, reducing GDPPC through the possibility of a steady state of high poverty. In this case, higher GDPPC might mean a structure that is less adaptable and stable, implying that there are more factors that may increase it (Moghari et al., 2016).

Thirdly, poverty has a strong statistically significant positive correlation with economic vulnerability. The potential for poverty increases to increase economic vulnerability operates through several interrelated channels. High poverty is commonly linked to a high percentage of the population in a delicate economic situation, which leads to, among other things, a general reduction in demand and, as a result, a reduction in the consumption of goods and services (Whelan et al., 2008). In other words, negative demand shock can restrict the potential for economic growth and create systemic risks (Al-Mamun and Mazumder, 2015). Secondly, people living in poverty may lack access to important services like healthcare and education and they may, therefore, be unable to contribute largely to the overall framework of society, in which humans create value through the creation of human capital (Verick, 2009). According to Maître et al. (2012), a large proportion of the population with relatively low knowledge and expertise is erythematous. In other words, it restrains his ability to develop and preserve the economy's competitive advantage. Finally, high poverty rates are largely linked to political instability and social unrest. Thus, they can incidentally create an unfair competition environment, friendly investment both locally and internationally, and create increased risks to the economy (Basu and Nolen, 2005; Pareliussen, 2014).

4.8 Conclusions and Policy Implications

In conclusion, the research explored the intricate relationships between various socio-economic factors and economic vulnerability. The study has analyzed the data using the Moments Quantile Regression (MMQR) method using panel data from 70 nations between 2009 and 2022. Internally Displaced Persons often have positive impact on economic vulnerability. The study suggests that the policymakers should formulate comprehensive strategies to mitigate the vulnerabilities that have been identified, including specific actions to lessen internal migration, encourage sustainable economic expansion, and fortify social safety nets.

4.9 Future Work

Furthermore, research on the impact of Internally Displaced Persons be broadened and deepened to also reflect other aspects of being affected by displacement. Social cohesion dynamics within host communities in the context of IDPs could be subject matter to investigate as there are strains or even enhancements as a result of displacement. Besides, psychological well-being, resilience, and various coping mechanisms, as well as mental health needs, may also be explored. There is a great issue of gender that may include changes in gender roles, access to resources, and other aspects of vulnerability for different genders to gender-based violence. In addition, environmental impacts and access to justice for IDPs will also be of help to put the multifaceted nature and impact of displacement into perspective to provide for better evidence-based attention and interventions targeting displaced people and host communities.

Note

1 Aberrations of normality are abundant in statistics that result from various causes, first of which is an insufficiently sized sample. In suitable cases, the presence of outliers or natural non-normality of the data generating process may be involved. Moreover, specific phenomena display naturally non-normal distributions, like income or population sizes. Correct identification and swift adequate action is mandatory due to their influence on the validity of statistical analyses, which prompts the use of non-parametric tests or transformations to guarantee correct inference.

References

Al-Mamun, A., & Mazumder, M. N. H. (2015). Impact of microcredit on income, poverty, and economic vulnerability in Peninsular Malaysia. *Development in Practice, 25*(3), 333–346.

Barrientos, A., Hulme, D., & Nino-Zarazua, M. (2009). *Will the green shoots blossom? A new wave of social protection in Sub-Saharan Africa*. Manchester, UK: Brooks World Poverty Institute, University of Manchester.

Basu, K., & Nolen, P. J. (2005). *Vulnerability, unemployment and poverty: a new class of measures, its axiomatic properties and applications*. SSRN.

Blomquist, J., & Westerlund, J. (2013). Testing slope homogeneity in large panels with serial correlation. *Economics Letters, 121*(3), 374–378.

Canh, N. P., & Thanh, S. D. (2020). Domestic tourism spending and economic vulnerability. *Annals of Tourism Research, 85*, 103063.

Chambers, R. (1989). *The state and rural development: Ideologies and an agenda for the 1990s* (No. 269, p. 24). Institute of Development Studies at the University of Sussex.

Chan, S., & Huff Stevens, A. (2001). Job loss and employment patterns of older workers. *Journal of Labor Economics, 19*(2), 484–521.

Dershem, L., Gurgenidze, N., & Holtzman, S. (2002). Poverty and vulnerability among internally displaced persons in Georgia: An update of their current status and circumstances. *The World Bank*.

Guerrier, G., Zounoun, M., Delarosa, O., Defourny, I., Lacharite, M., Brown, V., & Pedalino, B. (2009). Malnutrition and mortality patterns among internally displaced and non-displaced population living in a camp, a village or a town in Eastern Chad. *PLoS One, 4*(11), e8077.

Guillaumont, P. (2004). 'On the Economic Vulnerability of Low Income Countries'. In L. Briguglio and E. J. Kisanga (eds), *Economic Vulnerability and Resilience of Small States*. Malta: Islands and Small States Institute and London: Commonwealth Secretariat. 54–57.

Holzmann, R., & Jorgensen, S. (1999). *Social protection as social risk management*. Washington, DC: The World Bank.

IDMC (2018) *Global report on internal displacement 2018*. Geneva: Internal Displacement Monitoring Centre, p. 120.
Johnson, R. J., Antonaccio, O., Botchkovar, E., & Hobfoll, S. E. (2021). War trauma and PTSD in Ukraine's civilian population: comparing urban-dwelling to internally displaced persons. *Social Psychiatry and Psychiatric Epidemiology*, *57*, 1–10.
Kim, G., Torbay, R., & Lawry, L. (2007). Basic health, women's health, and mental health among internally displaced persons in Nyala Province, South Darfur, Sudan. *American Journal of Public Health*, *97*(2), 353–361.
Leus, X., Wallace, J., & Loretti, A. (2001). Internally displaced persons. *Prehospital and Disaster Medicine*, *16*(3), 116–123.
Lu, J., Zhang, M., Zhang, J., Xu, C., & Cheng, B. (2021). Can health poverty alleviation project reduce the economic vulnerability of poor households? Evidence from Chifeng City, China. *Computers & Industrial Engineering*, *162*, 107762.
Machado, J. A., & Silva, J. S. (2019). Quantiles via moments. *Journal of Econometrics*, *213*(1), 145–173.
Maître, B., Nolan, B., & Whelan, C. T. (2012). Low pay, in-work poverty and economic vulnerability: A comparative analysis using Eu-Silc. *The Manchester School*, *80*(1), 99–116.
May, J., & Norton, A. (1997). "A difficult life": The perceptions and experience of poverty in South Africa. *Social Indicators Research*, *41*(1), 95–118.
Moghari, M., Faridzad, A., & Khorsandi, M. (2016). The impact of economic vulnerability and resilience on GDP among selected OPEC countries. *Economic Development Policy*, *4*(2), 77–106.
Moser, M. A., & MacLeod, D. (Eds.). (1996). *Immersed in technology: Art and virtual environments*. Mit Press.
Nguyen, C. P., & Dinh Thanh, S. (2022). Nexus between energy poverty and economic vulnerability: Evidence from low and middle income economies. *Energy Sources, Part B: Economics, Planning, and Policy*, *17*(1), 2056264.
O'Brien, K., Hayward, B., & Berkes, F. (2009). Rethinking social contracts: building resilience in a changing climate. *Ecology and Society*, *14*(2), 1–18.
Ollenburger, J. C., & Tobin, G. A. (1998). Women and postdisaster stress. In *The gendered terrain of disaster: Through women's eyes* (pp. 95–107).
Olwedo, M. A., Mworozi, E., Bachou, H., & Orach, C. G. (2008). Factors associated with malnutrition among children in internally displaced person\'s camps, Northern Uganda. *African Health Sciences*, *8*(4), 244–252.
Owoaje, E. T., Uchendu, O. C., Ajayi, T. O., & Cadmus, E. O. (2016). A review of the health problems of the internally displaced persons in Africa. *Nigerian Postgraduate Medical Journal*, *23*(4), 161–171.
Pareliussen, J. (2014). Overcoming Vulnerability of Unemployment Insurance Schemes. OECD Economics Department Working Paper No. 1131. 2014(27)
Pesaran, M. H., & Yamagata, T. (2008). Testing slope homogeneity in large panels. *Journal of Econometrics*, *142*(1), 50–93.
Platt, T. (1991). Essay review: The anthropologyof astronomy: World Archaeoastronomy. *Journal for the History of Astronomy*, *22*(16), S76–S83.
Roberts, B., Ekezie, W., Jobanputra, K., Smith, J., Ellithy, S., Cantor, D., ... & Patel, P. (2022). Analysis of health overseas development aid for internally displaced persons in low-and middle-income countries. *Journal of Migration and Health*, *5*, 100090.
Sheikh, M. A. (2021). *Forgotten citizens: Internally displaced persons camp population density and multidimensional poverty in Northern Syria*. PhD Thesis submitted to the Faculty of the Graduate School of Arts and Sciences of Georgetown University.
Singh, K. P., Bhoopathy, S. V., Worth, H., Seale, H., & Richmond, R. L. (2015). Nutrition among men and household food security in an internally displaced persons camp in Kenya. *Public Health Nutrition*, *19*(4), 723–731.

Turnip, S. S., & Hauff, E. (2007). Household roles, poverty and psychological distress in internally displaced persons affected by violent conflicts in Indonesia. *Social Psychiatry and Psychiatric Epidemiology*, *42*, 997–1004.

UNCT Ukraine. (2019). Five years into the conflict: Displaced people in Ukraine need long-term solutions to housing and employment challenges—Ukraine. [UN Country Team in Ukraine]. https://ukraine.iom.int/news/five-years-conflict-displaced-people-ukraine-need-long-term-solutionshousing-and-employment-challenges

UNHCR. (2015). *Worldwide displacement hits all-time high as war and persecution increase*. UNHCR. https://www.unhcr.org/news/stories/worldwide-displacement-hits-all-time-high-war-andpersecution-increase

UNHCR. (2023a). *Surviving shelling, displacement, flooding, and now fearing the harsh winter – the stark realities of life in Southern Ukraine*. UNHCR Ukraine. https://www.unhcr.org/ua/en/64635-the-stark-realities-of-life-in-southern-ukraine.html

UNHCR. (2023b). Ukraine strategy 2024. https://reporting.unhcr.org/operational/operations/ukraine

Verick, S. (2009). Who is hit hardest during a financial crisis? The vulnerability of young men and women to unemployment in an economic downturn. IZA Discussion Paper No. 4359 August 2009

Vogel, S. (2004). *"When the little dawn was grey": Cabaret performance and the Harlem Renaissance*. New York: University.

Whelan, C. T., Nolan, B., & Maitre, B. (2008). Consistent poverty and economic vulnerability. In *Quality of life in Ireland: Social impact of economic boom* (pp. 87–103). Dordrecht: Springer Netherlands.

5 Herdsmen-Farmer Conflict-Induced Internal Displacement, Humanitarian Crisis, and Effects on Development in Benue State – Nigeria

Rita Iorbo

5.1 Introduction

The herdsmen-farmers conflict is a notorious reoccurring conflict between the Fulani herdsmen of northern Nigeria and crop-farming communities across Nigeria over access to land and water resources for crop farming and animal herding. The conflict is most intense in the Middle Belt region (also known as Central Nigeria and North Central Nigeria) where Benue State is the most affected with persistent large-scale destruction of property, farms, mass killings, displacement of crop farmers, and occupation of crop-farming communities (Tiwo, 2023).

This conflict has grown from short-term seasonal contested access to land and water resources, accusations of open grazing and destruction of crops; cattle rustling and farmers' encroachment on grazing routes (Gernyi, 2017; Amnesty International, 2018; United Nations Trust Fund for Human Security, UNTFHS, 2019; Sule, 2021; Ekanem, 2022 and Ogu et al., 2023) to a full-blown conflict linked to the Fulani expansionist and land-grabbing agenda (Ogbette et al., 2018 and Odey & Ajor, 2020). Legislative initiatives at the federal and state government levels to address the root cause of this conflict have failed to materialise (Ogu et al., 2023; Nasiru, 2018 and Andzenge & Iorbo, 2022). As such, the conflict has protracted and forced an estimated 1.5 million people into internal displacement, destroyed private, and public infrastructure (Tiwo, 2023). Additionally, the herdsmen-farmer conflict continues to induce humanitarian crisis, reverse developmental progress, impoverish the displaced population, and undermine security in affected communities (Ake et al., 2023).

Thus, the objective of this study was to examine the effects of the herdsmen-farmers conflict on the displaced population and on socio-economic development in Benue State as well as the response of government and humanitarian organisations. It is important for this study to examine the effects of the herdsmen-farmers conflict and humanitarian response on the development of Benue State and make recommendations for sustainable rehabilitation. The rest of the chapter is structured into literature review, methodology, findings, best practices, conclusion, and recommendations.

DOI: 10.4324/9781032694337-8

5.2 Review Of Literature

5.2.1 Internal Displacement and Internally Displaced Persons

The Kampala Convention (2012) defines internal displacement as "the involuntary or forced movement, evacuation or relocation of persons or groups of persons within internationally recognized state borders" (p. 7). While internally displaced persons are the people "who have been forced or obliged to flee or to leave their homes or places of habitual residence…" due to conflicts, violence, natural disasters, etc. and who have fled to safer locations within the same country for protection and assistance. It is called internal displacement, and the affected populations are internally displaced placed persons because they have not left their country to seek protection and assistance from a foreign country. Therefore, governments of the displacement-affected States have primary responsibility under their constitution and international obligations to guarantee the safety, well-being, and sustainable rehabilitation of displacement-affected people and communities.

5.2.2 Herdsmen-Farmers Conflict-induced Internal Displacement in Benue State

There is no singular agreed total population of persons displaced by the herdsmen-farmers conflict in Benue State. Depending on which state or non-state stakeholder is reporting the situation, no mention is often made of this driver of internal displacement in Nigeria. While the Benue State Government reports a staggering 1.5 million IDPs across 21 of 23 local government areas in Benue because of the herdsmen-farmers conflict and other forms of violence (State Emergency Management Agency, SEMA, 2022), the United Nations High Commission for Refugees [UNHCR] (2023) indicates that there are 489,245 IDPs in Benue. Timeline reports of the conflict show that between 2013 and 2023, about 6,000 people including children, nursing mothers, pregnant women, and security operatives have been killed by the herdsmen-farmers conflict (Vanguard News, 2023). Additionally, private and public infrastructure such as school buildings, churches, houses, farm barns, marketplaces, worship centres, healthcare facilities, among others were burnt completely in more than 200 communities (Ameh, 2018, Obi et al., 2021; Aver & Iorbo, 2023 and Vanguard News, 2023).

In the area of wasted developed human capacity for food security, as many as 53,000 farmers who had been trained and provided farm inputs and implements by the International Fund for Agricultural Development for advancing food security were affected by the persistent herdsmen-farmers conflict (Ede, 2023). These trainees and tens of thousands of other farmers who were part of the Benue farming community guaranteeing national food security have been displaced into camps for several years and no longer engage in farming. This reversal of sustainable progress in food security has significantly affected Benue and Nigeria's food production.

The conflict has also displaced small off-farm business owners who engaged in different commercial activities and trade in affected Benue State communities (Nomor & Ominyi, 2021). Other economic activities affected by this conflict include the loss of farmlands. According to Ukase and Jato (2022) and Ngbede and Mohammed (2023), the impact of the herdsmen-farmers conflict on economic and political development in Benue State is enormous and will take several years to recover. They identified the Fulani herdsmen occupation of ancestral lands as a significant economic setback since land, which is a major means of production and capital of crop farmers, had been taken away. Furthermore, the destruction of food, infrastructure, loss of livelihoods, and mass displacement have disrupted economic activities with the population and communities not being able to produce consumable goods or perform economic activities.

Several studies have examined the impacts of the herdsmen-farmers conflict on food security among IDPs in Benue State. Findings show that all participants were farmers with between 6 and twenty-one years of farm experience prior to displacement and had farm sizes ranging from one to seven hectares. Their income ranged between N251,000 and N1,000000 and above annually from farming which they used to meet their educational, healthcare, and other family needs. However, the displaced have suffered total loss of farms and access to farmlands due to the herdsmen-farmers conflict. The study concludes that the persistent conflict has reversed efforts in poverty eradication, food security, economic sustainability, loss of lives and property, and continues to threaten the means of survival of the affected population, Benue communities, poses a challenge to sustainable development and national food security (Uza et al., 2022, Obi, 2023 and Ifedayo, 2023).

Other studies reveal that the herdsmen-farmers conflict has affected quality education, led to significantly reduced school enrollment, discontinuation of education, and closure of schools due to insecurity and lack of financial capacity of displaced parents to enrol their children in school and meet other needs (Ekperechukwu & Carla, 2021 and Adeyi, Adamu & Itodo, 2024). Moreover, despite huge socio-economic losses incurred by the affected populations due to the herdsmen-farmers conflict, Iorbo et al. (2024) found that there has not been justice or restitution for affected populations and their communities. As a result, there has been an increased dependence on humanitarian aid across displacement-affected communities.

5.2.3 Humanitarian Crisis

Humanitarian crisis also known as humanitarian emergency is any humanitarian misfortune caused by conflicts or natural disasters, which may require the collaborative assistance of organisations or countries to alleviate human suffering and assist affected population to overcome the shocks of such humanitarian misfortune (Ginting et al., 2022). Humanitarian crisis is a major disruption to functional human societies that causes widespread loss or damage to people or to their socio-economic environment (United Nations International Strategy for Disaster Reduction, [UNISDR], 2004) and account for mass population displacement. According to Anderson and Gerber (2018), there are four phases of humanitarian crisis. These include pre-emergency, acute emergency, post-emergency, and recovery phase. They suggest that the response to humanitarian crisis should transition from saving lives measures to assisting the affected population to return or resettle. At the recovery phase, response efforts should focus on rebuilding affected communities with the aim of assisting the population to restore capacity for socio-economic functioning while also ending humanitarian aid dependency.

The herdsmen-farmers conflict in Benue State has induced a huge humanitarian crisis, led to substantial loss of lives, destruction of livelihoods, private and public social infrastructure that disrupted social services. Over 1.5 million people have fled their communities and ancestral homes to safer locations where they live without any sustainable means of livelihoods, adequate shelter, nor access to continuous education, healthcare, and personal well-being (Ameh, 2018; Kwaghtser, 2019). Receiving communities also face huge challenges due to the sudden influx of mass population with overbearing effects on scarce resources (SEMA, 2022). Beyond dire humanitarian crisis, this conflict has left substantial negative effects on socio-economic development across critical sectors in Benue State in particular, and Nigeria (Iorbo et al., 2024).

5.3 Methodology

This qualitative study was conducted amongst IDPs in two displacement camps – one official and another unofficial camp in Benue State, Nigeria, as well as among 11 humanitarian workers. Participants were purposively selected based on their knowledge of the conflict, displacement, and humanitarian response. They took part in the study after granting oral and written consent to be interviewed and digitally recorded. Interviews were transcribed and analysed using thematic analysis. Two major themes emerged from the analysis. They are the effects of the conflict on socio-economic development which has five sub-themes, namely education, shelters, healthcare, food security, and livelihoods and internal revenue. The other was the response to conflict-induced internal displacements. Secondary data were used to generate another theme – best practices on response to conflict-induced internal displacement and humanitarian crisis. The themes are presented under study findings and discussed.

5.4 Study Findings

5.4.1 Effects of the Conflict on Socio-Economic Development

This section highlights the effects of the herdsmen-farmer conflict on five developmental sectors in Benue State. These are education, housing, livelihoods and economy, food security, and healthcare.

5.4.1.1 Education

The effects of the Fulani herdsmen-farmers conflict on education in Benue State and Nigeria can be seen from the loss of education infrastructure, illiteracy rates, out-of-school children's rates and the potential loss of human capital. According to the Benue State Emergency Management Agency, there is education facility deficit in Benue State. In host communities, the conversion of classrooms into displacement camps has limited access to continuous education. Despite policy stipulations to avail IDPs continuous education, over 400,000 IDP and non-IDP children in the local communities are out of school and do not have any hope of attaining basic primary education. Already, Nigeria ranks low in national literacy rates at 62.2% (Sasu, 2023) with an alarming 19.7 million out of school children (UNESCO, 2022). The deterioration of Nigeria literacy rates coincides with the years of insurgency in the northeast and the Fulani herdsmen-farmers conflict across the country (Tiwo, 2023 and Amao, 2023).

5.4.1.2 Shelters

According to Moore (2019), Nigeria has a widespread 20 million housing deficit. Benue State is one of the states with a disturbing housing deficit (Iorshase, 2021). However, the herdsmen-farmers conflict continues to undermine progress made in Benue rural communities in housing. The targeted burning of houses in over 200 communities across 21 of 23 local government areas in Benue State has not only rendered 1.5 million people homeless. It has also successfully reversed decades-long efforts made in those communities and continues to feed into the national housing deficit. Going by the formula adopted by the Benue SEMA (2021) in determining the IDP population in the State (which is total number of households multiplied by an average 5.5 persons per household), a total of 1.5 million IDPs divide by 5.5 represents at least 272,727 houses destroyed in conflict-affected communities in Benue.

5.4.1.3 Healthcare

The effects of the herdsmen-farmers conflict on healthcare delivery are multifaceted. Amidst a looming infrastructure deficit in Nigeria, healthcare facilities in the conflict-affected communities have been destroyed and rendered unusable. The loss of physical healthcare institutions, medical supplies like beds, laboratory equipment, medicines among others represent one facet. Another is the displacement of 1.5 million people including medical health workers with overbearing effects on limited healthcare and human resources in host communities. The last is the limited short-term response to the health sector in emergencies. Although Nigeria's health sector is not at its best, the situation in displacement contexts is disproportionately challenging. IDPs have lost livelihoods and no longer have financial resources to access basic healthcare.

Chapter 4 (4.3.1b) of Nigeria's National Policy (2021) on internal displacement commits to increasing infrastructure in host communities to accommodate the sudden influx of IDPs and to also recruit more workers to assist in healthcare service delivery. But host communities are also overstretched with the sudden influx of IDPs while interventions to help them better cope with such population influx is lacking. Benue SEMA (2022) estimates that it would require $500 million to meet the healthcare needs of displaced persons and members of the host communities. While healthcare infrastructure has been destroyed by conflict and available ones in host communities are inadequate, the $500 million Benue SEMA budget focuses on provision of health services to the exclusion of long-term rehabilitation of healthcare facilities. The conflict, the mass displacement population, and the poor humanitarian response cumulatively, continue to undermine this sector.

5.4.1.4 Food Security

The displacement of 1.5 million crop farmers and the occupation of Benue farming communities by the Fulani herdsmen has reduced food production in a state known as the food basket as majority of the affected population can no longer farm nor afford what they consume. As such, there is food insecurity amongst a people once known for food production in commercial quantities, who contributed to national food security. The precarious food situation triggered by this conflict has also contributed to food shortage and price inflation not just in Benue State but also in Nigeria. A report by the World Bank Group (2018) and World Bank (2023) shows an increasingly deteriorating food price inflation from 19.4% in 2018 to 25.8% in August 2023, due in part to insecurity and a weak economy.

With a decline in food production in Benue and other states affected by the Fulani herdsmen-farmers conflict as well as the Boko Haram terrorism in the northeast, Nigeria continues to grapple with national food insecurity. According to the International Trade Administration (2020), Nigeria is not just food insecure, but it is so bad that she spends $22 billion annually on importation of food and agricultural products to meet its national food needs. As of 2023, the United Nations warned of a widespread hunger crisis in Nigeria with 25 million people at high risk of food insecurity (United Nations Children's Fund, UNICEF, 2023). Among this population are millions of displaced farmers who should be producing assorted food in commercial quantities but who unfortunately are camped in displacement shelters and being spoon-fed. In July 2023, a state of emergency was declared on food insecurity by the Federal Government of Nigeria (Angbulu, 2023).

5.4.1.5 Livelihoods and Internal Revenue

The effects of the herdsmen-farmers conflict on livelihoods and internal revenue in Benue State can be felt in three aspects: (1) loss of personal and community infrastructure, livelihoods, and farmlands (major capital); (2) untargeted economic response of government and humanitarian agencies; (3) loss of potential internal revenue because of the conflict and displacement. Put together, the socio-economic cost of the herdsmen-farmers conflict is enormous (Ukase & Jato, 2022 and Uza et al., 2022). The decimation of communities and occupation of ancestral lands belonging to the crop farmers is a monumental loss. Accessing finances needed for rebuilding the ruined communities will consume huge financial resources that would have been channelled into developing other sectors.

Mass displacement has rendered an otherwise productive people humanitarian aid-dependent. According to Kwaghtser (2019), the herdsmen-farmers conflict in Benue State has led to a 56% reduction of economic activities in affected areas. This corresponds with the World Bank Group's (2018) report that the recurring herdsmen-farmer conflict in Benue State makes internal revenue generation difficult. Additionally, the Benue State Government has reportedly lost $14 billion due to property loss and humanitarian aid management (Nwakanma & Boroh, 2019), while the Federal Government of Nigeria loses $16 billion revenue annually because of the herdsmen-farmers conflict (Africanews. 2018).

5.5 Response to Conflict-Induced Internal Displacements

The response to the internal displacement and the humanitarian crisis is generally poor and greatly insufficient to make life comfortable and trigger recovery. IDPs face enormous challenges in new locations, including struggles for survival, integration, employment, and livelihood opportunities, accessing education, healthcare, and adequate shelters (Olarewaju et al., 2019, Omoraka, Ogoh & Audu, 2022 and Abari et al., 2022). A study of the lived experiences and social inclusion of IDPs shows poor response of government to the economic plight of the displaced. Rather than collaborate with IDPs for sustainable livelihoods recovery, government agencies assert their preferred vocational training without financial nor material assistance to help IDPs (Okeke-Ihejirika et al., 2020 and Titilope et al., 2021). As such, the measures have led to lack of livelihood opportunities to enable IDPs exit displacement situations.

5.6 Best Practices: The Case of Liberia and Uganda

War-torn Liberia and Uganda suffered enormous loss of socio-economic infrastructure with millions of persons forced to flee their homes and communities. After several years of protracted displacement, governments prioritised long-term durable solutions and ended humanitarian aid dependency. Liberia, in collaboration with international humanitarian organisations focused on socio-economic rehabilitation of the conflict- and displacement-affected communities (Eriksson, 2008). Owing to significant destruction of infrastructure and loss of livelihoods, interventions focused on reconstruction of houses, water wells, toilets, schools, and healthcare infrastructure including clinics and hospitals in affected communities was prioritised. The government targeted mass school enrollment of displaced students in public schools across different communities and provided furniture and study materials in schools.

Community-level micro-finance associations were established and displaced persons encouraged to join such associations and access micro-credits through their communities. Liberia strategically created livelihood opportunities for displaced youths by engaging them as construction labourers for reconstruction and rehabilitation of affected communities. The targeted rehabilitation of conflict and displacement-affected communities ensured that the communities were assisted to accommodate the displaced, the returnees, and members of the local communities. A total of 941 socio-economic community infrastructure projects were completed comprising 393 water wells, 303 latrines, 111 schools, 20 healthcare centres, 16 marketplaces among others (Eriksson, 2008).

In Uganda, majority of the displaced population were farmers whose displacement-affected national food security with record high hunger and poverty rates. Rather than persistently spoon-feeding displaced farmers, government and the international organisations focused on empowering displaced farmers to regain self-sufficiency and recover Uganda's national food security (Wandschneider & Hodges, 2005). Grains and seed banks were set up, and hybrid high-yielding variety of grains and vegetables, fertilizers and farm tools were distributed to 94,000 IDP households to assist them reach self-sufficiency and boost national food security (United Nations, 2005). Moreover, Uganda focused on rehabilitating social infrastructure and providing social services in local communities to help accommodate IDPs, returnees and the communities. Prioritised sectors for rehabilitation and reconstruction included health facilities, schools, and provision of livelihood opportunities (Norwegian Refugee Council, NRC, n.d.). To facilitate a less challenging humanitarian exit, the displaced were provided short-term humanitarian transit packages to help them integrate and stabilise in their new locations.

5.7 Conclusion, Implications, and Recommendations

The herdsmen-farmers conflict has disrupted socio-economic activities, wasted human capital and continues to reverse the many developmental strides recorded in Benue State, Nigeria. Previous developmental efforts made towards improving literacy rates, reducing poverty, increasing internal revenue, physical infrastructure, and boosting national food security have been disrupted by this conflict. Beyond the conflict, however, government's prioritisation of short-term measures of spoon-feeding over 1.5 million displaced farmers and investing huge monies in temporary shelters has significantly undermined socio-economic development. Additionally, the absence of continuous quality education for IDP children and their counterparts in host communities have negatively affected literacy attainment in Benue State and the Nigeria State.

The herdsmen-farmers conflict and the response of government and international humanitarian organisations have implications on development, food security, literacy attainment, and well-being. Prioritisation of humanitarian measures of spoon-feeding displaced farmers over sustainable rehabilitation deeply entrenches a culture of aid dependency while undermining communities' capacity to be food secure, thereby, leading to food insecurity and inflation of food prices. The lack of access to education for over 400,000 children challenges literacy attainment of the affected generation. Furthermore, critical development sectors including human capacity, socio-economic infrastructure, and social service delivery continue to diminish while humanitarian aid dependency thrives.

While efforts may be in place to resolve the herdsmen-farmers conflict, restore peace and security, it is recommended that the Benue SEMA, the Federal and Benue State humanitarian ministries should collaborate with relevant development and humanitarian agencies to deliver sustainable long-term solutions across the affected critical sectors. As per Cernea (2004), sustainable rehabilitation of displacement populations and communities should focus on reversing losses and damages incurred by the conflict. Therefore, government should shift focus from temporary to sustainable long-term measures aimed at recovery of IDPs agency, livelihoods, personal and community infrastructure. Taking example from best practices, Benue government, the Federal humanitarian ministry, and development partners should prioritise socio-economic rehabilitation. People with different skill sets should be assisted according to their expertise rather than subjecting them to new skill sets. Providing socio-economic infrastructure in affected communities will sustainably help to integrate IDPs and reduce the strain of mass population influx on limited resources of host communities. Long-term measures will provide opportunities for IDPs to contribute to community and national development while also recovering their livelihoods, rebuilding their agency, and exiting humanitarian aid dependency.

References

Abari, C. A., Chinta, T., & Bai-Tachia, M. Living Condition and Health of Children in Internally Displaced Persons' (IDP) Camps in Benue State, Nigeria. *FUDMA Journal of Politics and International Affairs*. ISSN: 2682-5406 (2022).

Adeyi, N., Adamu, M. I., & Itodo, S. M. Effect of Farmers-Herders Conflict on School Enrollment in Benue State. *Kashere Journal of Politics and International Relations*, 2(1): 145–157 (2024).

African Union Convention for the Protection and Assistance of Internally Displaced Persons in Africa (Kampala Convention), 23rd October 2009 (Entered into Force 6th December 2012). https://au.int/sites/default/files/treaties/36846-treaty-kampala_convention.pdf.

Africanews. Violent conflicts between Nomadic Herders and Farmers in North-central Nigeria Escalate. (2018, January 8). https://www.africanews.com/2018/01/14/violent-conflicts-between-nomadic-herders-and-farmers-in-north-central-nigeria//

Ake, M., Owoeye, G., Ajakaiye, O., Ayantunji, K. A. A., Apalowo, J., Popoola, O., & Joy, O. Herders Farmers Crisis and Food Security in Nigeria-A Case of Benue State. *Baltic Journal of Law & Politics*, 16(1): 204–211 (2023).

Amao, O. B. A decade of terror: Revisiting Nigeria's interminable Boko Haram insurgency. In *Ten years of Boko Haram in Nigeria: The dynamics and counterinsurgency challenges* (23–41). Cham: Springer Nature Switzerland (2023).

Ameh, G. C.. Herdsmen Killings: Benue Govt Releases Timeline of Attacks. *Daily Post*. (2018, February 6). https://dailypost.ng/2018/02/06/herdsmen-killings-benue-govt-releases-timeline-attacks/

Amnesty International. *Harvests of death: Three years of bloody clashes between farmers and herders in Nigeria*. (2018). https://www.amnesty.org/en/wp-content/uploads/2021/05/AFR4495032018ENGLISH.pdf

Anderson, M., Gerber, M. Introduction to Humanitarian Emergencies. In: Townes, D. (eds). *Health in humanitarian emergencies: Principles and practice for public health and healthcare practitioners* (pp. 1–8). Cambridge University Press; 2018. United Kingdom.

Andzenge, D. T., & Iorbo, R. Victimisation by Policy Exclusion: The Case of Internally Displaced Persons in Nigeria. *Global Advances in Victimology and Psychological Studies*, 1(2): 55–60 (2022).

Angbulu, S. *Tinubu declares state of emergency on food security*. Punch Nigeria. (2023, July 13). https://punchng.com/tinubu-declares-state-of-emergency-on-food-security%E2%81%A3/.

Aver, T. T., & Iorbo, R. The Dynamics of Victims of Farmers-Herdsmen Violent Clashes in Benue State, Nigeria. *Global Advances in Victimology and Psychological Studies*, 2(1): 2–11 (2023). https://gavps.jibs.edu.in/index.php/gavps/article/view/42/24

Cernea, M. M. Impoverishment risks, risk management, and reconstruction: A model of population displacement and resettlement. In *UN Symposium on hydropower and sustainable development* (Vol. 27) (2004, October). Bejing: United Nations. https://www.un.org/esa/sustdev/sdissues/energy/op/hydro_cernea_population_resettlement_backgroundpaper.pdf

Ede, A. Insecurity Hampers Agricultural Activities in Benue- IFAD. *Daily Asset*. (2023, November4).https://dailyasset.ng/insecurity-hampers-agricultural-activities-in-benue-ifad/

Ekanem, E. A. Resource Scarcity and Fulani Herdsmen/Tiv Farmers' Crisis in Benue State, Nigeria. *European Journal of Conflict Management*, 3(1): 1–18 (2022). https://doi.org/10.47672/ejcm.1056

Ekperechukwu, E. C., & Carla, A.B.U. Agro–pastoralist Conflicts in Benue State Nigeria: Hazards and Imperative for Human Rights Protection. *International Journal of Management, Social Sciences, Peace and Conflict Studies (IJMSSPCS)*, 4(3): 241–253; ISSN: 2682-6135 (2021).

Eriksson, H. Assessment of SIDA Support through UNDP to Liberia Recovery and Rehabilitation. *Sida Evaluation* 2008: 50 (2008). https://cdn.sida.se/publications/files/sida48040en-assessment-of-sida-support-through-undp-to-liberia-recovery-and-rehabilitation.pdf

Gernyi, G. A. Ethnic and Religious Identities Shaping Contestation for Land Based Resources: The Tiv-Farmers and Pastoralists Conflicts in Central Nigeria until 2014. *Journal of Living Together*, 4(1): 136–151 (2017). https://www.icermediation.org/wp-content/uploads/2019/04/George-A.-Genyi-Ethnic-and-Religious-Identities-Shaping-Contestation-for-Land-Based-Resources-The-Tiv-Farmers-and-Pastoralists-Conflicts.pdf

Ginting, S., Kitreerawutiwong, N., & Mekrungrongwong, S. Food Access, Food Consumption, and Children's Nutritional Status of Smallholder Farmer in Sinabung's Eruptions-Prone Areas, Indonesia. *Ecology of Food and Nutrition*, 61(3): 319–336 (2022).

Ifedayo, T. E. Herders-Farmers Conflict and the Search for Peace in Benue State, Nigeria. *International Journal of Peace and Conflict Studies*, 8(1): 43–53 (2023).

International Trade Administration. (2020). *Nigeria food and agriculture*. https://www.trade.gov/market-intelligence/nigeria-food-and-agriculture.

Iorbo, R., Sahni, S. P., Bhatnagar, T., and Andzenge, D. T. Social Inclusion and Justice for the Internally Displaced by the Herdsmen-Farmers Conflict in Benue State,

Nigeria. *Journal on Migration and Human Security*, 12(2): 1–14 (2024). https://doi.org/10.1177/23315024241239585

Iorshase, J. *Benue moves to mitigate housing deficit*. (2021, February 21). https://thevoicenewspaper.ng/benue-moves-to-mitigate-housing-deficit/.

Kwaghtser, P. A. Impact of the Conflict between Farmers and Herdsmen on Food Production in the Agro-ecological Zone-B of Benue State, Nigeria. *Ianna Journal of Interdisciplinary Studies*, 1(1): 56–64. EISSN: 2735-9891 (2019).

Moore, E. A. Addressing Housing Deficit in Nigeria: Issues, Challenges and Prospects. *Economic and Financial Review*, 57(4): 201–222 (2019). https://dc.cbn.gov.ng/efr/vol57/iss4/15/.

Nasiru, J. Miyetti Allah Vows to Resist Benue Anti-grazing Law, Asks Buhari to Warn Ortom. *The Cable*. (2018, May 19). https://www.thecable.ng/miyetti-allah-vow-to-resist-benue-anti-grazing-law-asks-buhari-to-caution-ortom.

National Policy. *National Policy on international displaced persons*. Federal Government of Nigeria (2021). https://www.refworld.org/pdfid/632af49b4.pdf

Ngbede, A., & Mohammed, I. S. Effect of Farmers-herders Conflict on Agricultural Productivity in Benue State. *Lapai International Journal Administration*, 6(2): 21–40 (2023).

Nomor, D. T., & Ominyi, S. O. Impact of Herdsmen-farmers' Conflict on Small off-Farm Businesses in Benue State. *Journal of Economics and Allied Research*, 6(3): 51–61. ISSN: 2536-7447 (2021)

Norwegian Refugee Council (n.d.). *Report on the consultations with former IDPs in Gulu/Amuru & Kampala districts*. https://www.un.org/internal-displacement-panel/sites/www.un.org.internal-displacement-panel/files/summary_report_for_consultations_with_former_idps_uganda.pdf

Nwakanma, E., & Boroh, S.E. Demography of Conflict and the Herders-farmers Crisis in Nigeria. *The Nigerian Journal of Sociology and Anthropology*, 17(2): 28–40 (2019). https://d-nb.info/1242921257/34.

Obi, E. N. Effects of Farmers-Herders Conflicts on Food Security in Agatu Local Government Area of Benue State, Nigeria. *KIU Journal of Social Sciences*, 9(3): 159–168 (2023).

Obi, S. E., Odikpa, S., Jeremiah, E. S., Emeje, A. Y., & Godwin, O. The Implication of Farmers-Herders Conflicts on the Socio-Economic Development of Omala LGA, Kogi State, North Central Nigeria. *International Journal of Qualitative Research*, 1(1): 61–72 (2021).

Odey, J. S., & Ajor, J. O. Herdsmen as the Spiritual Arm of Fulani Expansionist Quest: A Threat to Integration in Nigeria. *International Journal of Recent Innovations in Academic Research*, 4(9), 10–20 (2020).

Ogbette, A. S., Attama, A. O., & Okoh, J.O. Fulani-Herdsmen and Farmers Crises under Buhari's Administration: Causes, Effects and Its Management (2015–2018). *International Journal of Peace and Conflict Studies*, 5(2): 44–53 (2018).

Ogu, E. C. S., Augustine, O. O., & Udeh, C. O. State Policy Action and Farmers-Herders Conflicts in Benue State, Nigeria. *International Journal of Innovative Development and Policy Studies* 11(2): 73–87 (2023).

Okeke-Ihejirika, P., Oriola, T. B., Salami, B., Obiefune, M., Ejike, N., Olutola, A., & Irinoye, O. Beyond Poverty Fixation: Interrogating the Experiences of Internally Displaced Persons in Nigeria. *Third World Quarterly*, 41(9): 1476–1497 (2020).

Omoraka, J. E., Ogoh, A. O., & Audu, Y. A. An Appraisal of the Management of Internally Displaced Persons (IDPS) in Benue State, North-central Nigeria, 2015-2022. *Zamfara Journal of Politics and Development*, 3(3): 14–14 (2022).

Sasu, D. D. *Literacy rate in Nigeria in selected years between 1991 and 2018*. Statista (2023). https://www.statista.com/statistics/1268372/literacy-rate-in-nigeria/

SEMA, Benue State Emergency Management Agency. *Benue State humanitarian response plan*. Document. (2022). Retrieved October 13, 2023. https://communitylinks.org.ng/2022/10/11/benue-state-humanitarian-response-plan/.

SEMA. Benue State Emergency Management Agency. *Benue State contingency plan 2019-2020*.(2021).https://www.christianaid.org.uk/sites/default/files/2022-08/nigeria-e4e-benue-contingency-plan-june2019.pdf.

Sule, P. E. Open Grazing Prohibitions and the Politics of Exclusivist Identity in Nigeria. *Africa Review*, 13(51): 539–555 (2021).

Titilope, A. G., Ahmad Zakuan, U. A., & Osman, N. The State of Conditions and Challenges Faced by Internally Displaced Women (IDW) in Nigeria: A Social Inclusion Perspective. *Journal of International Studies*, 17: 1–21 (2021). https://doi.org/10.32890/jis2021.17.1

Tiwo, R. A. Pastoralists and Farmers Conflict in Benue State: Changes in Climate in Northern Nigeria as a Contributing Factor. *World Journal of Advanced Research and Reviews*, 17(3): 325–344 (2023). https://wjarr.com/sites/default/files/WJARR-2023-0402.pdf

Ukase, P. I., & Jato, T. P. Socio-Economic Consequences of Conflict: The Predicament of Internally Displaced Persons in Benue State. *African Journal of Social Sciences and Humanities Research*, 5(5): 10–26 (2022). https://papers.ssrn.com/sol3/papers.cfm?abstract_id=4245731

UNESCO. *Out-of-school numbers are growing in sub-Saharan Africa*. (2022). https://unesdoc.unesco.org/ark:/48223/pf0000382577.

UNHCR. *Nigeria: All population snapshot*. (2023). https://data.unhcr.org/ar/documents/download/104216

United Nations. *UN to provide seeds, tools and training to help war-displaced in Uganda*. 5th May (2005). https://news.un.org/en/story/2005/05/136912.

United Nations International Strategy for Disaster Reduction, UNISDR. *Priority Areas to Implement Disaster Risk Reduction*. (2004). https://www.unisdr.org/2004/wcdr-dialogue/terminology.htm

UNTFHS (United Nations Trust Fund for Human Security). (2019). Transitioning From Humanitarian Relief to Long-Term Development: Addressing the Herdsmen-Farmers Conflict in Nigeria. Last accessed September 4, 2024. https://www.un.org/humansecurity/hsprogramme/herders-farmers-conflict/

UNICEF (United Nations Children Education Fund). (2023). 25 million Nigerians at high risk of food insecurity in 2023. Last accessed September 4, 2024. https://www.unicef.org/press-releases/25-million-nigerians-high-risk-food-insecurity-2023#:~:text=ABUJA%2C%2016%20January%202023%20%2D%20Nearly,carried%20out%20twice%20a%20year

Uza, D., Idyorough, A. E., Ugbem-Onah, C., & Nwafor, S. C. Internal Displacement of Farmers and Food Losses in Benue State, Nigeria. *Research on Humanities and Social Sciences*. ISSN 2225-0484 (Online), 12(10): 50–60 (2022). https://core.ac.uk/download/pdf/524587834.pdf.

Vanguard News. 6,000 killed, Communities Sacked, 2m Farmers Displaced: Buhari Days Darkest for Benue. (2023, April 29). https://www.vanguardngr.com/2023/04/6000-killed-communities-sacked-2-million-farmers-displace-buhari-days-darkest-for-benue/

Wandschneider, T., & Hodges, R. Local Food Aid Procurement in Uganda: A Case Study Report for EC PREP (UK Department for International Development). (2005). https://assets.publishing.service.gov.uk/media/57a08c5ce5274a31e0001178/LocalFoodAidUgandaReport.pdf.

World Bank. *The World Bank in Nigeria: Overview*. (2023). https://www.worldbank.org/en/country/nigeria/overview

World Bank Group. *Nigeria biannual economic update: Connecting to complete*. (2018). https://documents1.worldbank.org/curated/en/769551524576691390/pdf/WP-NigeriaBiannualEconomicUpdateAprilFinalVersion-PUBLIC.pdf

6 The Afghan Conundrum

'Just' War, Fragmented Sovereignties, and Political Double Binds

Ambreen Agha

6.1 Introduction

A "just war"[1] (Walzer, 1977) is premised on the notion of legitimate authority that rests on the person of the sovereign with ethical questions like "when," "why," and "how" to engage in war, especially in forbidding social, cultural, and geographical terrains. The U.S. invasion of Afghanistan in October 2001 (Operation Enduring Freedom until 2014 and Operation Freedom's Sentinel from 2015 until withdrawal in 2021) began with citing of the joint resolution as the legal rationale for waging the "War on Terror" with the support of NATO and non-NATO allies in response to al Qaeda's 9/11 terror attacks in the U.S. Within this theoretical framework of "just war," the U.S. legitimized successive military interventions in Afghanistan, producing conditions that led to multiple and fragmented sovereignties with both state and non-state actors emerging as contenders to sovereignty, more visible with the withdrawal of the American forces and the eventual fall of Kabul to the Taliban on August 15, 2021 (hereafter, the Fall).

In context to the Fall, this chapter aims to assess the impact of U.S. presence – military and non-military – in Afghanistan over the last 20 years from a double bind theoretical framework,[2] specifically pertaining to paradoxical situations that emerge in war settings and the dilemma around questions of political allegiance amid contested sovereignties, and unequal development. There have been several studies to understand the role of double binds in philosophy, politics, and war (Renov 1983; Hijri 2021, Leonard, 21). This chapter argues that owing to prolonged decades of war, creation of successive plaint governments, excessive dependence on aid economy that served few in proximity to the Presidential Palace, and the sudden abandonment of the commitment to "liberation" and "democracy" produced political dilemma among the ethnically and economically diverse Afghans.

These social, psychic, political, and economic dependencies on international donors, primarily the U.S., exposes the vulnerabilities of social groups at the intersection of class, politics, ideology, and territorial landscape. In the backdrop of the military withdrawal in August 2021, the chapter looks at how class politics and state's (in)action led to the birth of this situation that encircled the

DOI: 10.4324/9781032694337-9

Afghans in periodic cycles of violence amid U.S. quest for hegemony in the region and questions of power and legitimacy with two main contenders of sovereignty – the state and the Taliban – where the former dependent on the U.S. and latter hostile to its presence. Premised on this dual reality of dependence and hostility, the state and the non-state actor(s) cultivate allegiance and consent among their support base, producing double bind situations with fewer to limited options, each carrying its own structures of oppression that "expose one to penalty, censure or deprivation" (Hijri, 2021), irrespective of the choices they make.[3]

From the perspective of double binds and the *longue durée*[4] of war, foreign invasion, development efforts, and successive rounds of negotiations for peace, the primary focus of the chapter is to explore the impact of the 20-year long relationship between the domestic (Afghan government) and the external players (U.S. primarily) on the Afghan population. It analyses the implications of the hegemonic state building and reconstruction projects in Afghanistan exploring who were the beneficiaries of these effort and who was left out. In doing this, the first section of the chapter will focus on the international reconstruction, a robust aid economy[5] and the (asymmetrical) developmental model that it produced. Prior to the Fall, 75% of Afghanistan's fragile economy was dependent on foreign assistance (HRW, 2022). The situation worsened with the imposition of sanctions after the Fall that contracted the country's GDP by 40% with food emergency that left more than 90% of Afghans suffer from food insecurity (HRW, 2022). The second part of the paper looks into the situation and the conditions that led to the swift transfer of power to Taliban – by analyzing Taliban's cultivation of propaganda, linked to the mobilization of kinship narrative around civilian casualties and developmental model. It constructed new categories for political legitimacy and consensus based on collective memory and experience. This section furthers the argument for community-based development for domestic and international partners that would build partnership between the state and the communities across urban-rural divide, thus leading to fair distribution of national resources. In continuation to this, the third section focuses on the ethnic fault lines that exist alongside different ideas of nationalism impinging the construction of nationalist imaginaries.

6.1.1 Methodology

In this chapter, I have used theoretical framework of double binds to understand the political and social crisis in Afghanistan and the dilemma that it reproduces for Afghans. The argument that the chapter advances is derived from primary and secondary sources. Among primary sources, local, regional, and international newspapers as well as national and international reports have been used for analysis.[6] Secondary sources used include books, and scholarly articles on the subject that add persuasiveness to the argument with additional layer of interpretation and analysis.

6.2 Development as Ideology and Liberal Ascendancy

In the assessments that followed on the cost of war in Afghanistan, the Watson Institute's Costs of War Project[7] reported that the United States spent USD 2.313 trillion in its war in Afghanistan since the invasion in 2001. The question that arises here is, what did liberal intervention yield in terms of security and stability with the Taliban takeover in 2021? The first scenes that appeared after the Fall were of defacement of women's images, attacking beauty shops in Kabul, of fear that gripped artists, media personnel, and women, and more worryingly the immediate collapse of the Afghan security forces that bolstered Taliban's tactical offensives in Kabul. The violence, intimidation, and revenge attacks revived the memories of the 1990s, where the Taliban imposed austerity measures in areas under their control and influence.

The mayhem that ensued in Kabul was symbolic as it is the center of political power and epicenter of infrastructure development and economic activity. It bears the imprints of external development – in terms of foreign investments and rapid urbanization – that left out a significant part of the rural population living in underdevelopment and deprivation. This inflow of foreign aid created asymmetries of wealth and power, widening the gap between the urban and the rural with unfair distribution of power and resources. Major portion of investments came from the U.S. with USD 131 billion spent on reconstruction effort alone since 2002 across four areas: funding, security, governance, and economic and social development (SIGAR, 2021, p. 34). The reconstruction efforts included international community's contribution of billions of dollars towards urbanization and infrastructure development with Kabul as the cosmopolitan center that led to the emergence of military-bureaucratic establishment, an embodiment of state power. The infrastructural investments continued despite the precarious security situation that was the result of opposition that these political projects generated on grounds of social and ideological differences.

In the years of liberal dominance in world politics post the fall of communism, Afghanistan served as a site for reinforcing American hegemony in the form of economic/development aid programs. As part of the long history of American foreign policy (Fukuyama, 2006, p. 2),[8] the nation-building intervention aided imperialism – the national pursuit of bolstering domination and hegemony – rather than empowering nations it claims to be benefiting (Wood: 291, p. 166). Despite this "Failure of Institutional Memory" (Fukuyama, 2006, p. 1), the U.S. made same mistakes each time in its new nation-building intervention. Seen as a "fanciful objective," Walt (2018) argues that the U.S. engagement in Afghanistan was a failure that turned into a "fruitless but never-ending effort" attempting to replace the (structures of) power "with a modern, Western-style constitution and corresponding set of political institutions." The underlying objective of this mission is to provide (liberal) order to the world and justify occupation of territories, which is tied to the ideology of orientalism that deploys the narrative of ontological and epistemological differences, prioritizing racial hierarchy and naturalizing Western superiority between the "invented collective identities of the West and the Orient/East" (Said, 1979, p. 2).

6.2.1 Aid, Alliances, and American Hegemony

In wielding America's normative power, the Western-style governance structures were implanted with the dual approach of force and consent. While force was employed through military strategies completely overlooking the overwhelming presence of the Taliban in areas of operations that killed innocent civilians, categorized as "collateral damage," consent was drawn on achieving material success through infrastructure development and commitment to "support democracy and women's rights."[8]

Firstly, the use of force led to the strengthening of the Taliban. Harm to civilians by U.S. and Afghan forces led to a significant growth of the Taliban that undermined the war effort, further straining of U.S.-Afghan relations (Walt, 2018). The anger against U.S. forces increased over time with the use of disproportionate and indiscriminate force by paramilitary forces who fired into homes without any provocation (Gaston, 2010). These counterinsurgency strategies terrified the local communities against foreign forces who operated with impunity, exacerbating mistrust in U.S. policies and international presence. Secondly, the forging of consent encouraged urbanization with Kabul ranking fourth in the list of fastest-growing cities and urban areas during the period 2006–2020 (City Mayors Statistics, 2021). To this end of building a broad-based productive economy for creating employment opportunities, the Afghanistan National Peace and Development Framework (2017–2021) was developed in consultation with international partners. This was in line with the National Development Framework (NDF, 2002) that made the development of private sector as one of its goals with renewed emphasis on investment in infrastructure and policy reforms to boost private sector in a predominantly rural society.[9] The conflicting alliances that grew around this development model show the incorporation of urban Afghanistan into a world system dominated by Western capitalism that radically altered the old system and relations, leaving behind the majority of rural Afghans impacted by the disproportionate impact of development. If history is a lesson, the economic development through 1950s into the 1970s had "disastrous consequences"[10] (Shahrani, 2009, p. 547).

The roots of this model of aid and private investment in conflict societies lie in the liberal-democratic framework of development that encourages constitutionalism and unrestrained capitalism. This model of liberal internationalism (Keohane, 2002), where liberal peacebuilding is the only option in war-ridden societies (Fukuyama, 2006), prescribes political liberalism (in the form of democratic reforms with emphasis on human rights, individual freedom), and economic liberalism (self-interest in a free-market economy) that enable market privatization and foreign investments to create global liberal governance structures that act as deterrents to war and, instead, "facilitate cooperation and foster habits of working together" (Keohane, p. 30). With the Kantian belief that "the spirit of commerce cannot coexist with war,"[11] the export of liberal development model to war-torn countries is seen as a triumph of international liberalism to sustain peace, "fostering pluralism in economics and politics, and promoting international cooperation" (Keohane, 2012, p. 126). As a doctrine of international institutions for social progress, international liberalism's commitment toward privatization and development in Afghanistan had an asymmetrical effect along the clearly defined rural-urban divide in the country, where the major beneficiaries were the elite and the upper-middle class in Kabul and other urban cities, while the majority of the population – remote and rural – remained systemically excluded. In fact, the urban transition in Afghanistan is mainly because of insecurity, unemployment, and lack of access to public services in rural areas. This gap led to "rural-urban migration to avail opportunities and services accessible to the urban residents, adding economic and employment stress on the limited resources in urban settings" (Ahmadi, 2019, p. 10).

Afghanistan's experience with the liberal international order leaves us with questions about intervention and the use of force that remain contested. The spate of economic reforms that entrenched private players facilitating economic development[12] reinforced "power differential" between social groups on class lines (urban and rural matrix) along with repression of women through "social reproduction" of structures and systems that preserved social roles of masculine domination (Krais, 2006) compounded by wartime sexual violence against women and children (UNAMA, 2021).[13] Despite the awareness about sexual abuse in the form of *bacha bazi*[14] (pederasty), the practice is linked to oppression of women (Prey & Spears, 2021) in the face of militarized masculinities, structural gender inequalities, and insecurity.

6.3 Contested Sovereignties, Masculinity, and Muslimness

The grievances that strengthened Taliban foothold are civilian casualties, abuse of power, misuse of resources, and asymmetrical development benefiting few along ethnic and class lines. While Kabul emerged as the cosmopolitan center with a thrust of modernization, the structures of power remained unchanged in rural areas due to a lack of development. These grievances became a propaganda tool for the Taliban who fostered solidarity by mobilizing women's figuration and civilian casualties at the hands of the foreign forces to invoke fraternal solidarities. Earlier in the 1990s, Taliban forged attachments through narratives of "protecting" young boys from *bacha bazi* (Schneider, 2014) that increased their influence among the local village communities. Taliban used the figure of the "violated young boys" to build fraternal and paternal ties that bind the men of the community together. By employing the rhetoric of "collective humiliation" over the bodies of young boys and women, Taliban gave call to avenge the past injury inflicted on the community.

The practice of *bacha bazi* had resurfaced after the overthrow of the Taliban in 2001, and all efforts to abolish the practice failed with government complicity and negligence.[15] In this backdrop where the elite and educated engaged in practices like *bacha bazi*, the Taliban successfully projected itself as the "savior" of the community and legitimized their declaration of *jihad* against state institutions, security personnel, and foreign forces. The Taliban forged political attachments "nurtured through performance of Islamo-masculinity and intensified through recourse to kinship metaphors, affect and memory" (Moolji, 2021, p. 5). It is through the melding of masculinity and Muslimness that Taliban emerged as one of the most powerful contenders of sovereignty in Afghanistan, mimicking the state in many forms – owning a flag, an anthem, overseas political office, and judicial bodies (Moolji, 2021).

During the 20 years of War on Terror, the Taliban did not recognize the legitimacy of the Afghan government and emerged as a non-state performer of sovereignty following the overthrow in 2001. This contested terrain of sovereignties was further strengthened over the conceptualization of the political and construction of the social with emphasis on the question of women in an Islamically regulated society. The position and role of women in rural Afghanistan is determined by patriarchal kinship arrangements that give primacy to tradition, tribal customs, and [Muslim] religiosity, resisting any forms of modernization that threaten patriarchal authority. The expression of masculinity and power mobilized the allied public to their idea of the political.

6.3.1 Asymmetrical Development and Construction of New Identities

The rigid social stratification and gendered spaces led to a deep disconnect that existed between the urban social landscape and the remote, rural topography. During the period of war and reconstruction, the Taliban made inroads over the asymmetrical development, U.S.-brokered political arrangements, and construction of new identities – the outward-oriented cosmopolitan citizen with primary allegiance to a global moral community and the inward-oriented rural ethnic Afghan adhering to the tribal code – each inhabiting a "social world of accumulated history" (Bourdieu, 1986, p. 241). The former being the primary beneficiary of economic reforms and urbanization, and the latter a hapless onlooker. It is here that Pierre Bourdieu's notion of "capital"[16] is applied to understand the construction of new identities, where the cosmopolitan social agent is a product of objectified and institutionalized cultural capital, representing competence and authority by accruing qualifications through access to education that later transforms into objectified and embodied capital.[17]

Contrary to the embodiment of the cosmopolitan citizen emerges the figure of the Taliban, who wears rugged traditional clothes, eats cheap food, and an embodiment of poverty, portrayed as the "vanguard of Afghan tradition and culture." This gives them a higher social prestige[18] – defined as reputation for competence to fight the occupiers, and an image of honorability – among the local communities who have lost trust in the U.S. project of "emancipation" and "development" that widened the gap between the rural and the urban, where the former lacked education opportunities, access to healthcare and electricity, while the latter benefited from international aid worth billions of dollars.

This model of development led to stress on the urbanized spaces that saw a rise in urban slums and flow of internal migration, which reflects increasing income inequality between rural and urban Afghans that constitute a total of 24% of total population (UN Habitat, 2018, p. 1), and 40% living in poverty, mostly in rural areas. However, this doesn't mean that poverty and exclusion are features of rural areas alone (UN Habitat, 2018).[19] There were concerns about a substantial share of population expected to move below the poverty line in the months to come with an estimated 10 million Afghans vulnerable to fall into poverty, and deterioration of food security situation (The World Bank, 2021). Capitalizing over decades of partial deliverance, disproportionate accumulated wealth, and material grievances, the Taliban built a support base (Glinski, 2020) through propaganda and psychological war that culminated in the eventual collapse of Kabul.

Afghanistan's political leadership overlooked the fact that major rebellions in the country have their origins in rural areas owing to political neglect and hasty economic reforms that favored the urban over the rural, where majority of the people interact with local community leaders more than the national political elites and their failure to cultivate nationalist imaginaries.

6.4 Mapping Nationalist Imaginaries?

The problem in the long history of violence and conflict in the country lies in the taxonomy of the discipline that categorized Afghanistan as a "post-conflict" state in 2001 with the launch of the U.S. invasion that uninstalled Taliban from power. Despite the numerous proclamations on the "post-conflict rebuilding" in Afghanistan, the conflict continued to exist, however, the nature and players changed and evolved. In the political history of modern Afghanistan, conflict has existed along the lines of ethnicity and questions of sovereignty.

Historically, Afghanistan has been characterized by diverse ethnic, tribal, and sectarian identities, where each group has impeded the process of building a national consciousness – a pan-Afghan unity that cuts across the deep divisions – that would bring social political transformations. These divisions were visible in the execution of American project of democratization and liberation of "oppressed" Afghan women. During the election period in 2018, a bitter ethnic row erupted over the creation of new electronic identity cards where the national identity was defined as "Afghan," which was seen by the minority ethnic groups an equivalent to Pashtun, a group that has been the most powerful in Afghanistan's politics. The designation of holder's identity as "Afghan" was challenged by Tajiks, the second largest ethnic group in the country, because they saw this move as an entrenchment of Pashtuns in politics (Reuters, 2018).

President Ghani, who fled the country with the Fall, left behind a fractious Afghanistan that existed during and before the War on Terror – a nation torn by old schisms and new divides. During his tenure, disrupted with Taliban takeover, Ghani's government peddled an ethnonationalist agenda favoring the dominant Pashtuns in political appointments that were seen as biased and discriminatory to ethnic minorities. In November 2017, documents leaked from Public Order Department of Minister of Interior regarding the establishment of a 500-member anti-riot unit revealed that the Tajiks were singled out from joining this force (Bezhan, 2017). While the officials in the Ministry dismissed it as a "typing error," the angry reaction from the Tajiks reflected the historical injustices and systematic discrimination to ethnic minorities. These experiences led to a crisis of national identity and delayed the consolidation of Afghan identity that supersedes ethnic divisions in practice of politics.

The controversies over identity and the simmering resentment over politics of exclusion reveals the long-standing ethnic tensions that are further exacerbated by class fragmentation across urban and rural divide. Successive Afghan governments political manipulations widened institutional fissures and encouraged unchecked corruption that was manipulated by the Taliban in forging solidarities. With Taliban in power, public spaces are gendered and socially stratified. The challenge lies in mapping nationalist imaginaries that privilege the national over ethnic identities that were patronized and pandered by successive political leaderships for political gains. In a scenario where the war took a psychological form – with demoralized Afghan security forces, deepening of the crisis of political legitimacy with the president fleeing the chaos at home – the Afghans continue to face the trauma of everyday violence.

6.5 Conclusion

Through the study of Afghanistan, this chapter argues that state formation is a continuous process where old forms break down and are replaced by new forms or older forms with new capacities. Afghanistan's trajectory of development indicates that the theoretical field of development or the Western model of development has been in disorder, lacking consensus on critical questions about authority, accountability, and access. The current crisis has been years in making with no ready answers to the challenges posed by modernization and development theory. In the face of mounting challenges posed by the ferocity of a resurgent Taliban, ISIS-induced insecurity, and limited political options, the future of Afghans dwells in conformity or confrontation, each producing and reinforcing structures of oppression through this current regime of penalty, culture of censure, and tyranny of deprivation. Given this situation on ground, what may be of relevance is deepening development – a community-based approach – that identifies structures of domination and oppression both internally and externally and engages with social and political forces that resist such domination.

Notes

1 In attempting to build a defense of the modern theory of just war, American political philosopher Michael Walzer in his 1977 book, *Just and Unjust Wars: A Moral Argument with Historical Limitations*, explored the conditions and reasons for waging a war as well as the ethical limitations of war (*jus ad bellum* [the justice of war] and *jus in bello* [justice in war]) centered on the moral dilemmas of war – the underlying tensions of fighting well and winning the war. This influential work remains to be the standard theory in the just was theoretical tradition, despite the criticism it received, specifically his conclusion that the 1967 pre-emptive strike by Israel against the Arab nations was justified. However, despite the criticisms, the just war theory has served as providing a legitimate rationale for the U.S. military interventions in the wake of 9/11 in countries like Afghanistan and Iraq.

2 The double bind theory was first developed by Gregory Bateson in 1956 to understand the causes of the medical condition of schizophrenia and post-traumatic stress disorder (PTSD). In his study, Bateson expanded on the simpler understanding of double binds as "conflicting demands" to focus on the "hidden systems that control behaviour" (Gioia, 2020). He looked into how demands are imposed, who imposes them and what the subject on whom the demand is imposed makes of the situation. Bateson's theory of double bind was later applied to other areas like art, poetry, organizational behavior, and postwar situations among others.

3 In this chapter, I have applied Sakina Hijri's "Oppressive Double Binds" to understand the Afghan dilemma. She argues that the double binds exist in virtue of oppression wherein the double binds are both a product of as well as reinforce oppressive structures. Conceptualizing double binds as choice situations, Hijri argues that no matter what a person does, they become a mechanism for their own oppression.

4 *Longue durée* is a term coined by French historian Fernand Braudel, who defines it as "the history of long, even very long, duration in contrast with episodic time" (see, Braudel: 1980, 25).

5 Afghanistan has largely been an aid economy that has been in the form of development aid, foreign investments, military, and non-military reconstruction efforts, among others. To encourage investments, the government focused on bilateral and multilateral trade agreements along with trade-related reforms in different sectors of construction, communication, and logistics (see, Shirzad & Nusrat, 2018, p. 20).

6 Primary sources – Reports: U.S. Agency for International Development (USAID), United Nations Assistance Mission in Afghanistan (UNAMA), Special Inspector General for Afghanistan Reconstruction (SIGAR), Afghanistan National Peace and Development Framework (ANPDF) among others. Newspapers: Tolo News, the *New York Times*, Al Jazeera, Reuters.

7 The Cost of War Project is a research project at the Watson Institute for International and Public Affairs at Brown University that documents and analyses the human (casualties and civil liberties) and financial costs of US military interventions in Iraq, Afghanistan, and Pakistan in the name of War on Terrorism post-September 11 terror attacks.

8 The new nation-building efforts taken by the U.S. and international community increased since the end of the Cold War in 1989 with one new national building intervention every two years. Having toppled the Taliban regime in 2001, the U.S. was claimed to construct a "fully democratic political order" (Fukuyama: 2006).

9 Afghanistan National Peace and Development Framework (2017–2021), Food and Agriculture Organisation of the United Nations, p. 19, https://faolex.fao.org/docs/pdf/afg148215.pdf.

10 Afghanistan's earliest major agricultural development effort – the Helman Valley project – that was contracted to an American company was precedent setting for

three reasons: firstly, for its large-scale "white elephant" characteristics; secondly, its justification for political (benefiting the Pashtuns) rather than economic and rational grounds; and lastly, its heavy reliance on foreign loan and capital investments. Moreover, development projects have been ill-conceived by successive governments in Kabul. Their efforts to finance expensive projects triggered unrest and upheaval (see Shahrani in Robinson 2009 & Rakove, 2023).

11 For Immanuel Kant, who was the spokesman of the three versions of international liberalism – republican, commercial, and regulatory – republics were constitutional governments based on the principles of freedoms of individual rule of law and equality of citizens (Keohane in Hovden, 2002, p. 17).

12 Afghanistan witnessed economic growth and progress made with the inflow of aid, mainly from the U.S. As per the USAID, June 4, 2021, the U.S. announced an "additional humanitarian assistance of USD 266 million on June 4, 2021, in the face of continuing conflict and rising food insecurity." It further stated that the total U.S. humanitarian assistance for Afghanistan is more than USD 543 million since Fiscal Year 2020.

13 UNAMA recorded a total of 270 cases of sexual and gender-based violence. Of these, 18 were conflict-related sexual violence that affected nine boys, five women, and four girls. Violence against three girls were attributed to the Taliban. Apart from Taliban, members of Afghan National Army, Afghan National Police, and Afghan local police were also implicated in sexual violence.

14 *Bacha Bazi* translates into "boy play" where young boys are dressed as girls for "entertainment" of elite Afghan men (politicians and security forces), who force and sexually abuse these boys for prolonged hours. They continue to operate and carry on this form of traditional abuse with the complicity of U.S. forces who have been asked to ignore these issues in the name of local culture. The men owning *bachas* were those who held power or stature in their society. This relationship between the owner and the bacha terminates upon growing a beard that signifies "manhood," which would make him less attractive and useful for sexual entertainment. The other aspect of bacha bazi or bacha posh is to transform 3–4-year-old daughters into boys for next 10+ years. The girls are presented as boys and are encouraged to emulate boys. But upon attaining adolescence, these young girls-turned-boys had to dump their male identities and adapt to the acceptable form of "feminine behavior." This sudden transition has had psychological impact on young girls with many of them remaining puzzled about their identity (Prey & Spears, 2021, HTT-Unclassified, Bedi, 2021, & Nordberg, 2014).

15 A 2014 Report by AIHRC assessed that bacha bazi is prevalent among people who pay bribes or are related to law enforcement personnel, judges, or prosecutors, thus exempting them from prosecution. The practice is common among the literate and those with higher education. Despite Article 427 prohibiting rape and pederasty, the existing laws do not address the problem of bacha bazi.

16 French anthropologist Pierre Bourdieu's theory of capital talks about four main forms of capital – social, cultural (embodied, objectified, and institutionalized), economic, and symbolic. According to him, cultural capital is the knowledge, skill, and behavior that an individual gains in a social cultural context through pedagogic action (Bourdieu & Passeron, 1977; Bourdieu in Richardson, 1986).

17 Objectified cultural capital would imply material comfort, which can be of cultural significance. Poverty is associated with revolutionaries, who are considered as heroes. Going to universities adds skills which is a kind of embodied cultural capital. And the sharing of cultural capital forms a collective identity, which leads to social capital – the art of networking, to know or be connected with people who have power. When groups share their capital, it becomes part of their collective capital, and by joining a group, one gains access to collective capital that can buy higher position in society. Moreover, economic capital is the most important form of capital as it can be turned into other forms of capital over time (Bourdieu: 1986).

18 Social prestige explains Bourdieu's concept of symbolic capital, which is a value that indicates recognition and legitimization of other forms of capital – social, economic, and cultural. Since capital elevates the social status only if it is recognized, it becomes the most important form of capital (Bourdieu: 1986).
19 An estimated 28% of total urban population lives under the poverty line with the urban poor relying on irregular day labor (UN Habitat, 2018).

References

Afghanistan National Development Framework (NDF) (2002), Government of Afghanistan Policy Document, in Afghanistan National Development Strategy, Vol. 1, https://mof.gov.af/sites/default/files/2021-05/ANDS.pdf

Afghanistan National Peace and Development Framework (2017–2021), Food and Agriculture Organisation of the United Nations, https://faolex.fao.org/docs/pdf/afg148215.pdf

Ahmadi, Naqibullah, (2019), Drivers of Urban Transition in Afghanistan and the Country's Urban Future, Policy Brief, (51). *OSCE Academy*. https://osce-academy.net/upload/file/51_DRIVERS_OF_URBAN_TRANSITION_IN_AFGHANISTAN_ENG.pdf

Bezhan, Frud, (2017), Leaked Memo Fuels New Allegations of Ethnic Bias in Afghan Government. *Radio Free Europe/Radio Liberty*, https://gandhara.rferl.org/a/afghanistan-alleged-ethnic-bias/28865186.html

Bourdieu, Pierre, (1986), The Forms of Capital, in J. Richardson (ed.), *Handbook of Theory and Research for the Sociology of Education*, Greenwood, Westport.

Bourdieu, Pierre & Passeron, Claude, (1977), *Reproduction in Education, Society and Culture*, Sage Publications, London.

Braudel, Fernand, (1980), *The Structures of Everyday Life: Civilization and Capitalism, 15th to 18th Century*, Volume 1, Harper & Row, New York.

City Mayors Statistics, (2021), The world's fastest growing cities and urban areas from 2006 to 2020, http://www.citymayors.com/statistics/urban_growth1.html

Fukuyama, Francis (ed.), (2006), *Nation-Building Beyond Afghanistan and Iraq*, John Hopkins Press, Baltimore.

Gaston, Erica, (2010), Outsourcing the Dirty War in Afghanistan, *Open Society*. https://www.opensocietyfoundations.org/voices/outsourcing-dirty-war-afghanistan

Gioia, Ted, (2020), Why Gregory Bateson Matters, *Los Angeles Review of Books*. https://lareviewofbooks.org/article/why-gregory-bateson-matters/

Glinski, Stefanie, (2020), Report, Feeling Abandoned by Kabul, Many Rural Afghans Flock to Join the Taliban, *Foreign Policy*. https://foreignpolicy.com/2020/09/24/taliban-kabul-rural-afghans-join-peace-deal/

Hijri, Sukaina (2021), Oppressive Double Binds, *Ethics*, 131(4), 643–669.

HTT - Pashtun Sexuality, Unclassified, (2021), https://info.publicintelligence.net/HTT-PashtunSexuality.pdf

Human Rights Watch, (2022, August 4), *Afghanistan: Economic Crisis Underlies Mass Hunger*,https://www.hrw.org/news/2022/08/04/afghanistan-economic-crisis-underlies-mass-hunger

Keohane, M. (2002), Moral Commitment and Liberal Approaches to World Politics, in Eivind Hovden & Edward Keen (ed.), *The Globalization of Liberalism*, Palgrave Macmillan, U.K.

Keohane, Robert, (2012), Twenty Years of Institutional Liberalism, *International Relations*, 26(2), 125–138.

Khoja-Moolji, Shenila, (2021), *Sovereign Attachments: Masculinity, Muslimness, and Affective Politics in Pakistan*, University of Chicago Press, United States.

Krais, Beate, (2006), Gender, Sociological Theory and Bourdieu's Sociology of Practice, *Theory, Culture & Society*, 23(6), 119–134.

Mackenzie, James & Sediqi, Qadir, (2018) Afghan president launches new ID cards amid row over ethnicity, *Reuters*, https://www.reuters.com/article/us-afghanistan-politics-idUSKBN1I40RG

Nordberg, Jenny, (2014), The Underground Girls of Kabul: In *Search of a Hidden Resistance in Afghanistan*, Deckle Edge.

Prey, Emily & Spears, Kinsey, (2021), Gendered Analysis of the U.S. Withdrawal and Bacha Bazi in Afghanistan, *Newlines Institute*.

Rakove, Robert, (2023), Developing Afghanistan Since 1950, Asian History, in *Oxford Research Encyclopedia*, Oxford University Press, Oxford.

Renov, Michael. (1983), Leave Her to Heaven: The Double Bind of a Postwar Woman, *Melodrama*, 35(1), 28–36.

Said, W. Edward, (1979), *Orientalism*, Penguin Random House, U.K.

Schneider, Emily, (2014), The Underground Girls of Kabul, *Foreign Policy*. https://foreignpolicy.com/2014/10/15/the-underground-girls-of-kabul/

Shahrani, Nazif M., (2009), Afghanistan to 1919, in Robinson, Francis, (Ed.). *The New Cambridge History of Islam: The Islamic World in the Age of Western Dominance*, Volume 5, (203–211) Cambridge University Press, Cambridge.

Shirzad, Fazalrabi & Nusrat, Rabia, (2018), Investment in infrastructure and employment in Afghanistan: Review of Past and Present Investment Plans, Report jointly published by Liaison Office, *TLO & International Alert*. https://www.international-alert.org/app/uploads/2021/08/Afghanistan_InvestmentInInfrastructureEmployment_EN_2018.pdf

The World Bank in Afghanistan, (2021), https://www.worldbank.org/en/country/afghanistan/overview#1

UN Habitat, (2018), Discussion Paper, *Afghanistan's Urban Future*, https://unhabitat.org/sites/default/files/download-manager-files/1424269536wpdm_Afghanistan%20Urban%20Future.pdf

UNAMA, *Sexual Violence in Conflict*, (2021, March 30), https://www.un.org/sexualviolenceinconflict/countries/afghanistan/

Update Reconstruction, (2021 April), Quarterly Report to Congress, *Special Inspector General for Afghanistan Reconstruction (SIGAR)*. https://www.sigar.mil/pdf/quarterlyreports/2021-04-30qr-section2-funding.pdf

Walt, Stephen M., (2018, July 9), It Still Doesn't Get Worse Than Afghanistan, *Foreign Policy*. https://foreignpolicy.com/2018/07/09/it-still-doesnt-get-worse-than-afghanistan

Walzer, Michael, (1977), *Just and Unjust Wars: A Moral Argument with Historical Limitations*, Basic Books, United States.

World Bank Group Afghanistan Development Update, (2021, April), *Setting Course to Recovery*, https://thedocs.worldbank.org/en/doc/e406b6f24c2b7fdeb93b56c3116ed8f1-0310012021/original/Afghanistan-Development-Update-FINAL.pdf

7 Impact of the Cross-Strait Relations Tensions on Global South

The Case of China and Taiwan

Manoj Kumar Panigrahi

7.1 Introduction

'Global South' has chiefly felt the brunt of the great power politics, from colonisation to being caught between the major powers' power struggles. The immediate effect of conflicts from one region to another has a broader effect on the nations that are either geographically closer or economically intertwined with the conflicting parties.

This chapter will study the People's Republic of China (PRC) China and Republic of China (ROC) Taiwan relations and its effect on the 'Global South'. The relationship between China and Taiwan is also known as 'cross-strait relations'. Separated by the Taiwan Strait, *The Economist's* May 2021 edition, Taiwan has been described as 'The most dangerous place on Earth' (Economist, 2021). The president of Taiwan, Tsai Ing-wen, responded by showing confidence on Taiwan's unity and core values as an important pillar to face challenges (Ing-wen, Twitter [Now X], 2021)

7.1.1 Aim and Importance of the Study

This chapter argues that a cross-strait crisis brings back the 'power politics' into foreplay. First, 'Global South' countries must choose between democratic values and economic development to address their pressing developmental issues. To do so, the countries' exports after declaring their recognition of the PRC as the legitimate authority over Mainland China have been analysed since 2016. Second, it paves the way for a supply chain disruption and economic slowdown in a conflict. Taiwan, being a leader in the production of niche semiconductor technology, can lead to a reduced supply of such high-tech chips, ultimately having a catastrophic effect on the world economy, especially the 'Global South'. It risks an acute downturn in global economic activity. At a time when the global economy is reeling from the impact of the COVID-19 pandemic and the ongoing Ukraine-Russia conflict, another major conflict would further push it into a more profound crisis. Therefore, it is essential to understand the effect of a cross-strait conflict on the Global South.

DOI: 10.4324/9781032694337-10

7.1.2 Literature Review

Although there is scholarly work present on the economic impact of the cross-strait conflict and the bilateral trade ties between Taiwan and China notably (Liu, 2023; Chen, 2016; Magcamit & Tan, 2015), there lacks a significant gap in analysing the economic growth of the countries which switched diplomatic relations from Taiwan to China, except a particular book chapter which analysed Solomon Island's switch from Taiwan to China in 2019 (Aqorau, 2021).

The chapter considers 'power' as the basis of the argument. Robert Dahl has defined 'power' as a skill set to get others to do what they otherwise would not do (Dahl, 1957, pp. 202–203). For this chapter, the actors exerting power are nation-states. Power can be exerted in multiple ways via economy, natural resources, human capital, and defence, primarily known as 'hard power'. Following Dahl's work, Joseph Nye defined a new form of power, 'soft power'. According to Nye, soft power projection occurs when one country gets other countries to *want* what it wants (Nye J. S., 1990, p. 14). Though soft power has primarily been limited to cultural influences, Nye developed 'smart power', which is a combination of both 'hard and soft' powers (Nye J. S., 2009, p. 1). The case study given in this chapter will show how China has exerted its economic and diplomatic power or, in the words of Nye, 'smart power' in its favour by exerting its influence on the 'Global South' countries.

Nevertheless, the influenced countries do not always get along with the powerful nations. The less powerful nation aligns with another powerful nation to *balance* its interaction with the approaching powerful entity. The Cold War period is one of the examples to show such alignment, where countries mostly were aligned with the USA or Soviet Russia, and a handful of the remaining were determined to stay non-alignment.

7.2 Overview of Cross-strait Relations

The Japanese surrender of 1945 led to a series of events in Taiwan closely related to cross-strait affairs. The surrendering of Taiwan (or Formosa as it was known then) by Japan to ROC leadership on 28 April 1952 via 'The Treaty of Taipei' led to the formal transfer of Taiwan to ROC (UN, 1952, p. 38).

The conflict traces its roots to the civil war between the Nationalists led by Chiang Kai-shek of Kuomintang (KMT) and the Maoists led by Mao Zedong of the Chinese Communist Party (CCP) in China, which saw the KMT's defeat and later moved to Taiwan in 1949. Soon after, in 1949, there was an attempt by PRC soldiers to control the Kinmen/ Quemoy offshore islands under ROC, but being repulsed by the ROC forces gave a particular pause in the military actions by the PRC towards ROC soldiers (Yu M., 2016, p. 92). Other significant military actions by China against Taiwan were seen in 1955, 1958, and 1996, widely known as 'The Taiwan Strait Crisis'. It was not until August 2022 that another significant military action was conducted by China. The military action of firing missiles overland Taiwan and some of them landing in Japan's Exclusive Economic Zone (EEZ) brought up the severity of the issue where a geographically closer third nation faced such missile landings. In response to the missile landings, Japan's Foreign Minister Hayashi Yoshimasa blamed China for seriously affecting the peace and stability of the region and the international community (MOFA-Japan, 2022).

Such escalation incidents have also led to the changing perception of identity among local Taiwanese citizens over the years. As per the survey conducted by the Election Study Centre, National Chengchi University, Taiwan, since June 1992, there have been significant changes in people's perceptions. Table 7.1 explains how Taiwanese perceptions of identity and independence versus status quo have changed until June 2023. The available results show that a solid Taiwanese identity has formed over the years, contrasting the percentage of people who want independence. As the status quo has largely maintained the peace, it has been the most preferred response compared to declaring independence from Taiwan (NCCU, 2023).

Another aspect which closes 'Global South' with cross-strait affairs is the presence of more than half a million foreign workers in Taiwan, primarily from Indonesia, the Philippines, and Vietnam. Their safety during a conflict, which might call for their emergency evacuation, can embroil Southeast Asia in the conflict. Huang Xilian, the Chinese ambassador to the Philippines, warned of the safety of the 150,000 Overseas Filipino Workers (OFW) in Taiwan if the conflict arises (Xilian, 2023). Such statements echo China's position on Taiwan, which it emphasises as one of its 'core issues' (Hua, 2023).

Taiwan's stronghold over the niche semiconductors technology and peace in the Taiwan Strait are closely associated with the Global South's growth and prosperity. The supply chain of goods, which saw disruption due to COVID-19, can be disrupted during a conflict or a blockade of the Taiwan mainland. The following section will reflect on the economic aspect of whether countries from the 'Global South' gained by legitimising the PRC authority of Mainland China and Taiwan.

Table 7.1 Taiwanese Perceptions on Identity and Independence vs. Status Quo

Survey Question		*Year*	
		June 1992 (%)	*June 2023 (%)*
Identity	Taiwanese	17.6	62.8
	Chinese	25.5	2.5
Independence vs. Status Quo	Independence	3.1	4.5
	Status Quo	9.8	32.1

Source: Election Study Centre, National Chengchi University (NCCU, 2023).

7.2.1 Democracy Values versus Economy Growth

As the introductory section discusses, countries use their power to influence other countries' behaviour. The chapter argues that China used its economic and political power to steer countries to derecognise ROC/Taiwan as a country and establish diplomatic relations with itself. Such a switch of diplomatic relations legitimises China's narrative on the 'One China Principle', which states that 'there is only one China, and the PRC is the sole representative of the mainland' (Taiwan Affairs Office, 2023). This interpretation is also known as the '1992 Consensus', which stated two different understandings of 'One China'. According to the Taiwanese version, 'One China' refers to the establishment of ROC in 1912. However, no written agreement exists, as stated by the Mainland Affairs Council of Taiwan (MAC-Taiwan, 2023).

The derecognition of ROC as a country representing China was accelerated in 1971 through the UN, primarily due to the support of the USA. In 1971, UN Resolution No. 2758 specifically mentioned the authority of the PRC over mainland China from the ROC (UNGA, 1971).

7.2.2 Research Methodology

Only 13 countries recognise Taiwan as a country, down from 22 in 2016. Table 7.2 shows the export of goods to China by those countries that switched diplomatic recognition from ROC to PRC from 2016 until 2023—the countries who switched their diplomatic recognition in this time hail from the more prominent 'Global South'. The timeline is chosen from 2016 to 2023 because President Tsai Ing-wen of the Democratic Progressive Party (DPP) came to power in 2016 until her last tenure as president in 2024. DPP as a party is considered a pro-independence party, and during her inaugural speech in 2016, President Tsai did not acknowledge the earlier agreed '1992 Consensus' and sought the cross-strait to be more on a mutual understanding and respect (Ing-wen, 2016). The non-acceptance of the '1992 Consensus' created uneasiness in China as it did not align with the PRC's views.

One of the limitations of the data in Table 7.2 is the unavailability of the official data for Kiribati, which has been marked as 'NA'. Studying the switch of these recognitions helps to understand whether it benefitted these 'Global South' countries, or they were simply lured into the promise of getting benefits from the Chinese market access. The base year of comparison to such is selected a year before the countries switched their ties to show before and after comparing their exports to China.

7.2.3 Discussion

Along with the analysis of the table, the following conclusion on the switching ties could be drawn:

Table 7.2 Export of countries to PRC post switching of the diplomatic relations from ROC to PRC (2016–2023)

Year and name of country switching diplomatic ties to PRC		*Amount in Exports to PRC (in Millions USD)*							
		2015	*2016*	*2017*	*2018*	*2019*	*2020*	*2021*	*2022*
2016	São Tomé and Príncipe[b]	0.0119		0.123		NA	0.0184		
2017	Panama[a]		35.5	42.6	49.41	59.7	370.06	1,199.2	1532.7
2018	Dominican Republic[a]			190.6	188.4	276	181.82	244.3	355.31
	Burkina Faso[a]			10.06	13.09	13.92	2.63	19.83	1.54
	El Salvador[a]			47.1	85.63	51.8	50.01	61.19	47.50
2019	Solomon Islands[a]				380.3	287.3	286.97	200.3	188.51
	Kiribati[a]				NA	1.41	0.16	NA	NA
2021	Nicaragua[a]						12.5	16.5	15.2
2023	Honduras[a]							14.12	10.62

Source: The data were compiled through two open-source databases.

Notes

a International Monetary Fund (IMF, 2023)

b For Nicaragua and São Tomé and Príncipe Trading Economics (TradingEconomics, 2023)

a *São Tomé and Príncipe (STP)*

The STP data shows that since it switched ties to the PRC in 2016, it has only managed to increase its exports marginally. Historically, the diplomatic relations between STP and PRC have been uneven since its independence on 12 July 1975. Later, on 6 May 1997, it severed its ties with PRC and switched to ROC. However, later, in 2016, upon its request for further aid being declined by the ROC/Taiwan government, it switched its recognition to the PRC again. Such action taken by the STP saw a sharp response from the Taiwan president's office. It blamed China for engaging in 'dollar diplomacy' and pressing its version of the 'One China Principle' (President-ROC, 2016). Since it severed ties with ROC, STP has received substantial financial aid from the PRC (MacaoNews, 2022).

b *Panama*

Panama significantly increased its exports to China since the 2017 switch. Since then, the country has gained a valuable market for its products and resources in China. In 2018, Panama and China launched their talks on the Free Trade Agreement (FTA) (OAS, 2018). Establishing diplomatic relations can be seen as a crucial diplomatic win as it has been crucial for larger political gains. Since 2017, Panama also received multiple aid and investments from China, which has assisted in infrastructure projects and revamping its military (Ellis R. E., 2023).

c *The Dominican Republic*

Since May 2018, the country has sought cooperation with China in several sectors. A month after switching the ties, China assured them of a 600 million USD loan to improve the country's electricity (Reyes, 2018). As of this writing, China has failed to provide the promised amount (Ellis E., 2023). However, the Dominican Republic has doubled its exports to China since 2018. Taiwan's government blamed a 3.1 billion USD investment and aid from China for the switch of relations. Taiwan's foreign minister, Joseph Wu, stated, 'It was a cost that Taiwan could not match' (Yu & Blanchard, 2018).

d *Burkina Faso*

Like STP, Burkina Faso, after its independence in 1960, established ties with ROC in 1961, but this was not until an internal coup led to the switching of relations to the PRC in 1973. Then, the PRC provided the military government with first aid of 50 million USD to the coup in 1987, bringing back pro-ROC leadership, which led to the switch of ties back to ROC in 1994 (Noubel, 2023). Later in 2018, when the next switch of ties occurred, Burkina Faso President Roch Marc Cristian Kabore, during his visit to Beijing, showcased his support to PRC (Xinhua, 2018). As per Table 7.2, the export of Burkina Faso to China saw a continuous rise from 2018 except in 2020 and 2022, reflecting an uneven relation between the two nations. Such roller coaster switching of ties and trade volume exposes the thin trade on which the ties are being maintained.

e *El Salvador*

El Salvador and the PRC signed a joint communiqué on 21 August 2018, establishing bilateral relations between the two countries (MOFA-PRC, 2018). The catch is like other countries: Any country resuming diplomatic relations with China needs to recognise the PRC as the sole representative of China, with Taiwan being a part of it. The post-establishment of ties followed the same pattern of promises of significant investments and loans for the growth of the El Salvadoran economy. However, according to the data in Table 7.2, trade declined in 2022 compared to 2021. A noteworthy moment was seen in the bilateral relationship in November 2022 when both sides announced pursuing an FTA for larger economic growth. Such promises of economic growth have been questioned by Ricardo Castañeda, senior economist at the Central American Institute of Fiscal Studies, who put his concerns as 'The possibilities that an economy like El Salvador's could benefit from a FTA with China are very small' (Castañeda, 2023).

f *Solomon Islands*

The decision was made after a discussion to accept the 8.5 million USD in development funds offered by China (DW, 2019). Nevertheless, the switch was described as something which would give the Solomons 'greater leverage over traditional regional powers and to escape sanctions put on it by Australia and New Zealand following a 2006 military coup' by the country's Prime Minister Manasseh Sogavare (Sogavare, 2019). The formation of diplomatic relations between the two has also led to the signing of a 'Comprehensive Strategic Partnership' (MOFA-PRC, 2023a). The agreement will allow China closer ties with the Pacific country.

g *Kiribati*

Kiribati in the past had diplomatic relations with the PRC from 1980 until 2003. In 2003, it established relations with Taiwan and continued to do so until 2019 (MOFA-PRC, 2019). Comparing the trade export benefits of Kiribati to China is one of the limitations of the paper, which could not be provided. Soon after the diplomatic switch happened, Kiribati was granted a Most Favoured Nation (MFN) by China, which will allow goods to be exported to China from Kiribati duty-free, increasing their competitiveness (HKTDC, 2020). However, the importance of Kiribati is well noticed given its closeness to the significant military base of the USA in Hawaii.

h *Nicaragua*

Nicaragua and the PRC had diplomatic relations from 1985 until 1990. Post which Nicaragua recognised Taiwan as a country until both Nicaragua and China established their diplomatic relations in 2021 (MOFA-PRC, 2021). As per the trade data, Nicaragua has increased its trade exports to China with a slight reduction in 2022. Beyond trade and diplomatic relations, it has assisted China in becoming an observer in regional forums such as the Central American Parliament (PARLACEN) (Lopez, 2023). It led to the expulsion of the Taiwanese delegate from the regional body, leading to the further shrinking of international space for Taiwan.

i *Honduras*

Honduras is the latest country to switch the recognition from Taiwan to China in March 2023 (MOFA-PRC, 2023b). The reason for the switch, as claimed, was the refusal from the Taiwan side to respond to 2.5 billion USD as requested by the Honduran side. However, the Foreign Ministry of Taiwan denied such requests (MOFA-ROC, 2023). Eduardo Enrique Reina, Honduran foreign minister, described the switch as 'pragmatism, not ideology' (Lai, 2023). The exports between Honduras and China will need another two to three years to analyse whether the switch benefitted Honduras.

According to the data in Table 7.2, the 'Global South' nations had uneven growth, whereas in some countries it benefitted, but in others it did not in terms of exports. Beyond trade, China has used its economic power to invest and give financial loans to countries that have also pledged to join its Belt and Road Initiative (BRI) project, which promises economic growth to the participant countries.

7.3 Supply Chain Disruption and Economic Slowdown

The previous section described how the economic prospects with China mattered more than the democratic values to change the diplomatic ties between 'Global South' countries and Taiwan and China. As the world has entered the digital age, the importance of semiconductors has grown with each passing day. Chris Miller, author of *Chip War*, mentioned that it was in the 1980s when the first idea of chips as modern crude oil emerged (Miller, 2023).

Semiconductors have been crucial in all significant electronic equipment and have made them irreplaceable across sectors in the industrial and daily lives of the world's citizens. The world rightly felt the importance of semiconductors during the COVID-19 pandemic in 2020–2021, which saw a decline in production and global supply chain disruption, leading to a significant gap in supply and demand.

Taiwan-based Taiwan Semiconductors Manufacturing Company (TSMC), which supplies 90% of high-end chips worldwide, is crucial element supporting global growth. It is debated that the likelihood of a full-scale war on Taiwan is less due to the importance of the supply chain of the semiconductors that originate from Taiwan. The dependence of China and other countries on Taiwan's semiconductor production has led to the term 'Silicon Shield' (Cronin, 2022). It is argued that, as semiconductors are essential for everyone's growth and running of crucial industries, going to war in the Taiwan Strait is a loss to all. However, semiconductor-producing countries have tried diversifying their production from China and Taiwan. It is where 'Global South' countries such as India and Vietnam are considered preferred investment destinations.

During any conflict, the free movement of goods and people stand limited, leading to an increase in the price of the goods and, in some situations, even creating shortages. For example, in the Ukraine-Russia war, which created a shortage of wheat and a price increase. It has also led to long air flight durations proving costlier and lengthier for air traffic and cargo movement. On similar grounds, a cross-strait conflict can be disastrous to the world again and is not limited to the 'Global South' countries.

A survey conducted by *Commonwealth Magazine*, a Taiwan-based English media, shows how the business leaders of the 2,000 Taiwanese companies' CEOs see the potential cross-strait conflict and if they have any Plan B. In response to whether they fear a war between Taiwan and China within the next five years? Sixty percent of the respondents responded in the affirmative. Moreover, to find an alternate place of investment, 59.4% of the CEOs still want to invest in Taiwan, 26.5% in Southeast Asia, 7.5% in North America, and surprisingly 4.4% in India (Lu, 2023). The survey reflects that Southeast Asia is the first choice for Taiwanese executives to invest outside of Taiwan, given their similarity in culture and geographical distance to Taipei. Though the third favourite choice is North America, Taiwanese companies will face certain limitations, such as higher wages and taxes to invest, compared to the other destinations. Taiwanese investors have seen India as a complex place to invest mainly because different regions have diverse regulations, languages, and working cultures.

Chen Chern-chyi, deputy minister of Economic Affairs of Taiwan, in August 2023, stated that the investments by Taiwanese companies in January–June 2023, stood at 2.126 billion USD in NSP countries, compared to 1.9 billion USD in China (Chern-chyi, 2023). This investment increase can be understood as companies looking for more neutral investment areas to shield themselves from a cross-strait conflict.

Additionally, a report released in 2023 by the Economist Intelligence Unit (EIU) titled 'Conflict Over Taiwan: Assessing Exposure in Asia' identifies Asian countries and economies at different risk factors if any fallout happens in the Taiwan Strait. As per the EIU assessment, the Philippines has the highest overall exposure risk to a cross-strait conflict, given its proximity and high economic trade volume with China (EIU, 2023, p. 2). Additionally, Table 7.3 reflects the top 15 countries exposed to a conflict over Taiwan in terms of geopolitical and economic pressure. Of the 15 countries, nine countries from the Global South have the highest geopolitical and economic pressure due to a conflict over the Taiwan Strait. It also brings back the earlier argument about the safety of Filipino and other Southeast Asian migrant workers in Taiwan who are working in several sectors of Taiwan's economy. Their repatriation before and during the Taiwan conflict will expose the Southeast Asian countries' capabilities to organise such large rescue operations.

Table 7.3 Top 15 Countries Level of Exposure to Cross-Strait Conflict

Sl. No.		*Type of Exposure*		
		Highest Geopolitical Exposure	Highest Economic Exposure	
1	Highest Exposure	Japan	Hong Kong	Highest Exposure
2		Philippines	South Korea	
3		South Korea	Laos	
4	Severe Exposure	Australia	Vietnam	
5		Vietnam	Cambodia	
6		Thailand	Philippines	
7		Hong Kong	Thailand	
8		Malaysia	Japan	
9		New Zealand	Myanmar	
10	High Exposure	India	Malaysia	
11		Singapore	Singapore	Severe Exposure
12	Moderate Exposure	Bhutan	Australia	
13		Nepal	Maldives	
14		Myanmar	Indonesia	
15		Cambodia	New Zealand	

Source: (EIU, 2023, p. 3).

7.4 Conclusion

The chapter employed the argument of 'power' by studying the cross-strait relations between Taiwan and China. Using powers in terms of economy and diplomacy to let the 'Global South' countries choose between democracy and economic growth brings out hard facts. Through the cases studied, the chapter drew a few conclusions. First, it reflects those countries looking for their interest. Second, not what is promised by the country gets delivered, like the loans and financial aid. China used its economic growth story to lead the country to switch diplomatic relations in its favour.

China was also prosperous in making the countries, as mentioned in Table 7.2, join the BRI, its flagship global economic outreach programme. Similarly, growing protectiveness among the technologically advanced countries will affect the growth of the 'Global South' countries. Such technology would come at a cost to those who lack such advancements. It can also lead to a monopoly of such technologies by a few and cause a slow pace of growth among those who cannot. As peace lies an advantage to all the parties, the 'Global South' countries need to mitigate the global conflicts and steer their economic and national growth. The usage of 'smart power' by China's leadership has led to countries making decisions favouring China, even at the cost of their exports.

Finally, the chapter aimed to create a further debate and work on the economic implications for countries switching diplomatic ties in return for economic growth. Additional research on the topic can be done by conducting a comparative study on how the exports and imports changed by the countries studied in this chapter with Taiwan and China.

References

Aqorau, T. (2021) Solomon Islands' Foreign Policy Dilemma and the Switch from Taiwan to China. In: Editor, G. Smith, & T. Wesley-Smith, *The China Alternative: Changing Regional Order in the Pacific Islands* (pp. 319–348). ANU Press.

Castañeda, R. (2023, October 17). *China Embeds Itself in El Salvador*. Diálogo. https://dialogo-americas.com/articles/china-embeds-itself-in-el-salvador/, last accessed 2023/11/4.

Chen, C.-K. China-Taiwan Economic Ties and the 2012 Taiwanese Presidential Election. *American Journal of Chinese Studies*, *23*(1), 77–96 (2016).

Chern-Chyi, C. (2023, August 17). *Southbound tops China investment*. Taipei Times. https://www.taipeitimes.com/News/biz/archives/2023/08/17/2003804844, last accessed 2023/10/05.

Cronin, R. (2022, August 16). *Semiconductors and Taiwan's "Silicon Shield"*. Stimson. https://www.stimson.org/2022/semiconductors-and-taiwans-silicon-shield/, last accessed 2023/11/29.

Dahl, R. A. (1957) The Concept of Power. *Behavioral Science*, *2*(3), 201–205.

DW. (2019, September 21). *Solomon Islands establishes ties with China*. DW. https://www.dw.com/en/solomon-islands-establishes-diplomatic-ties-with-china/a-50527170, last accessed 2023/12/15.

Economist. (2021, May 21). The most dangerous place on Earth. *The Economist*. https://www.economist.com/leaders/2021/05/01/the-most-dangerous-place-on-earth, last accessed 2022/11/5.

EIU (2023). *Conflict over Taiwan: assessing exposure in Asia.* London. Economist Intelligence Unit.

Ellis, E. (2023, October 31). *The Evolution of Chinese Engagement with the Dominican Republic.* Centre for Strategic and International Studies. https://www.csis.org/analysis/evolution-chinese-engagement-dominican-republic, last accessed 2023/11/21.

Ellis, R. E. (2023, March 25). *China's Uneven Military, Political, and Commercial Advance in Panama.* The Diplomacy https://thediplomat.com/2023/03/chinas-uneven-military-political-and-commercial-advance-in-panama/, last accessed 2023/11/18

HKTDC. (2020, July 24). *China Grants Most-Favoured-Nation Status to Kiribati.* HKTDC Research. https://research.hktdc.com/en/article/NDgwNTA1OTg1, last accessed 2023/11/10.

Hua, C. (2023, April 27). *Taiwan question is the core of the core interests of China.* Embassy of the People's Republic of China in the Islamic Republic of Iran. http://ir.china-embassy.gov.cn/eng/sgzc/202304/t20230427_11067744.htm#:~:text=highly%20appreciates%20it.-,Taiwan%20question%20is%20the%20core%20of%20the%20core%20interests%20of,history%20will%20end%20in%20failure, last accessed 2023/12/5.

IMF. (2023, December 1). *Trade Data.* International Monetary Fund. https://data.imf.org/?sk=388dfa60-1d26-4ade-b505-a05a558d9a42, last accessed 2023/12/19.

Ing-wen, T. (2016, May 20). *Inaugural address of ROC 14th-term President Tsai Ing-wen.* Office of the President Republic of China (Taiwan). https://english.president.gov.tw/News/4893, last accessed 2023/12/2.

Ing-wen, T. (2021, April 30). *Twitter (Now X).* Twitter (Now X): https://twitter.com/iingwen/status/1388099630529880065?fbclid=IwAR2mbLBPElfdqTkeUdzfiikpZkP57-RMOAK5cE91xz5LNk9QjsXpGKSqx88_aem_AVVFQQqVhFQiY6vZCGvFJDVZhLfkeCGEYK4DtsvL61abyDWkHEPXmYdZx4kkb1supu5wzFfBhK63olvkbVLgs6rL, last accessed 2023/10/09.

Lai, M. (2023, October 6). *Honduras Ditches Taiwan for China.* Foreign Policy Research Institute. https://www.fpri.org/article/2023/10/honduras-ditches-taiwan-for-china/, last accessed 2023/11/10.

Liu, K. (2023) Cross-Strait Relations Between Taiwan and Mainland China: The Economic Imbalance and its Implications. *China Report*, *59*(2), 133–153.

Lopez, I. (2023, August 22). *Central America parliament expels Taiwan, makes China permanent observer.* Reuters. https://www.reuters.com/world/americas/central-america-parliament-expels-taiwan-makes-china-permanent-observer-2023-08-22/, last accessed 2023/11/16.

Lu, P. (2023, December 13). *60% of Taiwan CEOs fear outbreak of war.* Commonwealth Magazine. https://english.cw.com.tw/article/article.action?id=3584&utm_source=email_edm&utm_medium=email&utm_term=email_edm-english_edm, last accessed 2023/12/20.

MacaoNews. (2022, July 5). *China to invest US$100 million in São Tomé international airport expansion.* Macao News. https://macaonews.org/lusofonia/china-to-invest-us100-million-in-sao-tome-international-airport-expansion/, last accessed 2023/9/12.

MAC-Taiwan. (2023). *Former MAC Minister Chen Ming-tong's Comments on the 1992 Hong Kong Talks.* Mainland Affairs Council, Republic of China (Taiwan). https://www.mac.gov.tw/en/cp.aspx?n=34591B13E0BCBF3E, last accessed 2023/12/2.

Magcamit, M., & Tan, A. C. (2015) Crouching tiger, lurking dragon: Understanding Taiwan's sovereignty and trade linkages in the twenty-first century. *International Relations of the Asia-Pacific*, *15*(1), 81–112.

Miller, C. (2023) Chip War: How semiconductors became the new oil with Chris Miller. (P. Chapman, Interviewer) HC Insider.

MOFA-Japan. (2022, August 4). *Extraordinary Press Conference by Foreign Minister HAYASHI Yoshimasa* [Press Release]. https://www.mofa.go.jp/press/kaiken/kaiken24e_000149.html, ast accessed 2023/12/6.

MOFA-PRC. (2018, August 21). *Wang Yi Talks About the Establishment of Diplomatic Relations Between China and El Salvador*. Minsitry of Foreign Affairs of the People's Republic of China. https://www.fmprc.gov.cn/mfa_eng//wjb_663304/zzjg_663340/ldmzs_664952/xwlb_664954/201808/t20180823_593586.html, last accessed 2023/11/4.

MOFA-PRC. (2019, September 28). *Joint Communiqué on the Resumption of Diplomatic Relations Between the People's Republic of China and the Republic of Kiribati*. MOFA-PRC. https://www.fmprc.gov.cn/mfa_eng/wjb_663304/wjbz_663308/activities_663312/201909/t20190928_476734.html, last accessed 2023/11/9.

MOFA-PRC. (2021, December 10). *Communiqué on the Resumption of Diplomatic Relations Between The People's Republic of China and the Republic of Nicaragua*. Embassy of the People's Republic of China in El Salvador. http://sv.china-embassy.gov.cn/exp/Hoy/202112/t20211210_10466240.htm, last accessed 2023/12/1.

MOFA-PRC. (2023a, July 11). *Joint Statement on Establishing a Comprehensive Strategic Partnership Featuring Mutual Respect and Common Development For a New Era Between the People's Republic of China And Solomon Islands*. Embassy of the People's Republic of China in the Kingdom of Sweden. http://se.china-embassy.gov.cn/eng/zgxw_0/202307/t20230711_11111191.htm, last accessed 2023/11/9.

MOFA-PRC. (2023b, March 26). *Joint Communiqué on the Establishment of Diplomatic Relations Between the People's Republic of China and the Republic of Honduras*. Ministry of Foreign Affairs of the People's Republic of China. https://www.fmprc.gov.cn/eng/wjdt_665385/2649_665393/202303/t20230326_11049278.html#:~:text=26%2012%3A31-,The%20People%27s%20Republic%20of%20China%20and%20the%20Republic%20of%20Honduras,of%20signature%20of%20this%20communiqué, last accessed 2023/12/7.

MOFA-ROC. (2023, March 23). *https://www.mofa.gov.tw/News_Content.aspx?n=95&s=99944&create=1 [Translation: Regarding the denial of Honduras seeking $2.5 billion in aid from Taiwan, the Ministry of Foreign Affairs responded as follows:]*. Ministry of Foreign Affairs Republic of China (Taiwan). https://www.mofa.gov.tw/News_Content.aspx?n=95&s=99944&create=1, last accessed 2023/12/7.

NCCU. (2023, July 12). *Trends of Core Political Attitudes*. Election Study Centre, National Chengchi University. https://esc.nccu.edu.tw/eng/PageDoc?fid=7424, last accessed 2023/11/10.

Noubel, F. (2023, June 6). *Taiwan and Burkina Faso: A Tumultuous History of Cooperation and Estrangement*. The News International. https://international.thenewslens.com/article/186130, last accessed 2023/10/5.

Nye, J. S. (1990) Soft Power. *Foreign Policy*, *80*, 153–171.

Nye, J. S. (2009) Get Smart: Combining Hard and Soft Power. *Foreign Affairs*, *88*(4), 160–163.

OAS. (2018, January 16). *Panama-China*. Foreign Trade Information System. http://www.sice.oas.org/TPD/PAN_CHN/PAN_CHN_e.ASP, last accessed 2023/11/5.

President-ROC. (2016, December 21). *Statement on termination of diplomatic relations with Sao Tome and Principe*. Office of the President Republic of China (Taiwan). https://english.president.gov.tw/NEWS/5048, last accessed 2023/12/21.

Reyes, R. P. (2018, June 11). *The US$ 600 million that China will lend to RD for electricity will have a rate of between 2 and 3% interest*. Listin Diario. https://listindiario.com/la-republica/2018/11/06/540652/los-us-600-mm-que-prestara-china-a-rd-para-electricidad-tendran-tasa-entre-el-2-y-3--de-interes.html, last accessed 2023/12/17.

Sogavare. (2019, September 17). *'Dollar diplomacy': Taiwan condemns China after Solomons switch*. Al Jazeera. https://www.aljazeera.com/news/2019/9/17/dollar-diplomacy-taiwan-condemns-china-after-solomons-switch, last accessed 2023/11/14.

Taiwan Affairs Office, P. (2023). *The One-China Principle and the Taiwan Issue*. Taiwan (ROC). http://www.china.org.cn/english/taiwan/7956.htm, last accessed 2023/12/1.

TradingEconomics. (2023, December). *Honduras Exports to China*. Trading Economics. https://tradingeconomics.com/honduras/exports/china, last accessed 2023/12/24.
UN. (1952, April 28). *Treaty of Peace between the Repuiblic of China and Japan*. UN. https://treaties.un.org/Pages/showDetails.aspx?objid=08000002801526ae, last accessed 2022/11/5.
UNGA. (1971, October 25). *Restoration of the lawful rights of the People's Republic of China in the United Nations*. United Nations Digital Library. https://digitallibrary.un.org/record/192054?ln=en, last accessed 2023/12/4.
Xilian, H. (2023, April 16). *Remarks by Ambassador Huang Xilian at the 8th Manila Forum*. Embassy of the People's Republic of China in the Republic of the Philippines. http://ph.china-embassy.gov.cn/eng/sgdt/202304/t20230416_11060060.htm, last accessed 2023/12/1.
Xinhua. (2018, September 1). *China, Burkina Faso agree to open new chapter of bilateral friendly cooperation*. Xinhua News. http://www.xinhuanet.com/english/2018-09/01/c_137434550.htm, last accessed 2023/10/2.
Yu, J. M., & Blanchard, B. (2018, May 1). *Taiwan says China dangled $3 billion to grab ally Dominican Republic*. Reuters. https://www.reuters.com/article/us-china-dominicanrepublic-taiwan/taiwan-cries-foul-as-china-snatches-ally-dominican-republic-away-idUSKBN1I22LN/, last accessed 2023/10/4.
Yu, M. (2016) The Battle of Quemoy: The Amphibious Assault That Held the Postwar Military Balance in the Taiwan Strait. *Naval War College Review*, *69*(2), 91–107.

Part III

Climate Change and Environmental Sustainability in the Global South

8 Gender-Just Transition and Green Growth Nexus

Perspectives from Africa

Hebatallah Adam

8.1 Introduction

Africa's share of global greenhouse gas (GHG) emissions amounts to a mere 7.2%, with Nigeria and South Africa collectively responsible for a quarter of that (1.8%) (UNDP, 2022). However, Africa bears the brunt of the adverse impacts of climate change, as stated by the Intergovernmental Panel on Climate Change (IPCC) in 2021. Diverse factors contribute to Africa's climate vulnerability, including limited economic diversification, inadequate dissemination of technologies and information necessary for supporting adaptation efforts, and a heavy reliance on agroecosystems for sustenance. Consequently, the adaptability of African livelihood systems is highly restricted.

African women are disproportionately affected by the impacts of climate change. They are particularly vulnerable to the effects of climate change due to their reliance on natural resources, such as water and fuels, for their livelihood. Limited access to these resources can have catastrophic consequences for women's lives. In rural areas of Africa, for instance, women are responsible of collecting water for their families. When climate change dries up water sources, women are compelled to travel further, which can be hazardous and costly (Awiti, 2022). To achieve sustainable development, addressing gender inequalities within climate change policy is not only a moral imperative but also an economic decision. Climate policies can become more inclusive, effective, and resilient by promoting gender equality, empowering women, and addressing the needs of marginalised communities (Denton, 2002; Maduekwe et al., 2019). Overall, the literature review emphasises the importance of identifying the gendered nature of climate change and the need for gender-sensitive policies and actions.

Our thorough analysis of the current knowledge of literature has revealed a contextual research gap for the topic of gender-just transition and green growth in the African context. Numerous scholarly sources provide significant perspectives on gender disparities and inequities in Africa, specifically in education, employment, and agriculture. The extant scholarly works have examined inclusive green growth in particular sectors, such as the energy industry. Therefore, it is imperative to conduct further studies on the intersection of

DOI: 10.4324/9781032694337-12

gender, green growth, and sustainable development in Africa to acknowledge and address the existing disparities and inequalities.

This study examines how gender inequality is a cause and a consequence of slow progress towards achieving green growth objectives. By analysing extant literature and empirical evidence, this study aims to develop a conceptual framework that illustrates how gender equality may foster green growth and vice versa.

This research paper begins with a thorough review of the relevant literature. The second section displays the outcomes of the data analysis and index evaluation. We utilised secondary data from a variety of index analyses, such as the World Economic Forum's Global Gender Gap Report (2022), the African Development Bank's Africa Gender Index (2019), the UNDP's Gender Inequality Index (1995–2020), the Notre Dame Global Adaptation Index (1995–2020), and the Global Green Growth Institute's Global Green Growth Index (2010–2021). From 1995 to 2021 is the time frame under consideration. We conclude with policy recommendations for promoting a gender-just transition in Africa.

8.2 Literature Review

8.2.1 Gender Inequality and Climate Change in Africa

Gender inequality is prevalent in Africa, impacting many facets of life, including education, employment, land ownership, and political participation. Azuh et al. (2017) found that the prolonged underdevelopment of sub-Saharan African nations is due to the failure to include women in all aspects of life, as gender disparities are linked with poverty, slower economic growth, weakened governance, and decreased standards of living. Despite efforts to address gender inequality in Africa, this problem persists in many regions of the continent, impeding development and progress. Moreover, women and men from different socioeconomic backgrounds, ages, and social statuses may be disproportionately affected by any change (including climate change). This disproportionate impact is caused by several factors, including existing gender inequality and discrimination, unequal access to resources, and gendered social norms and roles (Rao et al., 2016). Goh (2012) explains that due to social and cultural norms about gender roles and their lack of access to and control over assets, climate change has a greater negative impact on women.

Women in Africa bear a disproportionate burden of the consequences of climate change, primarily because of their societal roles as primary caregivers, limited access to resources and decision-making power, and persisting gender inequalities. These vulnerabilities can lead to increased vulnerability to risks and perpetuation of the cycle of gender inequity. Remteng et al. (2021) state that the phenomenon of climate change is exacerbating the pre-existing gender disparities and vulnerability in Africa. According to previous studies conducted by Rao et al. (2016), Awiti (2022), and Bob and Babugura (2014), it has been emphasised that women are more susceptible to the adverse effects of climate change, particularly in domains such as land and natural resource accessibility, agricultural production, food and nutrition security, health, water and energy, and disasters caused by climate change, migration, and conflict. Alexander et al. (2011) explains that women are also more vulnerable to environmental hazards due to their predominance in agriculture and environment-related occupations.

8.2.2 Gender-Just Transition for an Inclusive Green Growth

The inclusive green growth development model considers economic growth's effects on both genders, male and female. Kabeer and Natali (2013) assert that gender equality is a crucial component of economic development, and it is vital to ensure that both genders reap equal benefits from growth. The study of Cabeza-García et al. (2018) has emphasised the significance of gender-related factors in fostering inclusive economic growth. This type of growth is characterised by the equal inclusion of both men and women.

The implementation of a Just Transition strategy is crucial in ensuring gender equality by facilitating equivalent job opportunities for women in sectors that have traditionally been dominated by men, such as the energy and construction industries. This involves establishing mechanisms within Just Transition policies that facilitate the incorporation of women not directly employed in high-emission sectors by providing alternative employment opportunities and enhancing social protections. Ensuring that employment across all sectors adheres to the principles of fairness, decency, and adequate support for women and their families (Smith & Koning, 2020).

A just transition has the potential to yield significant positive impacts for society in terms of creating environmentally sustainable employment opportunities while also advancing gender equality (Becker & Shadbegian, 2008). According to Dominish et al. (2019), allocating resources towards environmentally sustainable production, consumption, and management of natural resources can create many quality employment opportunities within the green industries. Just transition policies have the potential to generate substantial improvements in employment quality and income levels across a variety of industries, including agriculture, construction, recycling, and tourism. These enhancements result from adopting more productive processes and creating sustainable commodities and amenities (Guidelines for a Just Transition Towards Environmentally Sustainable Economies and Societies for All, 2015).

8.3 Research Methods

The primary purpose of this research is to assess the status of gender inequality in Africa to the advancement of green growth. Furthermore, the study examines how gender considerations have been incorporated into African countries' Nationally Determined Contributions (NDCs). The study aims to offer policy recommendations for facilitating a gender-equitable transition in the African setting. The study also aims to contribute to the current knowledge base and provide significant perspectives for policymakers, practitioners, and other stakeholders involved in sustainable development initiatives in Africa by addressing the research objectives.

This research employs hybrid methods consisting of data analysis and index evaluation. We relied on secondary data from a variety of index analyses, including the World Economic Forum's Global Gender Gap Report (2022), the African Development Bank's Africa Gender Index (2019), the UNDP's Gender Inequality Index (1995–2020), the Notre Dame Global Adaptation Index (1995–2020), and the Global Green Growth Institute's Global Green Growth Index (2010–2021). The period under consideration is from 1995 to 2021.

The research methods include an extensive review of the relevant literature about the topic. This study draws upon existing literature on gender inequality and inclusive green growth in Africa. Consequently, the methodology employed in this research entails thoroughly examining the existing pertinent literature.

8.4 Results and Discussion

8.4.1 Gender Inequality in Africa

8.4.1.1 Global Gender Gap Index

The Global Gender Gap Report 2022, published by the World Economic Forum, assesses the progress of 146 nations on the Global Gender Gap Index, which measures countries' performance on a scale of 0 to 100 based on the extent to which the gender gap has been reduced (World Economic Forum, 2022). Countries are classified based on their current level of gender equality across four distinct domains: economic opportunities, education, health, and political empowerment. The report included 40 African countries in 2022, of which 18 were below the global average (0.681), and the remaining 22 were above it. Africa's average is 0.683, marginally greater than the global average (see Figure 8.1). Africa has closed 68.3% of its gender gap by 2022 (Figure 8.2).

Rwanda, Namibia, South Africa, Burundi, and Mozambique are ranked first through fifth. Benin, Algeria, Mali, Chad, and Congo (Democratic Republic of) have the lowest rankings (see Figures 8.3 and 8.4).

In 2022, sub-Saharan Africa holds the sixth-highest regional score, reducing its gender gap by 67.9%. It ranks above the Middle East and North Africa, and South Asia regions.

Sub-Saharan Africa ranks lowest in the world for educational attainment, with a persistent gender gap of 0.853% (and Africa 0.8873). Although the subindex score has experienced a slight increase of 0.9%, the region still encounters hindrances that impede its ability to achieve equality (see Table 8.1).

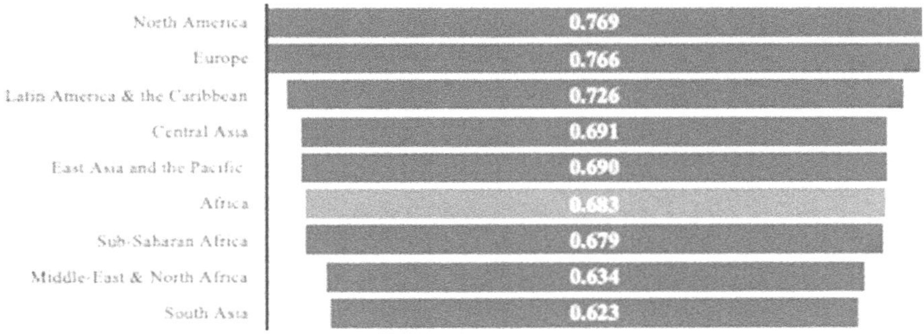

Figure 8.1 Global Gender Gap Index – Regional Performance 2022.

Source: Author's own contribution based on data from World Economic Forum (2022).

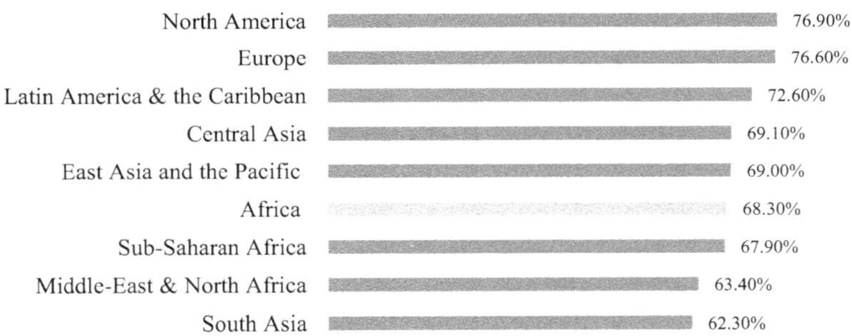

Figure 8.2 Global Gender Gap Index – Gender gap Closed to 2022, by Region.

Source: Author's own contribution based on data from World Economic Forum (2022).

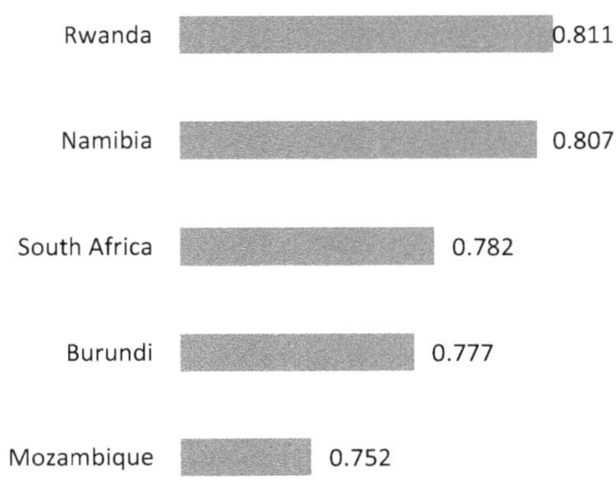

Figure 8.3 Highest Rank African Countries – Global Gender Gap Index 2022.

Source: Author's own contribution based on data from World Economic Forum (2022).

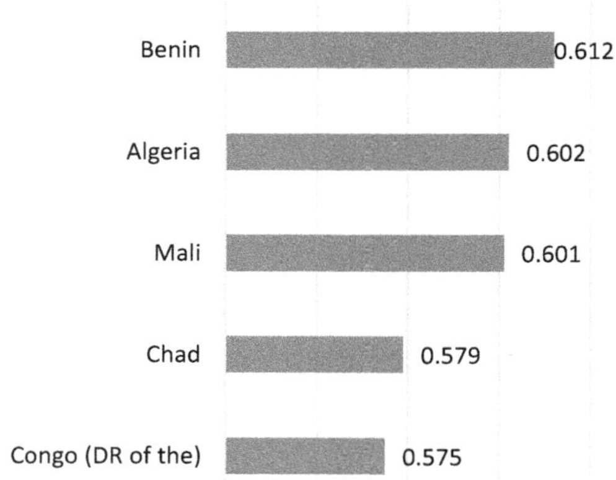

Figure 8.4 Lowest Rank African Countries – Global Gender Gap Index 2022.

Source: Author's own contribution based on data from World Economic Forum (2022).

Table 8.1 Global Gender Gap Index – Regional Performance 2022, by Subindex

Region	*Overall Index*	*Economic Participation and Opportunity*	*Educational Attainment*	*Health and Survival*	*Political Empowerment*
North America	0.769	0.774	0.997	0.969	0.337
Europe	0.766	0.702	0.995	0.970	0.398
Latin America & the Caribbean	0.726	0.645	0.995	0.976	0.287
Central Asia	0.691	0.682	0.988	0.974	0.118
East Asia and the Pacific	0.690	0.722	0.954	0.952	0.133
Sub-Saharan Africa	0.679	0.677	0.853	0.972	0.213
Middle-East & North Africa	0.634	0.460	0.962	0.964	0.151
South Asia	0.623	0.357	0.932	0.942	0.262
Africa	0.683	0.659	0.887	0.973	0.211

Source: Author's own contribution based on data from (World Economic Forum, 2022).

8.4.1.2 *Africa Gender Index*

The 2019 Africa Gender Index Report comprehensively analyses gender equality and women empowerment across Africa. It investigates the various dimensions of economic, social, representation, and empowerment, as well as political and institutional factors (African Development Bank and United Nations Economic Commission for Africa, 2020). According to the 2019 Africa Gender Index scores, which range between 24.0% and 79.7%, the average score is 48.6%.

Namibia, Lesotho, South Africa, Rwanda, and Seychelles are among the highest-ranking nations, while Niger, Sudan, Mauritania, Chad, and Comoros are at the bottom (see Figures 8.5 and 8.6).

The report thoroughly analyses 51 African countries, revealing that 28 fall below the African average (0.488), while the remaining 23 exceed it. Achieving gender equality in Africa, particularly in the Sahel region (Burkina Faso, Chad, Mauritania, Mali, and Niger), remains a major obstacle, despite the continent's significant progress in women's participation within the index's scope.

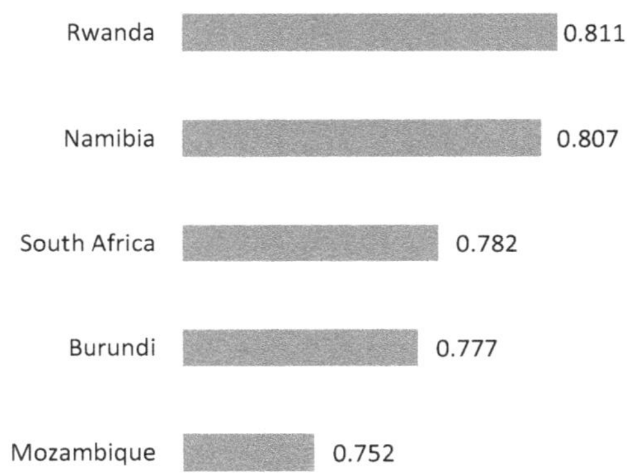

Figure 8.5 Highest Rank African Countries – Africa Gender Index 2019.

Source: Author's own contribution based on data from (African Development Bank and United Nations Economic Commission for Africa, 2020).

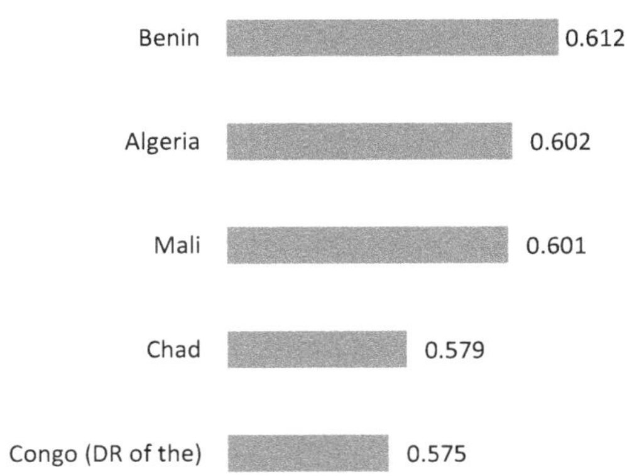

Figure 8.6 Lowest Rank African Countries – Africa Gender Index 2019.

Source: Author's own contribution based on data from (African Development Bank and United Nations Economic Commission for Africa, 2020).

At the regional level, gender inequalities exhibit significant disparities (see Figure 8.7). With a score of 61.3%, Southern Africa demonstrates lower levels of inequality between women and men, followed by East Africa, which achieves a regional score of 51.8%. North, Central, and West Africa, on the other hand, have the lowest regional average scores at 40.3%, 42.1%, and 43.7%, respectively, indicating a significant presence of gender inequality.

Countries with higher scores tend to exhibit more gender equality across all three dimensions. Despite this, North Africa demonstrates greater gender equality in social parameters, including health and education indicators. Women's participation in the economy and leadership positions significantly lags that of males.

Table 8.2 shows the gender disparity regarding indicators on the African continent, revealing diverse facets of gender inequity. The gender gap in basic education has been significantly reduced, with a closure rate of 96.2%. This indicates a near parity in the enrolment rates of both genders in basic education. However,

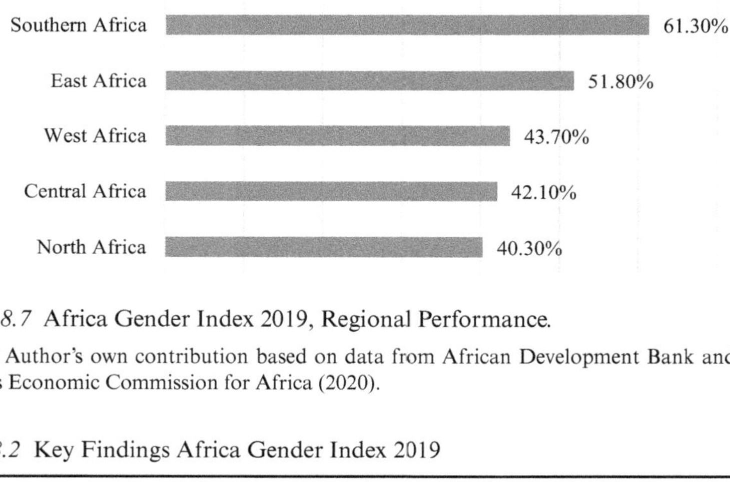

Figure 8.7 Africa Gender Index 2019, Regional Performance.

Source: Author's own contribution based on data from African Development Bank and United Nations Economic Commission for Africa (2020).

Table 8.2 Key Findings Africa Gender Index 2019

Gender Gap Indicators	*Gender Gap at Indicator Level (%)*
Basic Education	96.2
Youth Literacy	86.8
Youth in Work	90.3
Vulnerable Employment Gender Gap	70.7
Participation in Business Gap	44.3
Access to Credit	73.4
Access to Ownership	22.9
Top Managers in Firms	22.9
Parliamentarians	25.3
Managers, Professionals, Technicians	41.4

Source: African Development Bank and United Nations Economic Commission for Africa, 2020.

gender disparities are evident in the realm of STEM education and literacy rates, with a lower participation rate of females compared to their male counterparts. When examining formal employment in commerce and business, the gender gap among young individuals in the labour force is currently at 90.3%. Nonetheless, a significant discrepancy arises, underscoring a broader gender divide and suggesting that adolescent females have a 70.7% higher probability of participating in precarious and informal labour.

Gender inequality in Africa is significantly influenced by unequal land rights. The restricted credit availability for women constitutes a noteworthy obstacle to their engagement in agriculture, agribusiness, and entrepreneurial activities. The credit access gender disparity is reported to be 73.4%, whereas the gender gap in home and/or land ownership is estimated at 22.9%. The insufficiency of economic means often constrains female farmers to a pattern of poverty and subsistence agriculture, especially when faced with the difficulties presented by climate change.

Senior decision-making positions in the private sector remain predominantly occupied by males, leading to a considerable gender disparity, as evidenced by the Africa Gender Index score of only 22.9%. Similarly, the parliamentary representation is predominantly male, with few exceptions, leading to a gender disparity of 25.3%. According to the Africa Gender Index, men hold a higher percentage of positions in administration, professional work, and technical work in Africa, with a score of 41.4%.

8.4.1.3 UNDP's Gender Inequality Index

The United Nations Development Programme (UNDP, n.d.-b) designed the Gender Inequality Index (GII) to assess gender inequality through the lenses of reproductive health, empowerment, and the labour market. Maternal mortality ratio and adolescent birth rates are used to evaluate reproductive health. The evaluation of empowerment is based on two metrics: the percentage of parliamentary seats held by each gender and the proportion of the population with at least a secondary education. The measurement of labour market participation is based on the male and female labour force participation rates. The Gender Inequality Index (GII) measures gender disparities on a scale of 0 to 1, where higher values indicate more pronounced gender inequality. The GII is a tool for evaluating advancements in gender parity and pinpointing domains that necessitate targeted measures to mitigate gender disparities.

The 2020 Gender Inequality Index scores for Africa range from 0.259 to 0.69, with an average score of 0.537. In contrast, the average Global Gender Inequality Index (GII) stands at 0.344 (see Figure 8.8). These findings indicate that the level of inequality in Africa surpasses those observed globally.

The Central African Republic (0.69), Chad (0.688), Nigeria (0.68), Liberia (0.65), and Sierra Leone (0.634) were the African countries with the highest levels of gender inequality in 2020.

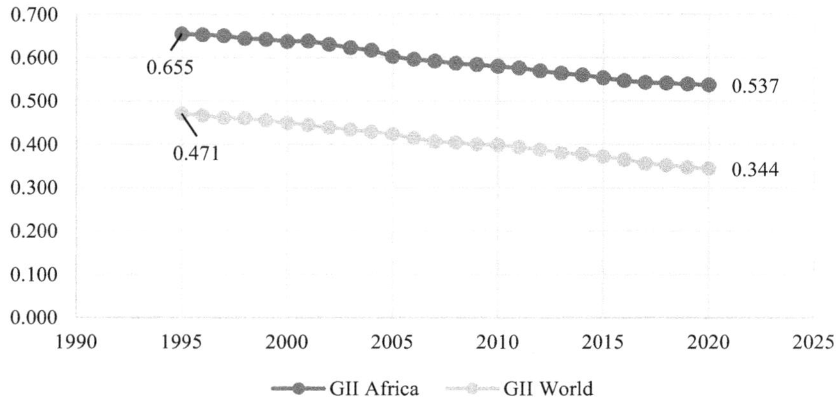

Figure 8.8 UNDP's Gender Inequality Index for Africa and the World, 1995–2020.

Source: Author's own contribution based on data from (UNDP, n.d.-b).

8.4.2 Green Growth in Africa

8.4.2.1 Notre Dame Global Adaptation Index (ND-GAIN)

The Notre Dame-Global Adaptation Country Index (ND-GAIN) is a comprehensive analytical tool that integrates a country's susceptibility to climate change and other global challenges with its readiness to enhance its capacity to withstand adverse impacts (University of Notre Dame's Environmental Change Initiative, n.d.). The average ND-GAIN index for African nations remained consistently below the global average from 1995 to 2020 (see Figure 8.9). The average ND-GAIN index for Africa in 2020 was 39.52 points, while the global average was 49.11 points.

The ND-GAIN Country Index encompasses two primary adaptation dimensions: vulnerability and readiness. The dimension of vulnerability pertains to evaluating a nation's susceptibility, responsiveness, and resilience in confronting the adverse impacts of climate change. On the other hand, readiness evaluates a nation's ability to efficiently utilise investments and translate them into tangible adaptation measures. The ND-GAIN Matrix serves as a visual representation of the relative capacity of nations to withstand and recover from various challenges. The y-axis represents the vulnerability score, while the x-axis represents the readiness score. The nations in the upper left quadrant of the ND-GAIN Matrix exhibit a considerable requirement for investments and innovative measures to augment their readiness, coupled with an imperative necessity for adaptation initiatives (University of Notre Dame's Environmental Change Initiative, n.d.).

Many African nations demonstrated an overlap of elevated vulnerability and diminished readiness indices. This indicates that these countries are especially

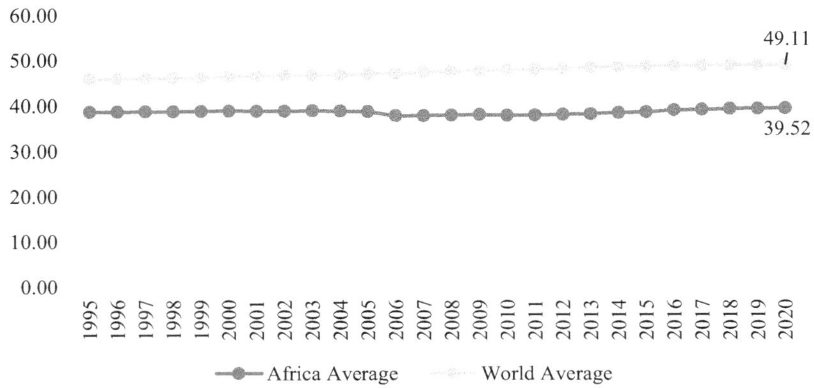

Figure 8.9 ND-GAIN's Average for Africa and the World, 1995–2020.

Source: Author's own contribution based on data from (University of Notre Dame's Environmental Change Initiative, n.d.).

Figure 8.10 Top Performers in Africa in ND-GAIN Country Index, 2020.

Source: Author's own contribution based on data from (University of Notre Dame's Environmental Change Initiative, n.d.).

vulnerable to the effects of climate change and encounter substantial obstacles in implementing effective adaptation measures.

According to the ND-GAIN Country Index (2020), Chad ranked last out of 182 assessed countries, scoring 26.69 points. In addition to Chad, the ten countries occupying the bottom positions in the index were the Central African Republic (27.17), Guinea-Bissau (30.55), the Democratic Republic of the Congo (31.08), Eritrea (31.08), Sudan (32.28), Niger (32.91), Zimbabwe (33.08), Liberia (33.78), and Somalia (34.15). In contrast, as shown in Figure 8.10, Mauritius, Morocco, Tunisia, Cape Verde, and Seychelles emerged as the top performers on the African continent, revealing a relatively reduced vulnerability to the effects of climate change.

8.4.2.2 Global Green Growth Index

The Green Growth Index (GGI) is a comprehensive composite index that measures a nation's progress towards attaining sustainability goals across four key facets of green growth: efficient and sustainable resource management, conservation of natural resources, generation of green economic opportunities, and fostering social inclusion. The Green Growth Index is a metric that measures performance levels on a scale of 1 to 100, where 1 represents the lowest level of performance, while 100 represents the highest level of performance. The comparison of the GGI index, along with its dimensions and indicator categories, is conducted against pre-established sustainability objectives. Hence, if a nation achieves a rating of 100 in the index, dimensions, or indicator categories, it has successfully attained the corresponding sustainability objective (Global Green Growth Institute, n.d.). The Green Growth Index (GGI) 2021 results for Africa indicate that the overall regional performance falls within the moderate to low range. As shown in Figure 8.11, the average GGI score for Africa is 48.59 points, which is lower than the global average of 55.72 points.

The analysis of GGI data spanning 11 years, from 2010 to 2021, indicates a minor improvement in Africa's performance regarding sustainability goals. As shown in Figure 8.12, the GGI encountered a modest increase of only 2.14% during this period, resulting in a score of 48.59 points in 2021 compared to 47.57 points in 2010.

All African nations performed moderately poorly on the GGI 2021 assessment except for Gabon, which scored 61.56 points. Tanzania (59.44), Botswana (57.9), Morocco (56.35), and Togo (56.21) emerged as the best performers in Africa after GabonAmong all GII dimensions, the green economic opportunities dimension scored the lowest in Africa in 2021, with an average score of 18.27 points due to the poor performance of the green investment indicator.

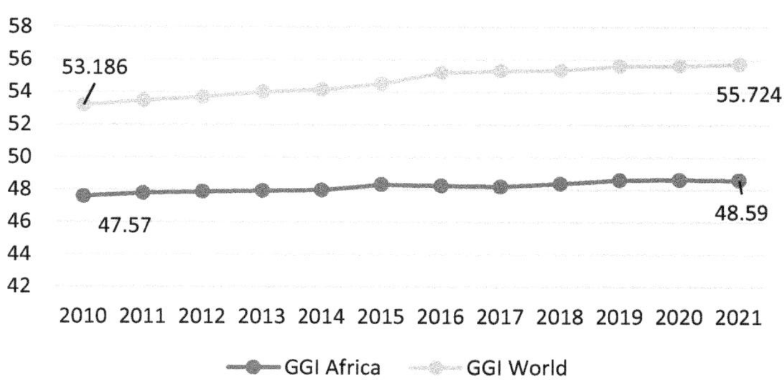

Figure 8.11 Green Growth Index for Africa and the World, 2010–2021.

Source: Author's own contribution based on data from (Global Green Growth Institute, n.d.).

Figure 8.12 Green Growth Index for Africa, 2010–2021.

Source: Author's own contribution based on data from (Global Green Growth Institute, n.d.).

8.4.3 Gender-Just Transition Initiatives and Actions in Africa

Per the Paris Agreement, all parties to the United Nations Framework Convention on Climate Change must furnish their Nationally Determined Contributions (NDCs) every five years. These commitments involve a comprehensive strategy encompassing adaptation and mitigation plans, including various economic sectors and stakeholders. Furthermore, they present a noteworthy prospect for integrating gender parity into climate initiatives substantially and comprehensively.

The UNDP's Climate Promise supports member countries of the Paris Agreement to increase the ambition of their national climate pledge, including advancing gender equality, and to translate their NDC goals into concrete action (UNDP, n.d.-a). A total of 44 African countries[1] have received assistance through the Climate Promise initiative of the UNDP to develop second-generation Nationally Determined Contributions (NDCs) by including measures to strengthen the adaptation aspects of their NDCs (UNDP, 2022).

In their initial and revised Nationally Determined Contributions (NDCs), most African countries have incorporated gender considerations. Nevertheless, the extent to which gender factors have been considered varies from country to country, indicating a range of profundity and comprehensiveness regarding gender integration. The widespread acknowledgement among African nations that climate change disproportionately impacts women and that women are essential drivers in furthering climate pledges is a notable sign of advancement.

The incorporation of gender perspectives into climate change policies has proven to be a difficult undertaking for most African nations. The absence of gender-segregated data posed a considerable obstacle in comprehending the distinct impacts of climate change on diverse genders. A further challenge pertained to the restricted participation of environment ministries, national climate change agencies, gender institutions, and women's and civil society organisations in formulating climate-related policies. Furthermore, African nations must prioritise including women's empowerment initiatives in their Nationally Determined Contributions (NDCs). These programmes should augment women's access to education, training, skill development, resources, green employment opportunities, and climate finance.

8.5 Conclusion and Policy Recommendations

The emergence of climate change poses a significant global challenge that requires immediate action to mitigate its effects. The need to reduce greenhouse gas emissions and mitigate the effects of climate change requires the transition to a low-carbon economy. Nonetheless, this transition must be carried out equitably and impartially, ensuring no person or group is excluded or disadvantaged. The concept of gender-just transition recognises the disparate impacts of climate change on individuals of various genders. It seeks to promote gender equality and female empowerment while transitioning to a low-emission economic model. Gender inequality is a prevalent issue in Africa that has far-reaching implications across various domains, such as education, employment, land ownership, and political participation. The problem persists in multiple sub-regions of the continent despite attempts to mitigate it, thereby hindering growth and development. Due to the intricate ways that climate change affects African women, a gender-sensitive approach must be implemented. Women are especially vulnerable to the effects of climate change because of their predominant role as primary caregivers, their restricted access to resources and decision-making, and their entrenched gender inequities. These issues must be addressed to guarantee that women are not left out of the battle against climate change.

The findings of our study on gender inequality in Africa indicate that the region's performance falls below the global average across all indices examined in the research, namely the Global Gender Gap Index, Africa Gender Index, and Gender Inequality Index. The green economy indices, namely the Notre Dame Global Adaptation Index and the Global Green Growth Index, indicate that the performance of African nations in this area ranged from moderate to poor. Most African nations have integrated gender considerations in their original and updated Nationally Determined Contributions (NDCs), although the degree of gender integration differs. Acknowledging the specific impacts of climate change on women and their crucial role in meeting climate obligations is a significant step forward. The absence of gender-segregated data, insufficient participation of relevant women and civil society organisations, and insufficient prioritisation of women's empowerment initiatives are significant obstacles to the integration of gender into climate change policies in Africa. The results of this study suggest that various policy recommendations can be proposed to facilitate a gender-just transition in Africa. These recommendations comprise:

1 Women's participation in formal employment: It is recommended that policies be established to address traditional gender role expectations concerning unpaid domestic labour, guarantee reasonable childcare and remunerated maternity leave, and allocate resources to infrastructural services that facilitate women's engagement in entrepreneurial activities.
2 Women's agency in the agricultural sector: It is imperative to institute policies that facilitate the enlargement of their land access and land rights, provide them with affordable credit, and guarantee their participation in the augmentation of cross-border trade.
3 Gender inequality in public and private leadership: To augment the number of women occupying leadership roles, it is imperative to undertake proactive measures. This may involve the adoption of gender-based quotas to enhance female representation in parliamentary bodies.
4 Gender and climate policy: It is imperative to establish robust coordination mechanisms that connect actors involved in climate and gender equality. Additionally, there is a need to bolster institutional capacity to achieve this objective.
5 Inclusive consultations: The collaborative consultation approach aims to empower women and marginalised groups, allowing them to adapt, enhance their resilience, and contribute to reducing greenhouse gas emissions.
6 Women's access to climate finance, training, and skills: It is recommended that policies be implemented to promote their economic empowerment and engagement in a low-carbon economy.
7 Policy integration and implementation: Mainstreaming gender into policy formulation. Additionally, concerted endeavours should be undertaken to eradicate enduring gender disparities across all domains of the economy.

Note

1 Angola, Benin, Botswana, Burkina Faso, Burundi, Cabo Verde, Cameroon, Central African Republic, Chad, Comoros, Congo (Democratic Republic), Congo (Republic), Cote d'Ivoire, Equatorial Guinea, Eswatini (Swaziland), Ethiopia, Gabon, Ghana, Guinea, Guinea-Bissau, Kenya, Lesotho, Liberia, Madagascar, Malawi, Mali, Mauritania, Mauritius, Mozambique, Namibia, Niger, Nigeria, Rwanda, Sao Tome and Principe, Seychelles, Sierra Leone, South Africa, South Sudan, Tanzania (United Rep. of), The Gambia, Togo, Uganda, Zambia, Zimbabwe.

References

African Development Bank and United Nations Economic Commission for Africa. (2020). Africa Gender Index report 2019.

Alexander, P. A., Nabalamba, A., & Mubila, M. M. (2011). The Link between Climate Change, Gender and Development in Africa.

Awiti, A. O. (2022). Climate change and gender in Africa: A review of impact and gender-responsive solutions. *Frontiers in Climate*, 4. https://doi.org/10.3389/fclim.2022.895950

Azuh, D. E., Amodu, L. O., Azuh, A. E., Oresanya, T., & Matthew, O. (2017). Factors of gender inequality and development among selected low human development countries in sub-Saharan Africa. *Journal Of Humanities and Social Science (JOSR-JHSS)*, 22(02), 1-7. https://doi.org/10.9790/0837-2202040107

Becker, R. A., & Shadbegian, R. J. (2008). The green industry: An examination of environmental products manufacturing. US Census Bureau Center for Economic Studies Paper No. CES-WP-08-34.

Bob, U., & Babugura, A. (2014). Contextualising and conceptualising gender and climate change in Africa. *Agenda*, 28(3), 3–15. https://doi.org/10.1080/10130950.2014.958907

Cabeza-García, L., Del Brio, E. B., & Oscanoa-Victorio, M. L. (2018). Gender Factors and Inclusive Economic Growth: The Silent Revolution. In *Sustainability* (Vol. 10, Issue 1). https://doi.org/10.3390/su10010121

Denton, F. (2002). Climate change vulnerability, impacts, and adaptation: Why does gender matter? *Gender & Development*, 10, 10–20.

Dominish, E., Briggs, C., Teske, S., & Mey, F. (2019). Just Transition: Employment Projections for the 2.0 °C and 1.5 °C Scenarios BT. In S. Teske (ed.), *Achieving the Paris Climate Agreement Goals: Global and Regional 100% Renewable Energy Scenarios with Non-energy GHG Pathways for +1.5°C and +2°C* (pp. 413–435). Springer International Publishing. https://doi.org/10.1007/978-3-030-05843-2_10

Global Green Growth Institute. (n.d.). Green Growth Index. Retrieved April 20, 2023, from https://gggi-simtool-demo.herokuapp.com/SimulationDashBoard/global_overview

Goh, A. (2012). A literature review of the gender-differentiated impacts of climate change on women's and men's assets and well-being in developing countries.

Guidelines for a Just Transition Towards Environmentally Sustainable Economies and Societies for All, 23 (2015).

Intergovernemmental Panel on Climate Change (IPCC). (2021). Sixth Assessment Report Working Group 1 Regional Fact Sheet — Africa. https://www.ipcc.ch/report/ar6/wg1/downloads/factsheets/IPCC_AR6_WGI_Regional_Fact_Sheet_Africa.pdf

Kabeer, N., & Natali, L. (2013). Gender equality and economic growth: Is there a win-win? *IDS Working Papers*, 2013(417), 1–58.

Maduekwe, M., Morris, E. V., Greene, J., & Healey, V. (2019). Gender equity and mainstreaming in renewable energy policies—Empowering women in the energy value chain in the economic community of west African states (ECOWAS). *Current Sustainable/Renewable Energy Reports*, 6, 13–21.

Rao, N., Lawson, E. T., Raditloaneng, W. N., Solomon, D., & Angula, M. N. (2016). Gendered vulnerabilities to climate change: insights from the semi-arid regions of Africa and Asia. *Climate and Development*, 11, 14–26.

Remteng, C., Nkem, J. N., Mofor, L. A., & Murombedzi, J. (2021). Gender in the nationally determined contributions of African countries: a way forward for effective implementation of adaptation and mitigation strategies. *Ecofeminism and Climate Change*, 3(1), 2–22. https://doi.org/10.1108/efcc-01-2021-000.1

Smith, S. M., & Koning. (2020). Just Transition and Gender–A Review. In UN Women, Expert Group Meeting. https://www.unwomen.org/sites/default/files/Headquarters/Attachments/Sections/CSW/66/EGM/ExpertPapers/SamanthaSMITH_CSW66ExpertPaper.pdf

UNDP. (2022). The State of Climate Ambition: Regional Snapshot Africa.

UNDP. (n.d.-a). Climate Promise. Retrieved April 20, 2023, from https://climatepromise.undp.org
UNDP. (n.d.-b). GENDER INEQUALITY INDEX (GII). Retrieved April 15, 2023, from https://hdr.undp.org/data-center/thematic-composite-indices/gender-inequality-index#/indicies/GII
University of Notre Dame's Environmental Change Initiative. (n.d.). Notre Dame Global Adaptation Index. ND-GAIN Country Index. Retrieved April 15, 2023, from https://gain.nd.edu/our-work/country-index/
World Economic Forum. (2022). Global Gender Gap Report.

9 Climate Crisis and Its Impact on the Global South

The Case of Brazil and India

Priti Agarwal

9.1 Introduction

When discussing about Global South versus Global North, what strikes most is the unequal historical contribution to emissions. Historically, the Global North or the developed countries have been responsible for emissions which is evident if one tries to take a look at the cumulative carbon emissions (Ritchie 2019). However, in terms of consequences of climate change, it is the developing world, particularly the poorest countries and communities which has suffered more as these economies have limited institutional capacity and depend heavily on climate-sensitive agriculture (Nath and Behera 2011). Moreover, these economies are geographically located in regions which are more prone to the adverse impact of global warming. For instance, Bangladesh has low-lying coastal areas making it prone to floods and India is a tropical country wherein already high average temperatures are further intensified by global warming. Additionally, dependence on climate-sensitive sectors like agriculture can amplify the problem of food insecurity in these regions.

One catastrophic impact of climate change is the rise in frequency and intensity of natural disasters. Many countries in the Global South have high vulnerability because of their geographical location. For instance, Brazil has an extensive coastline which increases the risk of floods in the region. Many developing economies are densely populated, such as India, which increases the vulnerability of communities residing in informal settlements, for example. Natural disasters also have huge economic repercussions and economies take a long time to stabilize in the aftermath of a disaster. Botzen et al. (2019) point out that economic losses attributed to natural disasters are on the rise in recent decades. Developing economies suffer more being characterized by lack of resilient infrastructure, poorly constructed housing, poor early warning systems and limited institutional capacity for disaster resilience. For instance, Chinowsky et al. (2011) use empirical evidence to demonstrate that the relative impact of climate events is different in developed and developing economies.

Although one may argue that climate change does not cause natural disasters directly, certain types of extreme weather events can be attributed to it. For instance, warming of the Earth's surface increases the frequency and intensity

DOI: 10.4324/9781032694337-13

of cyclones, heatwaves, storms and heavy rainfall. Rising sea levels increases the likelihood of coastal flooding, especially in low-lying coastal belt. Climate change may lead to altered precipitation patterns with floods in one region versus droughts in another. While one cannot attribute extreme weather events solely to climate change, one cannot deny that climate change has exacerbated the risk of natural disasters. Studies such as Thomas and Lopez (2015) have tried to explore the link between anthropogenic climate change and natural disasters.

Developing countries of the Global South being particularly more vulnerable, this chapter mainly focuses on the impact of climate change on these economies, with emphasis on natural disasters which have happened in these economies. We select two economies in the Global South – Brazil and India. Brazil is an interesting case study as it has a rich biodiversity, which is the Amazon rainforest. It also has an extensive coastline which makes it susceptible to floods. India is also an interesting study since it has diverse climate zones – alpine in the North and tropical in the South. Hence, it is more prone to glacial melt, floods, heatwaves, droughts, cyclones among others. India also possesses an extensive coastline and rising sea level poses a threat to coastal areas.

9.2 Objectives and Significance of the Study

The study aims to analyse the disaster profile of two select economies – Brazil and India. We analyse the disaster mortality in these economies from natural disasters, such as floods, earthquakes, landslides, storms, extreme temperatures among others. The study also aims to explore the economic damages as percentage of GDP in these economies. Such an analysis is important in the context of the climate change impacts across the globe with developing economies being particularly hard hit. Anthropogenic climate change and rise in incidence and intensity of natural disasters are perhaps related, which the present study aims to explore using evidence from the literature.

9.3 Review of Literature

Before we delve into a detailed review of literature exploring the climate-disaster linkages, a section to enhance our understanding of what constitutes Global South will be useful since the chapter aims to explore the climate change impact on two select economies in the Global South. Section 'a' delves into 'what constitutes Global South' followed by Section 'b' which analyses the Climate Crisis in the Global South. Section 'c' explores the climate-disaster link as documented in the literature.

9.3.1 What Constitutes Global South?

The guidelines as to what constitutes Global South verses Global North is rather blurred. There is no clear definition. But broadly speaking, 'Global

South' refers to countries which are developing or less developed as compared to their counterparts in the Global North, which are more developed. According to UNCTAD ('United Nations Conference on Trade and Development'),

> regions in Africa, Latin America and the Caribbean, Asia (without Israel, Japan and South Korea) and Oceania (without Australia and New Zealand) mainly comprise the developing countries (broadly referred to as Global South) whereas the developed economies broadly comprise Northern America and Europe, Israel, Japan and the Republic of Korea, as well as Australia and New Zealand.
>
> (broadly referred to as Global North)

The Global South countries are mostly located in the southern part of the planet. However, the distinction is not really geographical. For example, Australia is bracketed in Global North although geographically, it is located in the Southern Hemisphere. So essentially, developing (South) and developed (North) economies are marked by political, social and economic differences. Some of the common characteristics of countries in the Global South are history of colonial exploitation, still in the process of industrialization, low per capita income, lack of capital and problems, such as unemployment and inequality. In this chapter, we mainly focus on two countries in the Global South, Brazil from South America and India from the Asian region.

9.3.2 Climate Crisis and Global South

Average global temperatures have increased by about 1 degree Celsius since 1880. According to the Paris Agreement (COP21 in France, 2015), global warming should be no more than 1.5 degree Celsius. Primarily driven by human activities, such as burning of fossil fuels and deforestation, the impact of climate change is widespread and far-reaching – rising average temperatures globally, melting glaciers, rising sea levels, extreme weather events (such as hurricanes, droughts, floods, heatwaves, wildfires,), ocean acidification (as oceans absorb CO_2 from the atmosphere), ecosystem disruption leading to loss of plant and animal species, reduced agricultural productivity, droughts and water scarcity, among others.

It is well documented in the literature that the highly industrialized Global North are largely responsible for emissions historically (e.g., Stoddard et al. 2021). Yet, the world as a whole and particularly the developing countries continue to suffer the disproportionate burden. In the context of climate change, history matters. Frumhoff et al. (2015) points out that industrialized nations have contributed the most to greenhouse gas emissions and they should be taking the lead in climate mitigation efforts. The important question is who has used up most of the carbon budget and how to ensure carbon justice. Hence, we take a look at the cumulative amount of CO_2 emitted between 1850 and 2021 rather than current emissions (Charts are analysed from Carbon Brief – 'Carbon

Brief analysis of figures from the Global Carbon Project, Carbon Dioxide Information Analysis Center UNFCCC, Our World in Data, Carbon Monitor, Houghton and Nassikas [2017] and Hansis et al. [2015]'). Considering 'territorial CO_2 emissions (cumulative)' mainly originating from fossil fuels, cement, land use change and forestry, US (20 percent), China (11.4 percent), Russia (6.9 per cent), Brazil (4.9 percent), Indonesia (4.1 percent), Germany (3.5 percent), India (3.4 percent), United Kingdom (3 percent), Japan (2.7 percent) and Canada (2.6 percent) rank higher up on the list, in that order ('Analysis: Which countries are historically responsible for climate change? – Carbon Brief'). During this period, geographically extensive nations, such as US, China and Russia, resorted to cutting down of their temperate forests for fuel and land, whereas European nations such as France, Germany and UK were driven by coal-fuelled industrialization. In the late 19th and early 20th centuries, Indonesia and Brazil (the rainforest nations) were deforested. Hence, these nations contributed to historical warming. China, India and Brazil (part of Global South) are among the developing economies which have historically contributed to emissions. However, when we consider 'cumulative emissions per capita', these countries are nowhere in top 20.

From the analysis of cumulative emissions above, it is clear that historically, the advanced industrialized nations have been responsible for carbon emissions and global warming, whereas the developing countries are bearing the disproportionate impact till date. These regions are witnessing increased incidence of extreme weather events such as droughts, floods, cyclones, heatwaves, etc. Global climate crisis has amplified the risk of climate disasters in the Global South. For instance, 2019 witnessed cyclones Idai and Kenneth in Southern Africa (Siwedza et al. 2021). Rising sea temperatures also increases the likelihood of droughts. East African region was hard hit by severe droughts in 2011, 2017 and 2019 wiping out crops and livestock and leaving many people homeless in this region (Ayugi et al. 2022). The South Asian countries such as India, Nepal and Bangladesh witnessed devastating floods and landslides during 2020–2022. These climate-induced natural disasters have huge impacts on the developing economies in terms of loss of agricultural crops affecting food security of millions of people. Overall, the economic growth of such economies is negatively impacted. Studies such as Ngcamu (2023) points out how climate change affects the vulnerable populations of the Global South, particularly children, women, elderly and disabled. These vulnerable groups are ill prepared when it comes to adapting to climate disasters. Mishra et al. (2023) also contend that Global South is more susceptible to impact of climate change than Global North because of the widely prevalent poverty and inequality in the region.

9.3.3 The Climate-Disaster Link

Disasters can be classified as climatological (wildfires, droughts), hydrometeorological (heat waves, storms, floods) and geophysical (earthquakes, volcanos).

Although 'climate change is not a necessary or a sufficient condition for disasters to occur' (Thomas and Lopez 2015, 10), yet various studies have tried to analyse the climate-disaster link. Published research has a consensus that human-induced climate change has taken place. Anthropogenic increase in greenhouse gas concentrations have led to rise in global average surface temperature (Thomas and Lopez 2015). Thomas and Lopez (2015) examine the link between climatological/hydrometeorological disasters on one hand and anthropogenic climate change on another hand. They analyse if there is a link between accumulated stocks of CO_2, average sea temperature and number of global natural disasters. They construct a model of disaster risk determination for the period 1971–2013 for 157 countries and conduct a regression analysis. Their findings suggest that there is a connection between high frequency of natural disasters and climate change/global warming. Precipitation deviations are found to have positive association with hydrometeorological events. Thomas (2017) also contends that global warming impact is visible in rising threat of climate-related disasters. Anderson and Bausch (2006) report that global warming will increase the likelihood of extreme events.

9.4 Research Methods

We select two economies in the Global South – Brazil and India, both of which are interesting case studies; Brazil being rich in biodiversity and having an extensive coastline, whereas India having diverse climate zones. Both these countries are vulnerable to natural disasters. Using data from Ritchie and Rosado (2022), we trace the disaster profiles of the Brazilian and Indian economies over the period 1970–2020. We use the mortality data and trace the disaster deaths in Brazil and India over this period. We also track the economic damages from disasters as a percentage of GDP in Brazil and India over this period. We also conducted a bibliometric analysis of studies on climate-related disasters in Brazil and India using the software 'Vosviewer'. The articles in the bibliometric study were extracted from Dimensions AI-scientific research database in December 2023 and January 2024 for Brazil and India, respectively.

9.5 The Case of Brazil

The Brazilian economy in South America is a developing economy. The GDP was 1.44 trillion dollars as of 2020 but the growth rates have been volatile with significant fluctuations over the last decade (WB 2021). All three sectors – agriculture, industry and services contribute to the Brazilian economy.

Brazil harbours more than one-third of the global tropical forests covering the 'Amazon forest, the Cerrado, the Atlantic forest, the Caatinga and the Pantanal wetlands'. A substantial portion of the Amazon rainforest lies in Brazil. These are often called the 'lungs of the Earth'. Known for its ecosystem biodiversity, rich flora and fauna, Brazil is abundant in natural resources. It also possesses an extensive coastline to the east (WB 2021). However, the

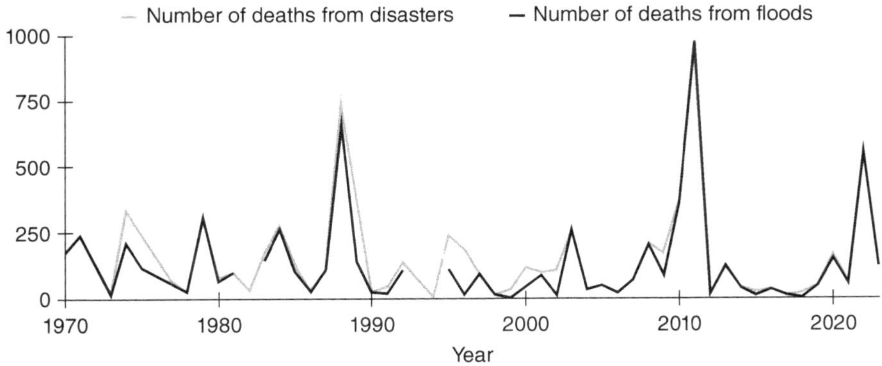

Figure 9.1 'Disaster Mortality in Brazil' (data from Ritchie and Rosado 2022).

Brazilian rainforest biodiversity is under threat due to timber production, agricultural and infrastructural development all of which add to the problem of carbon emissions and global warming. Brazil coastal areas are vulnerable to sea level rise impacting ecosystem and communities along the coast (Nicolodi and Pettermann 2011). Since 1980, temperatures have increased by 0.5 degree Celsius in the Amazon Basin. Winter temperatures are rising so is the number of warm days and nights. Extreme weather events such as droughts and floods have intensified and become recurrent (see Figure 9.1 for flood deaths). According to World Bank (2021), floods comprised more than 65 percent of natural hazards in Brazil in 1991–2010 period. Such vulnerability to climate impact presents a threat to its economic development (World Bank 2021). However, the ND-GAIN index ('Notre Dame Global Adaptation Initiative') ranks Brazil somewhat better. Brazil has a rank of 86 out of 181 countries (ND-GAIN index as of 2020) – low vulnerability and low readiness meaning that its vulnerabilities are manageable but improvement in readiness is required to adapt better to climate impacts. Adopting the Paris Agreement and submitting its NDC ('Nationally Determined Contribution'), Brazil agreed to decrease greenhouse gas emissions by 37 percent below 2005 levels by 2025.

9.5.1 Disaster Profile of Brazil

Categorizing natural disasters as droughts, earthquakes, volcanic activity, floods, glacial lake outbursts, storms and extreme temperatures, the data reveals that floods are mainly responsible for disaster deaths in Brazil, very few mortalities being from storms and extreme temperatures (data from Ritchie and Rosado 2022). Flood deaths do not show any consistency as we see wide year-on-year fluctuations, reflecting the uncertainty of natural disasters. The near overlap of flood deaths and disaster deaths show that floods are mainly responsible for disaster deaths. Brazil having an extensive coastline is highly prone to flood damages and climate change only exacerbates the risk. Droughts have also been a feature of the Brazilian economy on and off, the latest being

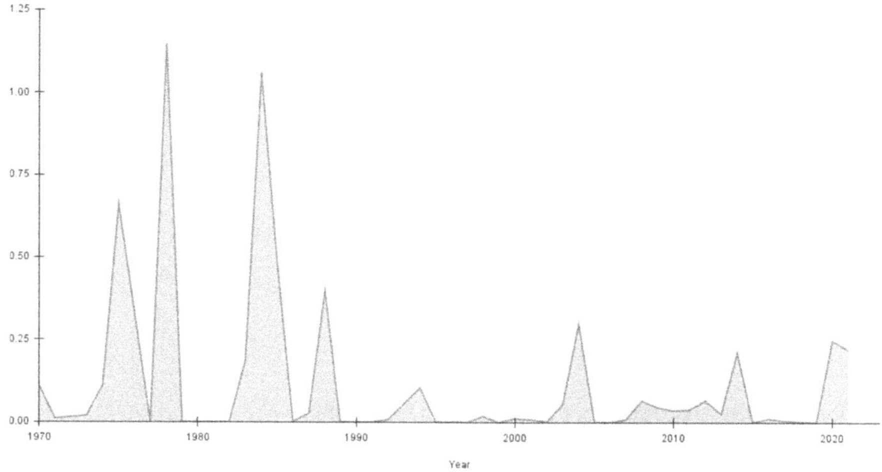

Figure 9.2 'Total Economic Damages from Disasters as a share of GDP in Brazil' (data from Ritchie and Rosado 2022).

the 2014–2017 Brazilian drought which affected the southeast Brazil, which was preceded by 2012 and 2010 (data from Ritchie and Rosado 2022). Total economic damages from disasters as a share of GDP (see parentheses) lies between 0 and 0.2 except for some outlier years as seen from Figure 9.2 (data from Ritchie and Rosado 2022). Natural disasters act as shocks which die out overtime, so the impact is felt in later years as well. In 2004, it was Hurricane Catarina. Since 1960s, unplanned urbanization is taking place which means building in unsafe areas such as floodplains. Between 2009 and 2014, 50,000 low-income households were destroyed by floods (World Bank 2021).

9.5.2 Studies on Climate Disasters in Brazil

Several studies on Brazil have pointed out that the risk of disasters increases due to climate change. Dalagnol et al. (2021) analysed to what extent climate change is to be blamed for an extreme precipitation event which occurred in Southeast Brazil in January 2020 which rendered more than 90,000 people homeless and imposed huge economic cost on the Brazilian economy. Debortoli et al. (2017) conducted simulation exercises within two global climate models and found that Brazil's vulnerability to floods and landslides increased. Seneviratne et al. (2012) points out that throughout the 21st century, global warming has intensified natural hazards in Northeast Brazil. Ferreira et al. (2023) points out that Brazil is vulnerable to impacts of climate change as it harbours more than a third of tropical rainforests worldwide. Climate change also has an impact on public health in Brazil. Chagas et al. (2022) conduct a study on the Brazilian water cycle and report that deforestation and water use has amplified the climate change effects on streamflow extremes. Various studies have also analysed the impact of disasters on the Brazilian economy. de Oliveira (2019) used the disaster dataset of Brazil and concluded that disaster damages have a negative impact on growth rate of municipalities in Northeast Brazil, having the greatest impact on agriculture and services.

We also conducted a bibliometric analysis of studies on climate-related disasters in Brazil using Vosviewer. The articles in the bibliometric study were extracted in December 2023 from Dimensions AI-scientific research database. The keywords used in the literature search were 'climate change', 'natural disasters', 'Brazil'. The search terms were combined with 'AND' logical operations to ensure that all the three search terms are present in the article. To select specific studies, we ensured that the search terms are present in 'title and abstract'. The search for articles covers the years 2000–2023. Our search yielded 80 publications.

The objective is to analyse how the existing literature talks about the linkages between climate change and natural disasters and the repercussions of these on the economy. For this, we conducted a 'keyword co-occurrence analysis' which is a network analysis. Typically, keyword co-occurrence networks are built on words retrieved from a publications' title and abstract. We chose 'binary counting' and restricted the 'minimum number of occurrences of a term' at 5. Out of 4,543 terms, 158 met the threshold. In Figure 9.3, we see that the round shape and bold text represents the weight of occurrence of the term. The thematic structure in the Figure 9.3 shows four clusters and the

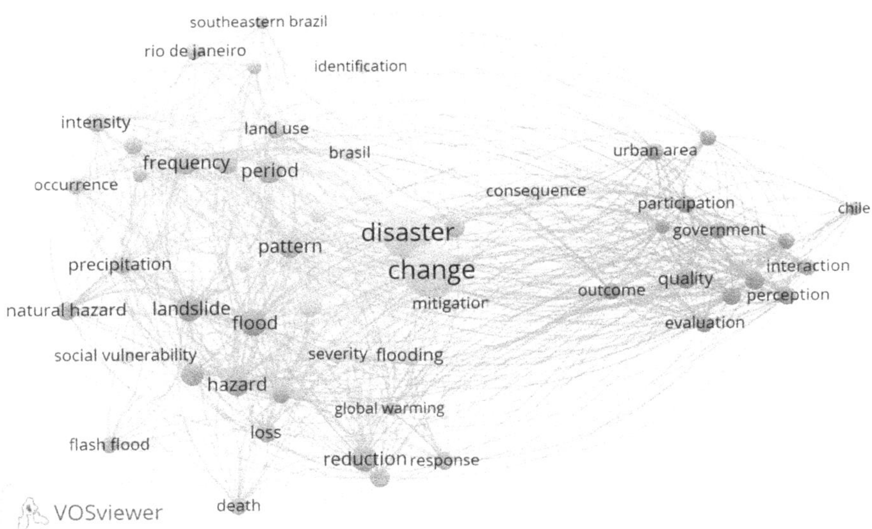

Figure 9.3 Keyword Co-occurrence analysis for Literature on Brazil's Climate Disasters.

interconnectedness between them through network lines. Keywords, such as 'disaster' and 'change' can be seen to be most important ones, the pattern highlighting the link between 'natural hazard', 'flood', 'landslide', 'social vulnerability', 'global warming', 'severity flooding', 'urban area' among others. Both the reviews – of select studies and bibliometric review highlight that climate change and natural disasters are linked and these have negative repercussions on the economy.

9.6 The Case of India

Situated in South Asia, India has a diverse topography with Himalayan range in the North and Deccan Plateau in the South. There are several major rivers including the Ganga, Yamuna, Godavari and more. India has a rich biodiversity being home to various national parks and wildlife sanctuaries. Enormous population and high population density increases India's vulnerability to natural disasters.

9.6.1 Disaster Profile of India

The data for India reveals that various types of disasters are responsible for disaster deaths, viz., floods, landslides, storms, earthquakes and extreme temperatures. Very few mortalities are reported from drought, volcanic activity, wildfires, fog, mass movement and glacial lake outbursts (hence not shown in Figure 9.4; data from Ritchie and Rosado 2022). Disaster deaths do not show any consistency as we see wide year-on-year fluctuations, reflecting the uncertainty of natural disasters. However, compared to Brazil, disaster mortality in India is much higher. In the Indian case as well, floods are mainly responsible for disaster deaths. Deaths from earthquakes shot up between 2000 and 2004 (see Gujarat Earthquake 2001). It is not surprising to note that extreme temperatures are also responsible for disaster deaths in India since it is a tropical country with average temperatures on the higher side. Average temperature over India has increased by 0.7 degree Celsius during 1901–2018 due to climate change. Sea-surface temperature has also witnessed similar warming for 1951–2015 (Source: Ministry of Environment, Forest and Climate Change, Press Information Bureau [pib.gov.in]). Total economic damages from disasters as a share of GDP (see parentheses) lies between 0 and 1 percent except for 1993 (deadly floods which affected several states) when it shot up to 2.82 percent and 2014 (Kashmir floods) when it increased to 1.15 percent (Figure 9.5 – data from Ritchie and Rosado 2022). The disaster shocks have lasting impacts and sometimes economic cost is felt in later years as well. Economic costs are higher in India as compared to Brazil which is mainly due to the lack of preparedness, improper infrastructure as well as high population density.

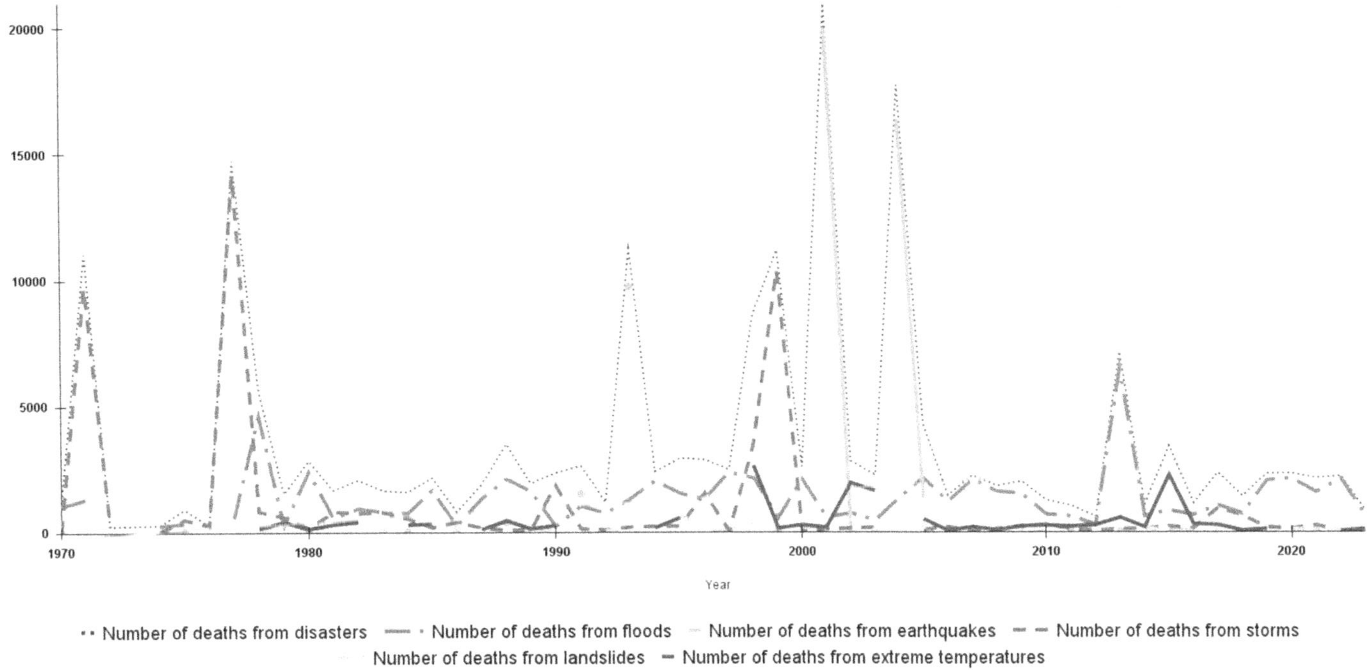

Figure 9.4 'Disaster Mortality in India' (data from Ritchie and Rosado 2022).

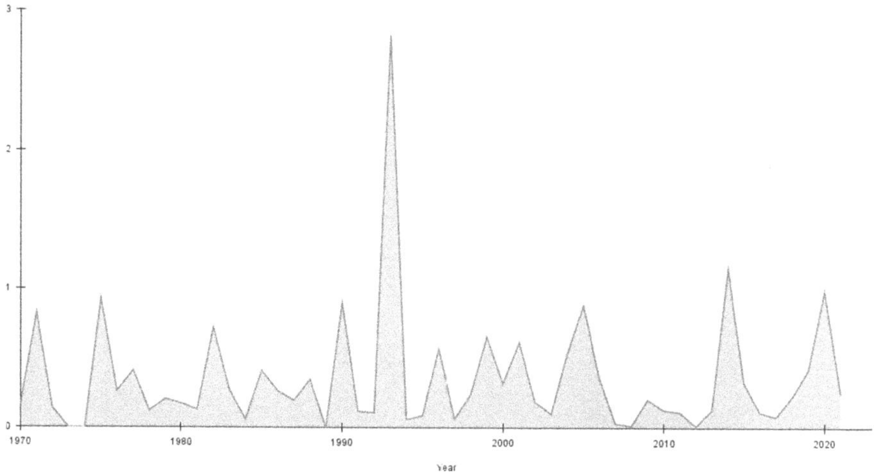

Figure 9.5 'Total Economic Damages from Disasters as a share of GDP in India' (data from Ritchie and Rosado 2022).

9.6.2 Studies on Climate Disasters in India

Several studies on India have analysed the impact of climate-induced disasters on various aspects such as human health, violent conflicts, etc. However, unlike Brazil's case, we did not find studies on India which have analysed the link between climate change and natural disasters. Purohit and Rout (2023) point out that 'Climate Induced Natural Disasters (CINDs)' have intensified and become more frequent in Odisha. Their independent variables include the 'indexed value of climate vulnerability' and 'adaptation coefficients' and dependent variable is 'mortality due to CINDs'. Conducting a regression analysis for studying the effect of climate change on human health, they find a significant positive relation between vulnerability coefficients and CIND mortality and a significant negative relation is found between adaptation coefficients and CIND mortality. Between 2000 and 2020, Odisha was found to be vulnerable to climate impacts as shown by greater vulnerability scores in Purohit and Rout (2023). Slettebak (2013) used data on Indian States (1956–2002) and showed that climate disasters increased the risk of riots and violence. Mall et al. (2011) point out that climate-induced disasters put poor, vulnerable populations at risk, particularly in developing countries such as India. Govind and Verchick (2015) conducted a case study of Surat in Gujarat which is susceptible to coastal flooding and suggest that local organizational methods should be integrated with overall climate adaptation goals. Parida et al. (2021) use panel data for Odisha – 30 districts (1999–2011) and show that better disaster adaptation measures help to mitigate disaster fatalities.

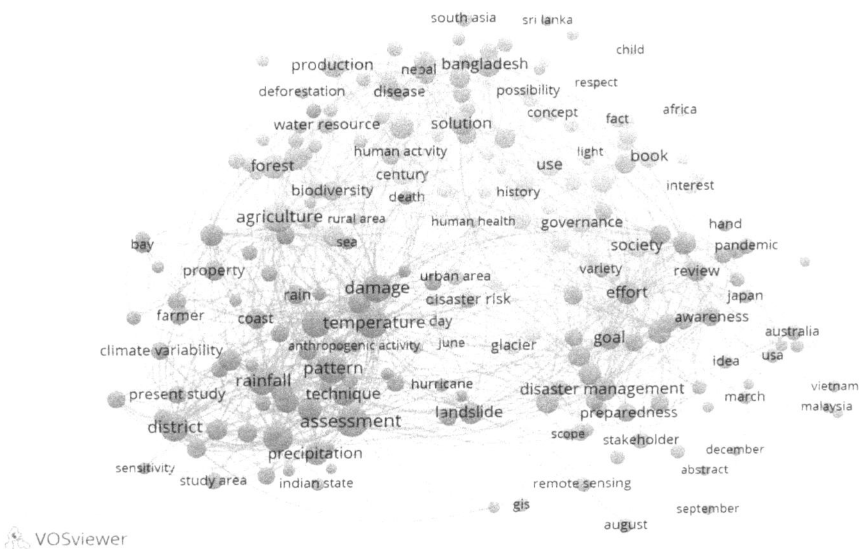

Figure 9.6 Keyword Co-occurrence analysis for Literature on India's Climate Disasters.

We also conducted a bibliometric analysis of studies on climate-related disasters in India using Vosviewer. The articles in the bibliometric study were extracted in January 2024 from Dimensions AI. The keywords used in the literature search were 'climate change', 'natural disasters', 'India'. The search terms were combined with 'AND' logical operations to ensure that all the three search terms are present in the article. To select specific studies, we ensured that the search terms are present in 'title and abstract'. The search for articles covers the years 2000–2023. Our search yielded 430 publications. For 'keyword co-occurrence analysis', we chose 'binary counting' and restricted the 'minimum number of occurrences of a term' at ten. Out of 14,723 terms, 371 met the threshold. In Figure 9.6, we see that the round shape and bold text represents the weight of occurrence of the term. The thematic structure in the Figure 9.6 shows four clusters and the interconnectedness between them through network lines. Keywords, such as 'damage', 'disaster management', 'preparedness', 'rainfall', 'temperature', 'human activity', 'biodiversity', 'agriculture', 'forest', 'human health', 'governance', 'climate variability', 'deforestation', 'Indian state', 'district', 'anthropogenic activity' among others can be seen to be most important ones. Both the reviews – of select studies and bibliometric review highlight that climate change as well as natural disasters have negative repercussions on the economy.

9.7 Conclusion and Policy Implications

The developed countries or the Global North have contributed more to carbon emissions historically; yet, the Global South or the developing economies have suffered the disproportionate impact, more so, since these economies lack the resources to adapt to climate change. Although climate change need not be the sole reason behind increasing intensity and frequency of natural disasters, one cannot deny that global warming and sea level rise might be responsible to some extent. The study started with the hypothesis the climate change-induced natural disasters are indeed taking place. Taking two cases – Brazil and India, two of the emerging economies in the Global South, we saw how they have faced unprecedented natural calamities ranging from floods, extreme temperatures, landslides, storms, earthquakes during 1970–2020 period. Few studies on Brazil have established the climate-disaster link while we did not find such a study for India. However, for both India and Brazil, existing studies as well as bibliometric review point out that disasters have huge consequences on the economy in terms of social vulnerability and economic losses. In the face of rising catastrophic climate disasters worldwide, disaster resilience (by activities, such as reforestation and prediction of extreme weather events) becomes important. Economies need to allocate higher budgetary funds to disaster risk reduction. Transition to a low carbon economy becomes all the more important. The area holds immense potential for future research as very few studies have explored the linkages between anthropogenic climate change and natural disasters.

References

Anderson, J., & Bausch, C. (2006, January 25). *Climate change and natural disasters: Scientific evidence of a possible relation between recent natural disasters and climate change* (Brief No. 02a/2006). IEEP (Institute for European Environmental Policy) and Ecologic.

Ayugi, B., Eresanya, E. O., Onyango, A. O., Ogou, F. K., Okoro, E. C., Okoye, C. O., Anoruo, C. M., Dike, V. N., Ashiru, O. R., Daramola, M. T., Mumo, R., & Ongoma, V. (2022). Review of meteorological drought in Africa: Historical trends, impacts, mitigation measures, and prospects. *Pure and Applied Geophysics*, 179(4), 1365–1386.

Botzen, W., Deschenes, O., & Sanders, M. (2019). The economic impacts of natural disasters: A review of models and empirical studies. *Review of Environmental Economics and Policy*, *13*, 167–188.

Chagas, V. B. P., Chaffe, P. L. B., & Blöschl, G. (2022). Climate and land management accelerate the Brazilian water cycle. *Nature Communications*, *13*, 5136.

Chinowsky, P., Hayles, C., Schweikert, A., Strzepek, N., Strzepek, K., & Schlosser, C. A. (2011). Climate change: Comparative impact on developing and developed countries. *The Engineering Project Organization Journal*, *3*, 67–80.

Dalagnol, R., Gramcianinov, C. B., Crespo, N. M., et al. (2021). Extreme rainfall and its impacts in the Brazilian Minas Gerais state in January 2020: Can we blame climate change? *Climate Resilience and Sustainability: Interdisciplinary Approaches towards Solutions for Climate Change*.

de Oliveira, V. H. (2019). Natural disasters and economic growth in Northeast Brazil: Evidence from municipal economies of the Ceará State. *Environment and Development Economics*, *24*(3), 271–293.

Debortoli, N. S., Camarinha, P. I. M., Marengo, J. A., et al. (2017). An index of Brazil's vulnerability to expected increases in natural flash flooding and landslide disasters in the context of climate change. *Natural Hazards*, *86*(2), 557–582.

Ferreira, M. M. A. Y. L. R., & Leite, C. C. J. (2023). *Impact of Climate Change on Public Health in Brazil*. Public Health Challenges. Wiley.

Frumhoff, P. C., Heede, R., & Oreskes, N. (2015). The climate responsibilities of industrial carbon producers. *Climatic Change*, *132*, 157–171.

Govind, P. J., & Verchick, R. R. M. (2015). Natural Disaster and Climate Change. In *International Environmental Law and the Global South: Comparative Perspectives* (Eds. S. Alam, S. Atapattu, C. G. Gonzalez, & J. Razzaque). Cambridge University Press.

Hansis, E., Davis, S. J., & Pongratz, J. (2015). Relevance of methodological choices for accounting of land use change carbon fluxes. *Global Biogeochemical Cycles*, *29*(7), 1230–1246.

Houghton, R. A., & Nassikas, A. A. (2017). Global and regional fluxes of carbon from land use and land cover change 1850–2015. *Global Biogeochemical Cycles*, *31*(3), 456–472.

Mall, R. K., Kumar, R., & Bhatla, R. (2011). *Climate Change and Disasters in India*. Vol. 4(1), *Journal of South Asia Disaster Studies*, SAARC Disaster Management Centre, New Delhi.

Mishra, S. K., Upadhyaya, P., Fasullo, J. T., et al. (2023). A need for actionable climate projections across the Global South. *Nature Climate Change*, *13*(10), 883–886.

Nath, P. K., & Behera, B. (2011). A critical review of impact of and adaptation to climate change in developed and developing economies. *Environment, Development and Sustainability*, *13*, 141–162.

Ngcamu, B. S. (2023). Climate change effects on vulnerable populations in the Global South: A systematic review. *Natural Hazards*, *118*, 977–991.

Nicolodi, J. L., & Pettermann, R. M. (2011). Vulnerability of the Brazilian coastal zone in its environmental, social, and technological aspects. *Journal of Coastal Research*, *27*, 1372–1379.

Parida, Y., Agarwal Goel, P., Roy Chowdhury, J., et al. (2021). Do economic development and disaster adaptation measures reduce the impact of natural disasters? A district-level analysis, Odisha, India. *Environment, Development and Sustainability*, *23*(5), 3487–3519.

Purohit, J., & Rout, H.S. (2023). Impact of climate change on human health concerning climate-induced natural disaster: Evidence from an eastern Indian state. *Climatic Change*, *176*, 109.

Ritchie, H. (2019). Who has contributed most to global CO2 emissions? Our World in Data. Retrieved from

Ritchie, H., & Rosado, P. (2022). Natural Disasters. Published online at OurWorldInData.org. Retrieved from: https://ourworldindata.org/natural-disasters 'Our World in Data' based on EM-DAT, CRED / UCLouvain, Brussels, Belgium – www.emdat.be (D. Guha-Sapir) [original data] – processed by Our World in Data (EMDAT-International Disaster Database- Centre for Research on the Epidemiology of Disasters)

Seneviratne, S. I., Nicholls, N., Easterling, D., et al. (2012). Changes in climate extremes and their impacts on the natural physical environment. In C. B. Field, V. Barros, T. F. Stocker, D. Qin, D. J. Dokken, K. L. Ebi, M. D. Mastrandrea, K. J. Mach, G.-K. Plattner, S. K. Allen, M. D. Tignor, and P. M. Midgley (Eds.), *Managing the Risks of*

Extreme Events and Disasters to Advance Climate Change Adaptation: A Special Report of Working Groups I and II of the Intergovernmental Panel on Climate Change (IPCC), Chapter 3. Cambridge University Press, pp. 109–230.

Siwedza, S., Mukonzo, S., Ngambi, C., & Shava, S. (2021). Impacts of Cyclones Idai and Kenneth and the 2019 Floods on the Insurance Sector in South Africa and Mozambique. In G. Nhamo & L. Chapungu (Eds.), *The Increasing Risk of Floods and Tornadoes in Southern Africa (Sustainable Development Goals Series)*. Springer.

Slettebak, R. T. (2013). Climate change, natural disasters, and post-disaster Unrest in India. *India Review*, *12*(4), 260–279.

Stoddard, I., Anderson, K., Capstick, S., Carton, W., Depledge, J., Facer, K., … Williams, M. (2021). Three decades of climate mitigation: Why haven't we bent the global emissions curve? *Annual Review of Environment and Resources*, *46*(1), 653–689.

Thomas, V. (2017). *Climate Change and Natural Disasters: Transforming Economies and Policies for a Sustainable Future*. Routledge.

Thomas, V., & Lopez, R. (2015). Global Increase in Climate Related Disasters. *ADB Working Paper Series, No. 466, November 2015*.

World Bank. (2021). *Climate Risk Profile: Brazil (2021)*. The World Bank Group.

10 Does the Global South's Economic Complexity and Environmental Policy Stringency Affect Its Carbon Footprint?

Nupur Nirola and Arth Agarwal

10.1 Introduction

The global landscape is undergoing a significant transformation in the patterns of economic growth in the past two decades. Emerging economies like Brazil, China, and India have experienced remarkable "growth in terms of trade and investment", altering the traditional dominance of the Global North (OECD, 2010; Nirola & Agarwal, 2024). However, this upsurged economic growth is imposing environmental costs, particularly concerning environmental degradation and carbon footprint.

Carbon footprints caused by the emissions of greenhouse gases pose "negative" externalities because most of the impacts of the emissions are not borne by those carrying out the industrial activities and, therefore, the costs are not borne by those responsible for the emissions. Apart from that, the negative impact of the industrial and trade activities in developed countries is transmitted to the people living in emerging and underdeveloped countries. Therefore, the emissions are "external" to the market, meaning that there is usually an ethical rather than an economic incentive for the economic agents – producers and consumers to cut their emissions. Consequently, excessive greenhouse emissions are causing market failure. In view of the market failure problem, these externalities need to be taken into account and should not merely be left to the open market forces. Over the past three decades, economies under the "Global South" have contributed substantially to carbon dioxide emissions due to their heavy reliance on fossil fuels for energy production, underscoring the urgent need for action to address climate change on a global scale.

On the contrary, the "Global South" economies are under the "energy poverty crisis". In response to this crisis, governments in these countries have implemented fiscal policies to subsidize the usage of fossil fuels (Nirola & Agarwal, 2024). However, such policies have distorted the market by disproportionately benefiting the better off further resulting in wasteful energy consumption (Fuhr, 2021; Nirola & Agarwal, 2024). More than 60% of the emissions in the Global South cluster come from China and India alone, while the top ten nations account for 78% of the emissions, with the remaining 120 countries contributing only 22% (Fuhr, 2021). Under these circumstances, the

DOI: 10.4324/9781032694337-14

government needs to enforce stringent environmental laws either through designing an emissions permit system, or levying Pigouvian taxes to control carbon emissions (Pigou, 1920, Haites, 2018; Tol, 2017 & 2018; Nirola & Agarwal, 2024).

Environmental policy stringency represents the stringent and effective measures enacted by the government to regulate environmental pollution, specifically targeting CO_2 emissions (Alsagr, 2023). By establishing specific targets, standards, and regulations, the government endeavors to drive reductions in CO_2 levels and incentivize stakeholders to adopt cleaner technologies and practices (Afshan *et al.*, 2022; Nirola & Agarwal, 2024). These policies serve a crucial role in raising public awareness about the adverse impacts of CO_2 emissions and nudging a positive behavioral change toward the adoption of energy-efficient practices (Schlindwein & Montalvo, 2023).

Given this background, we study the joint impact of environmental policies and the degree of economic complexity on the carbon emissions intensity in six major "Global South" economies, namely India, Brazil, Indonesia, China, South Africa, and South Korea from 2000 to 2020.

> Environmentally strict policies may have a negative effect on carbon emissions if these economies are growing and producing more complex products with a comparatively higher value-added for each unit of emission and if their production employs newer, more energy-efficient technologies.
>
> (Nirola & Agarwal, 2024)

By examining the intersection of sustainable development with carbon emission challenges in these economies, this research fills a critical gap by revealing the complex dynamics between strict environmental regulations and their impact on carbon emissions in the "Global South".

Our key findings demonstrate that stringent environmental policies and regulations lead to higher carbon emissions in these economies. However, as the industrial structure substantially changes toward knowledge-based production methods and technological advancement as these economies develop, the implementation of stricter policies mitigates carbon emissions. In practical terms, our findings suggest implementing stringent regulations alongside efforts to produce complex, high-end products using energy-efficient technologies. This roadmap offers a blueprint for policymakers in the "Global South" to embed environmentally friendly technology in diversifying exports, and reducing carbon footprints while fostering economic growth.

This research contributes significantly to the existing literature on environmental economics and offers actionable insights for policymakers. It highlights how nations can navigate the balance between growth and environmental stewardship, paving the way for sustainable development amidst rapid industrialization and increasing environmental awareness. Lastly, the broad spectrum of case studies in our research, encompassing countries from Latin

America (Brazil), Asia (India, China), and Africa (South Africa), comprising the Global South, enhances the generalizability of our findings. This diversified selection provides wider applicability across the diverse range of economies within the developing world, reflecting the varied contexts and challenges faced by these states.

10.2 Literature Review

10.2.1 Environmental Policy Stringency and Carbon Footprint

Studies by Dechezleprêtre and Sato (2017), Lægreid and Povitkina (2018), Mulatu (2018), Neves et al. (2020), and Khan et al. (2022) found that the adverse effects of carbon emissions are minimized through stringent environmental regulations as these policies discourage the use of environmentally harmful technologies, encouraging the adoption of green technology. This could influence the behavior of various stakeholders, nudging them toward adopting eco-friendly products. Wang and Shen (2016), Song et al. (2020) and Wu et al. (2020) have explored a similar relationship within Chinese provinces and found that environmental regulations notably reduce pollution emissions by fostering clean production sectors in these provinces. Another study by Danish and Khan (2020) found that environmental rules and regulations help cut greenhouse emissions in BRICS economies. Wolde-Rufael and Mulat-Weldemeskel (2021) studied the nexus in emerging economies and found Top of Form environmental stringent policies to be an effective measure in mitigating environmental degradation. Advanced economies have also shown a similar trend. Research by Shapiro and Walker (2018) argues that stricter environmental regulations were primarily responsible for the majority of the US 1990–2008 drop in air pollutant emissions. De Angelis et al. (2019) studied the impact of environmental stringency regulations on greenhouse gas emissions for a group of advanced economies and found it to be an effective policy instrument.

However, the other strand of literature is of the opposing view the counterproductive effect of increased emissions, commonly referred to as the "Green Paradox", may arise from implementing policies and regulations aimed at mitigating carbon emissions (Jensen *et al.*, 2015; Sinn, 2015 and Haites, 2018). These regulations predominantly target the demand side of fossil fuel consumption rather than the supply side of fossil fuel production. The underlying argument posits that environmental policy announcements entail a period of delay before they are implemented (Nirola & Agarwal, 2024). During this delay interval, fossil fuel owners may anticipate that heightened environmental regulations could diminish the demand for their resources. Consequently, these environmental regulations push resource owners to expedite the extraction of more fossil reserves. Fossil fuel producers perceive that these environmental rules could render their assets worthless, inclining them to intensify their production, exacerbating global warming instead of mitigating it (Nirola & Agarwal, 2024).

Imposing stringent environmental regulations on developing nations could have unfavorable repercussions and impede economic growth (Wang and Wei, 2020; The Phan, C. *et al.*, 2021). A study by Wolde-Rufael and Mulat-Weldemeskel (2020) states that the policies may also impose accounting costs on businesses, discouraging them from exploring innovations that could improve the quality of their environment and, as a result, from making environmentally friendly investments. To circumvent these additional costs, firms in developed countries engage in the practice of exporting the production of environmentally harmful goods to countries with comparatively laxer environmental regulations through advocacy and lobbying, a phenomenon often referred to as the "race to the bottom" theory (Haites, 2018; Mulatu, 2018). It states that developing nations, despite having stringent laws and regulations in place, allow such imports to enhance their international competitiveness and draw in foreign investment under the "race to bottom" hypothesis which leads to higher carbon emissions (Kim and Rhee, 2019). However, as these economies transit toward higher growth, they will be able to enact and enforce their stringent environmental laws and regulations, which further encourage the "usage of environment-friendly technologies" (Dechezleprêtre & Sato, 2017; Ferris *et al.*, 2017).

10.2.2 The Importance of Economic Complexity as a Mediating Factor

To unravel the differing effects, it is imperative to comprehend the "determining factors of carbon emissions", given the ambiguous relationship between the coherence of environmental policies and CO_2 emissions (Nirola & Agarwal, 2024). In recent times, there has been a considerable focus on economic complexity, coupled with the notion that technology innovation holds the potential to diminish global emissions (Nirola & Agarwal, 2024). Romero and Gramkow (2021) have characterized economic complexity as a "specific structural change in the production structure as it moves toward technological advancement and knowledge-based production processes" (Nirola & Agarwal, 2024). Classical development economists connect economic advancement with structural transformations, and the diversity and intricacy of the ensuing products and services indicating an enhanced capacity to produce and export more intricate, higher value-added products (Nirola & Agarwal, 2024).

A study conducted by Neagu and Teodoru (2019) found that nations attaining greater economic complexity experience a sharper decline in CO_2 emissions, attributed to variations in energy composition and efficiency (Bakhsh *et al.*, 2024). However, because export items required a large amount of energy to maintain, the economic complexity of the early export phase contributed to pollution (Afshan *et al.*, 2022). Economic complexity eventually leads to less pollution because of efficient technologies and a decrease in polluting resources. Thus, this connection is a mirror image of the environmental Kuznets curve with an inverted U shape. In other words, during the initial stages of exports, economic complexity results in greenhouse gas emissions due to extensive resource utilization. After a threshold point, it leads to reduced emissions through energy-saving and efficient technologies. This relationship, thus, mirrors the inverted U environmental Kuznets curve. Complex products use newer, more energy-efficient technology during manufacturing, and their value-added per unit of pollution is comparatively higher. The "Global North" has been the primary focus of an increasing number of research conducted in recent years that has looked at the environmental effects of economic complexity. Literature on developing economies is scarce.

From the overall literature survey, we found that complex goods increase economic efficiency by adopting high-end, technologically advanced products that bring more economic value for every unit of pollution emitted. Furthermore, more advanced economies may be able to produce commodities more efficiently and with less pollution by developing green innovations (Yirong, 2022). A study by Can and Gozgor (2017) examined the impact of economic complexity on France's carbon emissions from 1964 to 2014 and found economic complexity to be an effective factor in mitigating carbon emissions (Hu, G. et al. 2020). Similarly, Doğan et al. (2021) found a similar result for 28 OECD countries from 1990 to 2014. Neagu and Teodoru (2019) examined a similar nexus within the European Union and found that the initial advancements in economic complexity increased carbon emissions due to a higher proportion of energy consumption entailed in the production of more intricate goods, known as the scale effect. However, in the subsequent stages, a heightened level of economic complexity reduces carbon emissions owing to the predominance of technological effect, characterized by increased energy efficiency.

The remaining section of this chapter is structured as follows: Section 3 provides the empirical methodology and the main results. Section 4 presents the robustness checks before concluding in Section 5.

10.3 Methodology

10.3.1 Environmental Policy Stringency and Carbon Footprint

We are examining the impact of environmental policy stringency on CO_2 emissions with the mediating effect of the degree of economic complexity across a panel of six economies, namely India, Brazil, Indonesia, China, South Africa, and South Korea from 2000 to 2020.

A linear as well as non-linear interaction model is employed which is as follows:

$$\mathrm{CO}_{2it} = \alpha_0 + \beta_1 \mathrm{EPS}_{it} + \beta_2 \mathrm{EC}_{it} + \gamma \mathrm{X}_{it} + \eta_i + \mu_t + \mathrm{v}_{it} \tag{10.1}$$

$$\mathrm{CO}_{2it} = \alpha_0 + \beta_1 \mathrm{EPS}_{it} + \beta_2 \mathrm{EC}_{it} + \beta_3 \mathrm{EPS}_{it} \times \mathrm{EC}_{it} + \gamma \mathrm{X}_{it} + \eta_i + \mu_t + \mathrm{v}_{it} \tag{10.2}$$

Here, CO_{2it} represents carbon dioxide emissions across economies for different time periods, EPS_{it} represents environment policy stringency and EC_{it} represents the degree of economic complexity, and X_{it} includes control variables that affect environmental degradation based on literature. In this chapter, X specifically refers to GDP per capita, fossil fuel consumption, forest area cover, and population density; η_i are the time-fixed effects, v_i are the country fixed effects; and v_{it} refers to other influencing factors that are not reflected in the model, i.e., the white noise error term. A key part of the model is the interaction term $EPS_{it} \times EC_{it}$, which allows the effect of stringency to vary depending on the level of economic complexity present in economies.

We measure the linear effect of environment stringency on carbon emissions in Equation (10.1) while the non-linear effect of environment stringency through the economic complexity channel is measured in Equation (10.2). The coefficients of interest are β_1 and β_3. (Equation 10.2) necessary to calculate the marginal effects of environmental policy stringency on carbon emissions (Equation 10.3). It varies with the degree of economic complexity measure, i.e., how a 1-unit change in stringency affects carbon emissions (Equation 10.3). It varies with the degree of economic complexity measure, i.e., how a 1-unit change in stringency affects carbon emissions if economies become more economically complex. Consequently, the marginal effect is given by:

$$\frac{\partial CO_{2it}}{\partial EPS_{it}} = \beta_1 + \beta_3 EC_{it} \qquad (10.3)$$

where β_1 is the environmental policy stringency coefficient and β_3 the interaction term coefficient.

10.3.2 Main Results

Descriptive statistics are presented in Table 10.1.

We estimate Equation (10.1) and Equation (10.2) following the fixed effects technique. The results are presented in Table 10.2. To begin, we estimate the linear impact of stringent environmental policy on carbon emissions in the sample countries without considering the role of economic complexity within economies (fixed effects, columns 1&2).

The coefficient of environmental policy stringency is positive and statistically significant at 5% significance in all the estimated models, depicting that a one percentage point increase in environmental stringency increases carbon dioxide emissions by 0.688 percentage points. This implies that as environment degradation policies become stricter and more stringent for our Global South economies, it leads to higher carbon dioxide emissions in these economies. The results are in line with the "Green Paradox" literature suggesting that these policies despite being stringent are not helping these economies to reduce

Table 10.1 Descriptive statistics

Variables	*N*T*	*Mean*	*Standard Deviation*	*Min*	*Max*
EPS	126	1.343	1.027	0.167	3.611
CO_2 Emissions	126	4.899	3.682	0.884	12.22
Economic Complexity	126	40.44	19.50	3	73
Real GDP_{PC}	126	8,124	8,190	755.5	31,640
Fossil Fuel Consumption	90	73.31	12.92	51.32	90.57
Population Density	84	156.3	158.5	21.04	469.7
Forest Area Cover	126	37.50	18.45	14.06	65.93

Source: Author's calculation using Stata 15.

Table 10.2 Environment policy stringency and CO_2 emissions: Role of economic complexity

Dependent Variable: CO_2 Emissions	*Fixed Effects Model*		
	[1]	*[2]*	*[3]*
Real GDP_{PC}	1.287***	1.391***	1.405**
	[0.317]	[0.455]	[0.646]
Fossil Fuel Consumption	0.0836***	0.0747***	0.0995***
	[0.0186]	[0.0176]	[0.0207]
Population Density	0.0323***	0.0302***	0.0279***
Forest Cover Area	[0.0032]	[0.0031]	[0.0032]
	–0.018	–0.005	–0.018
	[1.205]	[0.995]	[0.988]
EPS	0.688***	0.514**	0.504***
	[0.247]	[0.0824]	[0.0882]
Economic Complexity		–0.0243**	–0.0194**
		[0.0094]	[0.0093]
EPS× Economic Complexity			–0.0119**
			[0.0057]
Constant	–24.74***	–16.37***	–10.88**
	[2.122]	[3.786]	[4.497]
Observations	60	60	60
R-squared	0.966	0.971	0.974
Year Fixed Effects	Yes	Yes	Yes
Country Fixed Effects	Yes	Yes	Yes

Notes: ***, **, and * denote statistical significance at 1%, 5%, and 10%, respectively. Standard errors are presented in []. EPS denotes Environment Policy Stringency.

carbon emissions. After adding economic complexity (Column 2), the estimated impact of a one percentage point change in stringency on carbon emissions decreases to 0.514 percentage points. That implies, that economic complexity acts as a significant determinant of environmental degradation in these economies and helps in mitigating it when added as control.

However, our main variable of interest is the multiplicative interaction between environmental policy stringency and economic complexity (Column 3). The results show that the compounding effect of environment stringent policies on carbon dioxide emissions gets weakened or mitigated with higher economic complexity in economies. However, these coefficients should not be interpreted in isolation. For a more holistic understanding, we look at the marginal impact of stringency on carbon emissions for varying degrees of economic complexity (Brambor *et al.*, 2006). Higher values signify higher complexity. The results are reported in Table 10.3. At each margin, an increase in economic complexity by 10 units mitigates the positive effect of stringency on environmental degradation.

10.4 Robustness Checks

10.4.1 Addressing the Endogeneity Concerns

The panel fixed effects method ignores the potential endogeneity of independent variables due to the dynamic specification of dependent variables. The estimation results may be inconsistent. There is a high likelihood that higher stringency, per capita real GDP, fossil fuel consumption, and forest area cover could be endogenously or inversely associated with carbon emissions. The system GMM approach "tackles the endogeneity issue by instrumenting the differenced endogenous variables with their available lags in levels: levels of the dependent and endogenous variables, lagged one or more periods; levels of the predetermined variables, lagged one or more periods" (Arellano and Bover, 1995). All the exogenous variables in the model are used as instruments (Jha *et al.*, 2024).

The system GMM estimate for the dynamic panel is:

$$\mathrm{CO}_{2i,t} = \alpha_0 + \alpha_1 \mathrm{CO}_{2i,t-1} + \beta_1 \mathrm{EPS}_{it} + \beta_2 \mathrm{EC}_{it} + \beta_3 \mathrm{EPS}_{it} \times \mathrm{EC}_{it} + \gamma \mathrm{X}_{it} + \eta_i + \mu_t + \mathrm{v}_{it} \tag{10.4}$$

$\alpha_1 \mathrm{CO}_{2i,\,t-1}$ represents the lagged value of the carbon emissions. The other variables have the same meaning as above. The system GMM results are presented in Table 10.4. The results align with fixed effects estimation results in Table 10.2, which further confirms the detrimental impact of environment stringent policies on carbon emissions and shows that the advancement of these economies toward higher economic complexity significantly reduces the emissions in the presence of stricter regulations.

10.4.2 Methods of Moment Quantile

As a second robustness check, we have employed the "Method of Moment Quantile", as an estimation regression method. It accounts for multiplicative interaction by controlling for distributional heterogeneity (Machado & Santos

Table 10.3 Marginal effects

Scales	*Fixed Effects Model*
Economic Complexity = 3	0.504***
	[0.088]
Economic Complexity = 13	0.385***
	[0.193]
Economic Complexity = 23	0.266***
	[0.142]
Economic Complexity = 33	0.147***
	[0.0735]
Economic Complexity = 43	0.028***
	[0.014]
Economic Complexity = 53	–0.091
	[0.094]
Economic Complexity = 63	–0.215
	[0.135]
Economic Complexity = 73	–0.329
	[0.185]

Note: Standard errors are reported in [].*, **, and *** denote significance at 10%, 5%, and 1 % levels, respectively.

Table 10.4 System GMM

Dependent variable: CO_2 Emissions	*[1]*	*[2]*	*[3]*
Lag of CO_2 Emissions	0.186***	0.189***	0.276***
	[0.066]	[0.054]	[0.045]
Real GDP_{PC}	1.386***	1.565***	1.288**
	[0.207]	[0.355]	[0.446]
Fossil Fuel Consumption	0.736***	0.747***	0.884***
	[0.019]	[0.0145]	[0.0207]
Population Density	0.0699***	0.0602***	0.0679***
	[0.0035]	[0.0032]	[0.0042]
Forest Cover Area	–0.020	–0.050	–0.382
	[0.205]	[0.995]	[0.988]
EPS	0.438***	0.630**	0.679***
	[0.145]	[0.032]	[0.075]
Economic Complexity		–0.0179**	–0.0199**
		[0.0064]	[0.0093]
EPS× Economic Complexity			–0.066**
			[0.0048]
Constant	–14.74***	–10.37***	–10.88**
	[2.122]	[2.786]	[2.497]
Observations	60	60	60
Number of instruments	5	5	5
AR(1)	0.000	0.000	0.000
AR(2)	0.269	0.354	0.157
Hansen test	0.999	0.998	1.000

Note: Standard errors are in parentheses. *, **, and *** measure statistical significance at the 10%, 5%, and 1% levels, respectively. Year and country fixed effects are included.

Silva, 2019). The estimates are robust to outliers in the outcome variable. The technique addresses the problem of asymmetric distribution by determining the distributional properties of several quantile values. The results are reported in Table 10.5. The coefficient of the interaction between environmental stringency and economic complexity is negative and statistically significant across 10–90% quantiles of the outcome variable showing that the rising environmental policy stringency is associated with decreasing carbon emissions largely at heightened levels of economic complexity.

10.5 Conclusion and Policy Recommendations

In this chapter, we study the degree to which an emerging economy's efforts to manufacture more complex products using newer and more energy-efficient technologies mediate the effect of stringent environment regulations on carbon emissions. A section of the existing literature is of the view that environment policy stringency may contribute toward the reduction in carbon dioxide emissions by encompassing diverse strategies such as emission reduction targets, "carbon pricing mechanisms, incentives for renewable energy adoption, and regulations governing industrial emissions" (Nirola & Agarwal, 2024). It is also possible that the reduction in emissions may not materialize because of the possibility of the "Green Paradox".

Our key finding is that countries like India, Brazil, Indonesia, China, South Korea, and South Africa can significantly reduce carbon emissions while fostering diversification and economic growth. The research suggests that while stringent environmental policies alone may not effectively reduce carbon emissions, integrating economic complexity can mitigate this issue. The positive coefficients of environmental policy stringency initially indicate a potential paradox, aligning with the "Green Paradox" concept. As economies become more technologically advanced and diversified in exports, they can better offset the environmental impact of stringent regulations. The analysis shows that higher economic complexity weakens the compounding effect of stringent policies on carbon emissions. Each increase in economic complexity diminishes the positive impact of stringency on emissions, emphasizing the importance of fostering technological advancement and diversifying exports. The robustness checks further support these conclusions, highlighting that as economies progress toward higher economic complexity, the detrimental impact of stringent policies on emissions diminishes.

This study's implications for policymakers and stakeholders in the "Global South" economies are significant. Policymakers may use this insight to align environmental policies with strategies promoting economic complexity, and fostering sustainable development while effectively reducing carbon footprints for a greener future. These emerging economies ought to lay more emphasis on embedding eco-friendly technology in their manufacturing process and diversify the range of products they export to mitigate their carbon

Table 10.5 Methods of Moment Quantile estimation

Quantile Range (10–30%)	*10%*	*20%*	*30%*
Real GDP_{PC}	0.652***	0.652***	0.973***
	(0.252)	(0.323)	(0.387)
Fossil Fuel Consumption	0.165***	0.165***	0.159***
	(0.004)	(0.0032)	(0.0067)
Population Density	0.0665***	0.0665***	0.0643***
	(0.0332)	(0.0017)	(0.0036)
Forest Area Cover	−0.018	−0.005	−0.018
	(1.205)	(0.995)	(0.988)
EPS	1.528***	1.528***	1.783***
	(0.186)	(0.191	(0.404)
EC	−0.091***	−0.091***	−0.092***
	(0.0067)	(0.0071)	(0.0149)
EPS × EC	−0.021***	−0.021***	−0.0243**
	(0.003)	(0.0047)	(0.0101)
Quantile Range (40%–60%)	40%	50%	60%
Real GDP_{PC}	0.663***	0.655***	0.845***
	(0.217)	(0.267)	(0.338)
Fossil Fuel Consumption	0.165***	0.159***	0.160***
	(0.0090)	(0.0075)	(0.0088)
Population Density	0.0236***	0.0109***	0.012***
	(0.0048)	(0.0041)	(0.0047)
Forest Area Cover	−0.004	−0.006	−0.015
	(0.883)	(1.367)	(0.996)
EPS	1.805***	1.674***	1.657***
	(0.540)	(0.452)	(0.529)
EC	−0.094***	−0.068***	−0.069**
	(0.020)	(0.0167)	(0.0196)
EPS × EC	−0.0289**	−0.032***	−0.031**
	(0.0134)	(0.0112)	(0.0132)
Quantile Range (70%–90%)	70*	80%	90%
Real GDP_{PC}	0.713***	0.916***	0.856***
	(0.387)	(0.309)	(0.318)
Fossil Fuel Consumption	0.163***	0.163***	0.175***
	(0.0038)	(0.0030)	(0.003)
Population Density	0.013***	0.015***	0.0245***
	(0.0021)	(0.0016)	(0.0026)
Forest Area Cover	−0.024	−0.038	−0.054
	(0.884)	(0.993)	(0.893)
EPS	1.567***	1.489***	1.600***
	(0.228)	(0.182)	(0.185)
EC	−0.062***	−0.058**	−0.068***
	(0.0084)	(0.0067)	(0.0066)
EPS × EC	−0.029***	−0.028**	−0.036***
	(0.0056)	(0.0045)	(0.0046)

Note: Standard errors are in parentheses. **p* value < 0.1. ***p* value < 0.05. ****p* value < 0.01.

footprint through the implementation of more stringent environmental laws and regulations.

Our study strongly suggests that achieving higher economic complexity can be an effective policy instrument toward achieving sustainable development in these economies. Future research will focus on investigating more accurately the channels through which environmental stringency influences carbon emissions and using more robust measures of economic complexity, such as the emissions intensity value of products that delve into the specific products linked with higher emission intensities, aiding in the formulation of policies aimed at mitigating carbon footprint.

References

Afshan, S., Ozturk, I., & Yaqoob, T. (2022). Facilitating renewable energy transition, ecological innovations and stringent environmental policies to improve ecological sustainability: evidence from MM-QR method. *Renewable Energy*, *196*, 151–160.

Alsagr, N. (2023). How does environmental policy stringency affect renewable energy investment? Implications for green investment horizons. *Utilities Policy*, *83*, 101613.

Arellano, M., & Bover, O. (1995). Another look at the instrumental variable estimation of error-components models. *Journal of Econometrics*, *68*(1), 29–51

Bakhsh, S., Zhang, W., Ali, K., & Anas, M. (2024). Energy transition and environmental stability prospects for OECD economies: The prominence role of environmental governance, and economic complexity: Does the geopolitical risk matter?. *Journal of Environmental Management*, *354*, 120358.

Brambor, T., Clark, W. R., & Golder, M. (2006). Understanding interaction models: Improving empirical analyses. *Political Analysis*, *14*(1), 63–82

Can, M., & Gozgor, G. (2017). The impact of economic complexity on carbon emissions: evidence from France. *Environmental Science and Pollution Research*, *24*, 16364–16370.

Danish, Ulucak R., & Khan, S. U. D. (2020). Relationship between energy intensity and CO2 emissions: does economic policy matter?. *Sustainable Development*, *28*(5), 1457–1464.

De Angelis, E. M., *et al.* (2019). Climate change and economic growth: the role of environmental policy stringency. *Sustainability*, *11*(8), 2273.

Dechezleprêtre, A., & Sato, M. (2017). The impacts of environmental regulations on competitiveness. *Review of Environmental Economics and Policy*, 11, 183–206.

Doğan, B., Driha, O. M., Balsalobre Lorente, D., & Shahzad, U. (2021). The mitigating effects of economic complexity and renewable energy on carbon emissions in developed countries. *Sustainable Development*, *29*(1), 1–12.

Ferris, A., Garbaccio, R., Marten, A., & Wolverton, A. (2017). *The impactsof environmental regulation on the US economy*. Oxford Research Encyclopedia of Environmental Science.

Fuhr, H. (2021). The rise of the Global South and the rise in carbon emissions. *Third World Quarterly*, *42*(11), 2724–2746.

Haites, E. (2018). Carbon taxes and greenhouse gas emissions trading systems: what have we learned?. *Climate Policy*, *18*(8), 955–966.

Hu, G., Can, M., Paramati, S. R., Doğan, B., & Fang, J. (2020). The effect of import product diversification on carbon emissions: New evidence for sustainable economic policies. *Economic Analysis and Policy*, *65*, 198–210.

Jensen, S., Mohlin, K., Pittel, K., & Sterner, T. (2015). An introduction to the green paradox: the unintended consequences of climate policies. *Review of Environmental Economics and Policy*.

Jha, S., Bhushan, S., & Nirola, N. (2024). Is geopolitical risk always detrimental to economic growth?. *Economic Change and Restructuring*, *57*(2), 25.
Khan, H., Weili, L., & Khan, I. (2022). Institutional quality, financial development and the influence of environmental factors on carbon emissions: evidence from a global perspective. *Environmental Science and Pollution Research*, 29, 1–13.
Kim, Y., & Rhee, D. E. (2019). Do stringent environmental regulations attract foreign direct investment in developing countries? Evidence on the "Race to the Top" from cross-country panel data. *Emerging Markets Finance and Trade*, *55*(12), 2796–2808.
Lægreid, O. M., & Povitkina, M. (2018). Do political institutions moderate the GDP-CO2 relationship? *Ecological Economics*, *145*, 441–450.
Levinson, A., & Taylor, M. S. (2008). Unmasking the pollution haven effect. *International Economic Review*, *49*(1), 223–254.
Machado, J. A., & Silva, J. S. (2019). Quantiles via moments. *Journal of Econometrics*, *213*(1), 145–173.
Mulatu, A. (2018). Environmental regulation and international competitiveness: A critical review. *International Journal of Global Environmental Issues*, *17*(1), 41–63.
Neagu, O., & Teodoru, M. C. (2019). The relationship between economic complexity, energy consumption structure, and greenhouse gas emission: Heterogeneous panel evidence from the EU countries. *Sustainability*, *11*(2), 497
Neves, S. A., Marques, A. C., & Patrício, M. (2020). Determinants of CO2 emissions in European Union countries: does environmental regulation reduce environmental pollution?. *Economic Analysis and Policy*, *68*, 114–125.
Nirola, N. & Agarwal, A. (2024). *Economic complexity and environment policy stringency in mitigating the carbon footprint: evidence from Global South*. Regional Studies Association Blog.
OECD. Publishing, Organisation for Economic Co-operation and Development Staff, & OECD Development Centre. (2010). *Perspectives on global development 2010: Shifting wealth*. Organization for Economic Co-operation and Development.
Pigou, A.C. (1920). *The Economics of Welfare*, fourth ed. Weidenfeld and Nicolson, London. 1938.
Romero, J. P., & Gramkow, C. (2021). Economic complexity and greenhouse gas emissions. *World Development*, *139*, 105317.
Schlindwein, L. F., & Montalvo, C. (2023). Energy citizenship: Accounting for the heterogeneity of human behaviors within energy transition. *Energy Policy*, *180*, 113662.
Shapiro, J. S., & Walker, R. (2018). Why is pollution from US manufacturing declining? The roles of environmental regulation, productivity, and trade. *American Economic Review*, *108*(12), 3814–3854.
Sinn, H. W. (2015). Introductory comment–the green paradox: A supply-side view of the climate problem. *Review of Environmental Economics and Policy*, 9, 239–245.
Song, M., Wang, S., & Zhang, H. (2020). Could environmental regulation and R&D tax incentives affect green product innovation? *Journal of Cleaner Production*, *258*, 120849.
Phan, C., Jain, V., Purnomo, E. P., Islam, M. M., Mughal, N., Guerrero, J. W. G., & Ullah, S. (2021). Controlling environmental pollution: Dynamic role of fiscal decentralization in CO 2 emission in Asian economies. *Environmental Science and Pollution Research*, *28*, 65150–65159.
Tol, R. S. (2017). The structure of the climate debate. *Energy Policy*, *104*, 431–438.
Tol, R. S. (2018). The economic impacts of climate change. *Review of Environmental Economics and Policy*, 12, 4–25.
Wang, H., & Wei, W. (2020). Coordinating technological progress and environmental regulation in CO2 mitigation: The optimal levels for OECD countries & emerging economies. *Energy Economics*, *87*, 104510.
Wang, Y., & Shen, N. (2016). Environmental regulation and environmental productivity: The case of China. *Renewable and Sustainable Energy Reviews*, *62*, 758–766.

Wolde-Rufael, Y., & Mulat-Weldemeskel, E. (2021). Do environmental taxes and environmental stringency policies reduce CO2 emissions? Evidence from 7 emerging economies. *Environmental Science and Pollution Research*, *28*, 22392–22408.
Wolde-Rufael, Y., & Weldemeskel, E. M. (2020). Environmental policy stringency, renewable energy consumption, and CO2 emissions: A panel cointegration analysis for BRIICTS countries. *International Journal of Green Energy*, *17*(10), 568–582.
Wu, H., Xu, L., Ren, S., Hao, Y., & Yan, G. (2020). How do energy consumption and environmental regulation affect carbon emissions in China? New evidence from a dynamic threshold panel model. *Resources Policy*, *67*, 101678.
Yirong, Q. (2022). Does environmental policy stringency reduce CO2 emissions? Evidence from high-polluted economies. *Journal of Cleaner Production*, *341*, 130648.

11 Climate Change and Living Conditions in the Global South

Evidence from Dynamic Panel Data

Ambrose Nnaemeka Omeje, Ravinder Rena, and Ikenna Paulinus Nwodo

11.1 Introduction

Climate change has been documented by scholars as one of the crucial determining factors of the living conditions of people, especially in the Global South, where some countries are found in tropical regions and semi-tropical regions, in which climate change effect makes them vulnerable. The predicament meted by climate change on the living conditions of the people in the Global South has undeniably far-reaching damaging and obvious impacts [1]. Some of these peoples' living conditions have been relegated with smaller number of them having the adaptive resources and/or the capacity to withstand these natural disasters [2]. Economies in Global South that are found in the Caribbean, Africa, Latin America, Oceania, and Asia have common income levels that ranges between low to medium, thereby, making them to be more marginalized in terms of their adaptation and/or response to climate change, hence worsening their living conditions economically, socially, politically, and otherwise [3].

Economic progress of Global South and that of the North in the previous two centuries has led to the human-led greenhouse gas (GHG) emissions which gives rise to climate change [2, 4]. The projected Global North contribution to GHG emissions is about 92% [1, 2], hence making them predominantly liable to the bulk of GHG emissions which greatly gives rise to climate change. However, the Global North also spread the footprints of its climate by establishing their industrial units across their borders, which also includes that of the Global South, thereby, contributing to variations in climate in the area [1].

A look at regional trends of the Global South's CO_2 emissions (kt), total greenhouse gas – GHG emissions (kt of CO_2 equivalent) and living conditions (proxied by GDP per capita [constant US$]) from 2020 to 2022 indicates that East Asia surpassed other regions in both 2020, 2021, and 2022 in emitting CO_2 (kt) and generating the GHG (see Figure 11.1). This is followed by South Asian countries between the periods 2020–2022. Again, countries in the Middle East and North Africa (MENA) assume the third position in emitting CO_2 (kt) and generating the GHG emissions for the years 2020, 2021, and 2022.

DOI: 10.4324/9781032694337-15

The fourth region is the Latin America, while the least region that contributes to CO_2 emission (kt) and GHG in the Global South is sub-Sahara African (SSA) region between the periods 2020–2022. This may be because SSA has the least mechanized or industrial economies compared to other regions and they rely mainly on agricultural production with crude implements, manual labour, and intermediate products that are still being used for industrial production(s). This period (2020–2022) was used just to show the current/immediate effects of emissions and their impacts on living conditions of the people. Figure 11.1 shows that climate change reduces living condition in the Global South. From 2020 to 2022, people's living conditions deteriorated for all the regions. Irrespective of who or which region emits the CO_2 and GHG emissions more, all the people in the Global South suffer similar deterioration in their living conditions.

However, governments in these regions have been making concerted efforts towards securing the environment by discouraging pollution to ensure green economy and to improve the living conditions of the people [6]. Some of the policy efforts by the Global South governments are the National Policy on Climate Change and Climate Change Policy Response and Strategy, enacting climate change legislations such as the Climate Change Act, among others. These policies and their implementations have not yielded the desired results. While different studies have looked at climate change and how it affects the Global South, they have failed to show how living conditions of the people is affected. The only studies related to the present study are country-specific study done for a developing country, Nigeria [7, 8], and emerging countries [9] with interest on climate change influence on life expectancy. It is on this note

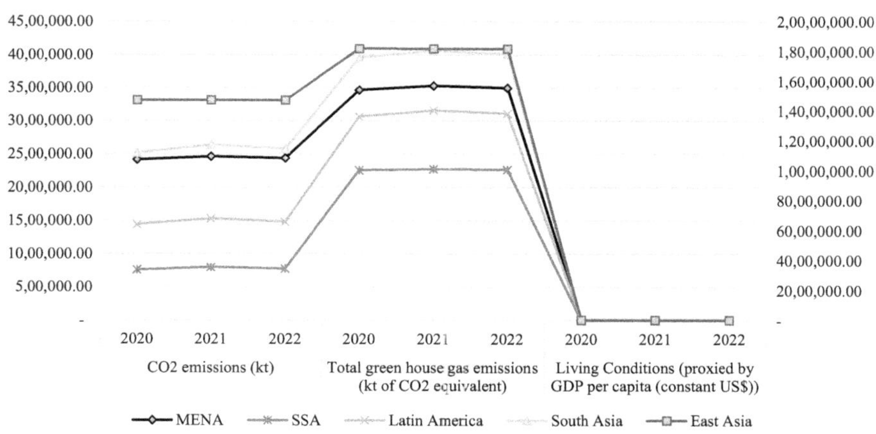

Figure 11.1 Regional Trend of Living Conditions, CO_2, and GHG Emissions in the Global South from 2020 to 2022.

Source: Authors' compilation from [5].

that this study examines climate change and living conditions in the Global South using evidence from dynamic panel data.

11.2 Literature Review

The theoretical foundation of this study is premised on the Person relative to Event (PrE) theory. This model has been applied to study disaster-associated conditions [10], such as climate change effects on the living conditions of the people. It was later modified by [11]. The theory posits that in determining what makes an individual to get prepared on the kind of steps and/or actions to take depends on how severe they rate the recurring event, and how they are affected by other varying factors, as well as erstwhile experience(s) on earthquake, climate change, and other natural disaster [10]. The model tries to envisage how rising levels of human threat with respect to resources could be sufficiently assessed relative to the size of intensifying problem-focused coping strategy of the threat. On the other hand, rising levels of threat with insufficient resources relative to amount of the threat make the problem-focused coping strategy to fall [11]. This theory assumed that any factor that should be associated and/or linked with this theory should be a threatening event. This theory is, therefore, relevant to our study since climate change is a threatening event that does not only threaten the existence of people and other living things in the Global South, but the world at large. Whatever threatens the existence of the Global South, also threatens the world at large.

In terms of empirical evidence, different studies have looked at climate change and how it affects the Global South. For instance, [12] used descriptive statistics to study how climate change affects Global South specifically in Africa. Empirical evidence revealed that 30–170 million persons would probably experience malnutrition and/or undernutrition worldwide in few years later, and Africa would make up three-quarter of this population. World Health Organization [13] examined how climate change influences health using descriptive statistics and panel data. It was found that there exists significant rise in the risks brought about by climate variations with more harsh impact on the Global South than anticipated.

Similarly, [2] used descriptive statistics and empirical review method to look at how variations in climate devastates Global South. Results show that the effects of climate change are more in India, Pakistan, Kenya, and Bangladesh. Variations in climate has posed devastating impacts on wheat, making different workers not to engage in outdoor-works, and exposing people more to severe health risks that could even lead to death.

Another study like [3] looked at different ways to mitigate climate change impact in Global South using descriptive statistics. Results indicate that member economies of Global South found within Latin America and the Caribbean, Asia, Oceania, and Africa recorded income levels that ranges between low and medium, which worsens their socio-political and economic equality. The study suggests that higher emitters of CO_2 such as UK, Germany, and Japan, need to assume responsibilities for previous emissions instead of shifting the cost and effect to the vulnerable countries. [14] reviewed different versions of the United Nations Framework Convention on Climate Change (UNFCCC) and Intergovernmental Panel on Climate Change (IPCC) reports to find out the climate change impact solutions available to Global South. Findings indicate that worldwide clean energy access remains the best solution to achieve sustainable socio-economic growth and development. In systematic literature review with the application of descriptive statistics, it was shown that climate change significantly and negatively affects the inhabitants of the Global South [15–18].

11.3 Methodology and Data

11.3.1 Methodology

The underlying theoretical framework for this study is Person relative to Event (PrE) theory. This theory is the most suitable because of the perceived risk associated with climate change and that of behaviour to prevent it by the Global South stakeholders. Our model is then built on this theory.

$$\text{lnliv} = f\left(\text{lncch}\right) \tag{11.1}$$

where lnliv = log of living condition proxied by gross domestic product (GDP) per capital in 2015 constant United States Dollars (US$), lncch = log of climate change proxied by carbon dioxide emissions (metric tons per capita), and f = functional form.

Consequently, Equation (11.1) is modified to include other relevant control variables following economic theory and represented in panel econometric form below.

$$\begin{aligned} \text{lnliv}_{it} &= \beta_{0,i} + \beta_{1,i}\text{lncch}_{it} + \beta_{2,i}\text{tra}_{it} + \beta_{3,i}\text{gfc}_{it} + \mu_{it} \\ \mu_{it} &= \alpha_i + \vartheta_{it} \end{aligned} \tag{11.2}$$

where tra = trade measured as trade (% of GDP), gfc = gross fixed capital formation (% of GDP), α_i= individual fixed effects that vary across cross-section (countries) but static across time, ϑ_{it}= error structure which is assumed to be uncorrelated across panel, $\beta_{0,i}$= constant that vary across panel (i), $\beta_i^{'}s$ = coefficient parameters, i = cross-sectional units, t = time dimension. Every other remains as defined earlier. i = 1, 2, 3, …, 11 and t = 1, 2, 3, …, 33.

Furthermore, due to inherent econometrics shortcomings of popular static models, such as fixed and random effect estimators, and pooled OLS, Dynamic Common Correlated Effect (DCCE) estimator of Dynamic Panel Data (DPD) is adopted for estimation in this study. This model is an extension of Panel Autoregressive Distributed Lag (PARDL) family such as the Mean Group (MG), Pooled Mean Group (PMG), and Augmented Mean Group (AMG) and has been proposed by [19]. The model draws heavily from the efforts of [20] Common Correlated Effect (CCE) approach. The model (DCCE) accounts for cross-sectional dependency inherent in long panel as in this study, possible endogeneity, and serial correlation by employing lagged dependent and independent variables. It uses the cross-sectional means of some of the variables or even all the variables entering the estimation equation to solve cross-sectional dependency problem in panels. DCCE is, therefore, symbolically represented as following Equation (11.2);

$$\begin{aligned}\Delta \text{lnliv}_{it} = {} & \beta_{0,i} + \beta_{1,i}\text{lnliv}_{it-1} + \beta_{2,i}\text{lncch}_{it} + \beta_{3,i}\text{tra}_{it} + \beta_{4,i}\text{gfc}_{it} \\ & + \sum_{r}^{p} \delta_{1,i}\overline{\Delta\text{lnliv}}_{i,t-r} + \sum_{l}^{q} \delta_{1,i}\overline{\text{lnliv}}_{i,t-l} + \sum_{j}^{m} \delta_{2,i}\overline{\text{lncch}}_{i,t-j} \\ & + \sum_{k}^{PT} \delta_{3,i}\overline{\text{tra}}_{it-k} + \sum_{h}^{g} \delta_{4,i}\overline{\text{gfc}}_{it-h} + \mu_{it}\end{aligned} \tag{11.3}$$

where the variables with overbars indicate the cross-sectional averages which could take different lags including zero while other items remain as defined earlier.

Finally, it is conventional to subject the dataset to various standard statistical and econometrics tests to establish its properties before estimation proper. This helps researchers to choose appropriate estimator. In this regard, this study employed descriptive statistics, and other second-generation econometrics tests such as Im-Pesaran-Shin (IPS) panel unit root, Pesaran cross-section dependency – CD [21], Westerlund panel cointegration and correlation matrix analyses. Other tests such as slope heterogeneity [21] and Jochman's within-group serial correlation are also employed.

11.3.2 Data

The data used in this study were accessed from [5]. The selected 11 Global South countries are Bangladesh, Brazil, China, Egypt, India, Indonesia, Mexico, Nigeria, Russia, Saudi Arabia, and South Africa covering the major regions in the Global South (SSA, South Asia, East Asia, Latin America & MENA), two for each bloc and Russia. The period is from 1990 to 2022. Therefore, $n = 11$, $T = 33$, and $T \times n = (11 \times 33) = N = 363$ observations. N = overall group observations, n = between group observation and T = within group observations.

11.4 Results and Discussion

11.4.1 Descriptive Statistical Analysis

Table 11.1 presents the descriptive statistics of the variables. The results indicate that the mean of living condition (lnliv) and climate change (lncch) are8.24%and0.88%. Grossfixedcapital(%ofGDP)–gfcandtrade(%ofGDP)–tra have a mean of 24.07% and 45.41%. These implies that the trade and gross fixed capital in these economies are quite high relative to the living condition and climate change that are largely small. In terms of the standard deviation (Std.Dev.), the overall mean deviation is 0.97 and 1.19 for lnliv and lncch, whereas the between and within group mean deviations for lnliv are 0.95 and 0.34. These imply that lnliv and lncch exhibit moderate fluctuation around their mean values. Again, gfc and tra std.dev were calculated as 7.65 and 16.72 for the overall economy. Also, gfc has between and within group mean dispersion of 6.27 and 4.75, while that of tra stood at 13.14 and 11.05. Further statistics can be confirmed from the minimum and maximum values whereas the observation is classified as overall (363), between (11), and within (33).

11.4.2 Contemporaneous Correlation Analysis

The correlation matrix analysis indicates absence of high correlation between the variables used in this analysis. This is evident as none of the correlation coefficients are larger than 0.80 which is the threshold of high correlation. The study concludes that there is an absence of multicollinearity in the ensuing analyses. The results are presented in Table 11.2.

Table 11.1 Panel Descriptive Statistics

Variable	*Group*	*Mean*	*Std. Dev.*	*Min*	*Max*	*Observations*
lnliv	overall	8.235396	0.969175	6.200702	9.958858	$N = 363$
	between		0.949676	6.750759	9.822499	$n = 11$
	within		0.34226	6.8348	9.382155	$T = 33$
lncch	overall	0.884296	1.193156	−2.31118	2.848264	$N = 363$
	between		1.21264	−1.37221	2.58539	$n = 11$
	within		0.288292	−0.05468	1.722338	$T = 33$
gfc	overall	24.0744	7.645821	12.44601	53.12219	$N = 363$
	between		6.273322	16.46109	37.81123	$n = 11$
	within		4.752143	9.967256	48.92072	$T = 33$
tra	overall	45.4051	16.71893	15.1556	110.5771	$N = 363$
	between		13.14041	24.37512	71.04971	$n = 11$
	within		11.0506	15.37244	102.6142	$T = 33$

Source: Authors' computation using STATA 15.

Table 11.2 Matrix of Correlations

Variables	*(1)*	*(2)*	*(3)*	*(4)*
(1) lnliv	1.000			
(2) lncch	0.743	1.000		
(3) gfc	−0.272	−0.162	1.000	
(4) tra	0.469	0.570	−0.052	1.000

Source: Authors' computation using STATA 15.

Table 11.3 Im-Pesaran-Shin (IPS) Panel Unit Root Test Result

Variable	*IPS (level)* t-*tilde-bar Statistic*	*IPS (level)* p-*value*	*IPS (First diff)* t-*tilde-bar Statistic*	*IPS (First diff)* p-*value*	*Remarks*
lnliv	−0.3127	1.0000	−3.1339	0.0000	*I*(1)
lncch	−1.5567	0.3219	−3.6608	0.0000	*I*(1)
tra	−1.5784	0.2901	−3.8432	0.0000	*I*(1)
gfc	−1.9952	0.0108	—	—	*I*(0)

Source: Authors' computation using STATA 15.

11.4.3 Panel Unit Root Tests

Table 11.3 presents the panel unit root test results. In the results, the variables were subjected to both level and first difference tests wherein it was found that except gfc, all the variables used in this analysis are stationary after first differencing. That is, lnliv, lncch, and tra are integrated of order one – *I*(1) while gfc is integrated of order zero – *I*(0).

11.4.4 Panel Cointegration Analysis

For cointegration analyses, Westerlund test approach was employed, and the results indicate reliable evidence in support of the null hypotheses which implies absence of cointegration. The result is presented in Table 11.4.

The Pesaran Cross-sectional Dependency (CD) test result is presented in Table 11.5. This test is most suitable for large T and small N. The results, however, indicate that the null hypothesis of no cross-sectional dependence is not favoured given the small p-values ($p < 0.01$) which are identified for all the variables.

11.4.5 Testing for Slope Heterogeneity

It is appropriate to test for panel heterogeneity. This helps to check the importance of country-specific analysis. This test is advanced by [22] and have been applied by [20]. The result presented in Table 11.6 indicate that the slope coefficients differ across country thus the groupwise and country-specific analyses are estimated.

Table 11.4 Westerlund Cointegration Test

Statistic	P-*values*	*Decision*
1.2385	0.1078	No Cointegration

Source: Authors' computation using STATA 15.

Table 11.5 Cross-sectional Dependency (CD) Test

Variable	*CD-test*	p-*value*	*Average joint* T	*Mean* ρ	*Mean abs*(ρ)
Lnliv	35.454	0.0000	33	0.83	0.83
Lncch	14.31	0.0000	33	0.34	0.67
Gfc	3.879	0.0000	33	0.09	0.41
Tra	7.299	0.0000	33	0.17	0.38

Source: Authors' computation using STATA 15.

Table 11.6 Slope Heterogeneity Test

	Delta	p-*value*
	22.001	0.000
adj.	23.885	0.000

H_0: slope coefficients are homogenous
Source: Author's computation using STATA 15.

11.4.6 Regression Results

The regression results are present in Table 11.7 for the 11 selected economies. The results show that the lagged value of living condition (lnliv), climate change (lncch), and gfc, are a statistically significant whereas trade (tra) is statistically insignificant. Specifically, lagged value of living condition is found to decrease the living condition of the 11 Global South economies. That is if past value of living condition is increased by 1%, then the living condition presently will decline by about 0.41% on the average ceteris paribus. This result is surprising but cannot be unconnected with the state of the living condition in the Global South whose economies are largely characterized by the poor or negative growth, volatile exchange, and inflation rates. All these factors including over reliant on the Global North for technology imports including expatriate professionals export jobs to the Global North leaving the Global South in persistent economic woes thus past value of living condition could not improve the present living conditions of the Global South.

Similarly, climate change (lncch) appears to improve the living condition of the Global South significantly. That is, 1% increase in lncch is associated with about 0.13% rise in the living condition of the Global South. This result is particularly striking as one would expect climate change to worsen the living

Table 11.7 DCCE Results (Groupwise)

Dependent Variable	*D.lnliv*
Gfc	0.00619*** (0.00237)
Tra	−0.000717 (0.000455)
Lncch	0.130** (0.0648)
L.lnliv	−0.408*** (0.0717)
Constant	0.444 (1.020)
Observations	341
Number of groups	11
R-squared	0.417
CD Statistic	−1.36
CD Probability	0.1744
Jochman's within-group correlation test	
Ch-sq (527)	11.000
Probability > Chi-sq	1.000

Source: Author's computation using STATA 15.

Notes: Standard errors in parentheses; $***p < 0.01$, $**p < 0.05$, $*p < 0.1$.

condition of the people, but this is not however the case in this study. But the result is not, however, unfounded owing to the economic configuration of the Global South. The argument is that climate change is not induced by the activities in the Global South but by the Global North industrial and manufacturing activities even though, some companies have crossed from Global North to Global South. Since Global South has low industrial and manufacturing activities compared to the Northern counterpart, it then implies that industrial activities in the Global South do not contribute significantly to emissions and climate distortions.

Additionally, companies migrating down South have introduced cleaner technologies for industrial activities as posited by the Green Haven Hypothesis thus improved climate change. Another likely important reason for this result is that dirty companies receive heavy environmental tax from the government which is then used to clean the environment and ultimately improve people's living condition. This argument is justified in the pollution haven hypothesis theory. This then implies that as the activities of these companies keep polluting the environment, government will have more money through environmental taxes to clean up the environment for people's well-being. This result validates the earlier findings by [9, 23] but largely infirm studies by [8, 18]. Furthermore, trade (tra) is statistically insignificant with negative association to living condition. Though statistically insignificant, this justifies the fact that globalization impede the living condition in Global South because most foreign-traded items outcompete the local products. This pushes most local industries out of business thus bickering unemployment and stunted economic growth. For gross fixed capital (gfc), the results show that living condition increases significantly as gfc increases. This implies that 1% rise in gfc will increase the living condition in the Global South by about 0.6% on the average ceteris paribus. While this result is expected, it follows economic theory since investment in the physical capital will translate into economic expansion which ultimately improve peoples' well-being.

R-square indicate that 41% variations in the living condition are jointly accounted for by the independent variables. The within-group correlation test of Jochman which accounts for serial correlation indicate evidence in support of no serial correlation as the *p*-value of the Chi-sq statistic is greater than 0.05. This result is found on the lower part of Table 11.8.

Results from country-specific analyses show that the lagged value of living condition (lnliv) is statistically significant for all the countries except Egypt. Aligning with the overall results, the relationship is negative for all the countries. Climate change is only statistically significant for Saudi Arabia with positive association to living conditions. The relationship remains negative

Table 11.8 Individual Country Results

Countries	*l.lnliv*	*Lncch*	*Tra*	*gfc*	*Cons*
Bangladesh	−0.2124**	−0.0198	0.0005	0.0070**	−2.1199*
	(0.0981)	(0.0461)	(0.0005)	(0.0040)	(1.1889)
Brazil	−0.9248***	0.0245	−0.0041***	0.0169***	4.5542***
	(0.1253)	(0.0546)	(0.0011)	(0.0025)	(1.1819)
China	−0.1645***	0.0526	0.0009	−0.0007	−2.0186*
	(0.0340)	(0.0942)	(0.0009)	(0.0015)	(1.1454)
Egypt	−0.1443	0.0902	−0.0007	0.0057***	−1.6630***
	(0.0937)	(0.0613)	(0.0005)	(0.0012)	(0.5547)
India	−0.4710***	0.2978*	−0.0021	0.0070	−2.0023
	(0.1672)	(0.1714)	(0.0019)	(0.0045)	(1.6911)
Indonesia	−.3325**	0.0405	−0.0019***	0.0127***	−2.6594**
	(0.1325)	(0.0818)	(0.0006)	(0.0035)	(1.0289)
Mexico	−0.5960***	−0.1918	0.0011	0.0196***	7.6751***
	(0.1858)	(0.1781)	(0.0009)	(0.0045)	(1.6180)
Nigeria	−0.2124	0.0634	−0.0004	−0.0022	0.0432
	(0.1464)	(0.0928)	(0.0010)	(0.0025)	(1.7927)
Russia	−0.4158***	0.3688	0.0002	−0.0008	−1.6034
	(0.1455)	(0.1950)	(0.0009)	(0.0057)	(1.0575)
Saudi Arabia	−0.3820***	0.5985***	−0.0010	−0.0042	1.6357
	(0.1323)	(0.2266)	(0.0017)	(0.0043)	(2.0080)
South Africa	−0.6270***	0.1044*	−0.0003	0.0071**	3.0462***
	(0.1849)	(0.0621)	(0.0008)	(0.0035)	(0.9284)

Source: Author's computation using STATA 15.

Notes: Standard errors in parentheses; *** $p < 0.01$, ** $p < 0.05$, * $p < 0.1$.

for all the countries except for Bangladesh and Mexico. These means that whilst climate change decreases living condition in Bangladesh and Mexico, it improves living condition in Brazil, China, Egypt, India, Indonesia, Nigeria, Russia, Saudi Arabia, and South Africa. These results cannot be far from the economic configuration of the countries of the global south. These findings could also be because of the type of emission that constitute climate change in these economies. Statistics shows that most developing economies emit more methane than CO_2. For instance, four (Mauritius, Sao Tome and Principe, South Africa, and Seychelles) out of 48 SSA emit more methane than CO_2 and SSA is a major regional bloc in Global South [24]. Trade is significant with negative correlation for Brazil and Indonesia such that 1% increase in trade decreases living condition by 0.4% and 0.1%, respectively, on the average. The reason for the inverse association remains as discussed earlier in the overall country discussion. Other countries where living condition and trade exhibit inverse link are Egypt, India, Nigeria, Saudi Arabia, and South Africa. These implies that trade reduces living condition in these economies while it insignificantly improves living conditions in Bangladesh, China, Mexico, and Russia. Additionally, gfc significantly improves living conditions in Bangladesh, Brazil, Egypt, Indonesia, Mexico, and South Africa. That is, living condition will on the average increase by about 0.7% in Bangladesh, 1.7% in Brazil, 0.6% in Egypt, 0.13% in Indonesia, 0.2% in Mexico, and 0.7% in South Africa for 1% increase in climate change. Climate change will insignificantly induce living condition in India but insignificantly reduce living condition in China, Nigeria, Russia, and Saudi Arabia. These results are interestingly and largely consistent with the countrywide results earlier discussed.

11.5 Conclusion and Policy Recommendations

This study demonstrated the relationship between climate change and living condition in Global South employing various second-generation econometrics approaches on long panel dataset. Panel unit root results indicate that all the variables are of first-order except gfc which is of zero-order. Also, results from the cointegration test indicate no evidence of cointegration while cross-sectional dependency test show reliable evidence of cross-sectional dependence. Slope heterogeneity result shoes supporting evidence that the panels are dissimilar. The countrywide analyses based on DCCE show that climate change appeared to significantly improve the living condition of the Global South. On the part of country-specific analyses, climate change appears to improve the living condition in most of the economies (Brazil, China, Egypt, India, Indonesia, Nigeria, Russia, and South Africa) though statistically insignificant. However, in Saudi Arabia, climate change significantly improves the living condition of the people.

It is suggested as policy option that policy stakeholders as well as individual governments of the Global South make concerted effort in reducing climate change emissions by regulating and monitoring the activities of local firms and multinationals. This is notwithstanding the fact that climate change appears to improve living condition in the Global South. This can be done by constantly updating the policies that govern emissions as well as tax burden meted on policy violators. Another important policy option is that government of Global South economies should always be cautious while attracting foreign multinationals especially those from Global North that seem to wield enormous power beyond the control of the host economy. Finally, there should be economic and political agenda for a more coordinated policies for all the economies in the Global South to challenge and thwart the dominance of the Global North.

Since the economies of the Global South are at different levels of development, the results are bound to vary across these economies. The study suggest that future researchers can model economies with similar behaviour and features. The topic can be extended to ECOWAS and sub-Saharan African regions. The main limitation of this study is poor data availability that characterize developing economy which dominate the Global South. This suggests that more countries would have been included in the analysis if data were available.

References

1. Bandera, G. (2022): How climate colonialism affects the Global South. Fair Planet. Available Online at: https://www.fairplanet.org/story/how-climate-colonialism-affects-the-globalsouth/#:~:text=The%20Global%20South%20is%20experiencing,planet%20warms%3B%20droughts%20in%20Madagascar
2. Huq, S., Adow, M.: Climate change is devastating the Global South. Aljazeera Opinions/Climate Crisis. (2022). Available Online at: https://www.aljazeera.com/opinions/2022/5/11/climate-change-is-devastating-the-global-south
3. Kelly, N.: Climate justice in the context of the Global South. Open Access, Open Science, MDPI, (2022). Available Online at: https://blog.mdpi.com/2022/10/26/climate-justice-global-south/
4. Sen, R.S.: Climate Change in the Global South: Trends and Spatial Patterns. In: *Linking Gender to Climate Change Impacts in the Global South*, pp. 1–25, Springer Climate, Springer, Cham. (2018). Doi: https://doi.org/10.1007/978-3-319-75777-3_1
5. World Bank: *World Development Indicators*. (2023). https://databank.worldbank.org/reports.aspx?source=World-Development-Indicators
6. Ifelunini, I.A., Ugwu, S.C., Ichoku, H.E., Omeje, A.N., Ihim, E.: Determinants of fertility rate among women in Ghana and Nigeria: Implications for population growth and sustainable development. *Etude de la Population Africaine/African Population Studies*, 32(2), 4125–4133 (2018).
7. Amuka, J. I., Asogwa, F.O., Ugwuanyi, R.O., Omeje, A.N., Onyechi, T.: Climate change and life expectancy in a developing country: Evidence from greenhouse gas (CO2) emission in Nigeria. *International Journal of Economics and Financial Issues*, 8(4), 113–119 (2018). ISSN: 2146-4138, Available Online at: http://www.econjournals.com
8. Osabohien, R., Aderemi, T., Akindele, D.B., Okoh, J.I.: Carbon emissions and life expectancy in Nigeria. *Research Square Preprint*, 1–10 (2020). Doi: https://doi.org/10.21203/rs.3.rs-80181/v1

9. Mahalik, M.K., Le, T.H., Le, H.C., Mallick, H.: How do sources of carbon dioxide emissions affect life expectancy? Insights from 68 developing and emerging economies. *World Development Sustainability*, 1(100003), 1–10 (2022). ISSN 2772-655X, Doi: https://doi.org/10.1016/j.wds.2022.100003
10. Mulilis, J.P., Duval, T.S.: PrE (Person-Relative-to-Event) Theory of Coping with Threat. *Educational Resources Information Center (ERIC)*, (028876), 1–16 (1998). Available Online at: https://files.eric.ed.gov/fulltext/ED424543.pdf
11. Duval, T.S., Mulilis, J.P.: A Person-Relative-to-Event (PrE) Approach to Negative Threat Appeals and Earthquake Preparedness: A Field Study1. *Journal of Applied Social Psychology*, 29(3), 495–516 (2006). Doi: https://doi.org/10.1111/j.1559-1816.1999.tb01398.x
12. Babugura, A.: Climate change and the Global South: The case of Africa. The Cairo Review of Global Affairs (2021). Available Online at: https://www.thecairoreview.com/essays/climate-change-and-the-global-south-the-case-of-africa/
13. World Health Organization – WHO: *Climate change*. World Health Organization Publications (2023). Available Online at: https://www.who.int/news-room/fact-sheets/detail/climate-change-and-health
14. Jacob, V.A.: What is the way forward for the Global South in the era of climate change? *Wisconsin International Law Journal*, 37(1), 1–15 (2020). Available Online at:https://wilj.law.wisc.edu/jus-gentium/what-is-the-way-forward-for-the-global-south-in-the-era-of-climate-change/
15. Atkinson, C.L., Atkinson, A.M.: Impacts of climate change on rural communities: Vulnerability and adaptation in the Global South. *Encyclopedia*, 3, 721–729 (2023). Doi: https://doi.org/10.3390/encyclopedia3020052
16. Ngcamu, B.S.: Climate change effects on vulnerable populations in the Global South: A systematic review. *Natural Hazards*. 118, 977–991 (2023). Doi: https://doi.org/10.1007/s11069-023-06070-2
17. Marquardt, J., Fünfgeld, A., Elsässer, J.P.: Institutionalizing climate change mitigation in the Global South: Current trends and future research. *Earth System Governance*, 15(100163), 1–15 (2023). ISSN 2589-8116, Doi: https://doi.org/10.1016/j.esg.2022.100163
18. Omeje, A.N., Mba, A.J., Obodoechi, D.N., Ukwueze, E.R., Urama, C.E. COVID-19, Environmental Pollution, and Climate Change Nexus in Sub-Saharan Africa. In: Das, R.C. (ed.) *Economic, Environmental and Health Consequences of Conservation Capital*, Chapter 18, pp. 241–258. Springer, Singapore. (2023). Doi: https://doi.org/10.1007/978-981-99-4137-7_18
19. Chudik, A., Pesaran, M. H.: Common correlated effects estimation of heterogeneous dynamic panel data models with weakly exogenous regressors. *Journal of Econometrics*, 188(2), 393–420 (2015).
20. Pesaran, M. H.: Estimation and inference in large heterogeneous panels with a multifactor error structure. *Econometrica*. 74(4), 967–1012 (2006).
21. Pesaran, M. H.: Testing weak cross-sectional dependence in large panels. *Econometric Reviews*, 34(6–10), 1089–1117 (2015).
22. Pesaran, M. H., Yamagata, T.: Testing slope homogeneity in large panels. *Journal of Econometrics*, 142(1), 50–93 (2008).
23. Bhutto, N.A., Chang, B.H., Adeel, S., Seelro, A.D., Qureshi, M.U.: Global warming, economic development and their impact on the life expectancy: An empirical evidence from Pakistan. *Ciencia de datos para la Economía Aplicada/Studies of Applied Economics*, 41(1), 10–25 (2023). Doi. https://doi.org/10.25115/sae.v41i1.7875
24. Joint Research Centre of the European Commission – JRC: EDGAR - Emissions Database for Global Atmospheric Research. Accessed on EDGAR - The Emissions Database for Global Atmospheric Research. (2023). (europa.eu)

Part IV

Technological Advancements and Digital Divides in the Global South

12 Digital Divide

Understanding the Disparities between Global North and Global South

Igor M. Stepnov, Petr I. Kasatkin, and Tatiana V. Kolesnikova

12.1 Introduction

Digital transformation of the world economy is a global process of the 21st century. Digitalization occurs through the introduction of information technologies into the life of society, production processes and public administration. The year 2020 saw an exponential growth in the spread of digital technologies in the world. It was driven by the constraints that accompanied the COVID-19 pandemic [1]. Production downtime, value chain interruptions, logistics crises, and social distancing have increased the use of digital technologies in work, education, telemedicine, and e-commerce [2].

The revolution of digital technology is sharpening the competition between states in the international economy. The disparity between the economic development of the Global North and the Global South has a correlation with technological innovation. On the one hand, new technologies allow states to increase labor productivity and economic growth. On the other hand, the most economically developed states are able to ensure the creation and the dissemination of new technologies. At the same time, developing economies have fewer opportunities for technological breakthroughs due to lagging technologies and lack of investment and financial capacity. This determines the risk of preservation of the technological backwardness of developing economies.

12.2 Literature Review

Certain aspects of the digital development of countries have been widely studied by Evtodieva [3], Yalcintas, Alizadeh, 2020 [4], Cory [5], Augusto and Nichols [6]. Digitalization has been considered as an economic growth driver for developing countries in the works of Chengetana and Chikati [7], Sabir, Niyaz and Bakhtiyar [8], Lee and Roh [9]. Digitalization has also been explored in relation to other global trends by Fouquet [10] and Reuven Avi-Yonah [11].

Technological sovereignty has been viewed through the prism of protectionism by Fajgelbaum, Goldberg, Kennedy and Khandelwal [12], Gilbert, Koska, Oladi [13], Khmeleva [14], Shastitko, Meleshkina, Markova [15], Vasiliev, Aganbegyan [16], Ikejiaku and Dayao [17].

DOI: 10.4324/9781032694337-17

At the same time, financial aspects of technological development have been examined by Kasatkin, Kovalchuk and Stepnov [18, 19], managerial aspects of technological development have been identified by Klepach [20], the issue of human resources have been studied by Miraliev and Kamolov [21], and industrial factors have been described by Pane and Patunru [22]. The aforementioned works and other academic researches allow us to generalize the obtained scientific results and formulate strategies for the implementation of digital transformation of states depending on the level of their technological development.

12.3 Methodology

This research was based on the methods of collecting, grouping and analyzing information to highlight the differences in technological development of countries depending on the level of their income. This allowed us to conclude that the lower the level of income in the states, the lower their level of digital accessibility.

A comparative analysis of the volume of digital exports has concluded that developed countries supply significantly more digital services to the world market than developing countries. At the same time, the dynamic analysis of these indicators allowed us to determine that the share of developing countries in international digital trade is increasing. The analysis of the dynamics of state regulation of the digital industry made it possible to determine that information security is a top-priority task of the state. To develop digital development strategies, the analysis of cause-and-effect relationships and the method of inductive reasoning have been employed, which made it possible to achieve the goal of the research.

12.4 Results and Discussion

12.4.1 Risks of the Digital Divide of States between Global North and Global South

To determine the risks of digital divide between the Global North and the Global South, the authors have analyzed the digital development of countries in the Global North and Global South, foreign trade in digital products, and government regulation of digitalization in different countries.

The analysis of the distribution of countries by the level of income and digital development is based on the 2023 ICT Development Index statistics. Digital development indicators have been broken down into five groups: 90–99%; 80–89.9%; 70–79.9%, 50–69.9%, 20–49.9%. The distribution of countries with different levels of development and income by groups is shown in Figure 12.1.

As can be seen from Figure 12.1, the highest level of digital technology development corresponds to high-income economies. In 90–99% group, there

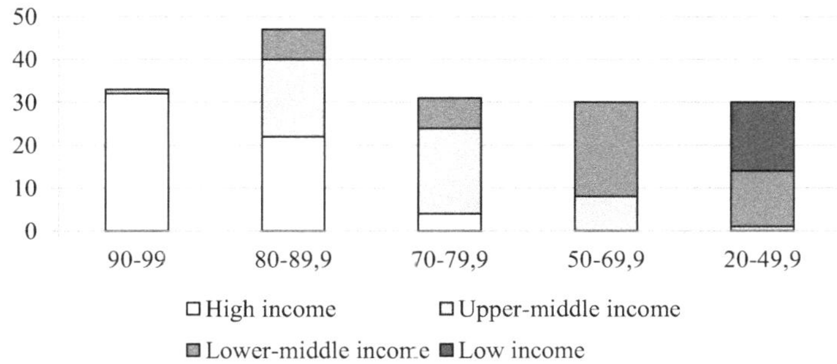

Figure 12.1 Country groups by digital development level, 2023, number of countries.

Source: Compiled by the authors according to the 2023 ICT Development Index [23].

are 32 high income economies and one upper-middle income economy. The lowest level of digital technology development corresponds to low-income economies. In 20–49.9% group, there are 16 low-income economies, 13 lower-middle income economies and one upper-middle income economy. Thus, the lower the level of income in the states, the lower the level of digital accessibility. These results could be explained by the fact that high-income countries have more financial and investment resources to create and attract digital technologies. However, it cannot be definitively concluded whether digital technologies are produced in all high-income countries or imported from abroad. At the same time, low-income countries are unable to ensure digital accessibility due to a lack of technological and financial resources.

The availability of domestic digital production can be traced through exports of digital products, as exports are derived from domestic production. The distribution of digital exports among developed and developing countries is shown in Figure 12.2.

The total export volume of digital products in the world has increased from US$ 168.1 billion in 2005 to US$ 912.9 billion in 2022. Thus, the volume of international digital trade has grown 5.4 times, indicating the rapid growth of the digital industry and its spread in the world. The overwhelming volume of digital product exports is carried out by developed countries. At the same time, the ratio of export volumes among countries is changing towards an increasing share of developing countries. For example, in 2005, the export ratio was 4 to 1 (developed economies accounted for 80% of export, while only 20% of export came from developing economies). In 2022, the ratio was already 2.3 to 1 (69% and 31% from developed and developing economies correspondingly). The trend suggests that the share of developing countries in digital exports will increase in the short term. The regional distribution of digital product exports is presented in Figure 12.3.

In 2022, digital product exports were predominantly represented by developed countries in Europe (56%) and developing countries in Asia and Oceania

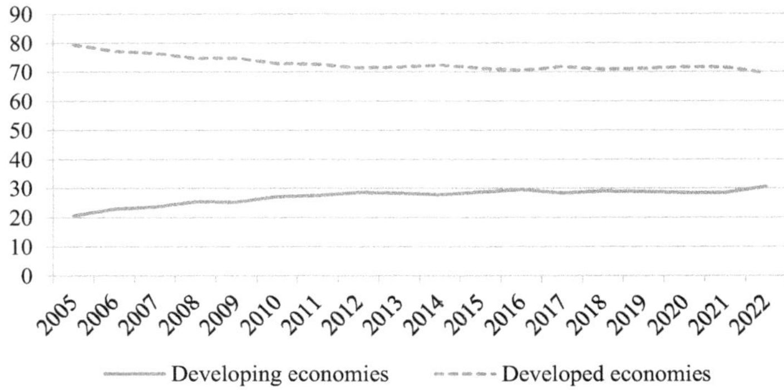

Figure 12.2 Distribution of digital technology exports by country groups, %.

Source: Compiled by the authors according to UNCTAD Statistics [24].

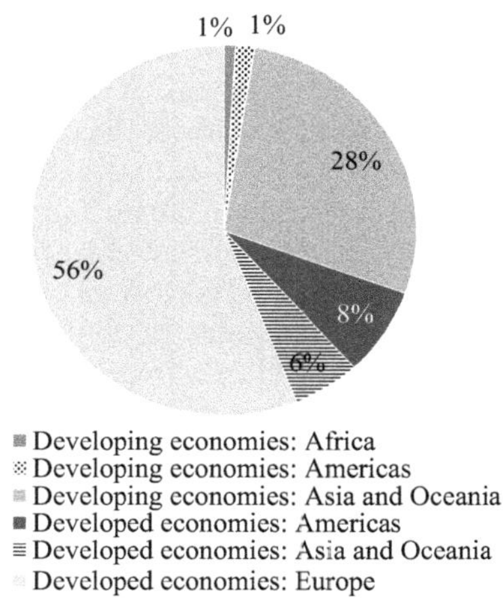

Figure 12.3 Distribution of digital technology exports by country and region, 2022, %.

Source: Compiled by the authors according to UNCTAD Statistics [24].

(28%), with the Americas region also being a major producer and exporter (8%). It should be noted that exports from Ireland (40%, USD 204 billion) are at the top of the exports from developed European countries, which could be explained by a virtually offshore position of this country. Among individual countries, the top three leaders of digital exports are as follows: India ($99 billion), China ($83 billion), and the United States ($55.5 billion). It is noteworthy that two countries in the Global South are world's leaders in digital exports. This is due to the fact that China and India are the largest economies among developing countries and have accumulated competitive advantages in digitalization.

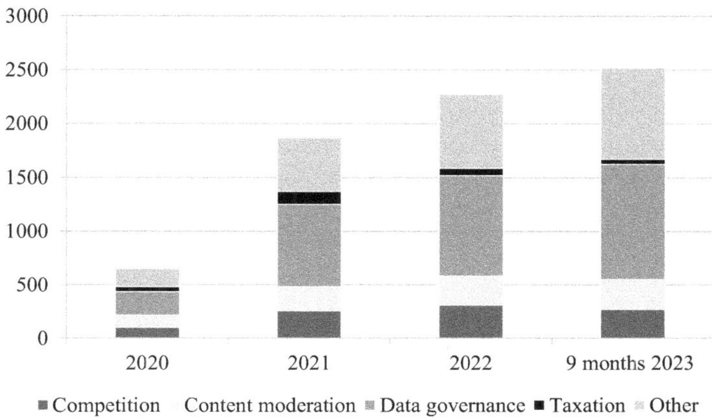

Figure 12.4 Spheres of state regulation in the digital industry around the world, 2020.–9M. 2023, number of regulatory decisions.

Source: Compiled by the authors based on Recent Activity. Digital Policy Alert [25].

The global digital transformation is accompanied by the strengthening of state regulation of the IT sector. In the period from January 1, 2020, to October 1, 2023, more than 18,000 acts of state regulation of the digital industry in the world were enforced (Figure 12.4).

In the structure of government regulation of the digital industry in the world, the prevailing instruments are those which are aimed at ensuring data protection and data governance. Their share in the total volume of solutions is 41%. Other instruments are less common: competition regulation (13%), content moderation (12%), taxation of digital activities (4%). This allows us to conclude that information security tasks are prioritized as part of digital security.

Two instruments of state regulation are particularly prominent among the instruments of state regulation: restrictions on cross-border data transfer, as well as data localization requirements. Access to information about users' shopping preferences allows global digital giants to create customized price offers. This creates a non-competitive environment for national companies that do not have such access [15]. The obligation of companies to store data within the country limits the ability of global digital giants to manage the collected and processed information.

The introduction of data localization requirements in countries which are actively developing digital technologies was carried out in the 2010s. For example, in Russia, localization of personal data of Russian citizens is mandatory from September 1, 2015 [26, 27]. According to the data by the Digital Policy Alert analytical portal, in the period from July 27, 2016, to October 1, 2023, the leading countries in introducing data localization requirements were India,

China, Indonesia, Pakistan, Turkey, and Vietnam. Corresponding requirements are also being introduced in the digital development flagship countries in the African region and in the Latin American region – South Africa and Brazil, Chile, Mexico correspondingly [25].

At the same time, the United States is the undisputed leader in the development of regulatory legislation. More than 1,300 U.S. regulatory acts include provisions regulating various aspects of digitalization. By comparison, Germany, which is the second largest country in terms of government interventions in the digital environment, has only 613 relevant amendments to regulations.

In the United States, the "CHIPS and Science Act" of August 9, 2022, provides for large-scale government support of the industry through budgetary funding ($52.7 billion) and administrative measures [28]. Notably, companies receiving government support are restricted in their ability to implement foreign operations in certain countries, particularly China. "The Foreign Investment Risk Review Modernization Act of June 27, 2018" restricts foreign companies from operating in the U.S. market. The share of foreign capital in U.S. corporations operating in the telecommunications sector is limited to 20% [29]. To a large extent, this law prevents the proliferation of Chinese companies (America and the EU are both toughening up on foreign capital). Regulation of investment transactions and control over technology transfer, the creation of attractive conditions for doing business in the country are aimed at commercialization of R&D results in the domestic market. This makes it possible to stick to "what is invented in America will be made in America" slogan [30]. Measures mirroring U.S. state protectionism of national digital manufacturing are implemented by the European Union within the framework of the "European Chips Act" of February 8, 2022, which provides for the allocation of 43 billion euros ($49 billion), aimed at increasing the industry's share in the international market from 10 to 20%.

It should be noted that digital transformation requires significant governmental efforts. However, full-fledged digital sovereignty can be achieved only if the country has its own national space technologies. The creation of a proprietary satellite system on Earth's orbit determines the ability to guarantee the independence and protection of information flows necessary for military, civil and commercial activities. Space actors at the beginning of the 2020s of the 21st century include more than 60 states that use space technologies in a limited range of areas: communications, navigation, scientific research, etc. At the same time, four states – the United States, Russia, China and India, as well as the European Union – use space activities in a much wider range of sectors. Achieving digital sovereignty is limited by a state's capabilities in outer space. Space technology is also predominantly concentrated in the countries of the Global North. This also limits the development potential of the countries in the Global South and hinders the reduction of the technology gap.

12.4.2 Defining the Tasks of State Regulation of the Digital Industry

The analysis of international experience in the development of digitalization allowed us to identify three public administration tasks.

The first task is *ensuring digital accessibility*, meeting the domestic demand for modern information technologies.

Digital accessibility can be achieved in two ways. The first is the development of domestic production. The second way is the development of international cooperation. It is important to note that these methods can be used in combination with each other. The basic condition for choosing a strategy is the availability and characteristics of the production potential of digital technologies and products. The development of domestic production is a natural task for digital technology-producing countries. States involved in the digital transformation, but without their own digital technologies, have to ensure access to them through international cooperation. This can be achieved in two ways: import of digital technologies and international investment deals.

The second task is *ensuring digital security*, reducing dependence on the risks of negative foreign impact on digital and information processes.

Ensuring digital security requires active government intervention. On the one hand, security in the digital industry plays the role of a guarantor in ensuring uninterrupted digital accessibility. In other words, if foreign suppliers refuse to supply information technology for any reason, the country's economic activity built on digitalization will be interrupted. However, the phenomenon of digital security, unlike security in other industries, is related to the product of the digital industry, which is knowledge. Thus, on the other hand, the management and control of information flows carried out by foreign actors can threaten the interests of national security. Information attacks, dissemination of fallible information, the way the Internet content is presented can be used to influence economic, humanitarian, cultural and political processes in society. In this context, digital security means limiting the negative foreign influence on public behavior. Thus, digital security is seen as ensuring uninterrupted digital accessibility and information security. Digital security requires state restrictions on the cross-border transfer of personal data and the creation of conditions for the development of national companies.

The third task is *ensuring international digital competitiveness* – selling proprietary information technologies on the international market.

Ensuring digital international competitiveness is even more challenging, as it forces domestic producers to adapt to the high standards of the global technology market, and requires the provision of export infrastructure and export support from the state.

12.4.3 Building Alternative Strategies for Digital Development

The choice of strategy for government regulation of digitalization depending on the level of development may differ for countries that are more technologically advanced – the notional Global North, and the less technologically advanced, the notional Global South. The proposed strategies for both groups of countries are shown in Figure 12.5.

The digital transformation strategy of the Global North can be represented by the following four stages.

The first stage of the digital transformation strategy of the Global North. Creating conditions for the development and implementation of the scientific potential, as well as for the conversion of theoretical developments into practical solutions; ensuring the introduction of information technologies into production; supporting the development of digitalization initiatives. State instruments include: state financing of R&D activities in the form of grants

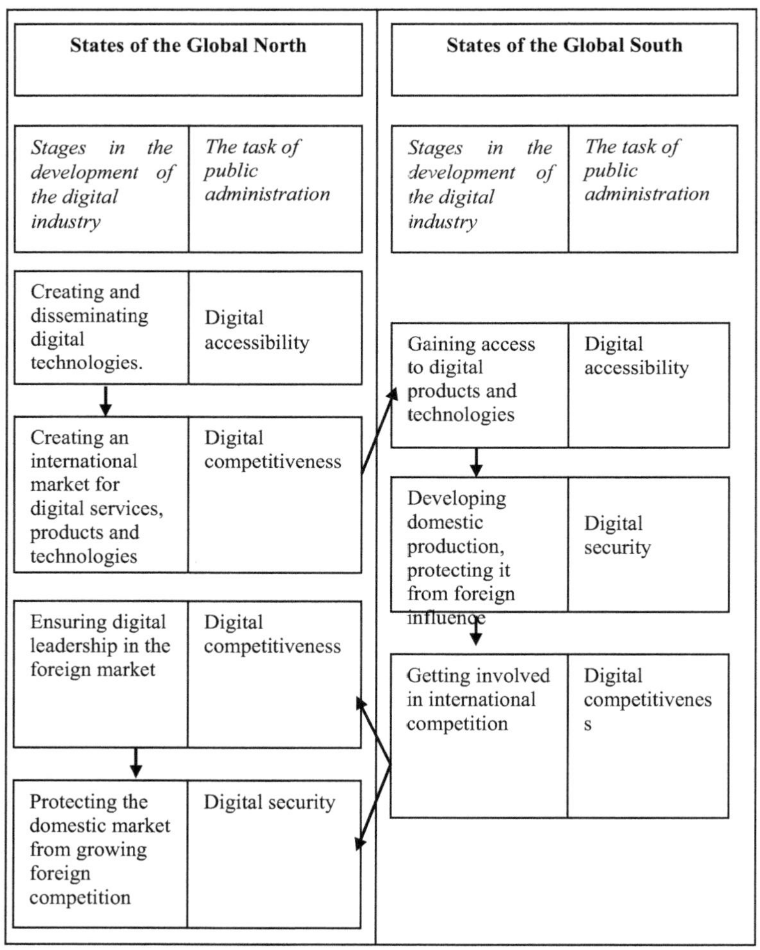

Figure 12.5 Models of Public Governance of Digital Transformation in the Global North and the Global South.

Source: Designed and compiled by the authors.

and subsidies, provision of tax benefits, subsidizing commercial loans for enterprises investing in R&D [19]. The spread of new technologies creates and satisfies domestic demand for digital products and services through domestic production. This has a positive impact on the productivity of the economy.

The second stage of the digital transformation strategy of the Global North. Creating an international market for digital services, products and technologies. At this stage, digital transnational corporations expand into foreign markets and are able to meet the demand in a large number of countries relatively quickly. The role of the state is to create non-discriminatory conditions of access to foreign markets.

The third stage of the digital transformation strategy of the Global North. Securing a leading position in the digital industry in the face of increasing international competition [12]. The proliferation of digital technologies is leading to the emergence of new players in the digital products market. New companies are emerging, including countries in the Global South. Government regulation in the Global North is aimed at creating conditions to ensure national competitive advantages. This is achieved through the use of mechanisms to protect patents and licenses of national companies.

The fourth stage of the digital transformation strategy of the Global North. Protecting the domestic market from rapidly growing foreign competition. The emergence on the national market of alternative suppliers of digital products from foreign countries reduces the share of domestic producers and creates risks of information vulnerability. The state regulation model in this aspect envisages the application of protectionist tools [13]. Protectionist tools include, in particular, moderation of investment deals, control over technology transfer, prohibition of the use of foreign technologies and products in state structures and individual industries, subsidizing demand for national software, administrative barriers, fiscal mechanisms.

Thus, the countries of the Global North are initiating international competition in the field of digital technologies. At the same time, growing competition from developing countries is forcing the countries of the Global North to apply measures to ensure digital security. In addition, the intensification of international competition requires developed countries to make increasing efforts to maintain leadership positions in the digital industry. This forces the countries of the Global South to respond to challenges and design their own digitalization management models.

For the countries of the Global North, maintaining digital leadership in international competition is paramount. Solving this problem leads to tackling the challenge of digital security.

The digital transformation strategy of the Global South can be described through the following three stages.

The first stage of the digital transformation strategy of the Global South. Creating conditions for attracting digital technologies into the country to meet the demand. In the state policy, the prevailing instruments are those which are aimed at ensuring the domestic market access to technologies which are in demand in the society and have no analogous domestic production.

The second stage of the digital transformation strategy of the Global South. Establishing a proprietary digital industry to ensure digital security. Within the framework of this task, the development of domestic production is a priority. Attracting foreign production, accompanied by technology transfer, makes it possible to improve the qualifications of specialists and adapt technological processes to the peculiarities of the national market. State support of enterprises is essential. It can be in the form of grants and subsidies, tax and credit incentives, data localization requirements, funding of training programs for the digital industry. The basis for the establishment and effective development of the digital industry is the development of human capital [16, 21], training and attracting qualified personnel in the field of information technology [3], all of which requires a comprehensive approach in public policy [20]. In addition, the state funding of scientific and research developments [18, 31] and support of related industries [14] play a crucial role.

Digital security is achieved by creating a system of protection against potential negative foreign impact on the industry in the aspect of dependence on foreign supplies, as well as in the aspect of ensuring information independence [4]. The model of state regulation envisages tax instruments [5], restrictive measures for the use of digital products of foreign companies, administrative barriers and budget financing.

The third stage of the digital transformation strategy of the Global South. Ensuring international competitiveness of the digital industry. The model may include subsidizing production and exports, creating export infrastructure, and facilitating investment deals aimed at the presence and expansion of national digital industry companies abroad.

Consistent implementation of the tasks of the Global South strategy makes it possible to ensure competitive positions for developing countries in digitalization.

It is important to understand the mutual influence and interdependence of the economic policies of the Global North and the Global South. The Global North creates and disseminates digital technologies, shaping the international market, which the Global South is gradually joining. For the countries of the Global North, the task of ensuring their own competitiveness in the international and domestic market determines the solution of the digital security task. However, for the countries of the Global South, the order of tasks is different. The digital dependence of these countries on the Global North does not provide an opportunity to enter foreign markets and conduct independent economic policy of the country. Therefore, for the Global South, digital security means a prerequisite for digital international competitiveness.

12.5 Conclusion

The study shows that the highest level of digital development corresponds to countries with high incomes. The lower the level of income in the states, the lower the level of digital accessibility. These results are due to the fact that high-income countries have more financial and investment resources to create and attract digital technologies. At the same time, low-income countries are not able to ensure digital accessibility due to the lack of these resources. The changing structure of digital product exports allows us to foresee an increase in the share of the Global South in production and exports. Although the developed economies collectively dominate international exports, two countries of the Global South, namely India and China, are the largest exporters. This is due to the size of their economies and competitive advantage in digitalization. However, increasing competition in the digital international market and the reluctance of developed countries to lose market share to developing countries creates the risk of digital underdevelopment.

The digital transformation strategies that have been proposed and substantiated in this chapter are based on the level of technological development of states and the state of international competition. This represents the fundamental conditions for decision-making in public administration. It is deemed that in the countries of the Global North and the Global South, the priority of the spheres of state regulation differs. For the countries of the Global North, the task of ensuring leading positions in the international market is the first priority, if solved, it will lead to the solution of the task related to ensuring digital security under increasing competition. For the countries of the Global South, the sequence of state regulation tasks is as follows: achieving digital accessibility, ensuring digital security, and developing digital competitiveness. This strategy is applicable given strong government support for the digital industry in developing countries.

The threat of a widening technological gap between Global North and Global South can be reduced by accelerating the implementation of the catch-up strategy for developing countries. In order to reduce the dependence on digital imports, it is necessary to develop a system of protectionist measures aimed at the development of national production. The need to develop measures to support the national digital industry determines the direction of further global research in the field of state economic management.

References

1. Khorana, S., Escaith, H., Ali, S., Kumari, S. and Do Q. The changing contours of global value chains post-COVID: Evidence from the commonwealth, *Journal of Business Research*, 2022, No. 153, pp. 75–86. (2022).
2. Thangavel, P., Pathak, P. and Chandra, B. Covid-19: Globalization – will the course change? Vision, 2022, Vol. 26, No. 1, pp. 7–10. (2022).
3. Evtodieva, M. G. Personnel and educational policy of Germany in the context of digitalization and development of Industry 4.0, *World Economy and International Relations*, Vol. 66, No. 11, pp. 50–59. (2022).
4. Yalcintas, A., Alizadeh, N. Digital protectionism and national planning in the age of the internet: The case of Iran. *Journal of Institutional Economics*, Vol. 16, No. 4, pp. 519–536. (2020).
5. Cory, Nigel. *The Ten Worst Digital Protectionism and Innovation Mercantilist Policies of 2018*. (2019).

6. Augusto, Alberto & Nichols, Augusto. *Predictions of the Impact of Digital Transformation in 2023 in the Business World*. (2023).
7. Chengetanai, Gibson & Chikati, Ronald. *Key Pillars for Digital Transformation of the Developing World*. 10.4018/978-1-6684-3901-2.ch007. (2022).
8. Sabir, R.A., Niyaz, A.M. and Bakhtiyar, A.G. Social benefits of digitalisation. Grima, S., Özen, E. and Boz, H. (Ed.) *The New Digital Era: Digitalisation, Emerging Risks and Opportunities (Contemporary Studies in Economic and Financial Analysis, Vol. 109A)*, Emerald Publishing Limited, Leeds, pp. 31–47. 10.1108/S1569-37592022000109A003. (2022).
9. Lee, M.-J. and Roh, T. Digitalization capability and sustainable performance in emerging markets: mediating roles of in/out-bound open innovation and coopetition strategy. *Management Decision*, Vol. ahead-of-print No. ahead-of-print. 10.1108/MD-10-2022-1398. (2023).
10. Fouquet, Roger. Thedigitalisation, dematerialisation and decarbonisation of the global economy in historical perspective: the relationship between energy and information since 1850. *Environmental Research Letters*, Vol. 19. 10.1088/1748-9326/ad11c0. (2023).
11. Avi-Yonah, Reuven. International taxation, globalization, and the economic digital divide, *Journal of International Economic Law*, Vol. 26, No. 1, March 2023, pp. 101–109, 10.1093/jiel/jgac068. (2023).
12. Fajgelbaum, P. D., Goldberg, P. K., Kennedy, P. J. and Khandelwal A. K. The return to protectionism, *Quarterly Journal of Economics*, Vol. 1 (135), pp. 1–55. (2020).
13. Gilbert, J., Koska, O. A., Oladi, R. Labor-eliminating technology, wage inequality, and trade protectionism, *Journal of Public Economic Theory*, Vol. 24(6), pp. 1249–1265. (2022).
14. Khmeleva, G. A. Measures to stabilize the technological development of Russian industry in the context of sanctions. Science of the XXI century: current directions of development, No. 1–2, pp. 68–71. (2022).
15. Shastitko, A. E., Meleshkina, A. I., Markova, O. A. The triad of market regulation: antitrust, industrial policy and protectionism in the optical fiber market. *Manager*, No. 1, pp. 47–61. (2021).
16. Vasiliev, A. N., Aganbegyan, A. G. World economy through the prism of changing technological structures and industrial revolutions. *Current problems of the development of economic, financial and credit systems: collection of materials of the X International Scientific and Practical Conference*, Belgorod, pp. 201–209. (2022).
17. Ikejiaku, B., Dayao, C. Competition law as an instrument of protectionist policy: Comparative analysis of the EU and the US. *Utrecht Journal of International and European Law*. Vol. 36, No. 1, pp. 75–94. 10.5334/UJIEL.513. (2021).
18. Kasatkin, P. I., Kovalchuk, Yu. A. and Stepnov, I. M. The financial component of the value of scientific publications, Higher Education in Russia, T. 31, No. 12, pp. 85–102. (2022).
19. Stepnov, I. M., Kovalchuk, Yu. A. The combinational nature of the updated model of technological breakthrough in Russia. *Innovation Management-2019: materials of the international scientific and practical conference*, Moscow, pp. 21–25. (2019).
20. Klepach, A. N. Scientific and technological complex of Russia: problems and prospects for development, Scientific works of the Free Economic Society of Russia, T. 232, No. 6, pp. 117–132. (2021).
21. Miraliev, K. M. and Kamolov, S. G. Human capital as the main resource of a modern organization. *III Gastev Readings: Collection of articles of the International Scientific and Practical Conference*, Moscow, April 14–15, 2021, *Moscow: Russian State University for the Humanities, 2022*, pp. 84–91. (2022).
22. Pane, D. D., and Patunru, A. A. The role of imported inputs in firms' productivity and exports: Evidence from Indonesia, *Review of World Economics*, Vol. 159. pp. 629–672. 10.1007/s10290-022-00476-z (2023).

23. The ICT Development Index, https://www.itu.int/en/ITU-D/Statistics/Pages/IDI/default.aspx, last accessed 2023/11/15.
24. UNCTAD Statistics, https://unctad.org/statistics, last accessed 2023/11/15.
25. Digital Policy Alert (DPA), Recent Activity, https://digitalpolicyalert.org/, last accessed 2023/11/15.
26. Federal Law RF dated July 27, 2006 No. 152-FZ "On Personal Data" (latest edition), https://www.consultant.ru/document/cons_doc_LAW_61801/, last accessed 2023/10/17
27. Federal Law RF of July 21, 2014 N 242-FZ "On amendments to certain legislative acts of the Russian Federation regarding clarification of the procedure for processing personal data in information and telecommunication networks" (with amendments and additions), https://base.garant.ru/70700506/, last accessed 2023/11/15.
28. H.R.4346 - Chips and Science Act. Public Law No: 117–167, Congress.Gov, https://www.congress.gov/bill/117th-congress/house-bill/4346/text, last accessed 2023/11/15.
29. H.R.5841 - Foreign Investment Risk Review Modernization Act of 2018, https://www.congress.gov/bill/115th-congress/house-bill/5841/text, last accessed 2023/11/15.
30. Dmitriev, S.S. Resetting the course to restore the industrial potential of the United States, *World Economy and International Relations*, Vol. 66, No. 8, pp. 61–69. (2022).
31. Klepach, A. N. Social and technological challenges of the Russian economy, Scientific works of the Free Economic Society of Russia, T. 230, No. 4, pp. 103–112. (2021).

13 Examining the Interplay between Technology and Trade in South Countries through a Structural Gravity Model Estimation

Mamta Kumari

13.1 Introduction

The discourse on the development challenges and opportunities facing the South countries is ongoing. Understanding and sustainable solutions for such development challenges, like low per capita income, excessive unemployment, lack of capital, lack of technological advancement, less foreign exchange earnings, political instability, and financial dependency, are some of the major concerns for policymakers. The South countries are still far off from the North countries in terms of access to technological developments. As evident in the literature, technological innovation has led to boosting productivity and efficiency of human activities, job creation, increased investment, and overall economic growth. One of the benefits of technological advancement has also been explored and discussed in terms of trade promotion. There are numerous theoretical writings (Bardhan, 1982; Markusen & Svensson, 1985; Pugel, 1982; Spencer & Brander, 1983) and empirical evidence (Akpa & Chabossou, 2024; Guei, 2022; Lo & Lee, 2024; Sohail & Din, 2024; Xing, 2018; Xu & Zhan, 2023), which confirms that technological capabilities and advancement have significant influence on trade pattern.

Posner's (1961) competitive advantage doctrine and Vernon's (1966) product life cycle theory have supported the significance of technology in international trade. Moreover, Eaton and Kortum (2002) suggested a model that explains how technology and geographic barriers affect bilateral trade flows. Advanced and upgraded technology can lead to a decrease in both costs of international and intranational trade. However, whether technology largely increases international or intranational trade is a matter of importance. Earlier studies done in this context were not able to properly control unobserved multilateral resistance terms owing to country-specific and non-discriminatory features of technology variables (Huong & Park, 2023; Kersan-Škabić, 2021; Rodriguez-Crespo et al., 2021; Tandrayen-Ragoobur et al., 2023).

Therefore, the study endeavors to mitigate such methodological limitations, by identifying the influence of technology on international trade in relation to intranational ones under the theoretically consistent structural gravity model.

DOI: 10.4324/9781032694337-18

The study focuses primarily on the 131 South countries from 1995 to 2016. The South countries have witnessed significant development in terms of internet use and broadband access during the last few decades. The South countries' trade has also increased owing to the South-South cooperation movement. Therefore, it would be essential to see evidence of a relationship between South countries' trade and technology. The study employs ICT (Information and Communication Technology) development as a proxy for technology. The study finds that technology enhances international trade more relative to intra-national trade. This finding suggests that South countries should improve their technology infrastructure to boost trade openness.

The present study makes significant contributions to trade literature in general and South countries' literature in particular. First, the study identifies the direct effects of technological capability on bilateral trade within the theory consistent gravity model specification, thereby leading to unbiased estimates of trade impact of technology (Beverelli et al., 2023). Second, the approach used in the study controls the endogeneity issue of technology variable by including country-pair fixed effects that controls the overlooked endogenous variable and error term relationships. Third, the study provides empirical reinforcement for the positive relation between technology and international trade.

13.2 Literature Survey

This section assesses theoretical and practical literature concerning the relationship between technology and trade.

13.2.1 Theoretical Framework

In traditional as well as modern trade theories, the implications of the technological capability of any country in influencing its trade have been discussed. Traditional trade theories have counted technology as an exogenous factor, while modern literature has focused on endogenous characteristics of technology. This section discusses these two strands of literature.

13.2.1.1 Technology as an Exogenous Factor

The Ricardian model framework explains the role of country-level differences in technological capacities in determining specialization and trade. This model can be extended further to study several critical issues, such as technology gaps, product life cycles, multiple factors of production, and national welfare. Krugman (1979) predicted trade patterns in case of knowhow being transmitted from the North to South. Since, North has a comparative advantage in newly invented goods, they produce and export most of them, the South has a comparative advantage in old products. Markusen and Svensson

(1985) explained the trade pattern in the case of Hicks-neutral technological variations between two countries with identical endowments and taste. They found that countries export goods, which have large productivity advantages. Krugman's (1986) technology gap model has explained that advanced countries usually produce and export more technically advanced goods because their comparative advantage lies in the more innovative goods as the technological gap is less significant for the commodities experiencing the lengthiest technical advancement. Davis (1995) also showed that intra-industry trade takes place under perfect competitive markets and constant returns to scale due to small technological differences.

13.2.1.2 Technology as an Endogenous Factor

Technology is considered an endogenous factor in two cases when technological –progress results from incidental learning, and when it results from intentional investments. This stream of models assumes the transfer of knowledge while manufacturing output. However, the spillovers of knowledge can be across borders, within borders, or even between industries. Ethier (1982) found that international external economies lead to static increases in returns to scale, thereby affecting trade patterns.

In another case, when technologies are the result of intentional investments, a model has been presented to determine the trade-technology nexus. A model assumes that productivity increases owing to the increasing specialization of the production process. The interaction of profits accrues to the invention, and the cost of the invention determines the evolution of new products. The bearing of technological progress on trade is contingent on whether knowledge spillovers are local in scope or global in scope.

In his literature survey on the technology-trade nexus, Cheng (1984) found that most of the theoretical works are based on incorporating endogenous mechanisms of technological progress into the factor endowment model of international trade. In the theoretical landscape, both partial equilibrium models (Bardhan, 1982; Spencer & Brander, 1983) and general equilibrium models (Brecher, 1982; Markusen & Svensson, 1985; Pugel, 1982) have been developed to confirm the relationship between trade patterns and technological progress.

13.2.2 Empirical Literature

Based on the different theoretical frameworks discussed above, several empirical studies have been done concerning technology-trade nexus. Different studies have used different proxies for technological growth, like R&D expenditure, the number of patent applications, and capital formation. One of the significant proxies for technology development is the ICT indicators. Das et al. (2007) argued that the significant use of ICT tends to generate direct effects on trade through decreasing fixed and marginal trade costs. Studies have confirmed that the positive influence of ICT on export (Freund & Weinhold, 2002, 2004). Moreover, Fink et al. (2005) have found that communication costs affect bilateral trade significantly. Clarke and Wallsten (2006) have found an encouraging impact of internet penetration on trade from developing to advanced countries. Vemuri and Siddiqi (2009) suggested the beneficial effect of ICT infrastructure and internet usage on trade. Moreover, similar positive effect has been found in the case of exports of services (Choi, 2010). In the case of emerging countries, Liu and Nath (2013) have found a positive impact of internet subscriptions on emerging economies' trade.

Recently, several studies have been conducted concerning the technology-trade nexus. Akpa and Chabossou (2024) investigated the impact of ICT on cashew nut exports in Benin. They found a differential impact of mobile cellular telephone subscription and internet usage on their exports in the short- and long term. Lo and Lee (2024) found that digitalization and AI intensity facilitate international trade and play a significant role in explaining the trade pattern across countries. Yi et al. (2024) projected that a 1% increase in ICT improvement leads to a surge of mineral resources trade in OECD countries by 0.18% and 0.23% in the short- and long term, respectively. Sohail and Din (2024) found ICT to be one of the factors influencing trade in mineral resources in the world's primary mineral trading economies. Huong and Park (2023) supported the positive relation between ICT and intermediate input trade, which vary by factor intensity and income level of countries. Xiong (2023) observed that technology intensity (R&D intensity) promotes varieties of exported products primarily in technology-intensive sectors. Xu and Zhan (2023) provided evidence that an increase in innovation intensity facilitates China's manufacturing export competitiveness. Another study by Tandrayen-Ragoobur et al. (2023) suggested that improvements in soft infrastructure, including ICT infrastructure, facilitate intra-African trade. Using disaggregated-level data from eight OECD countries, Guei (2022) found the positive impact of innovation intensity (proxied by R&D expenditure) on trade performance. Xing (2018) found that access to ICT and e-commerce adoption improve the East African community's export performance. By setting up a trade model, Kuo and Lee (2018) observed the significant impact of technological differences on trade patterns. Kersan-Škabić (2021) attained a positive impact of using internet on the import of goods and services of Southeast European countries using gravity model. Luong and Nguyen (2021) investigated the impact of ICT on services trade and observed that ICT promotes trade in services. Rodriguez-Crespo et al. (2021) have also suggested that ICT improves bilateral exports. They have also noted the differential impact of several types of technology.

Therefore, existing theoretical frameworks and empirical literature confirm that technological progress and advancement matter for trade. The present study attempts to present evidence on the technology-trade nexus using theoretically consistent structural gravity estimation.

13.3 Data and Methodology

13.3.1 Econometric Specification of Gravity Model

To explore technology-trade nexus, the study applies the structural gravity model (a widely used model in trade literature). The gravity model was originally used to predict the bilateral trade flows between two countries grounded on Newton's law of gravity (Tinbergen, 1962). The basic version of gravity model is expressed as:

$$X_{ij} = C\frac{M_i M_j}{D_{ij}} \tag{13.1}$$

Where X_{ij} is the projected trade of goods and services between country i and j. C is a gravitational factor. M_i and M_j denote the economic sizing of country i and j, respectively. D_{ij} measures remoteness between two countries. Therefore, the model indicates that trade between countries is straight connected to their economic dimensions and indirectly to their remoteness. For econometric analysis, the same model has been used in its log-linear form. Later, several improvements and modifications have been made in the gravity model to provide its theoretical justification. Further, estimating the trade impact of country-specific variables becomes one of the challenges for gravity models. Therefore, some adjustments to structural gravity model have been made (Yotov et al., 2016).

Therefore, referring to Beverelli et al. (2023) and Yotov et al. (2016), the study employs augmented structural gravity specification with country-specific technology indicators. A composite index measuring countries' level of ICT development has been constructed. The composite index includes percentage of individuals using the internet, landline phone, and cell phone subscriptions per 100 people.

The augmented gravity specification is:

$$\begin{aligned} X_{ijt} = \exp[&\beta_1 \mathrm{ICT}_{it} \times \mathrm{BORDER}_{ij} + \beta_2 \mathrm{BORDER}_t^{\mathrm{BORDER}_{ijt}} \\ &+ \beta_3 \mathrm{GRAV}_{ijt} + \chi_{it} + \nu_{jt} + \mu_{ij}] \times \varepsilon_{ijt} \end{aligned} \tag{13.2}$$

In Equation (13.2), X_{ijt} denotes trade flows between exporter i and importer j at period t. It includes both internal and international trade flows of manufacturing goods only. The variable of interest is $\mathrm{ICT}_{it} \times \mathrm{BORDER}_{ij}$, which is an interaction between ICT_{it} (exporting country's ICT development score at time t), and BORDER_{ij} (international trade dummy taking value of 1 for international trade, otherwise 0). Therefore, the bilateral term, $\mathrm{ICT}_{it} \times \mathrm{BORDER}_{ij}$ estimates how ICT development impact international trade differently to intranational trade. The new bilateral term makes it possible to estimate the trade effect of technology, even in case of including country-year fixed effects. The positive coefficient signifies that ICT development facilitates international trade more as compared to internal trade. In contrast, the negative sign suggests that ICT development improves internal trade more as compared to international trade. This equation captures the impact of ICT development on the exporter side trade. However, it is noteworthy that the estimated value of the impact of ICT development on the exporter and importer side will be similar as a country's score of ICT development will be identical irrespective of being an exporter or an importer. The estimations with ICT development of importers and exporter sides have been reported in the robustness check section 4.2. The time-invarying determinants of trade flows are also included in the model to check whether the baseline results are consistent or not. $GRAV_{ijt}$ represents the determinants of trade costs that vary by time. They are RTA (a dummy variable taking the value of one if regional trade agreements have been formed between countries, otherwise zero) and WTO membership (a dummy variable taking the value of one if both countries are WTO members, otherwise zero). Moreover, $BORDER_{ijt}$ (time-varying border dummies) captures the globalization effect. This is an interaction between international trade dummy and different years of study. χ_{it} denotes the exporter fixed effects varied by time and v_{jt} denotes importer fixed effects varied by time. Both the effects control multilateral resistances and time-varying observed and unobserved exporter and importer-specific characteristics, respectively. The country-pair fixed effects are denoted by μ_{ij}, which absorb all time-insensitive bilateral determinants of trade costs and further, controls for potential endogeneity of technology variable. ε_{ijt} is a remainder error term. A similar specification has been used to estimate the trade impact of individual dimensions of ICT development indicator, separately. This will provide an understanding of whether trade impact varies by different facets of ICT development, and further which of the facets is having more impact or less impact.

The PPML estimation technique has been used to examine the influence of ICT development on trade. This PPML method approximates the gravity model in its multiplicative form. The method has two main advantages. First, it accounts for heteroskedasticity. Second, it enables the model to consider even zero trade flows (Silva & Tenreyro, 2006).

13.3.2 Data and Their Sources

The source for manufacturing trade data is the Structural Gravity Manufacturing Database. This database is provided by Monteiro (2020). This database offers international and internal trade data of manufacturing goods for 186 countries across the years 1980–2016. The data on time-invarying and time-varying determinants of trade flows is extracted from the USITC dynamic gravity dataset. Principal component analysis has been used to construct an index measuring countries' level of ICT development. The indicators used to

Table 13.1 Descriptive Statistics

Variables	*Observations*	*Average*	*Standard Deviation*	*Minimum*	*Maximum*
Trade flows (US$)	269, 956	5.90e+08	6.00e+10	0	1.38e+13
ICT development Index	4774	0.482	0.303	7.28e-08	1
WGI Index	3605	0.004	1.000	−1.838	2.470
GDP (in constant 2015 US $)	2160	1.22e+11	5.58e+11	2.97e+07	9.49e+12
GDP per capita (in constant 2015 US $)	2160	5937.462	9832.261	194.873	69679.09

Source: Author's own computation.

create an index are sourced from the World Development Indicators provided by the World Bank. Based on the readiness of trade flow data, this research employs panel data of 131 South countries over the period 1995–2016. The list of South countries is taken from the United Nations' Finance Centre for South-South Cooperation. Using principal component analysis, the governance index has been constructed. The indicators used to construct this index are sourced from the Worldwide Governance Indicators prepared by World Bank. A descriptive statistic for variables of interest has been illustrated in Table 13.1.

13.4 Results and Discussions

13.4.1 Empirical Findings

The baseline gravity estimation results are shown in Table 13.2. The exporter- and importer-year fixed effects are incorporated in all the calculations. Column (1) presents the results estimated from the standard OLS method. The results show expected signs of all bilateral trade proxies, except the common colony. The distance restricts trade between countries, while a common border and common language foster trade between them. Moreover, the impact of trade integration and being a member of WTO on trade is positively significant. The coefficient estimating the impact of ICT development on global trade relative to internal ones is insignificant with negative sign, suggesting that the OLS method is biased to estimate the gravity model as it excludes all zero trade flows and does not control heteroskedasticity. Therefore, the model has been estimated with the PPML method. The PPML method is applied with the exclusion and inclusion of country-pair fixed effects, and the resultant estimates are explained in columns (2) and (3) of Table 13.2, respectively. The estimations without country-pair fixed effects suggest that ICT development facilitates internal trade more than international trade, as the estimated coefficient is significant with a negative sign. Further, there are expected results for all bilateral trade cost variables, presence of the RTA, and WTO membership.

Table 13.2 Impact of Technology on Trade Using Structural Gravity Estimations

	(1)	*(2)*	*(3)*
	OLS	PPML	PPML with pair fixed effects
Border × ICT	−0.306	−0.782**	0.226***
	(1.153)	(0.328)	(0.059)
Distance	−1.539***	−0.291	
	(0.036)	(0.194)	
Common Colony	−0.190	1.427**	
	(0.265)	(0.601)	
Common Border	0.875***	0.407*	
	(0.106)	(0.215)	
Common language	0.838***	0.899***	
	(0.042)	(0.160)	
WTO membership	0.216**	1.787***	0.301***
	(0.088)	(0.179)	(0.084)
RTA	0.897***	0.297*	0.177***
	(0.048)	(0.171)	(0.054)
Constant	28.110***	27.545***	27.456***
	(0.617)	(1.464)	(0.078)
No. of Observations	190401	269956	254110
R^2	0.673		
Pseudo R^2		0.987	0.999

Note: Standard errors are in parentheses. They are clustered at country pairs. The outcome variable is bilateral trade in PPML estimates and logarithm of trade in OLS estimates. Time-varying border dummies are incorporated in all specifications, but not stated in the table due to brevity. ICT, Information and Communication Technology; FE, fixed effect. *, **, and *** denote that coefficient is statistically significant at 10%, 5%, and 1%, respectively.

The PPML results with country-pair fixed effects suggest a progressive impact of WTO membership and regional trade integration on international trade. Owing to the addition of country-pair fixed effects, the estimations of all time-insensitive bilateral trade cost variables are omitted. Moreover, the sign of a coefficient estimate of ICT development becomes positive and significant, suggesting that ICT development enhances international trade more as compared to internal trade. In other words, ICT development decreases international trade costs to a greater extent than domestic ones. Such a difference in results from previous estimates shows that inclusion of country-pair fixed effects controls all time-invarying measures of bilateral trade costs. It also accounts for potential endogeneity of technology variable, and thereby leads to unbiased estimates.

Statistically, the result implies that an increase in one unit of ICT development leads to a 25% ([exp (0.226) −1] ×100) increase in international trade in relation to internal trade. The results seem stable with the theoretical framework (Eaton & Kortum, 2002) and empirical literature (Akpa & Chabossou, 2024; Guei, 2022; Lo & Lee, 2024; Sohail & Din, 2024; Xing, 2018; Xu & Zhan, 2023), confirming the influence of technology on trade patterns. There can be several plausible reasons to explain the positive influence of ICT development on international trade flows. Firstly, using ICT may reduce fixed and marginal export costs and thus improve exports. These costs include those related to firms' abilities to gather knowledge about overseas markets and consumer tastes and communication costs with trading partners and customers overseas. Second, the use of ICT may reduce uncertainties in obtaining and transferring relevant material that is required for smooth international transactions.

Moreover, the reason behind facilitating international trade more than internal trade through ICT development can be twofold. First, international trade typically requires more access to ICT services as compared to domestic trade; thus, international trade might be more responsive to ICT development as compared to internal trade. Second, international transactions rely more on ICT services than domestic transactions. Therefore, any improvement in the level of ICT development will increase international trade more than internal trade.

Besides estimating impact of overall indicator on trade, the study has further assessed the effect of individual dimensions of the overall indicator on trade. The estimates are shown in Table 13.3. All the results have been estimated with PPML estimator, including exporter and importer fixed effects varied by time along with country-pair fixed effects. As is clear from Table 13.3, the results of all the individual dimensions are consistent with the main results. Comparing the results statistically, it is found that mobile cellular subscriptions are having the greatest positive impact on international trade flows, followed by use of internet by individuals and landline phone subscriptions. The increased number of cell phone, individuals having the internet, and landline phone subscriptions leads to a surge in international trade relative to internal trade by 13.9% (see column 3 of Table 13.3), 8.5% (see column 2 of Table 13.3), and 3.1% (see column 1 of Table 13.3), respectively.

13.4.2 Robustness Checks

The present study has also performed several robust checks. All the results have been calculated in a standard fixed-effects gravity regression. First, the study controls the effect of development levels of countries in the specified model to circumvent the problem of omitted variable bias. Thus, GDP and GDP per capita have been introduced in the specified Equation (13.2). Both variables have interacted with the international border dummy. As is shown in column (1) of Table 13.4, the inclusion of GDP in estimating the model does not alter the positive influence of ICT on trade. The result seems consistent once GDP per capita is included in the estimation (see column 2 of Table 13.4).

Second, the study further controls the effects of governance quality. The governance variable has interacted with the international trade dummy and was added to the model. The result has been shown in column 3 of Table 13.4. The result indicates that controlling the effect of governance quality does not modify the sign and significance of the ICT variable. However, it is noteworthy that the coefficient is smaller in magnitude than the main results.

Table 13.3 Impact of Technology on Trade (with Alternative Proxies for Technology)

	(1)	(2)	(3)
	Fixed Telephone subscriptions (FTS)	Individuals using the Internet (II)	Mobile cellular subscriptions (MCS)
RTA	0.173***	0.164***	0.150***
	(0.054)	(0.054)	(0.053)
WTO membership	0.285***	0.271***	0.274***
	(0.084)	(0.084)	(0.081)
Border × Fixed telephone subscriptions	0.031*		
	(0.017)		
Border × Individuals using internet		0.082***	
		(0.024)	
Border × Mobile cellular subscriptions			0.130***
			(0.027)
Constant	27.457***	27.446***	27.402***
	(0.079)	(0.076)	(0.076)
No. of Observations	254110	254110	254110
Pseudo R^2	0.999	0.999	0.999

Note: Standard errors are shown in parentheses. They are clustered at country pairs. The individual indicators have been used in logarithm form. *, **, and *** denote significance level at 10%, 5%, and 1%, respectively.

Third, the results of trade impact of ICT on the importer side have been reported in column 4 of Table 13.4. As the estimations suggest, the effect of importers' ICT development on trade is equivalent to impact of exporters' ICT development (as shown in column 3 of Table 13.2).

13.5 Conclusion and Scope for Future Research

The study focuses on re-evaluating the impact of technology on international trade in the context of South countries. Using theoretically consistent structural gravity estimation, the study provides a consistent and robust estimation technology-trade relationship. The study assesses the technology-trade relationship for the sample of 131 South countries during the years 1995–2016. The bilateral trade flow of manufacturing goods, including both international and internal trade, is treated as a dependent variable. The technology variable is proxied by three ICT development indicators, namely number of landline telephone and cell phone subscriptions per 100 people, and percentage of individuals using internet.

The gravity model results using the PPML estimation method suggest that the overall ICT development index facilitates international trade more as

Table 13.4 Robustness Check Results

	(1)	*(2)*	*(3)*	*(4)*
	GDP	GDP per capita	Governance	Importer ICT
WTO membership	0.234***	0.233***	0.346***	0.301***
	(0.084)	(0.083)	(0.087)	(0.084)
RTA	0.111**	0.109**	0.163***	0.177***
	(0.055)	(0.053)	(0.053)	(0.054)
Border × ICT	0.285***	0.278***	0.223***	
	(0.060)	(0.060)	(0.064)	
Border × GDP	0.466***			
	(0.167)			
Border × GDP per capita		0.399***		
		(0.141)		
Border × WGI			−0.015	
			(0.086)	
Border × Exporter ICT				
Border × Importer ICT				0.226***
				(0.059)
Constant	26.133***	27.159***	27.605***	27.456***
	(0.495)	(0.144)	(0.084)	(0.078)
No. of Observations	239773	239773	198866	254110
Pseudo R^2	0.999	0.999	0.999	0.999

Note: Standard errors are in parentheses, and they are clustered by country pairs. The variables GDP and GDP per capita are transformed into logarithm form. *, **, and *** denote significance level at 10%, 5%, and 1%, respectively.

compared to internal trade in South countries. The disaggregated findings show that the increased number of subscriptions of mobile cellular accelerates international trade the most, followed by individuals' internet usage and subscriptions of fixed telephone. The robustness of the results is proved.

Therefore, the findings of the study suggest that South countries should continue their efforts to develop their ICT infrastructure to increase their trade, leading to more development. Moreover, policymakers of South countries should focus more on policies that encourage citizens to purchase mobile cellular subscriptions, as this will promote international trade more as compared to other policy measures.

The study can be extended further in many ways. The present study has been conducted in the context of South countries. In future, a study can be performed to compare the technology-trade nexus between North and South economies. Moreover, the result of the study is merely applicable to the manufacturing sector. Therefore, studies can also be performed to evaluate the differential effects of ICT development on different manufacturing, agriculture, and service industries.

13.6 Policy Implications

The results of the study offer several policy implications. First, it provides evidence that South countries with poor ICT quality may significantly gain from digitalization. The proof of the trade-improving impact of ICT is especially notable for South countries that have been focusing on promoting their world trade. Therefore, policymakers need to incentivize the adoption of ICT technologies, such as by providing low-interest business loans, grants, and subsidies for communities, and tax exemptions for industries shifting to the digital sector. Second, the disaggregated results suggest that South countries may focus the most on policies that would promote the use of mobile cellular services, followed by policies to promote the use of the internet and subscription of landline telephone by their citizens, for promoting international trade.

References

Akpa, A. F., Chabossou, A. F.: Effect of information and communication technology on cashew nut export in Benin, *Research in Globalization*, 8, 100197 (2024).

Bardhan, P. K.: Imports, domestic production, and transnational vertical integration: A theoretical note. *Journal of Political Economy*, 90(5), 1020–1034 (1982).

Beverelli, C., Keck, A., Larch, M., Yotov, Y. V.: Institutions, trade, and development: identifying the impact of country-specific characteristics on international trade. *Oxford Economic Papers*, 76(2), 469–494 (2023).

Brecher, R. A.: Optimal policy in the presence of licensed technology from abroad. *Journal of Political Economy*, 90(5), 1070–1078 (1982).

Cheng, L.: International trade and technology: A brief survey of the recent literature. *Weltwirtschaftliches Archiv*, 120(1), 165–189 (1984).

Choi, C.: The effect of the Internet on service trade. *Economics Letters*, 109(2), 102–104 (2010).

Clarke, G. R., & Wallsten, S. J.: Has the internet increased trade? Developed and developing country evidence. *Economic Inquiry*, 44(3), 465–484 (2006).

Das, S., Roberts, M. J., Tybout, J. R.: Market entry costs, producer heterogeneity, and export dynamics. *Econometrica*, 75(3), 837–873 (2007).

Davis, D. R.: Intra-industry trade: A heckscher-ohlin-ricardo approach. *Journal of International Economics*, 39(3–4), 201–226 (1995).

Eaton, J., Kortum, S.: Technology, geography, and trade. *Econometrica*, 70(5), 1741–1779 (2002).

Ethier, W. J.: National and international returns to scale in the modern theory of international trade. *American Economic Review*, 72(3), 389–405 (1982).

Fink, C., Mattoo, A., Neagu, I. C.: Assessing the impact of communication costs on international trade. *Journal of International Economics*, 67(2), 428–445 (2005).

Freund, C., Weinhold, D.: The Internet and international trade in services. *American Economic Review*, 92(2), 236–240 (2002).

Freund, C. L., Weinhold, D. (2004). The effect of the Internet on international trade. *Journal of International Economics*, 62(1), 171–189 (2004).

Guei, K.: On the role of innovation and market structure on trade performance: Is Schumpeter right? *European Journal of Management and Business Economics*, 32(2), 241–256 (2022).

Huong, N. T. T., Park, D.: Impact of ICT development on bilateral intermediate input trade: Considering cross-country heterogeneity. *The Journal of International Trade & Economic Development*, 32(8), 1291–1311 (2023).

Kersan-Škabić, I.: Information and communication technology development and foreign trade in the region of South-East Europe. *South East European Journal of Economics and Business*, 16(2), 101–113 (2021).

Krugman, P.: A model of innovation, technology transfer, and the world distribution of income. *Journal of Political Economy*, 87(2), 253–266 (1979).

Krugman, P.: A 'technology gap' model of international trade. In: Jungenfelt, K., Hague, D. (eds.) *Structural Adjustment in Developed Open Economies*, pp. 35–61. Palgrave Macmillan UK, London (1986).

Kuo, K. H., Lee, C. T.: Technology advantage, heterogeneous talent and trade. *The Singapore Economic Review*, 63(05), 1307–1317 (2018).

Liu, L., Nath, H. K.: Information and communications technology and trade in emerging market economies. *Emerging Markets Finance and Trade*, 49(6), 67–87 (2013).

Lo, C. P., Lee, Y.: Digitalization, AI intensity, and international trade. *Annals of Economics and Finance*, 25(1), 251–273 (2024).

Luong, T. A., Nguyen, T. H.: The impact of ICT on service trade. *The Singapore Economic Review*, 66(04), 1073–1086 (2021).

Markusen, J. R., Svensson, L. E. O. (1985). Trade in goods and factors with international differences in technology. *International Economic Review*, 26(1), 175–192 (1985).

Monteiro, J-A.: *Structural Gravity Manufacturing Sector Dataset: 1980–2016*. World Trade Organization, Geneva (2020).

Posner, M. V.: International trade and technical change. *Oxford Economic Papers*, *13*(3), 323–341 (1961).

Pugel, T. A.: Endogenous technological change and international technology transfer in a Ricardian trade model. *Journal of International Economics*, 13(3–4), 321–335 (1982).

Rodriguez-Crespo, E., Marco, R., Billon, M.: ICTs impacts on trade: A comparative dynamic analysis for internet, mobile phones and broadband. *Asia-Pacific Journal of Accounting & Economics*, 28(5), 577–591 (2021).

Silva, J. S., Tenreyro, S.: The log of gravity. *The Review of Economics and Statistics*, 88(4), 641–658 (2006).

Sohail, M. T., Din, N. M.: How do digital inclusion and energy security risks affect mineral resources trade? Evidence from world-leading mineral trading countries. *Resources Policy*, 89, 104528 (2024).

Spencer, B. J., Brander, J. A.: International R & D rivalry and industrial strategy. *The Review of Economic Studies*, 50(4), 707–722 (1983).

Tandrayen-Ragoobur, V., Ongono, P., Gong, J.: Infrastructure and intra-regional trade in Africa. *The World Economy*, 46(2), 453–471 (2023).

Tinbergen, J.: *Shaping the world economy: Suggestions for an international economic policy*. Twentieth Century Fund, New York (1962).

Vemuri, V. K., Siddiqi, S.: Impact of commercialization of the internet on international trade: A panel study using the extended gravity model. *The International Trade Journal*, 23(4), 458–484 (2009).

Vernon, R.: International investment and international trade in the product cycle. *Quarterly Journal of Economics*, 80(2), 190–207 (1966).

Xing, Z.: The impacts of Information and Communications Technology (ICT) and E-commerce on bilateral trade flows. *International Economics and Economic Policy*, 15(3), 565–586 (2018).

Xiong, T.: The effect of technological intensity on international trade. *International Economics*, 176, 100456 (2023).

Xu, Z. Y., Zhan, M. H.: Technology innovation and the duration of export competitiveness. *Applied Economics Letters*, 30(10), 1381–1384 (2023).
Yi, C., Chao Ma, H., Zhao, K.: Impacts of digital economic transformation and green growth on trade flows of mineral resources. *Resources Policy*, 90, 104664 (2024).
Yotov, Y. V., Piermartini, R., Larch, M.: *An Advanced Guide to Trade Policy Analysis: The Structural Gravity Model*. WTO Publications, Geneva (2016).

Part V

Regional Cooperation and Integration among Regions of the Global South

14 Global Partnerships for a Sustainable Future

China's Role in Latin America's Energy Transition

Rafael Ferraz dos Santos, Victor Hugo Souza de Abreu, Sandra Oda, and Andrea Souza Santos

14.1 Introduction

The energy transition, driven by the need to reduce greenhouse gas emissions and tackle climate change, has become globally relevant [1]. Latin America, with its wealth of natural resources, has great potential for adopting clean energy sources like solar, wind, biomass, and hydroelectric power [2]. Effective implementation requires investments and advanced technologies, inviting international involvement, including from China [3]. China, one of the world's leading economic and energy powers, has faced significant environmental challenges due to rapid industrialization and urbanization, particularly air pollution and carbon emissions [4–6].

The Chinese government has boosted investments in clean energy projects globally, including Latin America, while also maintaining a significant presence in the oil and gas sector through trade agreements and partnerships with state-owned companies [5, 7–13]. This dual approach raises debates about the environmental impacts and contradictions between pursuing clean energy and relying on fossil fuels [14]. Sustainable development discussions have gained prominence since the UN's 1972 Environment Conference and the 1992 adoption of the concept, with the Sustainable Development Goals (SDGs) integrating environmental impacts into development debates [15]. Sustainability is defined as actions that do not compromise resources, ensuring their reproduction, and requires regulatory and political actions for sustainable development and economic progress [16]. The COVID-19 pandemic disrupted the global clean energy sector, particularly in China and the US, and a drop in oil prices hindered renewable energy progress, causing temporary setbacks in low-carbon production systems and delaying projects and goals [17–19].

This chapter analyses China's role in Latin America's energy transition, focusing on energy security, social development, and environmental progress. It explores the dynamics that influence China's impact on the region's energy landscape, offering insights crucial for policymakers, stakeholders, and researchers.

DOI: 10.4324/9781032694337-20

14.2 Methodology

The data collection process began with exploratory reading to compile a dataset from diverse sources, prioritized for their relevance and contribution to the research. This was followed by selective reading to ensure consistency and coherence in the content. A meticulous approach was maintained to ensure the quality and reliability of the materials, with detailed records including authorship and publication dates. In the synthesis and analytical reading phase, the data provided deep insights and a comprehensive perspective on the subject, considering potential implications for future stakeholders. This rigorous methodology, an extensive literature review, not only grounded the research in reliable sources but also revealed valuable insights into the implications and future prospects for stakeholders (Figure 14.1).

14.3 Literature Review

The concept of a world in dispute is common. However, cooperation can be found at all levels of organization. From simple to multicellular organisms, parasites, insects, and human beings, cooperation is part of every nature when it comes to the formation of a society.

Although historical energy transitions often resulted from the scarcity of dominant sources, reduced prices of alternatives, or advancements in extraction and generation technologies, the current transition includes the need to address global challenges requiring collective effort beyond supply security and economic efficiency [20]. Prioritizing local gains over broader considerations in state-level decision-making is likely to fail in the medium or long term, making it crucial to prioritize the common good over narrow interests [21]. The pursuit of sustainable development, emphasized by the UN's Sustainable

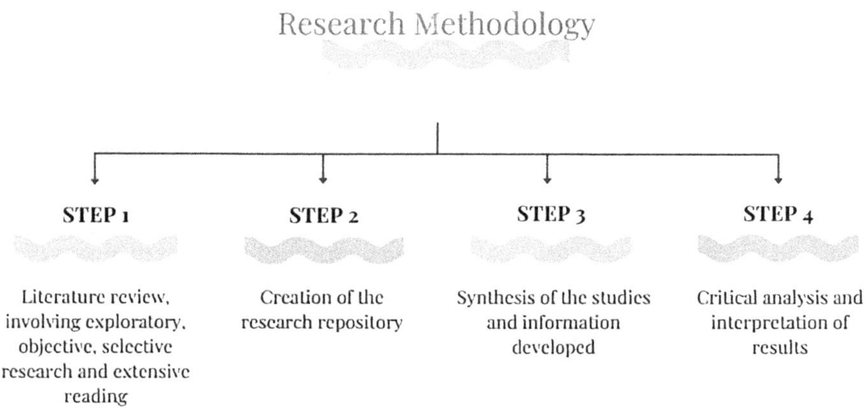

Figure 14.1 Stages of implementation of the methodology in the current study.

Source: Own elaboration (2024).

Table 14.1 Alignment of Sustainable Development Goals (SDGs) with Energy Transition Concepts, Source: Methodology Adopted by the Authors.

Sustainable Development Goals	*Energy Transition Concepts*
SDG 7: Affordable and Clean Energy	**Renewable Energy Sources**: Incorporating solar, wind, hydroelectric, and geothermal power to provide clean, accessible, and affordable energy.
SDG 11: Sustainable Cities and Communities	**Smart Grids and Urban Mobility**: Developing advanced power grids and promoting electric vehicles to enhance energy efficiency and reduce emissions in urban areas.
SDG 13: Climate Action	**Carbon Neutrality**: Striving for net-zero carbon emissions through the adoption of clean energy and carbon capture technologies.
SDG 15: Life on Land	**Biomass and Bioenergy**: Using organic materials for energy production to reduce dependency on fossil fuels and mitigate land degradation.

Development Goals (SDGs), addresses global challenges like poverty, inequality, climate change, and environmental degradation, with renewable energy central to achieving SDG 7 (Affordable and Clean Energy) and intersecting with other SDGs [22]. (See Table 14.1)

This section aims to explore the challenges of the energy transition and the relevance of the alliance between China and Latin America, two important players who, acting as protagonists of this transition and despite their differences, have been establishing promising and potentially beneficial agreements for both.

14.3.1 Energy Transition: Global Challenges and Implications

The energy transition can be defined as a process of transformation in which there is a significant change in the predominant sources of energy, from a matrix based on fossil fuels to a cleaner and more sustainable matrix, made up mainly of renewable sources [1, 23]. After decades of oil dominance, the need to mitigate the environmental impacts of greenhouse gas emissions and reduce dependence on fossil fuels is increasingly threatening the hegemony of hydrocarbons [24].

The transition to renewable energy faces several challenges. The existing fossil fuel-dependent infrastructure complicates integrating renewable sources, requiring investments in smart energy technologies to manage variability and intermittency [1, 25]. Although renewable energies are becoming more competitive, they still require significant initial investments and efficient technologies, posing financial challenges, especially for developing countries with limited resources [24, 26]. Energy security is another concern, as dependence on fossil fuels creates supply vulnerabilities. In the short and medium term, different energy sources must coexist, impacting socio-economic and environmental factors. Policies and market forces can accelerate low-carbon technology adoption, but the process is slow [3]. Political and ideological barriers also pose challenges, as the transition involves deep structural changes that may face resistance from established fossil fuel interests. Promoting informed debate is essential to find consensus and solutions considering different contexts [25, 27]. Societal perceptions and behavioral shifts are significant hurdles. Despite growing awareness of sustainability, cultural norms and consumer behaviors rooted in fossil fuel use persist. Overcoming these patterns requires technological innovation and comprehensive education to foster acceptance of renewable energy alternatives [27–29].

Moreover, geopolitical dynamics and global cooperation are essential, as energy markets are interconnected, and international collaboration is needed to address shared challenges like energy security, climate change mitigation, and equitable access to resources [30]. Diplomatic efforts and multilateral agreements are crucial in facilitating this transition. Innovation and research are also critical, with breakthroughs in renewable energy technologies, energy storage solutions, and energy efficiency necessary to overcome barriers and accelerate the transition [29, 31].

14.3.2 Latin America in the Context of the Energy Transition

The Latin American and Caribbean (LAC) region, comprising 42 countries with diverse geographical and ecological characteristics, is a key player in the global energy transition due to its abundant natural resources and renewable energy potential. The region's rich diversity in energy sources—solar, wind, biomass, hydroelectric, and geothermal—provides a strong foundation for adopting clean and sustainable energy [32]. However, challenges remain, such as the 14 million people without access to energy and the high socio-environmental impact of existing infrastructure, which conflict with the World Energy Council's (WEC) principles of security, equity, and sustainability [33, 34].

Hydroelectric power is the main source of energy generation in Latin America's energy matrix, accounting for 45% of the supply compared to just 16% globally. The region's large rivers and basins enable the construction of these plants, with significant capacities in countries such as Brazil, Argentina, Colombia, and Peru, although they remain vulnerable to climate variations [35]. Latin America also has great potential for solar and wind energy due to high solar radiation in areas like the Atacama Desert and northeastern Brazil, and constant winds along the Brazilian coast and Argentine Patagonia [34]. Additionally, biomass is a prominent energy source, supported by a strong agricultural and forestry industry, providing organic waste for biogas and bioenergy production. In Brazil, sugarcane is widely grown for ethanol and energy generation from bagasse [24].

Latin America recognizes the importance of coming together and taking action in the face of climate change. No single country or region can solve this issue alone. However, the region faces the complexity of its states, which are known for their volatility and where social actors influence governmental decisions. These dynamics deeply influence national policies and international interactions. Despite the consolidation of democracy in the region, it takes on various forms, often characterized by centralized, personality-driven, and occasionally authoritarian state systems [36].

14.3.3 The Chinese Presence in Latin America's Energy Transition

Chinese investments have significantly impacted the global stage, particularly in the energy sector, as they shift toward green policies to combat climate change [32, 37]. In Latin America, where the energy matrix includes fossil fuels and renewables like hydroelectric power, China has been a key player in transitioning to renewable energy sources, primarily since 2015 [38]. In Brazil, China has not only been the top trading partner since 2009 but also became the second-largest destination for Chinese investments in 2010 [39].

In Latin America, Chinese investments in renewable energies have been pivotal. Since 2021, the Chinese state-owned State Grid has controlled over half of Chile's electricity distribution through a controlling stake in Compañía General de Electricidad (CGE). In Brazil, the company has been the majority shareholder of Companhia Paulista de Força e Luz (CPFL) and CPFL Renováveis since 2017, with investments totaling R$17.36 billion [40]. China, despite its reliance on coal and oil and high socio-economic inequality, has been diversifying its energy sources as outlined in its recent five-year plans. From 2011 to 2020, Sino-Brazilian cooperation included 19 bilateral acts, with four focused on renewable energies [41]. The 13th Plan (2016–2020) emphasized economic openness and regulatory facilitation for Chinese investments abroad [39]. The 14th Five-Year Plan (2021–2025) focuses on sustainable industrial development, science, technology, the digital economy, transforming the energy matrix, mitigating climate change, and enhancing international relations [8].

Among the major Chinese investments in renewable energy over the last decade, notable projects include BYD's 2015 assembly plant for photovoltaic solar panels in Campinas, supported by a R$2.0 billion contribution from the Chinese development bank ICBC to Petrobras. In 2016, the Chinese state-owned State Grid's investments raised the country's annual investment volume to over R$10 billion for the first time. In 2017, the São Simão hydropower plant was acquired by State Power Investment Corporation (SPIC) in an auction for R$7.18 billion [42].

14.3.4 The Prospects and Dilemmas of Brazil in the Energy Transition

Brazil stands out for presenting significant advantages and facing common challenges in the region. Currently, the country distinguishes itself by using renewable sources for 48% of its energy matrix, in contrast to the global average of approximately 14%. Brazil excels even more in the electrical matrix, with 85% of its electricity coming from renewable sources, compared to the global average of around 30% [26].

Brazil's energy matrix, characterized by a diverse mix of renewable and non-renewable sources, is a significant geopolitical asset amid global climate change. This advantage involves complex interactions among governments, industry, academia, and civil society, requiring enhanced cooperation and dialogue to develop effective policies, foster technological innovation, and encourage public participation [43]. Prior to 2005, Chinese investments in Brazil were limited and aligned with sector-specific strategies of Chinese companies. However, since 2010, there has been a marked increase in the scale of investments and the presence of Chinese companies in Brazil, particularly in renewable energy and the electrical sector, leveraging Brazil's natural advantages and established infrastructure [44]. Over the past decade, foreign companies, especially from China, have participated more in Brazil's energy sector, facilitated by government-promoted auctions offering opportunities to acquire energy assets and export innovative technologies. While these investments bring economic and technological benefits, they also raise debates and challenges regarding national sovereignty and environmental impact. Proper regulatory supervision and thorough assessment of associated impacts and benefits are necessary for sustainable development [27].

Brazil has historically been key to regional energy integration due to its size and economic power, enabling significant regional projects even with modest domestic demand. However, Brazil's regional influence has waned due to several factors, including the political-economic turmoil during Dilma Rousseff's presidency (2011–2016), the Car Wash scandal, and the nationalist policies of former President Jair Messias Bolsonaro (2019–2022), who prioritized alignment with the United States and scaled back participation in multilateral organizations [6]. The current president, Luiz Inácio Lula da Silva, is actively working to restore Brazil's international stature and strengthen its global commitments through numerous international visits.

14.3.5 COP27: Significant Achievements and Urgent Pending Issues in the Fight against Climate Change

The United Nations Climate Change Conferences provide a platform for countries to negotiate and transition toward a sustainable global economy. At COP27 in Sharm el-Sheikh, Egypt, states renewed their commitment to limiting global temperature rise to below 2°C, emphasizing the 1.5°C goal from the Paris Agreement. Achieving these goals requires reducing greenhouse gas emissions across all sectors, especially energy. States were encouraged to promote renewable energy technologies, implement energy efficiency measures, reduce coal-fired power without carbon capture, and eliminate inefficient fossil fuel subsidies [45]. The summit highlighted the need for $4 trillion annually in renewable energy investments by 2030 to achieve zero emissions by 2050 and established a compensation fund for nations severely affected by climate change, with guidelines to be presented at COP28 [46]. In 2022, China funded nearly half of global low-carbon energy investment but resisted contributing to the international loss and damage fund, citing its developing country status. This disagreement underscores the need for broader financing options, possibly involving emerging countries or new financial structures like multilateral banks [45].

14.4 Results and Discussion

The approach between regions became more pronounced during the second decade of the 21st century, marked by a significant strengthening of relations through a surge in Chinese investments. Between 56% and 66% of these investments were directed at three key countries: Brazil, Chile, and Mexico. During this decade, these countries enhanced their importance as trade partners with China. For instance, in 2011, Chinese imports from these nations were 4.87% of the total. By 2020, this figure increased to 6.68%, as shown in Figure 14.2. This growth represents a 60% increase in the volume of dollars invested, highlighting the depth and dynamism of these economic connections.

Figure 14.2 illustrates this upward trajectory, highlighting the growing importance of Brazil, Chile, and Mexico in China's trade relationships. Figure 14.3 further emphasizes that while each of these countries may have a different level

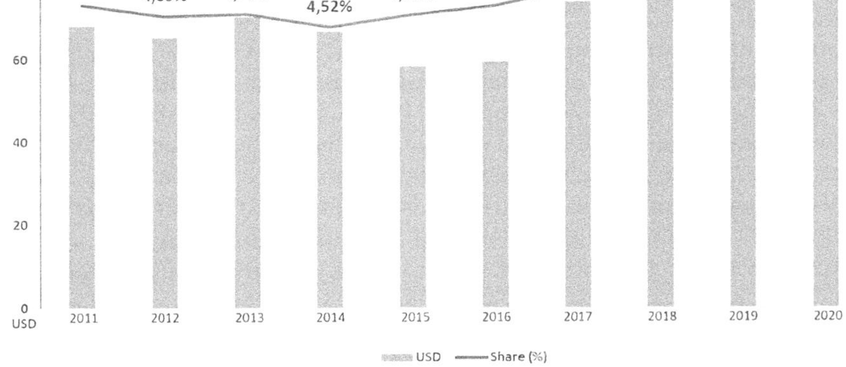

Figure 14.2 Accumulated imports from China to Brazil, Chile, and Mexico, in billions of US dollars.

Source: Adapted from Growth Lab [47].

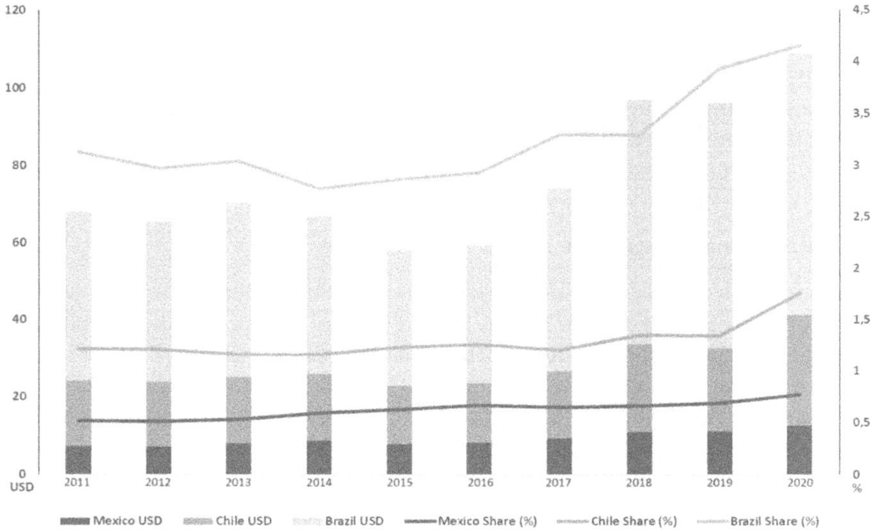

Figure 14.3 Segregated values of imports from China to Brazil, Chile, and Mexico, in billions of US dollars.

Source: Adapted from Growth Lab [47].

of significance in this progression, all three have experienced an upward trend, demonstrating the strengthening ties between China and Latin America [48].

This intensified relationship between China and Latin America presents various opportunities and challenges, from trade and economic cooperation to political and cultural exchanges. As these two regions continue to engage in increasingly diverse and multifaceted collaborations, both sides need to navigate this evolving landscape with a focus on mutual benefit and sustainable development [12].

During the progress made so far in China-Latin America relations, the energy agenda has taken on an increasingly prominent role. In 2011, China took first place in energy consumption [49], its sources are still mostly non-renewable, such as coal (58%) and oil (20%), as well as hydroelectric (8%), the latter, although renewable, has a significant environmental impact [50].

With a population of around 1.4 billion and projected economic growth of 5.82% by 2030 according to the Atlas of Economic Complexity [47], energy security is a major motivation for China to seek agreements that include the acquisition of oil, on which it is heavily dependent, making it the world's second-largest importer [14]. China's presence in Latin America dates back to the 1990s when the China National Petroleum Corporation signed its first international contract in Peru in 1993. Another significant milestone was in 1997 with the start of oil exploration in two Venezuelan fields. The largest increase in oil imports from the region occurred at the turn of the century; oil sent to China rose from 0.92% in 2003 to 13.42% in 2018 [51].

Latin America's strategic position enhances its appeal to China, not just as an alternative oil route to the tense Strait of Hormuz but also as a burgeoning hub for renewable energy. Although most oil from the region does not reach China due to refinery capacity limitations, Latin America offers a viable pathway via the Pacific Ocean, avoiding areas of frequent military tensions and tanker attacks [14, 52]. Concurrently, there has been a significant shift toward renewables in the region, driven by Chinese investments. The 35th edition of the Bulletin of International Economics and Policy by the Institute for Applied Economic Research [53] highlights China's substantial contribution to the global increase in photovoltaic capacity and its dominance in solar module production. Since 2019, Chinese firms have quadrupled the region's solar capacity from 363 megawatts to about 1.4 gigawatts by 2022 [53]. These results are summarized in Figure 14.4.

China has invested in several renewable energy projects in Latin America, including the Ituverava Solar Park in Bahia, the Punta Sierra Wind Farm in Chile, and the Cauchari Solar Park in Argentina. Table 14.2 outlines China's global investments, with a clear emphasis on wind and solar power projects in Latin America.

Notably, Latin America is in a privileged position in current Chinese planning. Compared to the Asian countries with which China has a massive presence, the Latin America region, given its potential described throughout this research, represents a small fraction of emissions derived from units sponsored by Chinese capital, in addition to presenting a higher percentage of projects from clean energy generation [56].

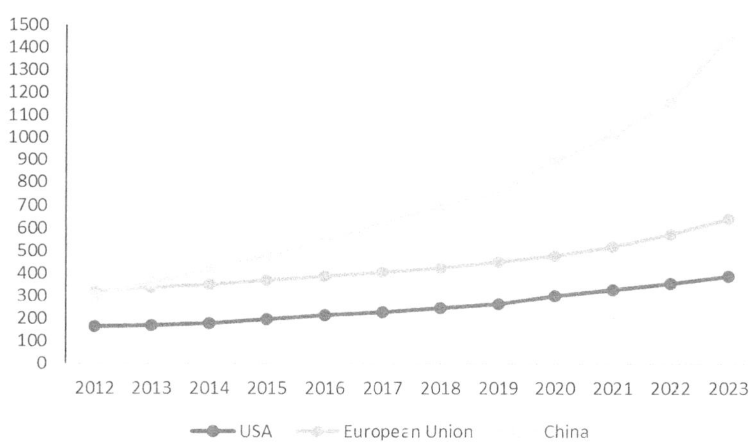

Figure 14.4 Installed electricity generation capacity, in GW, from renewable sources in China, the European Union, and the United States (2012–2023).

Source: Adapted from IRENA [54].

Table 14.2 Distribution of Power Generation Projects with Financing and/or Foreign Direct Investment (FDI) from China (2000–2023)

Energy Source	*North America*	*Latin America*	*Africa*	*Asia*	*Europe*	*Oceania*	*Total*
Wind	101	4.170	620	603	3.776	3.265	12.535
Solar	35	2.250	342	2.255	1.368	1.339	7.589

Source: Adapted from Global Development Policy Center [55].

The China-CELAC Forum, established in 2015, enhances cooperation, trade, and investment between China and Latin America and the Caribbean. In 2022, it focused on poverty reduction and development, leveraging China's expertise in eradicating extreme poverty and emphasizing the link between poverty reduction and environmental improvement [57]. During the 15th BRICS summit, Brazil's Economy Minister Fernando Haddad reaffirmed the country's commitment to clean energy and becoming a global exporter, promoting "neo-industrialization" by adopting new technologies and prioritizing sustainability. However, China's technological dominance challenges Brazil and Latin America's natural advantages in clean energy [58].

In the US, a consultancy by Wood Mackenzie reported a 17% reduction in solar energy generation capacity in the third quarter of 2022, linked to trade barriers and supply chain restrictions from the US Department of Commerce's anti-circumvention tariffs on Southeast Asian solar products [59]. China, with over 80% of the global share in solar panel manufacturing, challenges US policies to protect local industry. Haddad reaffirmed Brazil's role in the energy transition without threatening China's supremacy. Concerns about production concentration affecting developing nations highlight the need for attention to ensure technological and environmental advances drive social and economic progress in Brazil and Latin America [60]. Many Latin American economies rely on exporting natural resources while importing technology from advanced countries. To overcome this dependence, a strategy combining access to advanced foreign technologies with domestic technology development is needed.

14.5 Final Considerations

China's unique experience in the energy transition highlights its proactive approach to global climate challenges. The recent shift toward "green" capital in China is a testament to its capability to lead the global energy transition. It is crucial for global actors, especially those from the Global South, to remain vigilant of China's socio-environmental responsibility. The Sustainable Development Goals are a pragmatic starting point for significant advancements in areas such as poverty eradication, food security, health, education, and inequality reduction. These goals require collaboration for the well-being of the global population and the sustainable management of the planet's resources.

To ensure an inclusive and sustainable energy transition in Latin America, we need to strengthen local capacities and promote regional technological development. We must incorporate climate justice considerations, ensuring vulnerable communities aren't left behind. Support mechanisms must help communities adapt to climate change and transition to low-carbon economies, highlighting the need for equity.

Latin America's natural advantages extend beyond biodiversity and geographical complexity, making it a key player in global energy security and the transition to cleaner, more sustainable sources. The region's strategic position as an alternative transportation route for oil and other products underscores its significance. It is crucial to exploit energy resources in a way that promotes national sovereignty and critically analyze alternative models like China's. This is essential to ensuring a sustainable and sovereign energy future.

References

1. de Assis, T. F., Monteiro, T. G. M., de Abreu, V. H. S., D'Agosto, M. D. A., Santos, A. S.: Enabling the Green Bonds Market for Sustainable Transport Projects Based on the Measure/Monitoring, Reporting and Verification Method. In *Carbon Footprints of Manufacturing and Transportation Industries*, pp. 1–24. Springer Nature Singapore, Singapore (2022).
2. Roett, R., Paz, G.: *China's Expansion into the Western Hemisphere: Implications for Latin America and the United States*. 1st edn. Brookings Institution Press, Washington, DC (2008).
3. Ferreira, T. V. B., Machado, G. V.: The role of planning in the energy transition: more light and less heat. *Revista Brasileira de Energia*, 27(2), 123–135 (2021).
4. Yu, L.: China's strategic partnership with Latin America: a fulcrum in China's rise. *International Affairs*, 91(5), 1047–1068 (2015).
5. Bullock, G.: The belt and road initiative: China's rise, America's balance, and Latin America's struggle. *History Honors Papers*, 7, 4–213 (2020).
6. Fuser, I., Abrão, R. A. F.: Energy integration in South America: perspectives, impasses and obstacles. *Brazilian Journal of Latin American Studies*, 19(37), (2020).
7. Gachúz Maya, J. C., Urdinez, F.: Geopolitics and geoeconomics in the China–Latin American relations in the context of the Us–China trade war and the COVID-19 pandemic. *Journal of Current Chinese Affairs* 51(1), 3–12 (2022).
8. Ugarteche, O., De León, C.: China and the change of the energy matrix in Latin America: a global political economy approach. *Brazilian Journal of Political Economy* 42(2), 442–459 (2022).
9. Kuwayama, M., Rosales, O. China and Latin America and the Caribbean: building a strategic economic and trade relationship. *ECLAC* (2012).
10. Hogenboom, B., Baud, M., Gonzalez, V., Steinhö, R.: *China's Economic and Political Role in Latin America*. CEDLA–UvA, Amsterdam (2022).
11. Hsiang, A. C.: China rising in Latin America: more opportunities than challenges. *Journal of Emerging Knowledge on Emerging Markets* 1(1), 4 (2010).
12. Jenkins, R.: China and Latin America. In American hegemony and the rise of emerging powers. In: Regilme, S. S., Parisot, J. (eds.) *American Hegemony and the Rise of Emerging Powers – Cooperation or Conflict*, 1st ed, pp 182–197. Routledge, London (2017).

13. Ellis, R. E.: *The Future of Latin America and the Caribbean in the Context of the Rise of China*. Center for Strategic and International Studies, Washington, DC (2018).
14. Haffner, J. A., Maia, A. V.: Chinese energy security and the role of South America. *OIKOS* 21(3), 231–245 (2022).
15. Roma, J. C.: Os objetivos de desenvolvimento do milênio e sua transição para os objetivos de desenvolvimento sustentável. *Ciência e cultura* 71(1), 33–39 (2019).
16. De Faria, J. H.: Towards a critical theory of sustainability. *Organizations and Sustainability* (2014).
17. Kanda, W., Kivimaa, P.: What opportunities could the COVID-19 outbreak offer for sustainability transitions research on electricity and mobility? *Energy Research & Social Science* 68, 101666 (2020).
18. Priya, S. S., Cuce, E., Sudhakar, K.: A perspective of COVID 19 impact on global economy, energy and environment. *International Journal of Sustainable Engineering* 14(6), 1290–1305 (2021).
19. Manzanedo, R. D., Manning, P.: COVID-19: Lessons for the climate change emergency. *Science of the Total Environment* 742, 140563 (2020).
20. Cazalbón, A. Y. A., Kerr-Oliveira, L.: Integración energética en América del Sur: retrospectiva y desafíos en el contexto de la transición energética. *Revista tempo do mundo* 32, 61–96 (2023)
21. Liang, W.: Pulling the region into its orbit? China's economic statecraft in Latin America. *Journal of Chinese Political Science* 24(3), 433–449 (2019).
22. Dias, R.: O papel das energias renováveis no cumprimento dos ODS: oportunidades e desafios. *Recima21 - Revista Científica Multidisciplinar* 5(1), e514845 (2024).
23. de Assis, T. F., Ricci, L. M., Monteiro, T. G. M., de Abreu, V. H. S., D'Agosto, M. D. A., Santos, A. S.: Sustainable Transport Indicators and Mitigation Actions Applied to the Green Bond Principles. In *Carbon Footprints of Manufacturing and Transportation Industries*, pp. 139–169. Springer Nature Singapore, Singapore (2022).
24. De Abreu, V. H. S., Da Costa, M. G., Da Costa, V. X., De Assis, T. F., Santos, A. S., D'Agosto, M. D. A.: The role of the circular economy in road transport to mitigate climate change and reduce resource depletion. *Sustainability* 14(14), 8951 (2022).
25. Losekann, L., Tavares, F. B.: Política Energética no BRICS: desafios da transição energética (No. 2495). Text for Discussion (2019).
26. Delgado, F., Filgueiras, R.: A crise do setor de óleo e gás e os desafios da transição energética brasileira. *Revista Conjuntura Econômica* 76(04), 36–39 (2022).
27. Santos, A. S., de Abreu, V. H. S., de Assis, T. F., Ribeiro, S. K., Ribeiro, G. M.: An Overview on Costs of Shifting to Sustainable Road Transport: A Challenge for Cities Worldwide. In Muthu, S.S. (eds) *Carbon Footprint Case Studies - Environmental Footprints and Eco-Design of Products and Processes*, pp. 93–121. Springer, Singapore (2021).
28. De Assis, T. F., De Abreu, V. H. S., Carneiro, P. J. P., Marcio De Almeida, D. A.: Contribution of Best Practices to Promote Sustainable Urban Freight Transport. *Revista GEINTEC-Gestao Inovacao e Tecnologias* 11(4), 5928–5949 (2021).
29. Da Costa, M. G., de Abreu, V. H. S., de Assis, T. F., da Costa, V. X., de Almeida D'Agosto, M., Santos, A. S.: Life cycle assessment and circular economy strategies for electric vehicle: A systematic review on mitigating climate change and reducing resource depletion in road transportation. *Carbon Footprints of Manufacturing and Transportation Industries*, 113–137 (2022).
30. De Assis, T. F. D., Marujo, L. G., de Abreu, V. H. S., da Costa, M. G., Rodrigues, L. M., D'Agosto, M. D. A.: Best practices to support the transition towards sustainable logistics from the perspective of brazilian carriers. *Sustainability* 15(18), 13434 (2023).

31. De Abreu, V. H. S., D'Agosto, M. D. A., Angelo, A. C. M., Marujo, L. G., Carneiro, P. J. P.: Action Plan Focused on Electric Mobility (APOEM): A tool for assessment of the potential environmental benefits of urban mobility. *Sustainability* 15(13), 10218 (2023).
32. Shoujun, C.: Introduction: Sino-Latin American Relations in Strategic Transition. In *China and Latin America in Transition: Policy Dynamics, Economic Commitments, and Social Impacts*, pp. 1–11 (2016).
33. World Energy Council: *World Energy Trilemma Index*. World Energy Council, London, United Kingdom (2019).
34. González, A. B. P., Viglio, J. E., Da Costa Ferreira, L.: Energy Communities in Latin America: Towards an energy transition based on the notion of Good Living. *Development in Question* 20(58), (2022).
35. Godoy, E., Profeta, D., Chávez, J.: *The Future of Hydroelectric Power in the Face of the Climate Crisis in Latin America*. (2022)
36. Barroso, L. R.: Revolução tecnológica, crise da democracia e mudança climática: limites do direito num mundo em transformação. *Rei - Revista Estudos Institucionais* 5(3), 1234–1313 (2019).
37. Wise, C., Chonn Ching, V.: Conceptualizing China–Latin America relations in the twenty-first century: the boom, the bust, and the aftermath. *The Pacific Review* 31(5), 553–572 (2018).
38. Ugarteche, O., de León, C., García, J.: China and the energy matrix in Latin America: Governance and geopolitical perspective. *Energy Policy* 177, 113435 (2023).
39. Kroetz, M. E., Sanchez-Badin, M. R., Sato, L. M.: Os planos estratégicos chineses e seu impacto nos investimentos no Brasil: uma análise do setor de energias renováveis. *Conjuntura Austral* 13(61), 93–107 (2022).
40. Shutte, G. R.: *Oasis for Capital: Fertile Ground for the Gold Rush*. The Dynamics of Chinese Productive Investments in Brazil, Appris, Curitiba (2020).
41. Boa Nova, V. V. F., Khalil Jabbour, E. M., Cambuhy, M. C.: A nova economia do projetamento como estágio superior de intervenção do Estado chinês no território. *Geosul* 38(87), 69–93 (2023).
42. Santos, J. H.: *Chinese Investment in Brazil: An Analysis of the Brazilian Energy Sector in the Recent Period*. Course Conclusion Paper, Universidade Estadual de Campinas, Institute of Economics (2021).
43. Santos, F. M. Energy transition: Framework and challenges. *Revista Videre* 11(22), (2019).
44. Corrêa, A. P.: *Industrialização, demanda energética e indústria de petróleo e gás na China. China Em Transformação: dimensões econômicas e geopolíticas do desenvolvimento*, 189–236 (2015).
45. Instituto Brasileiro de Petróleo e Gás - IBP: *A COP-27 e Suas Implicações Para a Indústria de Energia*, IBP. (2022).
46. The Nature Conservancy: *COP27 Termina Com Acordo Histórico Para Perdas e Danos*. (2022).
47. Growth Lab: The Atlas of Economic Complexity. Homepage, https://growthlab.hks.harvard.edu/, last accessed 2023.
48. Miyakawa, S. S.: *The Chinese Rise and the Strategic Role of China-Latin America Economic Relations*. Course Conclusion Paper in Graduation in Economic Sciences, School of Economics, Administration, Accounting and Actuarial Sciences, Pontifícia Universidade Católica de São Paulo (2022).
49. Casal-Campos, A., Fu, G., Butler, D., & Moore, A. (2015). An Integrated Environmental Assessment of Green and Gray Infrastructure Strategies for Robust Decision Making. *Environmental Science & Technology*, 49 14, 8307–8314. https://doi.org/10.1021/es506144f.

50. Dudley, B. P.: BP statistical review of world energy 2019: an unsustainable path. *Energy Academy and Center for Economic Reform and Transformation*, 1–2 (2019).
51. United Nations.: *United Nations Commodity Trade Statistics Database (UN Comtrade)*. (2019).
52. Koch-Weser, I.: *Chinese Energy Engagement with Latin America: A Review of Recent Findings*. Inter-American Dialogue, Washington, DC (2015).
53. Instituto de Pesquisa Econômica Aplicada - IPEA.: *BEPI Boletim de Economia e Política Internacional*. (2023).
54. International Renewable Energy Agency - IRENA.: Renewable Capacity Statistics 2024. In: *International Renewable Energy Agency*. Abu Dhabi (2024).
55. Global Development Policy Center.: *Policy Research For A Better World*. (2023).
56. Nunes, T. G. A., Ungaretti, C. R.: Chinese financing of renewable energy projects in Latin America: An analysis in light of the challenges of climate change. *Bulletin of International Economics and Politics* 35, (2023).
57. Niu, H.: A new era of China-Latin America relations. *Anuario de integración* 11(2015), 39–51 (2015).
58. Agência Brasil. (2023, agosto 17). Haddad: Brics pode ser coerente sem antagonismo com outros fóruns. Agência Brasil. https://agenciabrasil.ebc.com.br/economia/noticia/2023-08/haddad-brics-pode-ser-coerente-sem-antagonismo-outros-foruns
59. Solar Power World.: Installed Solar Capacity down 17% from Last Year, but Still the Most-Installed Electricity Source in America. Homepage, solarpowerworldonline.com, last accessed 2023.
60. Van Barneveld, K., Quinlan, M., Kriesler, P., Junor, A., Baum, F., Chowdhury, A., … & Rainnie, A. (2020). The COVID-19 pandemic: Lessons on building more equal and sustainable societies. *The economic and Labour Relations Review*, 31(2), 133–157.

15 Foreign Direct Investment and Economic Development

The Case of Global South Economies

Ash Narayan Sah and Avisha Malik

15.1 Introduction

According to the World Bank, "Foreign direct investment (FDI) refers to investments made by investors outside of their domestic economies to obtain long-term ownership or effective control over a business enterprise." FDI serves as a catalyst for economic change and fosters growth (Philip et al., 2021; Yimer, 2023). It offers developed and emerging countries prospects for expansion, diversification, and integration into international markets. The significance of FDI is quite evident in the prospering economies of the Global South, particularly the group of 11 nations referred to as the GS-11. The GS-11 group consists of the original BRICS nations, namely Brazil, Russia, India, China, South Africa, and six recently added member countries: the UAE, Saudi Arabia, Iran, Ethiopia, Egypt, and Argentina. Together, these economies have emerged as a powerhouse in the global economic landscape (Chakraborty, 2018). The increasing impact of the GS-11 on the global economy has attracted significant attention, especially in the context of the recently held G-20 summit hosted by India (2023). The summit brought attention to the wide range of challenges faced by the Global South nations, including the complexity of multilateral trade negotiations, achieving financial stability, and promoting sustainable economic growth and development. To redress these issues, incoming investments from advanced nations play an essential role (Biørn & Han, 2017).

Further, Table 15.1 provides insights into the economic profiles of GS-11 nations, highlighting China as the world's second largest economy with a GDP of 17.7 trillion dollars. It is followed by India and Brazil, ranking fifth and ninth globally. Given the significance of the GS-11 nations, it is evident that this group will emerge as the hub of economic activity in the coming decades. Notably, India and China have large populations (see Table 15.1), which determines the size of the consumer market in the world. The other GS-11 member countries contribute substantially to the global population, making them prime destinations for foreign investors (Desbordes & Wei, 2017).

Next, examining the gross domestic savings as a percentage of GDP, China and India lead with 43.14% and 27.70%, respectively. In contrast, South Africa

DOI: 10.4324/9781032694337-21

Table 15.1 Economic profile of GS-11 nations

Country (2023)	*Population (in million)*	*GDP (US $ billion)*	*Gross Domestic Savings (% of GDP)*	*Trade Openness Index*	*FDI inflows (US $ million)*	*Inflation rate (in %)*	*Real Interest rate (in %)*
UAE	10.06	509.18	45.38	147.29	20,667	0.61	4.79
South Africa	61.53	380.91	18.67	53.11	19,286	4.34	3.91
Saudi Arabia	32.82	1,070	33.59	55.83	40,659	1.24	4.76
Russia	143.2	1,860	33.45	49.15	40,450	4.07	10.93
Iran	86.55	366.44	42.62	34.34	1,425	30.05	-7.05
India	1430	3,730	27.70	42.05	44,727	4.70	1.80
Ethiopia	105.75	155.8	18.94	23.62	4,259	14.39	7.20
Egypt	105.67	398.4	6.44	30.62	5,122	13.69	5.56
China	1410	17,700	46.08	37.30	344,075	2.00	1.45
Brazil	204.25	2,130	20.37	35.82	46,439	4.35	7.90
Argentina	46.76	621.83	23.26	31.63	6,903	40.85	92.15

Source: International Monetary Fund.

and Egypt lag behind, with savings rates of only 18.67% and 6.44%, respectively. The low savings rate ultimately results in a low level of domestic investment (Kapingura, 2018). This can lead to reduced funds for investment in infrastructure, health facilities, and other productive areas, hindering long-term economic development (Ribaj & Mexhuani, 2021). The trade openness index measures a country's engagement in foreign trade, calculated as the ratio of total trade to GDP. The index is highest for the UAE, reflecting its extensive integration into the global economy.

Furthermore, recent FDI trends reveal that China has attracted the highest FDI, amounting to $344,075 million. Other countries like Brazil, India, Russia, and Saudi Arabia have also attracted significant investment inflows, establishing the Global South as a leading choice for investors. In terms of inflation rates, Brazil, China, India, and Russia exhibit lower rates than the newly added GS-11 members. Notably, the UAE boasts an exceptionally low inflation rate of 0.61%, even lower than China's. Additionally, real interest rates in Brazil and Russia present attractive investment opportunities due to promising returns, contrasting with China and India's rates, which hover around 2%. The diverse economic profiles of GS-11 nations highlight their individual economic strengths, which will effectively contribute to the development of the Global South. Therefore, this chapter aims to explore the role of incoming FDI in the economic growth and development of Global South nations, particularly the GS-11. These countries collectively hold a substantial share of the world economy, and it is important to analyse the intricate dynamics between FDI and economic development within this group. This will yield invaluable insights into emerging economic trends, trade patterns, and investment flows. It will further help these nations formulate informed strategies to achieve sustainable development goals (SDGs) and utilise FDI to benefit their economies.

15.2 Review of Literature

All investments, whether domestic or foreign, are integral in sustaining economic growth and development in host nations (Chanegriha et al., 2020). In this regard, FDI emerges as the preferred choice for stimulating economies and emerging markets due to its perceived effectiveness (Philip et al., 2021). This is because FDI not only injects capital but also facilitates the transfer of skills, managerial expertise, technology, employment, and other essential resources (Aziz, 2022). This aids in catalysing economic development across multiple dimensions. Multiple studies have investigated the correlation between FDI and economic growth. The existing literature provides extensive evidence supporting the notion that FDI has a beneficial effect on the economies of host countries. The study by Mehic et al. (2013) found that FDI played a pivotal role in fostering economic growth in seven Southeast European countries from 1998 to 2009. Similarly, Omri (2014) discovered that FDI contributed to the growth of 13 MENA countries from 1990 to 2010 by accumulating the domestic capital stock. Owusu-Nantwi and Erickson (2019) observed a long-run equilibrium relationship between FDI and economic growth in a panel of ten South American nations from 1980 to 2015, with short-run bidirectional causality between these variables (Akadiri et al., 2020; Owusu, 2021; Nupehewa et al., 2022; Kumari et al., 2023). Saleem et al. (2020) also identified long-run cointegration between FDI, economic growth, and trade openness in five South Asian countries (Arvin et al., 2021; Banday et al., 2021). Numerous other studies have also examined the long-term nexus between FDI inflows and economic growth and reported a positive association between them (Saidi et al., 2020; Asafo-Agyei & Kodongo, 2022; Rao et al., 2023; Sobirov et al., 2023; Karahan & Çolak, 2024).

Furthermore, prominent economic theories like the Solow-Swan model and endogenous growth theory provide critical insights into economic growth dynamics. The Solow-Swan model posits capital accumulation as a primary driver of economic growth. FDI plays a vital role in this accumulation process by injecting crucial capital investment into host countries, thereby enhancing their productive capacity (Li & Tanna, 2019; Chanegriha et al., 2020). Conversely, the endogenous growth theory emphasises the significance of knowledge and technological progress in fostering long-term economic growth. FDI acts as a channel for multinational enterprises to transfer technologies, managerial expertise, and knowledge spillovers to domestic firms (Jude, 2016; Salim et al., 2017; Morita & Nguyen, 2021). Thus, existing literature affirms the essential role of FDI inflows in driving growth and sustained economic development.

15.3 Methodology

This study uses a descriptive methodology to analyse the nexus between FDI and economic development. The secondary data is collected from multiple sources, including the World Bank database, OECD statistics, and the International Monetary Fund. Descriptive tools like pie charts, bar graphs, and trend lines illustrate the findings. The scatter plot fitted with straight lines is used to demonstrate the relation between GDP per capita and FDI per capita in the case of Global South nations.

15.4 FDI Trends in GS-11 Economies

The GS-11 economies have evolved dynamically in the past two decades. With the addition of six new countries, the GDP share in the world economy has increased from 25.77% to almost 30% for these nations (see Figure 15.1). Their population share has also increased from 40.9% to 46% due to expansion (see Figure 15.2). This is mainly because the Global South economies include India and China, the two most populous countries in the world, providing foreign

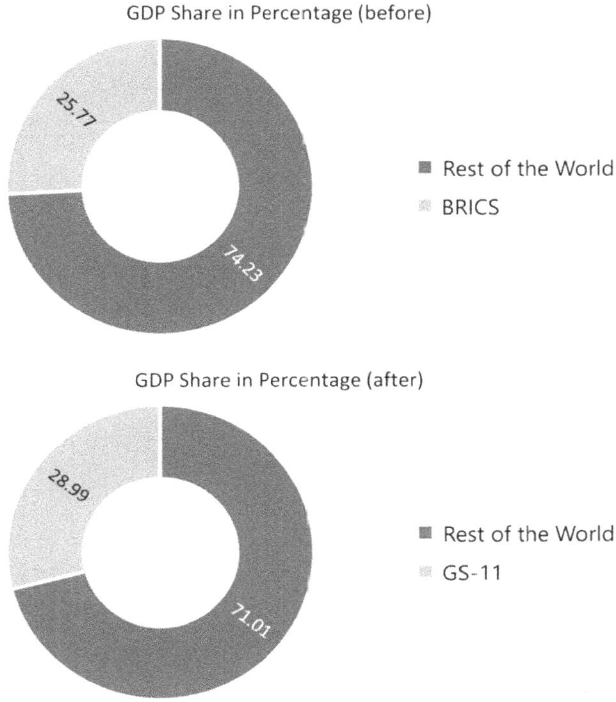

Figure 15.1 GDP shares in percentage.

Source: World Bank database.

investors with access to large consumer markets with increased purchasing power (Aziz, 2022).

In recent years, the group has witnessed significant growth in FDI inflows, signifying the attractiveness of these economies to foreign investors. The share of annual average FDI inflows in GS-11 countries from 2000 to 2022 (see Figure 15.3) shows that China receives the highest amount of inward FDI amongst all the nations. It attracts almost 53% of the FDI flowing into Global South nations. This is due to its large market size and export-oriented growth strategy (He, 2018). The government's significant domestic investment in infrastructure, technology, and manufacturing sectors has also attracted foreign investors in China (Kroeber, 2020).

Next, China is followed by Brazil, which attracts about 16% of the total incoming investment from abroad, largely owing to its abundant natural resources (Nistor, 2015). The country has the world's largest rainforest, spread over 500 million square kilometres, and is rich in mineral reserves, making it an attractive destination for FDI across various sectors. Over the past 20 years, India and Russia have received nearly equal amounts of FDI, with India

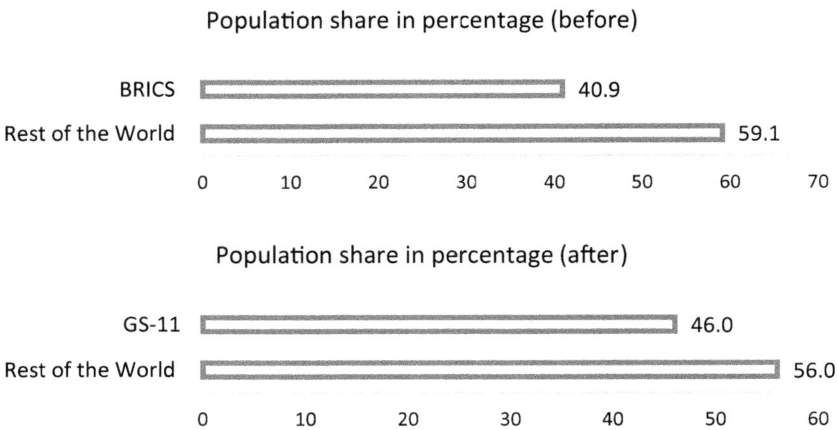

Figure 15.2 Population shares in percentage.

Source: World Bank database.

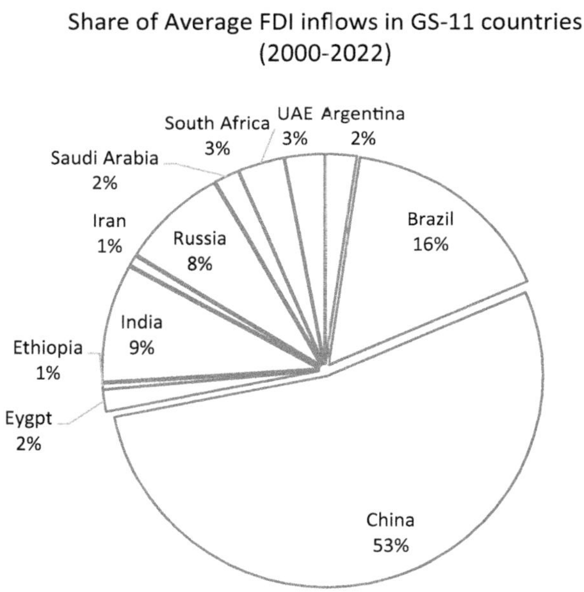

Figure 15.3 Share of annual average FDI inflows in GS-11 nations.

Source: World Bank database.

receiving 9% and Russia receiving 8% of the total FDI inflows. Multinational companies invest in India due to its growing consumer base, favourable economic reforms, and booming service sector. On the other hand, a significant flow of FDI into Russia is due to the ample supply of natural resources (oil, gas, and metals) and the availability of skilled labour (Domínguez-Jiménez & Poitiers, 2020).

Other nations in the GS-11 group have received comparatively lower FDI than China, Brazil, India, and Russia. Overall, the annual FDI inflows across GS-11 nations exhibit diversity, with varying degrees of investment. The incoming investment from abroad depends on each country's distinctive economic capabilities, sector-specific distribution, and policies for facilitating foreign investment. These inflows, irrespective of their scale, play pivotal roles in the comprehensive development and growth trajectories of these countries.

15.5 Impact of FDI Inflows on Economic Growth

FDI is critical in promoting economic growth by enhancing capital formation in host countries (Li & Tanna, 2019). This mechanism serves as a cornerstone in the development and expansion of economies. In recent years, foreign investors have significantly contributed to economic advancement by channelling their funds into various sectors. This influx of foreign investment has resulted in a substantial increase in the capital stock, which is pivotal for economic growth and development. Foreign investors, defined as individuals or entities from outside a country investing in projects or businesses within that country, bring essential capital that can be utilised to expand existing businesses, launch new ventures, or support infrastructure development (Odhiambo, 2022). Additionally, they introduce advanced equipment, machinery, and production techniques that may not be readily available domestically (Pece et al., 2015). This infusion of technology facilitates the acceleration of domestic industries in terms of competitiveness and efficiency. By adopting these advanced technologies, local companies can enhance production processes, cut costs, and deliver higher-quality goods (Sahoo & Dash, 2022).

Furthermore, FDI contributes to job creation, resulting in reduced unemployment rates and increased disposable incomes for the local workforce in GS-11 nations (Basu & Ghosh, 2017). It also plays a pivotal role in fostering the development of critical infrastructure in Global South countries, including transportation systems, communication networks, and energy grids (Rehman et al., 2023). By injecting capital and expertise, FDI significantly enhances the growth and improvement of these essential facilities in host nations. Enhanced infrastructure is crucial for driving economic growth by lowering production costs and enhancing market accessibility (Wang, 2019). Improved infrastructure, such as roads, bridges, and transportation systems, facilitates more efficient transportation of goods and services, reducing production costs and increasing market accessibility.

Moreover, FDI has the potential to stimulate domestic investment by encouraging partnerships between domestic companies and foreign investors. This collaboration allows domestic firms to benefit from the expertise and resources brought in by their foreign counterparts, thereby enhancing competitiveness and fostering economic growth. Additionally, FDI promotes economic diversification by attracting investments from abroad, particularly in less developed regions within the GS-11 bloc, thereby reducing overall regional disparities (Iammarino, 2018).

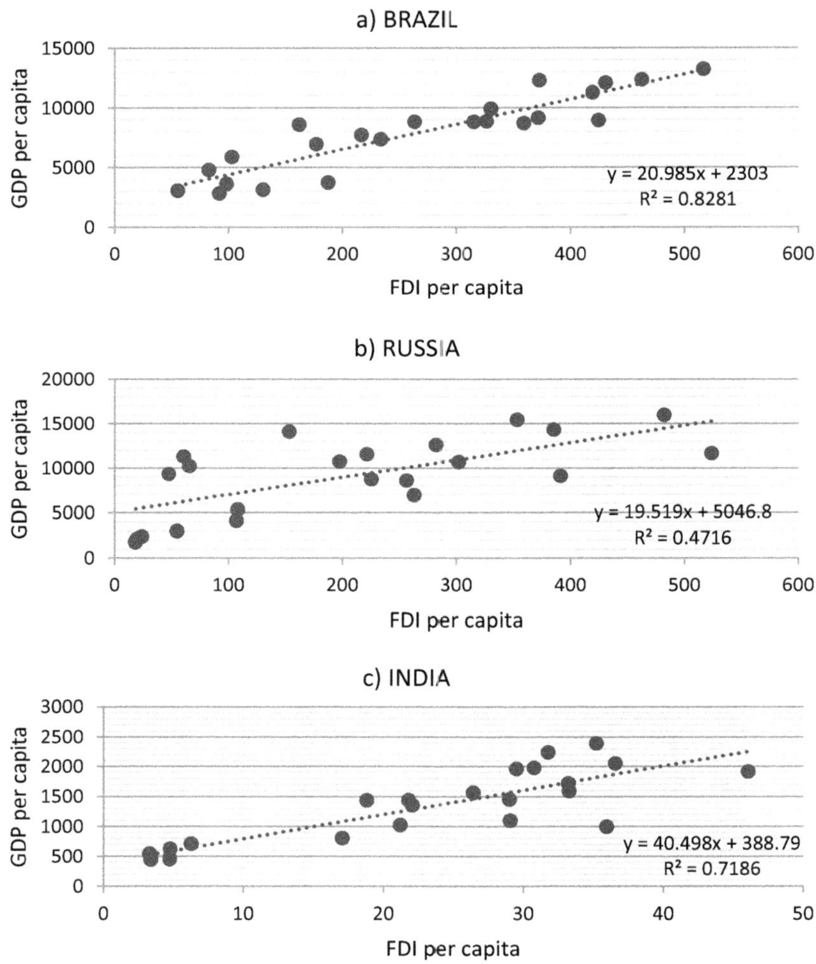

Figure 15.4 Correlation between GDP and FDI inflows.

Source: World Bank database.

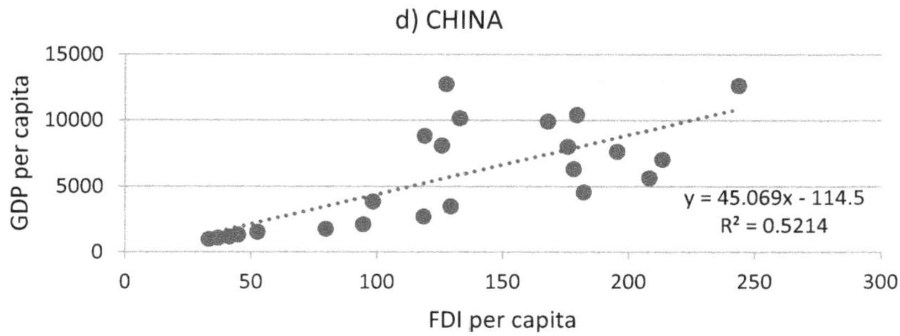

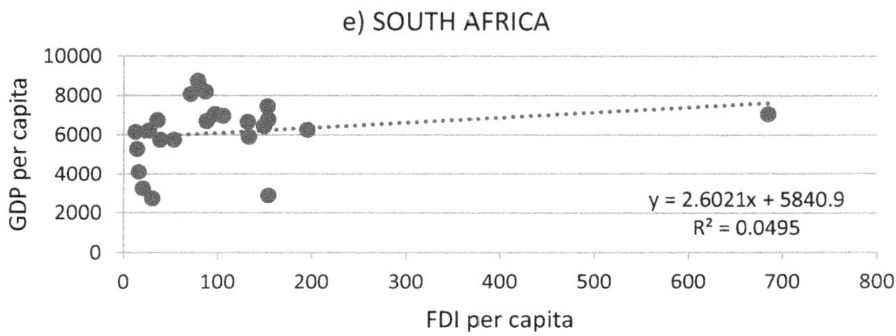

Figure 15.4 Continued.

To illustrate the relationship between economic growth and FDI inflows, the scatter plots featuring GDP per capita and FDI per capita are shown for selected Global South countries: Brazil, Russia, India, China, and South Africa (see Figure 15.4). The GDP per capita and FDI per capita are linearly positively related in the cases of Brazil, China, India, and Russia. The BRICS countries can exploit this positive relationship between GDP per capita and FDI per capita to promote their economic growth and development. However, in the case of South Africa, GDP per capita and FDI per capita data points do not exhibit any definitive pattern and lack a significant positive relationship. This is probably due to very high fluctuations in FDI receipts in South Africa.

15.6 Technology Transfer and Knowledge Spillovers

FDI facilitates the transfer of technology and knowledge from advanced nations to nations in the Global South. As the world has become interconnected on a global scale, the flow of capital across borders has intensified. When multinational corporations (MNCs) invest in GS-11 countries, they often bring modern technology, innovative processes, and managerial expertise in their pursuit of global opportunities. Technology transfer occurs through various channels, including greenfield investments in infrastructure, direct investment in R&D projects, and technology licencing agreements. Knowledge spillovers occur when local firms, suppliers, and employees interact with foreign investors, leading to the diffusion of knowledge and skills throughout the host country's economy (Morita & Nguyen, 2021). Local employees working for foreign firms often acquire valuable skills and training, which can be applied to other job opportunities, potentially boosting overall human capital. However, the extent of technology transfer and knowledge diffusion depends on factors like the host country's absorptive capacity, including its educational institutions and skilled workforce, and the openness of the local economy to foreign competition (Salim et al., 2017).

15.6.1 Case study: Information Technology (IT) Sector in India

By the turn of the 21st century, India had emerged as a global IT hub, largely due to FDI-driven technology transfer. FDI inflows in the IT sector surged from $25 million to $2 billion between 1990 and 2000, as per the UNCTAD report, 2020. Multinational IT corporations such as IBM, Oracle, and Microsoft introduced advanced software development techniques and innovative tools to the Indian IT sector. These foreign investors collaborated with local engineers and professionals to set up R&D units and software hubs in India. Indian employees gained exposure to international standards, acquiring skills in project management, software development, and quality control. This interaction facilitated the transfer of skills, technology, and knowledge, leading to the rapid evolution of India's IT industry and the emergence of indigenous firms like Wipro, Infosys, and Tata Consultancy Services (TCS). This transformation also fostered a vibrant ecosystem of entrepreneurship and innovation, with over 50,000 tech start-ups registered in India, according to a NASSCOM (2021) report. The Indian IT sector exemplifies how FDI can catalyse technology transfer and knowledge spillover, enhancing a country's capabilities and global competitiveness.

15.7 FDI's Contribution to Export-Oriented Growth

Multinational companies (MNCs) use FDI to set up production facilities in host countries. This is mainly done to utilise the local resources and secure entry to emerging markets (Kastratović, 2020). By doing so, foreign investors aim to capitalise on the market potential of the Global South countries. One of the key outcomes of this phenomenon is that it brings a significant amount of foreign currency into the host countries (Yimer, 2023). The export sector of the countries undergoes a series of technical improvements that increase their productivity manifolds. Such efficiency advancements due to the incoming FDI have contributed to the growth of export-led production of goods and services (Rao et al., 2023). When the GS-11 countries attract investments from advanced nations, they often witness a significant diversification of their exports. This is primarily because FDI brings new industries and products to the developing country's economy. This enables domestic firms to expand their

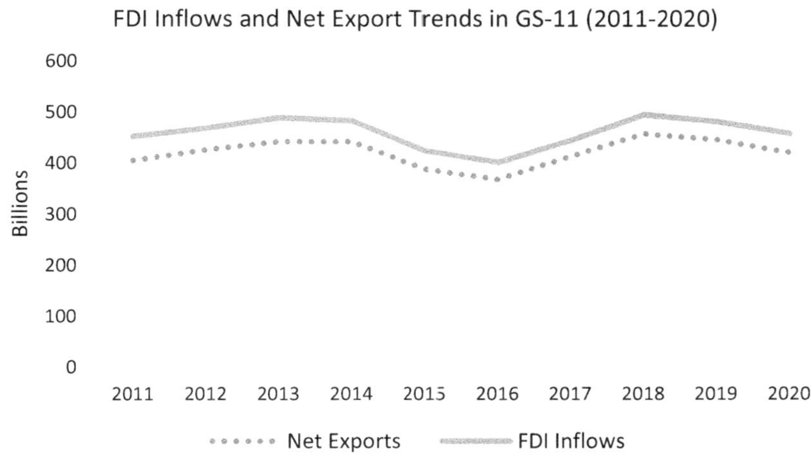

Figure 15.5 FDI inflows and net export trends in GS-11 nations.

Source: OECD statistics.

production capabilities and encourages them to improve the quality of their products. As a result, the variety of products and services a country can export widens, leading to increased economic opportunities and potential growth. This further lowers the overall unemployment rate by generating more local jobs (He, 2018). It improves the economic stability of these countries and enhances overall growth and development.

Further, the trends in FDI inflows and net exports for the GS-11 group between 2011 and 2020 closely track each other, exhibiting a strong correlation (see Figure 15.5). This correlation has significant implications for the net exports of the GS-11 economies. The countries in the Global South should focus on increasing FDI inflows to boost their net exports.

15.8 Linkages to Global Value Chains

The GS-11 nations focus on attracting investments from advanced economies to strengthen linkages with global value chains (GVCs), enabling integration into the global production network (Taglioni & Winkler, 2016). A global value chain can be defined as an industrial network for the production of goods and services spread across nations. Within this network, each country specialises in a unique step or set of processes contributing to the manufacturing process, which is crucial for its efficiency and reliability (Kano et al., 2020).

FDI often facilitates greenfield investments, establishing subsidiary units or manufacturing plants within host economies for GVC stages. Participation in GVCs provides GS-11 economies with economies of scale, specialised opportunities, and access to global markets (Baldwin & Lopez-Gonzalez, 2015), leveraging multinational firms' resources and expertise. Furthermore, GVCs depend on FDI-driven linkages for importing and exporting products along the value chain, benefitting both the host nation and the global network. All these factors have become a crucial aspect of their economic growth strategy and help to increase their global competitiveness.

15.8.1 Case study: Brazil's Agri-Sector: A Global Role Model

Brazil has emerged as a prominent source of agricultural raw materials within the global value chain, specialising in producing and exporting soybeans and meat worldwide. This success can be attributed to several factors. Firstly, Brazil benefits from ample arable land and favourable climate conditions, facilitating successful crop cultivation. Additionally, investments in technology and infrastructure have propelled the growth of its agricultural sector. In 2022, Brazil produced approximately 156 million metric tonnes of soybeans, becoming the world's largest soybean producer. It has now successfully expanded its reach to global markets, especially in China. In the same year, Brazil's soybean exports to China amounted to 53.6 million metric tonnes, with a total value of 31.8 billion dollars. This represents almost 70% of Brazil's overall soybean exports (USDA, 2023). Soybean meal and oil significantly contribute to these exports, benefitting the global food industry and livestock feed production. Agricultural technology in Brazil has notably advanced through FDI, enhancing agribusiness and sustainable farming methods, thereby increasing production and efficiency in the value chain. This sector substantially boosts Brazil's economy by generating employment, increasing export revenue, and ensuring food security.

15.9 Policy Implications

FDI has proven to be an essential catalyst propelling the economies of the Global South towards advancement and growth. To optimise their potential for economic development, these nations must align their strategies with the sustainable development goals (SDGs). Collaboration and partnerships with international investors will enable them to leverage their expertise and resources collectively. Policymakers should strike a delicate balance between domestic policies and international cooperation to maximise benefits. Developing comprehensive investment promotion strategies for GS-11 nations is crucial, involving creating a conducive environment for business and investment through simplifying administrative procedures, minimising red tape, and offering incentives such as tax breaks or subsidies to foreign investors. By closely monitoring FDI, policymakers can make informed decisions and devise strategies to maximise its positive effects. However, FDI alone may not be sufficient for economic development; it must be complemented by pro-growth policies such as fiscal stability, investment-friendly regulations, and modern infrastructure initiatives. Governments should invest in infrastructure expansion projects like transportation facilities, energy projects, telecommunications, and digital networks to improve connectivity and facilitate business operations. Additionally, introducing skill development programmes will enhance overall workforce efficiency. These strategies will enable Global South economies to achieve SDG-8 of economic growth and development through incoming FDI channels.

15.10 Conclusion

Globalisation has facilitated the rapid growth of FDI in developing nations as MNCs increasingly seek opportunities to expand their operations across international borders. Incoming FDI from developed nations serves as a potent force for economic transformation and expansion (Odhiambo, 2022), offering advanced and developing nations opportunities to prosper, diversify their economic activities, and integrate into global markets. This influx of investment has significantly reshaped the economies of the Global South, particularly the GS-11 countries, which now represent approximately half of the global population and control one-third of the world's GDP. FDI brings in modern machinery, advanced technology, managerial expertise, increased jobs, access to international markets, and much-needed capital resources. The GS-11 countries have gained significantly from foreign investors, particularly in terms of increased exports and enhanced capacity to produce goods and services.

This chapter comprehensively investigates the significant contribution of FDI inflows to the sustained growth and comprehensive development of the GS-11 nations, enabling them to establish themselves as key players in the world economy. From 2000 to 2022, China emerged as the largest recipient of FDI inflows in GS-11 countries, attracting about 53% of the total incoming investment in the Global South, followed by Brazil, India, and Russia with 16%, 9%, and 8%, respectively. The relationship between GDP per capita and FDI per capita is analysed for Global South nations, showing a positive correlation in Brazil, Russia, China, and India, with the impact of incoming investment evident in the overall economic growth and development. However, the relationship remains insignificant in South Africa, which is attributed to the high volatility in FDI inflows.

The chapter also explores the impact of FDI on knowledge spillovers and technology transfer, demonstrating how the GS-11 countries have utilised FDI to become more competitive globally. FDI has greatly enhanced export-oriented growth, leading to an incredible diversification of exports and opening up new avenues for economic growth. The GS-11 countries have also effectively used FDI to enhance connectivity with global value chains (GVCs), thereby enabling their integration into the global production network. These economies get access to global consumer markets and economies of scale and size via FDI-driven linkages with GVCs. Thus, this study establishes that FDI is essential for the long-term economic development of Global South countries.

In light of these benefits, policymakers should integrate sustainable development goals (SDGs) into measures aimed at attracting FDI through collaboration with international investors. Tailored policies responsive to individual countries' circumstances, needs, and characteristics will be conducive to long-term development and prosperity in the Global South economies. It is also essential to complement FDI with pro-growth policies like fiscal stability and investment-friendly regulations. FDI should be directed towards renewable energy, green technologies, and eco-friendly projects for sustainable economic development. Investing in infrastructure expansion projects and skill development programmes will further enhance overall workforce efficiency. Future research should also address the environmental impacts of FDI, particularly regarding climate change and increased carbon emissions.

References

Akadiri, A. C., Gungor, H., Akadiri, S. S., & Bamidele-Sadiq, M. (2020). Is the causal relation between foreign direct investment, trade, and economic growth complement or substitute? The case of African countries. *Journal of Public Affairs*, *20*(2), e2023. https://doi.org/10.1002/pa.2023

Arvin, M. B., Pradhan, R. P., & Nair, M. (2021). Uncovering interlinks among ICT connectivity and penetration, trade openness, foreign direct investment, and economic growth: The case of the G-20 countries. *Telematics and Informatics*, *60*, 101567. https://doi.org/10.1016/j.tele.2021.101567

Asafo-Agyei, G., & Kodongo, O. (2022). Foreign direct investment and economic growth in Sub-Saharan Africa: A nonlinear analysis. *Economic Systems*, *46*(4), 101003. https://doi.org/10.1016/j.ecosys.2022.101003

Aziz, O. G. (2022). FDI inflows and economic growth in Arab region: The institutional quality channel. *International Journal of Finance & Economics*, *27*(1), 1009–1024. https://doi.org/10.1002/ijfe.2197

Baldwin, R., & Lopez-Gonzalez, J. (2015). Supply-chain trade: A portrait of global patterns and several testable hypotheses. *The World Economy*, *38*(11), 1682–1721. https://doi.org/10.1111/twec.12189

Banday, U. J., Murugan, S., & Maryam, J. (2021). Foreign direct investment, trade openness and economic growth in BRICS countries: evidences from panel data. *Transnational Corporations Review*, *13*(2), 211–221. https://doi.org/10.1080/19186444.2020.1851162

Basu, S., & Ghosh, S. (2017). FDI in India: Understanding the implications for growth and job creation. *Journal of Management and Public Policy*, *9*(1), 5–16. https://doi.org/10.5958/0976-0148.2017.00005.1

Biørn, E., & Han, X. (2017). Revisiting the FDI impact on GDP growth in errors-in-variables models: a panel data GMM analysis allowing for error memory. *Empirical Economics*, *53*, 1379–1398. https://doi.org/10.1007/s00181-016-1203-4

Chakraborty, S. (2018). Significance of BRICS: Regional powers, global governance, and the roadmap for multipolar world. *Emerging Economy Studies*, *4*(2), 182–191. https://doi.org/10.1177/2394901518795070

Chanegriha, M., Stewart, C., & Tsoukis, C. (2020). Testing for causality between FDI and economic growth using heterogeneous panel data. *The Journal of International Trade & Economic Development*, *29*(5), 546–565. https://doi.org/10.1080/09638199.2019.1704843

Desbordes, R., & Wei, S. J. (2017). The effects of financial development on foreign direct investment. *Journal of Development Economics*, *127*, 153–168. https://doi.org/10.1016/j.jdeveco.2017.02.008

Domínguez-Jiménez, M., & Poitiers, N. F. (2020). An analysis of EU FDI inflow into Russia. *Russian Journal of Economics*, *6*(2), 144–161. https://doi.org/10.32609/j.ruje.6.55880

He, Y. (2018). Foreign direct investment, economic growth and employment: Evidence from China. *International Research in Economics and Finance*, *2*(1), 12. https://doi.org/10.20849/iref.v2i1.320

Iammarino, S. (2018). FDI and regional development policy. *Journal of International Business Policy*, *1*, 157–183. https://doi.org/10.1057/s42214-018-0012-1

Jude, C. (2016). Technology spillovers from FDI. Evidence on the intensity of different spillover channels. *The World Economy*, *39*(12), 1947–1973. https://doi.org/10.1111/twec.12335

Kano, L., Tsang, E. W., & Yeung, H. W. C. (2020). Global value chains: A review of the multi-disciplinary literature. *Journal of international business studies*, *51*(4), 577–622. https://doi.org/10.1057/s41267-020-00304-2

Kapingura, F. M. (2018). Relationship between foreign capital flows, domestic investment and savings in the SADC region. *Development Southern Africa*, *35*(4), 554–568. https://doi.org/10.1080/0376835X.2018.1487279

Karahan, Ö., & Çolak, O. (2024). The causality relationship between foreign direct investment and economic growth in RCEP countries. *Journal of Economic and Administrative Sciences*, *40*(1), 95–110. https://doi.org/10.1108/JEAS-04-2022-0112

Kastratović, R. (2020). The impact of foreign direct investment on host country exports: A meta-analysis. *The World Economy*, *43*(12), 3142–3183. https://doi.org/10.1111/twec.13011

Kroeber, A. R. (2020). *China's Economy: What Everyone Needs to Know*. Oxford University Press.

Kumari, R., Shabbir, M. S., Saleem, S., Yahya Khan, G., Abbasi, B. A., & Lopez, L. B. (2023). An empirical analysis among foreign direct investment, trade openness and economic growth: evidence from the Indian economy. *South Asian Journal of Business Studies*, *12*(1), 127–149. https://doi.org/10.1108/SAJBS-06-2020-0199

Li, C., & Tanna, S. (2019). The impact of foreign direct investment on productivity: New evidence for developing countries. *Economic Modelling*, *80*, 453–466. https://doi.org/10.1016/j.econmod.2018.11.028

Mehic, E., Silajdzic, S., & Babic-Hodovic, V. (2013). The impact of FDI on economic growth: Some evidence from Southeast Europe. *Emerging Markets Finance and Trade*, *49*(1), 5–20. https://doi.org/10.2753/REE1540-496X4901S101

Morita, H., & Nguyen, X. (2021). FDI and quality-enhancing technology spillovers. *International Journal of Industrial Organization*, *79*, 102787. https://doi.org/10.1016/j.ijindorg.2021.102787

NASSCOM. (2021). IT-BPM Industry in India: Strategic Review 2021. *National Association of Software and Service Companies*.

Nistor, P. (2015). FDI implications on BRICS economy growth. *Procedia Economics and Finance*, *32*, 981–985. https://doi.org/10.1016/S2212-5671(15)01557-9

Nupehewa, S., Liyanage, S., Polkotuwa, D., Thiyagarajah, M., Jayathilaka, R., & Lokeshwara, A. (2022). More than just investment: Causality analysis between foreign direct investment and economic growth. *Plos One*, *17*(11), e0276621. https://doi.org/10.1371/journal.pone.0276621

Odhiambo, N. M. (2022). Foreign direct investment and economic growth in Kenya: An empirical investigation. *International Journal of Public Administration*, *45*(8), 620–631. https://doi.org/10.1080/01900692.2021.1872622

Omri, A. (2014). The nexus among foreign investment, domestic capital and economic growth: Empirical evidence from the MENA region. *Research in Economics*, *68*(3), 257–263. https://doi.org/10.1016/j.rie.2013.11.001

Owusu, E. L. (2021). The relationship between foreign direct investment and economic growth: A multivariate causality approach from Namibia. *International Journal of Finance & Economics*, *26*(2), 2990–2997. https://doi.org/10.1002/ijfe.1946

Owusu-Nantwi, V., & Erickson, C. (2019). Foreign direct investment and economic growth in South America. *Journal of Economic Studies*, *46*(2), 383–398. https://doi.org/10.1108/JES-11-2017-0323

Pece, A. M., Simona, O. E. O., & Salisteanu, F. (2015). Innovation and economic growth: An empirical analysis for CEE countries. *Procedia Economics and Finance*, *26*, 461–467. https://doi.org/10.1016/S2212-5671(15)00874-6

Philip, L. D., Sertoglu, K., Akadiri, S. S., & Olasehinde-Williams, G. (2021). Foreign direct investment amidst global economic downturn: is there a time-varying implication for environmental sustainability targets?. *Environmental Science and Pollution Research*, *28*, 21359–21368. https://doi.org/10.1007/s11356-020-12053-8

Rao, D. T., Sethi, N., Dash, D. P., & Bhujabal, P. (2023). Foreign aid, FDI and economic growth in South-East Asia and South Asia. *Global Business Review*, *24*(1), 31–47. https://doi.org/10.1177/0972150919890957

Rehman, F. U., Sohag, K., & Saeed, T. (2023). Impact of Sectoral Infrastructure on Export and Foreign Direct Investment Inflow: Evidence from Selected South Asian Economies by Applying a New Global Infrastructure Index. *Journal of Infrastructure Systems*, *29*(1), 04022045. https://doi.org/10.1061/(ASCE)IS.1943-555X.0000724

Ribaj, A., & Mexhuani, F. (2021). The impact of savings on economic growth in a developing country (the case of Kosovo). *Journal of Innovation and Entrepreneurship*, *10*, 1–13. https://doi.org/10.1186/s13731-020-00140-6

Sahoo, P., & Dash, R. K. (2022). Does FDI have differential impacts on exports? Evidence from developing countries. *International Economics*, *172*, 227–237. https://doi.org/10.1016/j.inteco.2022.10.002

Saidi, S., Mani, V., Mefteh, H., Shahbaz, M., & Akhtar, P. (2020). Dynamic linkages between transport, logistics, foreign direct Investment, and economic growth: Empirical evidence from developing countries. *Transportation Research Part A: Policy and Pratice*, *141*, 277–293. https://doi.org/10.1016/j.tra.2020.09.020

Saleem, H., Shabbir, M. S., & Bilal Khan, M. (2020). The short-run and long-run dynamics among FDI, trade openness and economic growth: using a bootstrap ARDL test for co-integration in selected South Asian countries. *South Asian Journal of Business Studies*, *9*(2), 279–295. https://doi.org/10.1108/SAJBS-07-2019-0124

Salim, A., Razavi, M. R., & Afshari-Mofrad, M. (2017). Foreign direct investment and technology spillover in Iran: The role of technological capabilities of subsidiaries. *Technological Forecasting and Social Change*, *122*, 207–214. https://doi.org/10.1016/j.techfore.2015.09.012

Sobirov, Y., Jeong, J. Y., Karimov, M. U. U., & Bekjanov, D. (2023). Do FDI and trade openness matter for economic growth in CIS Countries? Evidence from panel ARDL. *Journal of East-West Business*, *29*(4), 345–374. https://doi.org/10.1080/10669868.2023.2242854

Taglioni, D., & Winkler, D. (2016). *Making global value chains work for development*. World Bank Publications. https://doi.org/10.1596/978-1-4648-0157-0

USDA. (2023). Brazil Soybean Transportation, Overview 2022. *United States Department of Agriculture*.

Wang, X. (2019). FDI and Infrastructure Improvement of ASEAN. *International Journal of Economics and Finance*, *11*(10), 140–147. https://doi.org/10.5539/ijef.v11n10p140

Yimer, A. (2023). The effects of FDI on economic growth in Africa. *The Journal of International Trade & Economic Development*, *32*(1), 2–36. https://doi.org/10.1080/09638199.2022.2079709

Part VI

Global South Countries' Perspectives and Experiences

16 Post-Pandemic Polycrises in Malaysia

A Bibliometric Review

Stephen T Homer

16.1 Introduction

Polycrisis occurs when multiple crises intersect, creating a complex and diverse issue. These crises could affect the economy, society, environment, politics, and health (Kotarski, 2023). Understanding polycrises and their effects on the Global South is crucial to solving their problems. Since Malaysia emerged from the COVID-19 pandemic and faced many post-pandemic issues, it is crucial to examine the applicability of polycrises to the current situation. Malaysia, an upper-middle-income country pursuing developed country status, is plagued by rapid urbanisation, poor transport infrastructure, and population congestion, including the loss of young adults from older urban districts and urban sprawl (Homer et al., 2023). Homer and Khor (2022) examine how the COVID-19 pandemic in Malaysia affected sustainable development. Following the Movement Control Order (MCO) and virus control measures, the study describes the track and trace app "MySejahtera." It also highlights the lockdown's effects on marginalised groups, non-citizens, and international workers. The psychological and economic effects of quarantine, such as business closures and unemployment, are discussed. This study is narrow because it addresses only one crisis and youth. The objective of this chapter is to explore the post-pandemic literature on crises within the Malaysian context through a bibliometric analysis of post-outbreak scholarly literature. The aim is to illuminate academic conversations about Malaysia's contemporary crises.

16.2 Literature Review

16.2.1 Defining Polycrisis

A polycrisis is a complex, multifaceted web of interrelated and simultaneous crises that profoundly affect Earth's natural and social systems. In "Homeland Earth: A Manifesto for the New Millennium," renowned philosopher and complexity thinker Edgar Morin coined the term "polycrisis" to describe our complex, interconnected problems. Morin calls it "interwoven and overlapping crises," illustrating how problems, antagonisms, and uncontrollable processes

DOI: 10.4324/9781032694337-23

contribute to our planet's crisis (Henig & Knight, 2023). Scholars like Tooze and Hobson have called polycrisis a symbol of our time. They argue that the term describes a complex system of escalating issues that form a crisis narrative (Henig & Knight, 2023). As a result, polycrisis provides a broad view of current issues that affect individuals, societies, and the planet.

Polycrises are multifaceted, like the COVID-19 pandemic, rising alcohol and drug deaths, income inequality, homelessness, geopolitical conflicts, economic instability, and environmental issues. Crisis after crisis has made it harder to provide essential services to vulnerable populations, especially those with substance use disorders (Carver et al., 2023). To solve these intersecting problems, innovative approaches and rethinking conventional strategies are needed. Polycrisis goes beyond Morin's framework, including catastrophic scenarios caused by multiple interconnected natural and social systems failing. Homer-Dixon and colleagues argue that a global polycrisis is a single macrocrisis caused by runaway failures in Earth's vital systems, threatening humanity's future (Homer-Dixon et al., 2022). This view emphasises the severity of interconnected crises and the need for global action to prevent disasters.

Polycrisis—the simultaneous occurrence of multiple crises, such as pandemics, natural disasters, geopolitical conflicts, and economic instability—is expanded by Kotarski (2023). This definition of polycrisis as global insecurity emphasises its pervasiveness and impact on human life. It highlights the interconnectedness of crises and their impact on global security. Polycrisis has also been observed in regional entities like the EU. Zeitlin et al. (2019) highlight the EU's economic, political, social, and environmental challenges over the past decade. These crises have strained EU institutions and member states, increasing political fragmentation and governance issues.

To sum up, a polycrisis is a confluence of crises that exacerbate each other, creating a massive challenge that transcends individual issues. It requires understanding these challenges' interconnectedness, prompting innovative solutions and global efforts to navigate and mitigate our current crisis landscape. Collective action, adaptive strategies, and a holistic approach are needed to address a polycrisis and protect societies and the planet.

Now that polycrisis has been defined, the following section discusses the impact of polycrises on society, thus explaining the issues and challenges faced in light of the complex, multifaceted phenomenon.

16.2.2 The Impact of Polycrises on Society

A polycrisis can irreversibly and catastrophically damage humanity's future. It can cause a runaway failure of Earth's natural and social systems, causing extreme complexity, nonlinearity, transboundary causality, and uncertainty. Polycrisis can affect living organisms' physical environments, interpersonal, intergroup, intercultural, and international areas, as well as individuals' hearts, minds, and souls (Oxford et al., 2023). The polycrisis has dramatically affected the EU. The crises have strained EU institutions and governance and politicised and fragmented the political system. EU-level grand bargains to solve the polycrisis have become more challenging due to new cleavages like the integration/demarcation cleavage. Politicisation has different domestic and supranational effects (Zeitlin et al., 2019).

Polycrisis is a web of interconnected crises that affect many aspects of human life and global stability. The COVID-19 pandemic, combined with rising substance use disorders, income inequality, and homelessness, has disproportionately affected vulnerable populations, making it harder to provide essential addiction services (Carver et al., 2023). Innovative addiction treatments have emerged from this convergence of crises, teaching us how to handle future crises. Polycrisis refers to a complex web of issues threatening the planet's livability, emphasising the need to address global issues in the Anthropocene (Henig & Knight, 2023). A global polycrisis could have severe and long-term effects on health, food security, economic stability, and social cohesion (Homer-Dixon et al., 2022). Parallel crises prolong insecurity and instability, increasing uncertainty in politics, economics, and social cohesion (Kotarski, 2023). These crises' scale and speed intensify distributional battles and reshuffle power dynamics, fostering political pathology and stifling creativity.

Polycrises are cascading, runaway failures of Earth's ecological, social, and personal systems that affect physical environments, intergroup dynamics, and individual well-being (Oxford et al., 2023). Crisis after crisis has strained institutional mechanisms in the EU, politicising and fragmenting the political system. Fragmentation has hindered EU-level polycrisis solutions (Zeitlin et al., 2019). These insights provide glimpses into the multifaceted effects of a polycrisis. Still, they emphasise the need for comprehensive analysis and global collaboration to identify causal mechanisms and develop actionable policies to mitigate intertwined crises. Polycrisis affects interconnected systems, requiring adaptive strategies that cross disciplines and prioritise collective action to protect societies and the planet.

16.3 Methodology

This section describes the methodology. Due to its peer-reviewed quality, SCOPUS was used to find relevant academic literature. The title, abstract, and keywords of MALAYSIA AND CRIS* were searched on SCOPUS. The term cris* was used to include broader crisis synonyms like crises. Since the entire database was searched without specific fields of study, the literature was diverse from 2020, when COVID-19 spread worldwide, to the present, post-pandemic recovery. Articles, only the final document type, and English papers were filtered. The initial data set had 517 articles. Social sciences (166 articles), economics, econometrics, and finance (136), business, management, and accounting (123), medicine (87), and environmental science (61) were covered in the initial data articles can be coded into multiple subject areas, so the numbers exceed

517. The output document was then searched for “crisis” and “crises” using Excel’s find function. Any instances where these terms did not appear were manually checked for relevance to the study. The “CRIS*” search term included technical, Latinized names for ecological or medical papers like “crispifolium” and “crispy.” After removing irrelevant papers, 465 papers were suitable for bibliometric analysis. The 465 articles were divided into 105 in 2023, 139 in 2022, 122 in 2021, and 99 in 2020.

16.4 Results

VOSViewer created a map based on the text data function used to analyse the document. This used the SCOPUS file type, including title and abstract fields, with full counting. A minimum number of occurrences was set at 23; this was following the 5% significance often adopted within statistical tests and to add rigour to this study, as 5% of the 465 papers equates to 23.25. Of the 11,916 terms within all abstracts and titles, 131 met the 23 co-occurrence requirements. Figure 16.1 presents the graphical output from VOSviewer.

Cluster one comprised 61 keywords. The number of links varied from 130, indicating that the keyword appeared in all the abstracts of other papers, to 18 links. The total link strength represents the overall strength of the co-authorship connections between a specific researcher and other researchers. In this cluster, COVID had the highest total link strength of 21,076, which is expected due to its dominant presence in the literature. On the other hand, E-learning had the lowest total link strength of 863. The frequency of the keyword “word” in all

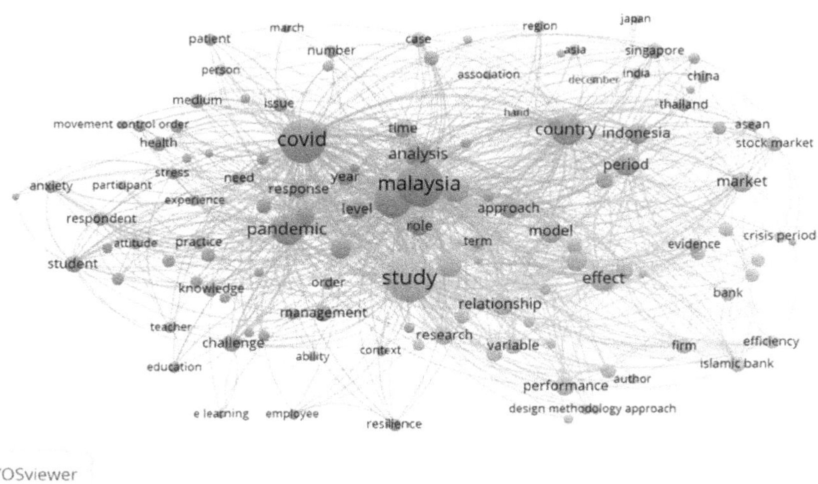

Figure 16.1 VOSviewer Output Image. (Author’s own work).

Table 16.1 Cluster One Results Table (Authors' own work)

Item	*Links*	*Total link strength*	*Occurrences*	*Item*	*Links*	*Total link strength*	*Occurrences*
Analysis	130	7067	239	Total	115	1220	38
Covid	130	21076	687	Experience	114	1537	55
Crisis	130	12902	491	Person	114	1732	54
Malaysia	130	19150	736	Questionnaire	114	1861	60
Pandemic	130	11918	367	Respondent	114	2329	67
Role	130	4133	145	Spread	113	1317	40
Factor	129	4063	132	Participant	112	1265	34
Level	129	4612	137	Interview	110	1255	42
Strategy	128	4110	131	Malaysian	110	931	33
Order	127	1622	57	Medium	110	2039	76
Year	127	2958	102	Resilience	109	1569	56
Knowledge	126	2409	79	Coronavirus disease	108	996	30
Importance	125	1525	54	Lockdown	108	1335	38
Issue	124	2189	80	Perception	108	1601	54
Management	124	2531	98	March	104	996	30
Response	124	2820	103	Business	102	1082	36
Context	123	1350	45	Attitude	100	1660	50
Outbreak	123	1830	54	Movement control order	100	1215	35
Challenge	122	3570	121	Anxiety	99	2126	56
Information	122	2094	76	Education	99	1547	50
Government	121	3088	106	MCO	98	1899	57
Health	121	2579	86	Stress	97	2422	60
Need	121	2291	73	Student	94	3009	102
Support	121	2086	65	Patient	83	1591	60
Number	120	1858	58	Teacher	80	1515	50
Practice	120	2093	74	Employee	75	1272	45
Life	118	1841	58	Preparedness	75	943	42
Survey	118	2006	57	Depression	68	901	24
Way	118	933	36	E-learning	58	863	28
Ability	117	933	33	Use	18	1306	51
Organisation	115	1258	44				

the abstracts varied, with Malaysia having the highest occurrence of 736, which is expected given it is a search term. In contrast, Depression had the lowest occurrence of only 24. Table 16.1 contains the complete results for this cluster.

Cluster two comprised of 37 keywords. The number of links ranged from 130 to 76 links; thus, although the cluster was more minor than Cluster One, the number of links remained higher per keyword, as Cluster One had a minimum of only 18 links. The total link strength for this cluster ranged from 24,874 for Study down to 796 for Pakistan. The number of occurrences presented and how many times the keyword appeared within all the abstracts ranged from 841 for Study; however, this is due to the academic language and not its relativity to the topic of this chapter through to 26 for Pakistan. The full results for this cluster can be found in Table 16.2.

Table 16.2 Cluster Two Results Table (Authors' own work)

Item	*Links*	*Total link strength*	*Occurrences*	*Item*	*Links*	*Total link strength*	*Occurrences*
Data	130	6642	216	Evidence	121	2544	83
Effect	130	6373	230	Design methodology approach	119	1729	45
Impact	130	8313	274	Originality value	118	1627	43
Implication	130	3246	95	Type	117	1435	53
Study	130	24874	841	Policymaker	111	1292	38
Model	129	5226	202	Investor	109	2705	82
Research	129	3889	131	Practical implication	109	1240	33
Relationship	128	4870	156	Financial crisis	108	1931	78
Sample	127	1500	55	Global financial crisis	108	2038	66
Insight	125	1597	47	Pakistan	107	796	26
Paper	125	4102	151	Author	106	1360	38
Risk	125	3190	105	Company	102	2032	78
Performance	124	3541	126	Bank	100	2053	81
Change	123	2130	78	Crisis period	100	1906	57
Literature	123	1649	53	Return	100	2002	67
Variable	123	3217	98	Firm	99	2173	90
Addition	122	1083	37	Efficiency	89	2409	65
Influence	122	1426	48	Islamic bank	76	2623	88
Value	122	2342	85				

Cluster three comprised of 31 keywords. The number of links ranged from 130 to 74, thus having a similar composition to Cluster Two. The total link strength for this cluster ranged from 11,170 for *Country* down to 693 for *December*. The number of occurrences presented how many times the keyword appeared within all the abstracts; this ranged from 384 for *Country* through to 23 for both *December* and *Hand*. The full results for this cluster can be found in Table 16.3.

Cluster four comprised only two keywords, making it the smallest cluster. *Development* and *World* had the number of links of 122 out of a possible 130, so it appeared in most abstracts. The total link strength for this cluster was 1,883 for *Development* and 1,394 for *World*. The number of occurrences was 75 for *Development* and 45 for *World*. The full results for this cluster can be found in Table 16.4.

16.5 Discussion

This section will discuss each of the clusters from the analysis before proceeding to discuss what is missing from the analysis.

Table 16.3 Cluster Three Results Table (Authors' own work)

Item	*Links*	*Total link strength*	*Occurrences*	*Item*	*Links*	*Total link strength*	*Occurrences*
Country	130	11170	384	Philippines	112	1789	53
Period	130	5668	174	Region	112	1714	54
Approach	129	3522	127	December	108	693	23
Time	129	4518	133	Hand	108	699	23
Term	128	1883	65	January	107	716	27
Indonesia	126	4814	159	China	106	1723	62
Economy	124	3023	110	India	105	1285	39
Case	123	2825	97	Asia	103	1248	47
State	123	1399	60	Southeast Asia	99	1017	33
Opportunity	121	1366	40	Vietnam	98	940	31
Article	119	1817	82	Japan	93	961	30
Future	118	1107	40	Volatility	93	2146	69
Association	117	1522	36	ASEAN	92	2033	62
Singapore	117	2570	87	Stock market	89	2912	91
Market	116	5057	164	GFC	74	1048	27
Thailand	115	2094	72				

Table 16.4 Cluster 4 Results Table (Authors' own work)

Item	*Links*	*Total link strength*	*Occurrences*
Development	122	1883	76
World	122	1394	45

16.5.1 Cluster 1: Humanistic

Cluster 1 focused on the COVID pandemic and its health impact; thus, this represented the humanistic side of polycrises. COVID and Pandemic have 130 connections; thus, co-occurrence is with every abstract in the sample, the same as the search terms of Crisis and Malaysia. Hence, even during the recovery period in the later publications, the pandemic is still a prominent feature to be discussed. Interestingly, there is also a grouping of keywords that look at addressing the crises; keywords such as Strategy, Management, and Response are all high in co-occurrence and are interlaced with keywords, such as Knowledge and Information, suggesting that there is a pursuit of data-driven decision making. The keyword Health is also prominent, with 121 co-occurrences and humanistic terms such as Need, Support, and Life closely clustered in the co-occurrence. However, the specific instances of the health issues are less prominent as they divide into specific areas, such as Attitude (i.e., Ghasemy & Frömbling, 2023), Anxiety (i.e. Rom et al., 2023) and Depression (i.e. Zakaria et al., 2022). This cluster also specifies the stakeholders directly, such as Students, Teachers, Employees, and Patients, but also indirectly highlights those impacted through a broader context, such as business or education. As a whole, this cluster focuses on the impact the COVID-19 pandemic has had on Malaysian society. It emphasises that although Malaysia is well into its recovery period, it still dominates the literature.

The COVID-19 crisis still dominates the literature, even in the recovery stages currently, as it has had a profound human impact, spanning health, social, economic, and psychological realms. It caused significant loss of life, overwhelmed healthcare systems, and led to unprecedented stress among frontline workers. Lockdowns and restrictions brought isolation and mental health challenges, while job losses and economic uncertainties deepened inequalities. Marginalised communities faced heightened vulnerabilities, and education disruptions widened gaps. This crisis underscored disparities in access to resources and healthcare, emphasising the need for resilience and equitable support systems. Addressing these multifaceted impacts demands comprehensive strategies centred on public health, social equity, and holistic recovery measures.

16.5.2 Cluster 2: Economic

Cluster 2 has the opposite view of crises compared to Cluster 1, with a data and numerical feel, looking towards policy and economic outputs. Many terms refer to the academic study approach, such as Data, Study, Research and Sample, which do not reflect the crisis' theme but are necessary to include in the interest of transparency. The theme becomes more apparent as the keywords of Risk, Performance, and Change reflect the policy and economic perspective. The more specific topics become apparent as the keyword co-occurrences behind to reduce. The economic crisis is emphasised through the keywords of Financial Crisis, Bank, Return, and Islamic Bank. This is further supported through Company and Firm, which, when considered with Investor, would further suggest the economic impact on publicly listed company share prices. The importance of financial crises stems from their impact on economies and communities in many ways. They cause economic downturns with falling GDP, rising unemployment, and falling consumer spending. After bank failures, credit availability is limited, limiting loans and investments. Asset prices plummet, reducing wealth and affecting investors and real estate. Government bailouts and stimulus initiatives transform fiscal landscapes. Crisis often causes psychological distress and economic damage, exacerbating social inequality. Their worldwide influence spreads economic instability. Policymakers boost financial systems through regulatory reforms. Industries that rely on credit and consumer spending suffer, reducing innovation and jobs. Understanding these repercussions is essential for devising practical solutions to mitigate and stabilise future financial crises.

16.5.3 Cluster 3: Geographical

Cluster 3 has a geographical focus, with the most prominent keyword being Country, closely followed by State. However, the focus is very much on Asia, with many countries listed within ASEAN, including Indonesia, Singapore, Thailand, Philippines, and Vietnam. The larger economic nations within Asia, namely China, India, and Japan, are clearly stated. This trend shows Malaysia's interdependence within Southeast Asia and the broader region. Yet, it does not go to the extent of including Western nations or other influential nations. Several studies contain comparative studies, such as Shah et al. (2023) comparing Islamic banking in Malaysia, Indonesia, UAE, and Pakistan and Jamil et al. (2023) comparing financial markets in Malaysia, Thailand, Singapore, Indonesia, and the Philippines.

Geographical proximity profoundly shapes the impact of polycrises, fostering interconnected vulnerabilities and opportunities. Neighbouring nations face shared challenges, experiencing spillover effects that amplify crises across borders. The COVID-19 pandemic showcased how proximity led to similar health risks and economic repercussions among interconnected countries. Climate similarities also render regions susceptible to analogous ecological crises. However, proximity offers collaboration prospects, enabling joint crisis management and policy responses. Leveraging regional alliances and cooperative frameworks can mitigate shared challenges effectively. Ultimately, geographical closeness is crucial in shaping the spread, intensity, and management of multifaceted crises, fostering vulnerabilities and collaborative resilience.

Another clear trend within this cluster is time, with the keywords Period and Time, having 130 and 129 links, respectively. Other keywords that demonstrate this theme are Term and Future, with the specific months of December and January indicating when the pandemic began to take effect.

16.5.4 Cluster 4: Global

Cluster 4 comprised only two keywords, Development and World; however, both are prominently seen with 122 links each, with Development occurring considerably more overall with 76 counts. With the term Development meaning a process that creates growth, progress, positive change or the addition of physical, economic, social, environmental, and demographic components and World indicating a global perspective or application, this cluster may be indicative of macro-level solutions to the polycrisis that affect the planet and subsequently Malaysia. However, a text search within the abstracts for Sustainable Development Goal returns only five results, while SDG returns only three. Only Nilashi et al. (2023) with "COVID-19 and sustainable development goals: A bibliometric analysis and SWOT analysis in Malaysian context" and Chua et al. (2022) with "Ecolinguistics for and beyond the Sustainable Development Goals" directly take the SDGs. Thus, the sustainable development goals were adopted by all members of the United Nations in 2015 to address the global crises, culminating in polycrisis. Yet, these high-level, macro solutions appear not to be prominent in the literature.

In the literature review section, Homer-Dixon et al. (2022) refer to a polycrisis regarding the runaway failures of Earth's vital natural and social systems that irreversibly degrade humanity's prospects. However, the present study's literature review shows a distinct lack of natural crisis. Despite many countries worldwide declaring climate emergencies and ecological crises, the Malaysian literature only refers to the social and economic systems developed by the latter. Keller et al. (2023) raised the ecological component within their study by looking at the biodiversity consequences of long-term active forest restoration in selectively logged tropical rainforests, referring directly to the mitigation of the ecological crisis within their abstract. The paper by Gan et al. (2023) used the index keywords of freshwater biodiversity crisis. Thus, there was no co-occurrence despite both papers having a similar topic: tropical rainforests. Furthermore, Evans et al. (2021) discussed palm oil plantations, which cause deforestation. The other papers discussed the term biodiversity crisis within the abstract. Thus, despite the similarities between the papers, there is limited co-occurrence. With only a tiny number focusing on the ecological side, they are foreshadowed by the other themes of humanistic and economic.

16.5.5 Practical Implications

16.5.5.1 Cross-sector Collaboration

The diverse and complex nature of polycrises requires cooperation among government agencies, academic institutions, civil society organisations, and the private sector. Through the collective collaboration and utilisation of knowledge and resources, a wide range of individuals and organisations can effectively tackle intricate problems in a comprehensive and integrated manner. Government agencies establish regulatory frameworks, academics provide research insights, civil society actively involves communities, and the private sector contributes technology and funding. By forming alliances, interventions can address underlying causes and alleviate effects across various domains. This cooperative method improves the efficiency of responding to crises and fosters the ability to withstand and recover from interconnected difficulties.

16.5.5.2 Sustainable Development

The study highlights the crucial incorporation of sustainability principles into crisis management strategies. This involves ensuring that policies are in line with the Sustainable Development Goals (SDGs), promoting environmentally friendly and strong infrastructure, and promoting sustainable practices in important sectors, such as agriculture, transportation, and energy. Societies can effectively tackle crises and simultaneously foster long-term environmental stewardship and socio-economic resilience by implementing these principles. This highlights the significance of taking proactive actions that not only reduce immediate effects but also support sustainable development objectives, guaranteeing a more resilient and environmentally aware future.

16.5.5.3 Risk Mitigation and Preparedness

It is crucial to implement proactive measures to mitigate and prepare for risks in order to enhance resilience against multiple crises. This entails developing risk assessment frameworks, contingency plans, and early warning systems to predict and mitigate the effects of crises. By implementing these tactics, communities can predict and alleviate the negative consequences of complex crises, thereby improving their capacity to endure and bounce back from disruptions. Implementing proactive measures not only reduces the intensity of crises but also facilitates prompt reactions, promoting the ability to recover and adapt in the presence of intricate difficulties.

16.6 Conclusion

This study examined Malaysian academic literature on crises to identify patterns and discussions about current crises. SCOPUS was used to find relevant academic literature for MALAYSIA AND CRIS* by searching for title, abstract, and keywords. Manually checking the output document for study relevance followed. A bibliometric analysis of 465 papers was undertaken for the following years: 105 articles in 2023, 139 in 2022, 122 in 2021, and 99 in 2020. The reviewed literature shows that the COVID-19 pandemic has a widespread impact on Malaysia's society, economy, and region, but it ignores urgent ecological crises. The literature's lack of natural crisis coverage suggests a blind spot in understanding and addressing the nation's complex issues. Promoting interdisciplinary collaborations, filling knowledge gaps, integrating global sustainability goals into regional frameworks, and turning research into policy are academic implications. Academics must adopt a more holistic and inclusive approach to studying and managing crises to help Malaysia and others address their complex issues.

16.6.1 Limitations and Future Research

This study's scope is limited to one country, but polycrises are macro events, and the geographical cluster reinforces this. This suggests that future research may analyse whole regions or even the world. The study focused on post-pandemic 2020 and, later, a short time frame for academic literature. Research themes may change more if studies examine events like the COVID-19 pandemic before and after.

References

Carver, H., Ciolompea, T., Conway, A., Kilian, C., McDonald, R., Meksi, A., & Wojnar, M. (2023). Substance use disorders and COVID-19: Reflections on international research and practice changes during the "poly-crisis". *Frontiers in Public Health*, 11, 1201967.

Chau, M. H., Zhu, C., Jacobs, G. M., Delante, N. L., Asmi, A., Ng, S., John, S. S., Guo, Q. & Shunmugam, K., (2022). Ecolinguistics for and beyond the Sustainable Development Goals. *Journal of World Languages*, 8(2), 323–345.

Evans, M. N., Müller, C. T., Kille, P., Asner, G. P., Guerrero-Sanchez, S., Bakar, M. S. A., & Goossens, B. (2021). Space-use patterns of Malay civets (Viverra tangalunga) persisting within a landscape fragmented by oil palm plantations. *Landscape Ecology*, 36, 915–930.

Gan, L. X., Tan, C. L., Ahmad, A. B., Cai, Y., & Yeo, D. C. (2023). Forest conversion adversely affects native Macrobrachium shrimp assemblages in tropical Malaysian streams. *Aquatic Conservation: Marine and Freshwater Ecosystems*, 33(1), 89–101.

Ghasemy, M., & Frömbling, L. (2023). Stay positive: Studying the change patterns in academics' job and life satisfaction during the Covid-19 pandemic through growth curve modeling. *Evidence-based HRM: A Global Forum for Empirical Scholarship*, 11(3), 271–294.

Henig, D., & Knight, D. M. (2023). Polycrisis: Prompts for an emerging worldview. *Anthropology Today*, 39(2), 3–6.

Homer, S. T., & Khor, K. S. (2022). Exploring the perceptions of Malaysian Gen Z towards the impact of COVID-19 on sustainable development. *Environmental Science and Pollution Research*, 29(57), 85700–85716.

Homer, S. T., Berezina, E., Chaouche, S. S., & Gill, C. M. H. D. (2023). Co-designing urban transport solutions with Southeast Asian young adults. *Transportation Planning and Technology*, 47(2), 147–169.

Homer-Dixon, T., Renn, O., Rockstrom, J., Donges, J. F., & Janzwood, S. (2022). A call for an international research program on the risk of a global polycrisis. Available at SSRN 4058592.

Jamil, I., Kogid, M., Lim, T. S., & Lily, J. (2023). Pre-and post-COVID-19: The impact of US, UK, and European Stock Markets on ASEAN-5 Stock Markets. *International Journal of Financial Studies*, 11(2), 54.

Keller, N., Niklaus, P. A., Ghazoul, J., Marfil, T., Godoong, E., & Philipson, C. D. (2023). Biodiversity consequences of long-term active forest restoration in selectively-logged tropical rainforests. *Forest Ecology and Management*, 549, 121414.

Kotarski, K. (2023). The new era of polycrisis and how to tackle it. *Future Europe Journal*, 3, 14–25.

Nilashi, M., Abumalloh, R.A., Mohd, S., Azhar, S.N.F.S., Samad, S., Thi, H.H., Alghamdi, O.A. & Alghamdi, A. (2023). COVID-19 and sustainable development goals: A bibliometric analysis and SWOT analysis in Malaysian context. *Telematics and Informatics*, 76, 101923.

Oxford, R. L., Perz, S. A., & Schultz, J. (2023). From Polycrisis to Peace. *Peace Research*, 55(1), 36–70.

Rom, F. M., Mahmud, A. A. E., Suainbon, R., & Miskan, M. (2023). Psychological impact and coping style among students of National Defence University of Malaysia during the COVID-19 Pandemic. *Bangladesh Journal of Medical Science*, 22(1), 105–114.

Shah, S. A. A., Fianto, B. A., Sheikh, A. E., Sukmana, R., Kayani, U. N., & Ridzuan, A. R. B. (2023). Role of fintech in credit risk management: An analysis of Islamic banks in Indonesia, Malaysia, UAE and Pakistan. *Journal of Science and Technology Policy Management*, 14(6), 1128–1154.

Zakaria, S. M., Abdullah, N., Md Akhir, N., Amin, A. S., Mohd Shukry, A. N. A., Abdul Rashid, M. R., & Wan Yusof, W. N. (2022). Perceptions of quality of life during the pandemic: A case study on B40 single mothers. *International Journal of Environmental Research and Public Health*, 19(19), 12219.

Zeitlin, J., Nicoli, F., & Laffan, B. (2019). Introduction: The European Union beyond the polycrisis? Integration and politicisation in an age of shifting cleavages. *Journal of European Public Policy*, 26(7), 963–976.

17 India's Quest for Leadership of Global South

Debendra Sahu

17.1 Introduction

Global interconnectivity and the resultant integrated global demand and supply chain have also integrated the crises worldwide. The political and economic crises in one state, one sector, and one aspect often spill over to another in no time. The convergence of a multitude of challenges emerging from geopolitical crises like the enduring conflict in Ukraine, post-COVID stagflation, employment crisis, illicit economic activity, debt crisis, resource rivalries, climate change, and increasing emissions forming a "polycrisis" that requires a comprehensive global response and multifaceted solutions. The COVID-19 crisis caused chronic and infectious health conditions, leading to lockdown of cities and closing of borders. This led to a prolonged economic downturn, which resulted in an employment crisis. The employment crisis ran the risk of proliferation of illicit employment activities. The same is true with interstate conflict, collapse of state, effecting large-scale involuntary migration. All in all, the interconnection of risk intensified the severity of individual risk (World Economic Forum [WEF], 2023). Global South has been the most affected by this "polycrisis" and is now searching for a solution of its own, not forced upon it by the West.

India has been at the forefront of articulating the voice of Global South since Narendra Modi's ascendancy to power in New Delhi. The External Affairs Minister of India, Subrahmanyam Jaishankar, called on Europe to prioritise global issues over its own. In its election manifesto of 2014, the Bharatiya Janata Party (BJP) emphasised India getting due recognition in global forums and institutions. The manifesto also talked about adopting "proactive diplomacy" to reclaim its status as *Vishwaguru* – Global Teacher (BJP, 2014). The 2019 election manifesto declared India's rise as the new reality and committed to positioning India as a leading force in shaping the global agenda while prioritising "First responder" roles during crises (BJP, 2019).

Against this backdrop, this chapter aims to analyse India's pursuit of a leadership role within the Global South by delving into the convergence of India's interest with its advocacy for the Global South. It explores the significance of India's solidarity with Global South and analyses India's diplomatic strategies

DOI: 10.4324/9781032694337-24

and policy approaches in addressing global challenges. In doing so, it contributes to existing literature on India's quest for leadership in this context by providing insights into India's aspirations and contributions to shaping the voice of Global South into a credible one in the new world order ridden with crises.

17.1.1 Literature Review

There has been a lot of scholarly debate on what constitutes the Global South. The term is not only about geography but also defines the developmental disparity between the Northern and Southern Hemispheres (Dirlik, 2007; Grovogu, 2011; Gray & Gills, 2016). Global South in this context includes the formerly colonised part of the world, united by developmental and political goals and belonging to geographic regions of Latin America, the Caribbean, Africa, Asia, and Oceania. Despite the debate surrounding the geographic and developmental definition of the term "Global South," the countries constituting Global South seek to have a voice of their own. Discussions on issues like Trade-Related Aspects of Intellectual Property Rights (TRIPs) underscored the divergent interests between Global North and Global South (Ntaba et al., 2021; Forman et al., 2023). Criticism of India among other developing countries, who were touted as "villains of Copenhagen" (Mark Lynas [2009] as cited in Hurrell and Sengupta, 2012) and described as a "major emitter, whose development choices are critical to the future of climate change but whose governments have proved to be obstructionist and negative" (Hurrell & Sengupta, 2012) also highlighted this divergence.

Irrespective of how "Global South" is defined, India's leadership role in the Non-Aligned Movement, colonial history, developmental journey, response to discriminatory "NPT" regime, and championing trade negotiations in the WTO makes India a vital constituent of Global South. In its ambition of achieving rising power status and the vision of a "Viksit Bharat" – a developed India by 2047, the 100th year of independence, India continues to build strategic and economic partnerships with developed countries. Concomitantly, India also seeks support from the developing countries of Global South. Literature surrounding India's role in Global South has been rich and varied, reflecting geopolitical dynamics and developmental challenges. Cooper (2021) sees this as India's ambivalence in India's foreign policy approach. This view has also been reinforced as "transitional identity" (Thakur, 2014, p. 1793), "two attitudes towards external reality" (Bhabha, 2017, p. 91), and as ambiguity in India's foreign policy by various other scholars (Mitra & Schottli, 2007). Discussion about India's engagement in multilateral forums as a "status seeking rising power" and as "champion of solidarity with other countries of the Global South" (Chakrabarti, 2017; Cooper, 2021) provided additional insight into India's diplomatic strategies.

There has also been literature focusing on China, the other claimant for leadership position. China aims to create an alternative world order (Murphy, 2022) by broadening its sphere of influence with infrastructure projects like the

Belt and Road Initiative (Pillsbury, 2019) and economic exchanges with political conditionalities (Char, 2016). Some work has been done on a comparative study of India's approach with that of China (Wagner, 2016; Cooper, 2021; Banik & Mawdsley, 2023). Despite these contributions, there remains a gap in the literature regarding a comprehensive analysis of India's quest for leadership role amidst interconnected crises. This chapter seeks to address this gap by providing a nuanced examination of India's policies and approaches within the context of contemporary challenges.

17.1.2 A Note on Methods

This chapter employs a qualitative research approach by examining existing literature, including scholarly articles, policy documents, and government reports. Primary sources, such as official statements, declarations, and press releases from Indian government agencies and international organisations, are also utilised to gather empirical evidence with the help of limited data. The analysis focuses on identifying key themes and patterns in India's diplomatic strategies, policy positions, and actions. Comparative analysis is also employed to elucidate India's responses and contribution within the broader context of global governance and South-South cooperation.

17.2 COVID-19 Crisis and Global South

The COVID-19 healthcare crisis, which soon spiralled into a livelihood crisis, affected Global South and Global North disproportionately. Figure 17.1 shows the percentage of informal employment in different regions of the world when COVID-19 struck in 2019. The share of countries in the Global South were much higher in the informal sector, with Central and Southern Africa at 86.3 per cent and sub-Saharan Africa at 84.9 per cent. This group of informal workers were without any basic protection like little or no job security, social sector benefits, low wages, and were unprotected by labour laws. Evidently, the countries from Global South were the hardest hit countries, and the workers from these countries faced the highest risk of falling into poverty. A major fallout of rising poverty is millions of children being forced into child labour.

Likewise, the Global South was also pushed into an unprecedented unemployment crisis among the youth during the pandemic. Figure 17.2 illustrates the comparison of proportion of youth not engaged in education, employment, or training (NEET) in 2018 and 2022. All the regions in Global South, with exception of Latin America and the Caribbean, saw an increase in proportion of NEET in 2022 in comparison to the pre-pandemic level in 2018. The difference in Oceania's data stems from Australia and New Zealand being included in 2018 and excluded in 2022.

Furthermore, Figure 17.3 highlights the very low proportion of social security protection for Global South countries vis-à-vis the high-income countries

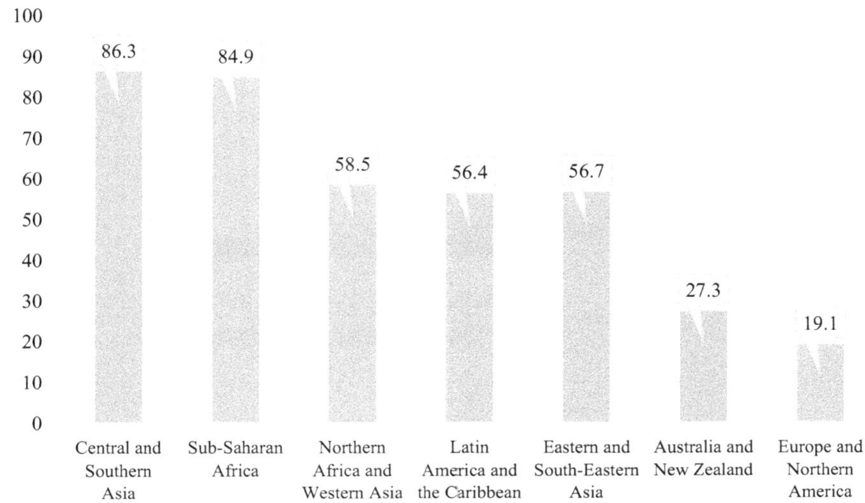

Figure 17.1 Informal employment in total employment by percentage in 2019.

Source: Goal 8, the Sustainable Development Goal Report 2021.

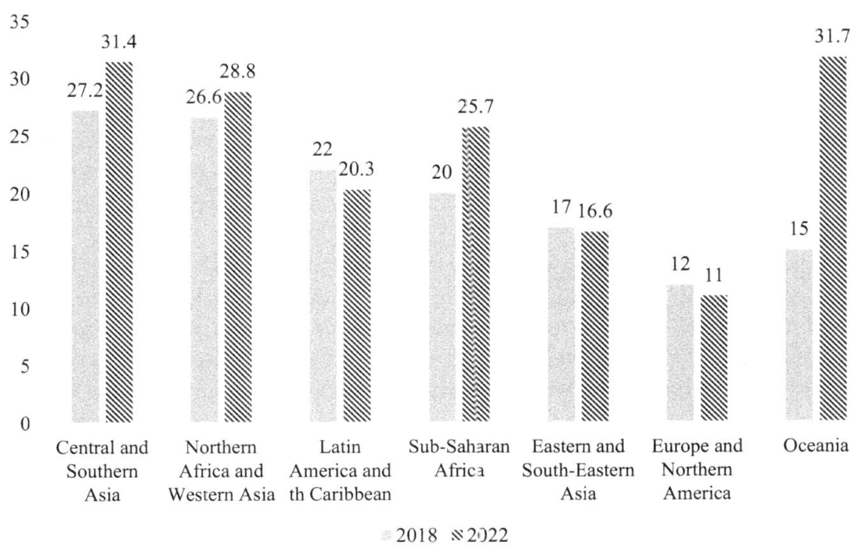

Figure 17.2 Proportion of youth not in education, employment, or training.

Source: Goal 8, the Sustainable Development Goal Report of 2019 and 2023.

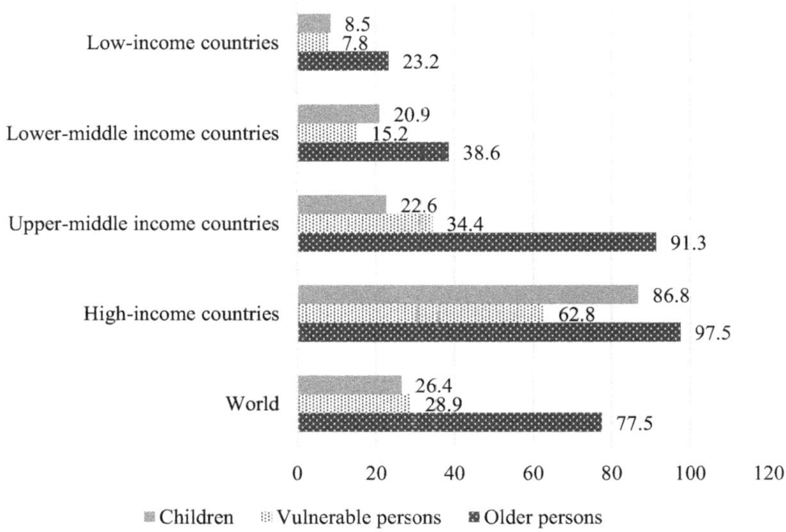

Figure 17.3 Proportion of children, vulnerable persons, and older persons covered by social protection cash benefits, 2020 (percentage).

Source: Goal 1, the Sustainable Development Goal Report of 2023.

of Global North. The national expenditure of lower-middle income countries for children and older persons also remains low (UN Statistics Division, 2023).

Figure 17.4 shows the proportion of unemployed persons receiving cash benefits to unemployed people. The high-income countries provided cash benefits to more than 50 per cent of unemployed people in comparison to less than 1 per cent for low-income countries and 5.5 per cent for lower-middle income countries.

It is evident from the discussion here that while the COVID-19 crisis affected all the countries in the world, developing and underdeveloped countries were struggling more to respond and mitigate the crisis. Naturally, these countries waited for COVID-19 vaccines to re-emerge from the ruptures of the crisis. It is natural that all countries prioritise their own citizens, but ignoring the health workers and vulnerable populations in low-income countries has wider ramifications. This not only widens the inequality gap that already exists but also has economic implications, as this will prolong the pandemic.

Table 17.1 illustrates bottom ten countries in terms of vaccinated population in all three categories of at least one dose, complete primary series and with one booster dose, are all from Global South with the sole exception of Ukraine because of the war. Similarly, countries from Global North dominate the list of top ten vaccinated countries in all three categories. This difference in mitigation of the crisis also validates the argument that Global South

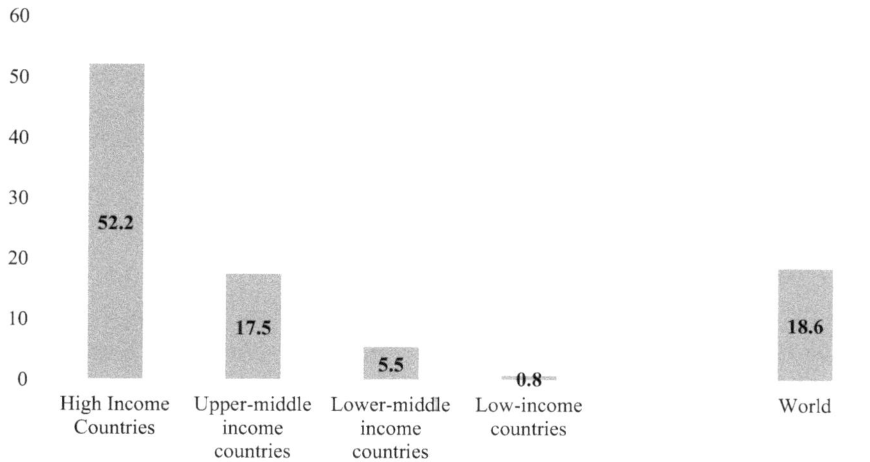

Figure 17.4 Proportion of unemployed persons receiving unemployment cash benefits, 2020.

Source: Goal 1, the Sustainable Development Goal Report of 2022.

Table 17.1 Bottom Ten Countries in Terms of Vaccinated Population as on November 26, 2023

At least one dose		*Complete primary series*		*At least one booster*	
Country	*% of Population*	*Country*	*% of Population*	*Country*	*% of Population*
Yemen	4	Yemen	3	Madagascar	1
Papua New Guinea	4	Haiti	3	Iraq	1
Haiti	5	Papua New Guinea	4	Algeria	1
Madagascar	10	Senegal	9	Venezuela	2
Congo	13	Madagascar	9	Ukraine	2
Gabon	14	Gabon	12	Uganda	2
Cameroon	14	Congo	12	Jamaica	2
Senegal	15	Cameroon	12	Gambia	2
Algeria	18	Syria	13	Libya	3
Syria	19	Equatorial Guinea	15	Guinea	3

Source: World Health Organization COVID-19 dashboard, 2023 (WHO, 2023).

needs to find solutions to its own problems and be a voice of its own. India was also hit hard by the COVID-19 pandemic. One of the convergences of India's challenges with that of Global South is the post-COVID potential jump in poverty. As per a report prepared for the UN virtual Inter-agency Expert Group Meeting on eradication of poverty, India led the chart of top ten countries by change in potential poverty headcount with about 46 million in 2019–2020, with all other remaining countries being from Global South (Kharas and Dooley, 2021). India's GDP declined 5.83 per cent in the financial year 2020–2021 before starting to recover (PIB, 2023a). However, India, being at the forefront of development of vaccines, took a human-centric approach to global cooperation along with the difficult task of vaccinating its huge population.

17.2.1 India's Vaccine Maitri

India launched the ambitious Vaccine Maitri programme with the belief in *Vasudhaiva Kutumbakam*. Prime Minister Modi committed that India's vaccine production will be used for humanity (Modi, 2020). This was an extension of an extraordinary supply of relevant drugs, personal protection equipment (PPE) kits, and other pharmaceutical and medical products around the world. Within days of starting the vaccination drive at home, India started to supply vaccines to the world, starting with its immediate neighbour Bhutan. It was soon expanded to Nepal, other immediate neighbouring countries, Gulf, and then smaller and more vulnerable nations, including reaching out to Africa (Ministry of External Affairs [MEA], 2021a). India continued its vaccine outreach programme despite call for "vaccine nationalism" at home and abroad. The government and Prime Minister Modi were also heavily criticised when its own citizens faced massive vaccine shortage at home. Notwithstanding the political and social criticism both at home and abroad, the government of the day continued to supply vaccines to the world. Table 17.2 illustrates the top ten recipient countries.

The list of 100 countries is heavily dominated by Global South countries. While the list of top ten countries in terms of vaccine supply from India also includes a few countries from Global North, when we consider the grants and COVAX obligation disregarding the commercial supplies, the list is all about

Table 17.2 Top Ten Countries in Terms of Vaccine Supply from India (in million)

S.N.	*Country*	*Grant*	*Commercial*	*COVAX*	*Total*
	Netherlands	–	113.62	–	113.62
	Australia	–	30.91	–	30.91
	Bangladesh	3.3	15.0	9.78	28.08
	Myanmar	3.7	17.5	–	21.2
	Nigeria	0.1	–	9.7	9.8
	Nepal	1.11	2.0	6.38	9.49
	Indonesia	–	9.01	–	9.01
	USA	–	8.07	–	8.07
	Morocco	–	7.0	–	7.0
	Canada	–	6.98	–	6.98

Source: COVID-19 Updates: Vaccine Supply (MEA, 2023).

the countries from Global South. Furthermore, during the peak of COVID-19 pandemic, the vaccine supply to 53 countries till March 2021 by India was all about Global South countries apart from Canada and Ukraine (MEA, 2021b). That too was restricted to commercial supplies only. A total of 47.1 million vaccines being sent to 51 Global South countries during the peak of COVID-19 crisis is evidence of India's solidarity with Global South. This *Vaccine Maitri* outreach was in line with world's need, India's growing status as a great power, and its aspiration for the leadership of the Global South. The world leaders, particularly from the Global South countries were effusive in their praise for India, showing gratitude and appreciating the selfless cooperation during such a need. The most noteworthy was the Brazilian President Jair Bolsonaro, who equated India's vaccine supply to the world with *Sanjeevani*, a medicinal herb brought by Lord Hanuman to save Lakshmana's life as per Hindu epic *Ramayan*. India was also not hesitant to showcase its vaccine outreach, particularly towards the Global South countries. The G20 presidency of India prominently featured India's approach during the COVID-19 pandemic.

17.3 TRIPs versus Public Interest

COVID-19 also saw a different form of vaccine nationalism over the Intellectual Property Rights (IPR) for vaccines. To facilitate equitable distribution of vaccines, India and South Africa jointly proposed a temporary waiver of TRIPs governing COVID-19 vaccines, diagnostics, and therapeutics for at least three years to make the critical products accessible and affordable for all. Significant work has been done to suggest how IPR protections might lead to delay in accessibility and affordability. Patents, for example, lead to monopoly and become a barrier to affordable medicines (Durkin et al., 2021). Trade secrecy, which prevents information flow also becomes a barrier to "decentralizing production or biological resources for treatment and vaccine development" (Durkin et al., 2021, p. 130). COVID-19 clinical trial data secrecy could have led to delay in vaccine development and obstruct information about infection and immune response. So, in a time of crisis like COVID-19, public interest should prevail over commercial considerations for waiver of TRIPs. Ntaba et al. (2021) suggest "access to COVID-19 vaccines and therapeutics is part of the human right to health." Durkin et al. (2021) prescribed "mandatory proactive disclosure" and "excluding public health information from scope of trade secret" when public interest outweighs private harm. While supporting the waiver, Forman et al. (2023) presented the case of pricing variability between developed countries and countries from Global South (see Table 17.3).

While the rationale for waiving IPR protections was supported by Global South countries, most developed countries outrightly rejected its waiver on various grounds like "no evidence of IPR as barrier" and "flexibility is already existing" (WTO, 2022), "malpractice by LDC" (USITC, 2023), "impact on investor appetite for biotechnology investment" and "it will not stop here" (Busch, 2023) to oppose TRIPs waiver. Over a year after it was initially

Table 17.3 Pricing Variability of COVID-19 Vaccines

Country/Region	*Price per dose (in USD)*	*Vaccine*
European Union	2.16	AstraZeneca
Bangladesh	4.0	AstraZeneca (SII)
South Africa	5.25	AstraZeneca
Uganda	7.0	AstraZeneca
Sri Lanka	15.0	Sinopharm

Source: (Forman et al., 2023).

proposed, a severely toned-down version of the initial proposal was adopted at the WTO ministerial conference (WTO, 2022). The scope of the waiver was limited to vaccines and did not extend to diagnostics and therapeutics as originally proposed by India and South Africa. In addition, the waiver was only for low- and middle-income countries except those with manufacturing capacity (Forman et al., 2023, p. 11). While it was decided to revisit the need to extend it to diagnostics and therapeutics in six months, subsequent meetings and actions with success not in sight, the WTO members failed the countries from Global South. The opposition to this TRIPs waiver for vaccines, diagnostics, and therapeutics by countries from Global North, particularly at a time when people were dying largely due to unavailability of therapeutics and vaccines, was a cause of concern.

With contrasting vaccine coverage data of Global North vis-à-vis Global South around that time, the WHO representatives told UK MPs that "this disease now fundamentally of poorer people and poor nations" (Ntaba et al., 2021). In contrast, India, despite being one of the top three affected countries in terms of COVID-19 cases and deaths, was exporting vaccines to the Global South and led the fight for TRIPs waiver. Vaccine nationalism and subordinating public health to private and commercial interests are how far justified, is the question and this question is not going to die down soon. But India's approach for TRIPs waiver has struck a chord with Global South countries, and India once again led the way to challenge the hegemonic position of the Global North.

17.4 Climate Change and Global South

The Intergovernmental Panel on Climate Change (IPCC) has already cautioned the world about a probable rise in mean temperature by up to 4 degrees by 2099 if nothing is done to curb fossil fuel emissions. Global problem of this scale needs fundamental cooperation between countries to arrive at global solutions. However, there is another deep divide between the Global North and South. India leads the fight, arguing that developed countries must compensate for the historic emissions they have caused, leading to climate change. An environment-friendly route to development for underdeveloped and developing countries will be costly in comparison to the developmental cost incurred by the developed countries. Coal versus solar energy, petrol cars versus electric cars, natural gas versus green hydrogen are all cases in point. A United Nation Development Programme (UNDP) report of 2011 stated that there are "900 cars per thousand people of driving age in the US, 600 in Europe and only 10 in India" (Uddin, 2017). The same report also noted two televisions per house in the US to less than one in ten houses in Uganda, and average lifestyle in Britain produces more greenhouse gases in two months than what a least developed country produces in a year (Uddin, 2017). While it is true that India has overtaken the European Union and became the third largest emitter of greenhouse gas, it is important to note that India has more than thrice the population of EU. US is still emitting more greenhouse gases than India. Furthermore, if per capita emission by country is considered, developed countries still dominate the list of top emitters, and India ranks way lower (see Figure 17.5).

The world's focus on climate change has coincided with the development ambition of developing and underdeveloped countries, and it is obvious that the countries from Global South also figure in the list of top emitters. However, a look at the top ten countries most affected by weather-related loss between 2000 and 2019 shows they are all from Global South other than Puerto Rico, which has been considered separately from the US in the report (see Table 17.4).

The Global Climate Risk Index, 2021, confirms that less developed countries are more affected by existing vulnerability due to climate change, which is another example of Global South being discriminately affected by crises. Critics argue this is exactly why Global South, particularly countries like

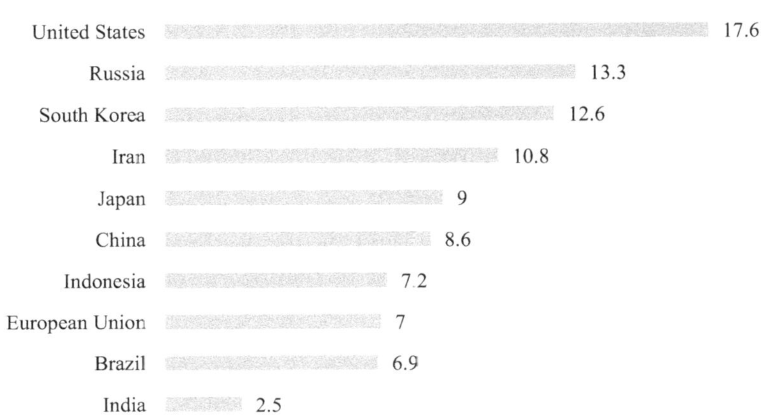

Figure 17.5 Per capita emission for the top ten total emitters, 2019, tCO2e/person.

Source: World Resources Institute, 2023.

Table 17.4 Top Ten Countries Most Affected by Weather-related Loss from 2000 to 2019

Climate Risk Index (CRI) 2000–2019	*Country*	*CRI Score*
1	Puerto Rico	7.17
2	Myanmar	10.00
3	Haiti	13.67
4	Philippines	18.17
5	Mozambique	25.83
6	The Bahamas	27.67
7	Bangladesh	28.33
8	Pakistan	29.00
9	Thailand	29.83
10	Nepal	31.33

Source: Global Climate Risk Index 2021.

India, must shift to low-carbon emission path of development. India, leading the Global South, calls it "double standard." The developing and underdeveloped countries of the Global South have made little contribution to the environmental owes vis-à-vis the developmental journey of developed countries of the North. Fighting deep poverty, the least developed world is not expected to remain where it is. Economic development is intrinsically linked to energy use, and that is why the "Kyoto Protocol" differentiation between economic development of countries and historical emission of CO_2 is an important differentiation, which is key to climate change negotiation and for the economic development of Global South countries.

India, despite its economic success in recent decades, still has its citizens below poverty line, an aspect common with many Global South countries. India continues to demand that developing countries of Global South should not be forced to cut their energy-related emissions for their economic growth. India, at the recently held COP 28 Climate Summit in Dubai, emphasised "equity" and "climate justice" as the basis for climate action (PIB, 2023b). India calls for action and funding arrangements by the developed world so that the developmental aspiration of Global South is not derailed. The Paris Accord, a commitment of 100 billion USD by the developed world, was in this line. However, it was side-tracked owing to pulling out of the US. While climate change cannot be left at the mercy of politics, Global South nations should not endure perpetual poverty due to insufficient funds and technology for low-emission development. India, with its growing aspiration for a leadership role, is starting to take proactive measures and partly committing to emission targets but, at the same time, refuses to make concessions for economic growth of the country. In the process, India leaves a template for the countries of Global South in their future course of development.

17.5 G20 Presidency of India and Global South

The G20 presidency of India in 2023, during the time of polycrisis, was a perfect occasion for the manifestation of India's aspiration. The global community, particularly the Global South countries, faced numerous challenges from the COVID-19 pandemic, economic stagflation, and rising external debt. However, the geopolitical crisis in Eastern Europe was threatening to make the G20 insignificant with the focus on Russia-Ukraine war. Jaishankar's "Europe's problem" analysis emphasises the importance of concerns other than geopolitical crisis in Europe. Furthermore, on the Ukraine crisis, India refused to take a side – the one the West wanted. India, nevertheless, succeeded in getting member countries to the table and came out with the New Delhi Declaration. With the deep divide over Ukraine apparent, coming out with a declaration that was agreeable to both sides was nothing sort of victory for India. This signifies the diplomatic clout that India has gained in recent times. For this, India worked very closely with other Global South countries like Brazil, South Africa, and Indonesia.

17.5.1 Voice of Global South Summit

With the assumption of G20 presidency in December 2022, India made efforts to take the views of most countries and issues concerning them to set the agenda of G20 through the "Voice of Global South" summit in January 2023. Critiquing the geopolitical tension in the West, Prime Minister Modi said, "geopolitical tensions distract us from focusing on our development priorities" (PIB, 2023c). He also announced the establishment of a Global South Centre for Excellence for the Global South Countries. The Centre of Excellence called the Development and Knowledge Sharing Initiative, abbreviated DAKSHIN, which means South in Hindi. Modi also emphasised the launching of "Global-South Science & Technology" initiative and the sharing of India's expertise with other developing nations. Targeting the youth of Global South, he also proposed a "Global-South Young Diplomats Forum" and "Global South Scholarships" to study in India (PIB, 2023c).

In terms of the outcome of the G20 presidency of India, the most important has been the historic inclusion of the African Union as a permanent member of the G20. The G20 New Delhi Leaders" Declaration also recognised the conflict in Ukraine and called for durable peace without specifying the aggressor. Apart from this, the G20 noted the green financing requirements to the tune of 5.9 trillion USD for developing countries. Among others, the declaration also emphasised on strengthening multilateral development banks, digital infrastructure, addressing debt vulnerabilities in developing countries and recommitting to achieve sustainable development goals. India through inclusion of the African Union, Voice of Global South Summit, and the New Delhi Declaration, has given prominence to the priorities of Global South and has successfully positioned itself as a champion of the developing world. Russian foreign minister aptly summarised and praised India's leadership and said it is "awakening of the Global South members of the G-20" and a win for Global South (Haider, 2023).

17.6 Conclusion

There is a disproportionate impact of crises on the Global South, which calls for collective response and solidarity among the countries of Global South. Historically, India has advocated that the voice of the developing world be heard and amplified its efforts in recent times. Through initiatives like the *Vaccine Maitri* programme and advocating for TRIPs waiver, India demonstrated not only its aspirations but also its commitment for the Global South countries during the time of crisis. Likewise, India refused to accept the one-sided inequitable Western prescription on climate change. India's stand exemplifies inclusivity, concern for development, and equity among nations. This strengthens the argument that India not only aspires but also leads the way for Global South towards positive changes. The G20 presidency of India also exemplified India's insistence on emphasising problems faced by the developing and underdeveloped countries in the world and making a case for global acknowledgement of such issues. At the G20, Indian efforts to ensure that Africa is an integral part of all global conversations, acknowledgement of green financing to the tune of 5.9 trillion USD for developing countries, Voice of Global South Summit, and the theme of "One Earth, One Family, One Future" has resonated with countries from the Global South.

There is no ambivalence in India's quest for leadership of Global South. It has been amply clear from many of Modi's, Jaishankar's, and other minister's views in public forums. This has also been emphasised by the ruling party, BJP's vision and domestic campaign. Going forward, India's aspiration as the leader of Global South will be tested by its role in humanitarian assistance, response in crisis, development cooperation, and inclusive diplomacy. With the other contestant for the role, China being seen as extending conditional development assistance to push its own agenda, India is the hope for "non-conventional" and "non-traditional" security in the Global South. To meet the expectation, India needs to enhance diplomatic outreach, foster deeper regional alliances, promote inclusive solutions, and prioritise initiatives that address shared challenges in the non-traditional domain. With Modi preparing for an unprecedented third term in 2024, whether India can obtain its desired place, commensurate with its civilisational status, economic, military, and demographic power, remains to be seen.

References

Banik, D. & Mawdsley, E. (2023). South-South cooperation and global development in a multipolar world: China and India in Africa. *Journal of International Development*, 1–10. https://doi.org/10.1002/jid.3789

Bhabha, H.K. (2017). *The Location of Culture*. Routledge Classics.

Bharatiya Janata Party (2014). *Election Manifesto 2014: Ek Bharat Shreshtha Bharat*. https://www.bjp.org/images/pdf_2014/full_manifesto_english_07.04.2014.pdf

Bharatiya Janata Party (2019). *Election Manifesto 2019: Sankalpit Bharat Sashakt Bharat*. https://www.bjp.org/files/2019-10/BJP-Election-english-2019.pdf

Busch, M. (2023, July 14). The market's response to the TRIPs Waiver. Wilson Center. https://www.wilsoncenter.org/article/markets%2Dresponse%2Dtrips%2Dwaiver?gad_source=1&gclid=Cj0KCQiA1rSsBhDHARIsANB4EJakvasxm8aNCml%2Du2lUML0ThpWXBSKzkdVjzNciUchUZt1ClExz8YsaAkU-EALw_wcB

Chakrabarti, S. (2017). Global South rhetoric in India's policy projection. *Third World Quarterly*, 38(8), 1909–1920, https://doi.org/10.1080/01436597.2016.1248931

Char, J. (2016). Aspiring to be a global power: China's activism in the Global South. In J. Braveboy-Wagner (Eds.) *Diplomatic Strategies of Nations in the Global South* (pp. 59–91). Palgrave Macmillan, New York.

Cooper, A.F. (2021). China, India and the pattern of G20/BRICS engagement: differentiated ambivalence between rising power status and solidarity with the Global South. *Third World Quarterly*, 42(9), 1945–1962. https://doi.org/10.1080/01436597.2020.1829464

Dirlik, A. (2007). Global South: Predicament and Promise. *The Global South*, 1(1), 12–23.

Durkin, A., Maria, P. A. S., Willmore, B., & Kapczynski, A. (2021). Addressing the Risks That Trade Secret Protections Pose for Health and Rights. *Health and Human Rights*, 23(1), 129–144.

Forman, L., Jackson, C., & Fajber, K. (2023). Can We Move Beyond Vaccine Apartheid? Examining the Determinants of the COVID-19 Vaccine Gap. *Global Public Health*, 18(1), 1–18. https://doi.org/10.1080/17441692.2023.2256822

Gray, K. & Gills, B.K. (2016). South-South cooperation and the rise of the Global South. *Third World Quarterly*, 37(4), 557–574. http://dx.doi.org/10.1080/01436597.2015.1128817

Grovogu, S. (2011). A Revolution Nonetheless: The Global South in International Relations. *The Global South*, 5(1), 175–190. https://doi.org/10.2979/globalsouth.5.1.175

Haider, S. (2023, September 10). Win for Global South, says Russian FM, praises India for G-20 summit statement success. *The Hindu*.

Hurrell, A., & Sengupta, S. (2012). Emerging Powers, North-south Relations and Global Climate Politics. *International Affairs*. 88(3), 463–484.

Kharas, H., & Dooley, M. (2021). *Extreme poverty in the time of COVID-19*, Prepared for the United Nations Virtual Inter-Agency Expert Group Meeting on the Implementation of the Third United Nations Decade for the Eradication of Poverty (2018–2027). https://www.un.org/development/desa/dspd/wp%2Dcontent/uploads/sites/22/2021/05/KHARAS_paper1.pdf

Ministry of External Affairs. (2021a). Injecting hope: fighting the Covid-19 pandemic together. https://indianembassy-moscow.gov.in/pdf/Covid_16_03.pdf

Ministry of External Affairs. (2021b, June 15). Covid-19 Updates: Vaccine Supply. https://www.mea.gov.in/vaccine-supply.htm

Ministry of External Affairs. (2023). Reply to unstarred question in Lok Sabha. https://sansad.in/getFile/loksabhaquestions/annex/175/AU2648.pdf?source=pqals

Mitra, S.K., & Schottli, J. (2007). The New Dynamics of Indian Foreign Policy and Its Ambiguities. *Irish Studies in International Affairs*, 18, 19–34. http://www.jstor.org/stable/25469813

Modi, Narendra (2020, September 26). *Text of PM's Address at the 75th United Nations General Assembly (UNGA) session 2020*. Prime Minister's Office. https://www.pib.gov.in/PressReleasePage.aspx?PRID=1659410

Murphy, D.C. (2022). *China's Rise in the Global South: The Middle East, Africa and Beijing's Alternative World Order*. Stanford University Press.

Ntaba, Z., Uprimny, R., & Yacoob, Z. (2021, November 30). Rich Countries Must Stop Blocking the COVID Vaccine Patent Waiver. *Al Jazeera*. https://www.aljazeera.com/opinions/2021/11/30/rich-countries-must-stop-blocking-the-covid-vaccine-patent-waiver

Press Information Bureau. (2023a). *GDP Growth*. Ministry of Statistics & Programme Implementation. https://pib.gov.in/PressReleasePage.aspx?PRID=1942795

Press Information Bureau. (2023c, January 13). *"Prime Minister Shri Narendra Modi's opening remarks at the concluding leaders" session of the Voice of Global South Summit*. Prime Minister's Office. https://pib.gov.in/PressReleasePage.aspx?PRID=1891102

Press Information Bureau. (2023b, December 09). *COP 28 national statement by Union Minister for Environment, Forest and Climate Change Shri Bhupender Yadav*. Ministry of Environment, Forest, and Climate Change. https://pib.gov.in/PressReleaseIframePage.aspx?PRID=1984434

Thakur, R. (2014). How Representative Are BRICS? *Third World Quarterly*, 35(10), 1791–1808.

Uddin, M. K. (2017). Climate Change and Global Environmental Politics: North-south Divide. *Environmental Policy and Law*, 47(3–4), 106–114.

United Nations Statistics Division. (2019). *The Sustainable Development Goals Report 2019*. https://unstats.un.org/sdgs/report/2019/The-Sustainable-Development-Goals-Report-2019.pdf

United Nations Statistics Division. (2021). *The Sustainable Development Goals Report 2021*. https://unstats.un.org/sdgs/report/2021/The-Sustainable-Development-Goals-Report-2021.pdf

United Nations Statistics Division. (2022). *The Sustainable Development Goals Report 2022*. https://unstats.un.org/sdgs/report/2022/The-Sustainable-Development-Goals-Report-2022.pdf

United Nations Statistics Division. (2023). *The Sustainable Development Goals Report 2023 Special Edition*. https://unstats.un.org/sdgs/report/2023/The-Sustainable-Development-Goals-Report-2023.pdf

United Stats International Trade Commission. (2023). COVID-19 Diagnostics and Therapeutics: Supply, Demand, and TRIPS Agreement Flexibilities. https://www.usitc.gov/publications/332/pub5469.pdf

Wagner, C. (2016). The Role of India and China in South Asia. *Strategic Analysis*, 40(4), 307–320. https://doi.org/10.1080/09700161.2016.1184790

World Economic Forum. (2023). *The global risks report 2023*. 18th Edition. https://www3.weforum.org/docs/WEF_Global_Risks_Report_2023.pdf

World Health Organization. (2023). *WHO COVID-19 dashboard*. Retrieved on November 26, 2023 from https://data.who.int/dashboards/covid19/vaccines?m49=001&n=c

World Trade Organization. (2022, July 6). TRIPS Council welcomes MC12 TRIPS waiver decision, discusses possible extension. https://www.wto.org/english/news_e/news22_e/trip_08jul22_e.htm

Pillsbury, M. (2019). *The Hundred-Year Marathon: China's Secret Strategy to Replace America as the Global Superpower*. Macmillan US.

18 Postcolonial Urbanism

Making and Unmaking of World-Class City in Amaravati

Maanvender Singh, Bikku, Aqsa Agha, Ugen Bhutia, and Chandna Deka

18.1 Introduction

In a globally integrated economic system phrases such as smart cities, world-class cities and futuristic cities have not only shaped the imaginaries of city-making discourse in the Global South but also set the tone on how global is imagined and produced (Ong, 2011; Roy, 2011b; Datta 2019). They become important sites to imagine, confirm and contest national and regional identities, which also justifies the restructuring of such urban spaces (Roy, 2011a; Upadhya, 2017). One of the key essences to understanding what shapes the imagination of such ideas is to recognise what Ong (2011) calls the "art of being global" (pp. 12, 23). The task, therefore, what Ong (2011) argues, is to imagine urban as an animated space with a range of speculative possibilities in terms of actors, institutions and practices. This calls for a continuous effort to resist the singular logic of global/world-class cities and move beyond labelling such projects as mere conjecturing of the neoliberal utopia or homogenous postcolonial experiments (Roy, 2011b, p. 309). The emphasis should also be on understanding the provincialisation (Chakrabarty, 2000) of city-making (Roy, 2011b, p. 310). In this context, our research locates the idea of Amaravati as the site of reorienting Telugu aspirations where the urban is imagined in various speculative possibilities (Goldman, 2023) and is constituted by practices of inter-referencing and solidarity with the Asian experience of urbanism (Ong, 2011, p. 18).

On 2 June 2014, Andhra Pradesh (AP) State in India was bifurcated, and the new state of Telangana was formed with AP, retaining its original name. Hyderabad (capital of the undivided state) was announced to remain the joint capital for the next ten years, during which AP was expected to pick a capital for them. Within one month, then chief minister of AP, Chandra Babu Naidu, announced he would build a new capital that he claimed would surpass even what Hyderabad had achieved.[1] Amaravati, a small village between Guntur and Vijayawada, was announced as new capital. It was projected as the next big thing in India, guided by the technocratic expertise of Singapore and Japan.

Amaravati needs to be located in this moment of despair, hope and desire. With the state's bifurcation, Amaravati becomes the site to reorient Telugu

DOI: 10.4324/9781032694337-25

identity. As discussed by Upadhya, the global developmental imaginary of Amaravati reflects the "older developmental imaginary that has shaped Andhra's regional identity" (Upadhya, 2017, p. 181). The Telugu identity, which Amaravati as capital so often evokes, is hegemonic and is crafted by either suppressing or marginalising other narratives of regional identity, something that was reflected in the popular demand for autonomy in Telangana movement that challenged the cultural and material dominance of coastal Andhra (Upadhya, 2017). The Telugu identity in the context of Amaravati is primarily defined by the cultural and material pathways created by the *Kamma*'s of coastal Andhra and their emergence as the transnational regional elite (Roohi, 2023).[2] Therefore, Amaravati reflects the political project from where emanates its idea as a global city and which it (the city) encourages in many ways. The construction of Amaravati emerges as a restoration project that aims to reclaim Telugu for both the present and future. The symbolic importance of building new wealth, named and planned in the ancient Buddhist site of the Satavahana Kingdom and the Pallava, is equally important.

18.1.1 Objectives and Methodology

The chapter is divided into three sections and builds on Roy (2011a) and Ong's (2011) framework of postcolonial urbanism. The first section provides an overview of the discourse on postcolonial urbanism in India and how the idea of urban space becomes inevitable and natural in different forms and meanings. The second section critically engages with the discourse of a world-class/global city in the context of Amaravati. We show how the world-class city is an important discursive trope that justifies how urban space is imagined and built. In the third section, we draw on the data obtained from the field employing qualitative field-based research methods and tools. We used unstructured and semi-structured in-depth interviews, focus group discussions, observation and case studies, in four villages, namely, Neerukonda, Kuragallu, Inavolu and Nowluru in the "Knowledge City" of Amaravati Capital Region, from August 2021 to December 2023. These four villages where educational institutions burgeoned were selected for this study to probe how individuals and communities experience various forms of social exclusion in the city-making process make sense of such ubiquitous ideas and offer their own meanings to the idea of world class.

18.2 Discussion: Postcolonial Desire and Inevitability of Urban

On 2 April 1952, the first prime minister of India Jawaharlal Nehru made a speech while announcing Chandigarh as the new administrative city of Punjab.

> Let this be a new town, symbolical of the freedom of India, unfettered by the traditions of the past – an expression of the nation's faith in the future....
>
> (cited in Khosla, 2015, 11)

Nehru's imperative to build something new was reflective of the anxieties and desires of a postcolonial state that was struggling with the aftermath of partition, refugee settlement and war coupled with a moribund economy. Through Chandigarh, Nehru was speaking of new assertions of a future vision that could break from the structures and ideas that he believed held a restrictive control on modern collectivities of the nation-state. Chandigarh offered solutions to the problems of the nation by extending its imagination beyond the confines of local and parochial. Ong's (2011) observation in this context is important; the city is imagined and built as a space of intervention to solve problems associated with modern life and national and regional interests (p. 10). However, it is not just the question of whether Chandigarh failed or succeeded in creating something new and just. It is the rationality expressed through the designs of a city and the production of knowledge about urban as true and universal becomes the problem (Foucault & Rabinow, 1984). The new values that the city claims to create easily become spaces of power and domination (Foucault & Rabinow, 1984). Therefore, as Nehru speaks of creating new values for a future nation, a dominant description of urban space emerges as inevitable and simultaneously desirable.

James Scott's (1998) concept of high modernism provides the framework for understanding why such highly motivated projects insist on the socio-economic reordering of society (p. 88). Scott (1998) locates fetishism to build something new as a faith in scientific authoritarianism that resists or eliminates the local knowledge (pp. 89–93). Self-confident in scientific rationality to improve the human condition, high modernism creates an episteme of planned and orderly (Scott, 1998). Therefore, Le Corbusier, the key architect of Chandigarh, disapproves of animated Indian streets. Instead, the organised symmetry of the human body becomes Corbusier's figure of rationality replicated in built form to achieve order, producing regimented dimensions in city planning.

In this, nationalist imagination of rural and urban binaries offers an insight into the indispensability of urban in the postcolonial desire for development. For instance, Aditya Nigam (2011) points out how M.K. Gandhi in *Hind Swaraj* presents an alternative to speed exhibited by an industrial society. Gandhi, according to Nigam (2011), in his critique of factory production, "enunciates an aesthetic of slowness" (p. 88). Gandhian alternative to the industrial hysteria of speed was to move towards self-sustaining villages and small-scale industries catering to more localised needs (Datta, 2019). More importantly, the Indian village for Gandhi was an important repository of economic, political and cultural and key constituent of self (Nandi, 2001, p. 16). Gandhi often counterposed villages with colonial cities as an alternative to the totalising discourse of capitalism and socialism (Jodhka, 2002). Nehru, on the other hand, while acknowledging the value of the rural in harnessing anticolonial energies, also believed that the village quintessentially was inept for modernity (Jodhka, 2002) and, therefore, the break that Nehru speaks of can only be achieved through urban space that is structured free of traditional orders This dichotomy widened post-1990s with the urban turn or digital turn in urbanism, imagining and governing cities through speed (Datta, 2019).

But did the experience of urban planning change as India transitioned from the state bureaucratic capitalism of the Nehruvian period to the neoliberal capitalism of the post-1990s? The debate oscillates between two homogenising teleology of urban experience in postcolonial India from the homogenising effects of neoliberalism in the formation of urban space to the subaltern response or resistance to the global (Ong, 2011, p. 2). Both readings largely extend Marxist understanding of urban space and, therefore, locate the Indian postcolonial experience of urbanism from the paradigms of catching up to the benchmarks of development (Ong, 2011, p. 2) or label the urban experiments in India as mimicking the neoliberal desires to leapfrog the stages of development and engineer something new that can disrupt the existing orders (Banerjee-Guha, 2020). There is also then a tendency in urban studies to suggest that the discourse on urbanism in India took a ruptural turn in the post-1990s with the imposition of a neoliberal framework (Banerjee-Guha, 2020).

While it is true that the neoliberal reasoning of urban planning has become omnipresent, and the world-class/global cities almost anywhere are being modelled by the transnational or global capital. However, the assumptions of homogenised planning at the behest of global capital and an equally homogenised subaltern response to such urban spaces miss an important point (Banerjee-Guha, 2020). The experiments of city-making in the Global South are not assembled under regimented commands of transnational capital. The ideas are rather communicated and drawn from a disparate spectrum of urban ideas. For instance, Peck, Theodore and Brenner (2009) point out the uneven and often contradictory process of neoliberalism that is geographically variable, and locally rooted in the distinctive crises or vernacular capitalism of regional South India (Upadhay, 2017). Ong (2011) argues that mobile technology of the neoliberal political economy allows neoliberal "borrowing, appropriations, and alliances" in varied ideological and political systems (p. 5). Therefore, brands Dubai and Singapore are circulated and consumed in Asia, Africa and other parts of the world as best practices in creating new or remodelling existing urban space (Haines, 2011, p. 164).

18.2.1 Amaravati and Framing of New City Narratives

In one of our visits to a Dalit colony of Neerukonda village in 2023, we asked a group of women about the "aspirations they had when Amaravati was first announced as the capital". One of the women responded in a tone of despair and diminishing hope. "We hoped that if Amaravati became like Hyderabad or Singapore, our children would find employment opportunities in software companies and their future would be secured".[3] The statement shows how the people on the margins became invested in the narratives of world-class city and appropriated the desire of belonging to the global. This is/was one of the key founding narratives of Amaravati. Regular localised media blitz was carried out to showcase the coming of global to Andhra and Andhra becoming global

(Ramachandraiah, 2016). In the same conversation, we were told that the APCRDA (Andhra Pradesh Capital Region Development Authority) officials would often take them to the panchayat office to show images and videos of Amaravati plan built on Singapore model and how it would be better than Hyderabad.[4] The peddling of these urban imaginaries stopped in 2019 when the newly elected government led by Jagan Mohan Reddy[5] either scrapped or put on hold most of the projects in Amaravati.[6] Jagan instead announced a plan to build three capitals as Amaravati was reduced to the status of legislative capital.[7] However, this order was reversed by the High Court of AP in 2022 and recently Supreme Court of India also refused to offer any immediate solution to the rumbling over the capital.[8] As the growling continues for the capital, the narratives from which the idea of Amaravati emanates remain firm in the state. These narratives now exist amidst angst of uncertainty.

We are proposing three main arguments that will help to deconstruct the narratives of Amaravati and their meanings. First, like other postcolonial experiments in city-making, Amaravati internalises the global discourse on urbanism and, therefore, is imagined as becoming part of the global. This leads to the transplantation of ideas, tools, experts, policy designs and planning models. However, this is not a mere imitation of the neoliberal logic of city building. Rather, Amaravati becomes a "field of intervention", a space of problem-solving as Ahiwa Ong (2011) notes and, therefore, "instantiate some vision of the world in formation" (p. 11). Second, the idea of Amaravati as a world-class city is not established solely from econometric forecasting of urban space. Such ideas require the propagation of a compelling futuristic vision (Ghertner, 2011, p. 281). In the case of Amaravati, such a vision is rooted in the idea of re-conceptualising and recreating a modern technocratic Telugu state. Thus, the city of Amaravati, both in imagined and built form, is tied to the stories of the regional modernity of Andhra (Upadhyay, 2017). This vision, however, exists in abstract form, offering a multitude of speculative and performative ideas of urban spaces. Lastly, we situate the Amaravati project in the grammar of speed, which has become essential and fundamental to neoliberal urban planning (Shaban & Datta, 2019). Speed both in conception and design is an essential trope in shaping new vocabularies of the urban (Shaban & Datta, 2019). Amaravati is no different in that sense it was/is conceptualised with a discourse of an urgent need for a global capital for the Telugu people.

18.2.2 Urban Imaginaries of Global

In 2014, the Government of India (GoI) appointed an Expert Committee in March to deliberate upon the alternatives for capital city in AP (Sivaramakrishnan, K.C et al, 2014).[9] One of the key terms of reference of the report was to advise on possible suggestions for the capital region without affecting the agricultural system (p. 12). The report had advised against the idea of building a greenfield capital particularly anywhere around Guntur-Vijayawada region as it happens to be the most fertile land in AP (p. 26).

However, these concerns were ignored and in December 2014, the governments of AP and Singapore signed a Memorandum of Understanding (MoU) to develop the new greenfield capital city in Guntur-Vijayawada region.[10] Singapore was expected to assist in designing the capital plan, act as a developer in some capacity and share the urban development expertise (Ramachandraiah, 2016). As the foundation stone of the new capital was laid in June 2015 by the prime minister of India Narendra Modi, Naidu made an emphatic statement on Amaravati.

> Every Telugu should feel proud of the new capital Amaravati, which should be the envy of every country in the world, which would be unparalleled in the history of India.
>
> (Cited in Ramachandraiah, 2016, p. 75)

We need to read the above statement through the framework of worlding practices (Ong, 2011, p. 12). Worlding is a set of practices or processes by which the city(ies) work, speculate and experiment to establish themselves and their vision as part of the global without fixating on a singular design of globality (Ong, 2011, p. 12). The claim of Amaravati to be the best in the world is made from a comparative framework where Singapore becomes the point of reference. Singapore is often reiterated as desirable in the vision statement of Amaravati.[11] The worlding practices are inherently speculative and disruptive in a way that some of these projects are disrupted by the very speculative nature that fuels such projects. This is also true in the case of Amaravati, where "speculative urbanism" justifies speculative development projects (Devabhaktuni, 2022). More importantly, worlding practices exhibit that the processes that create or imagine a "global situation are always in formation" (Ong, 2011, p. 12). Therefore, it becomes important to dissociate from any particular ideological underpinning from which worlding is homogenised (p. 12).

World-class cities are teleological projects of progress filtered through global systems of knowledge on urban planning. However, what is being imagined as global is locally adopted and appropriated, or there is a provincialisation of global (Narayanan, 2019). Amaravati, instead of mimicking, assembles and inserts some fragments of Singapore's experiments in city building and its functioning, such as water resource management, tourism, vertical farms and subsidised housing,[12] or Twin Tower project, expected to be developed by Shapoorji Pallonji in Velagapudi, inspired from Burj Khalifa.[13] Inter-referencing is an important methodological tool to understand how, in recent times, the urban experiments in the Global South have overlooked the metropolis hegemony and why Amaravati leans towards the Asian experience of urban planning, which Ong (2011) argues is a "distinctive vision of global" learning from the Asian experiences, in which inter-referencing becomes inevitable.

Singapore becomes synonymous with the urban utopian space that can resolve issues of urbanisation (Ong, 2011, p. 4). Singapore, as Ong (2011) argues, is a site of urban normativity, which inspires cities across Asia to translocate their urban planning model termed "urban modelling" (p. 14). However, the key aspects of worlding of Amaravati and its assertion as the best in the world are located in the regional developmental aspirations of Andhra (Upadhay, 2017). Therefore, Amaravati often claims to be the best in the world and on par with Singapore and, at times, better than Singapore.[14] The story of Singapore for Amaravati is significant as it tries to create a distinctive imprint on the global urban experience.

It is important to further deconstruct the future vision in which the city imagines and invests the self and the people and how one locates the confluence of the regional identity with the idea of being global in Amaravati (Upadhay, 2017). The city is an unbound phenomenon, not peculiar in the sense of distinctiveness to one claim (Sheppard et al., 2013). The future that the city aspires to is produced amid circulation of ideas and practices that are not solely bound to the local peculiarities or designed by the compulsions of national and global. This is not to imply that any attempt to understand the regional or local imaginaries of the city is a seamless exercise. What is important is to locate and understand the patterns of contestation and appropriation of world class in Amaravati and resist defining the city in the form of only peculiarities or abject differences from the other experiences. Similarly, locating the experience of city building in local/parochial or regional sensibilities does not mean that it creates or imagines a space of peculiarity or difference (Sivaramakrishnan & Agrawal, 2003).

It is the constant reiterating of Amaravati being better and bigger than Hyderabad that becomes important to understand here.[15] The project Amaravati is rooted in the regional histories of postcolonial in which the meanings that define the identity of a region are produced and redefined in a certain historical context. The bifurcation of AP is one such moment. For instance, the observations made by Ananya Roy (2011a) on how Tata Nano project shifted from Nandigram to Sanad in Gujarat represented the "confluence of Hindu fundamentalism and neoliberal nationalism" (p. 264). The project was a key moment in the history of Gujarat and the nation as new meanings were being drawn to the postcolonial imagination of development (Roy, 2011a, p. 264). Similarly, the formation of Amaravati needs to be historicised and located in the earlier projects of Telugu modernity such as the planning of Hyderabad as cybercity (Upadhay, 2017). Therefore, the idea that Amravati offers a new and more prosperous future to Telugu people is engineered with the confluence of vernacular neoliberalism and the aspirational middle class dominated mostly by the *Kammas*. An imaginary that is often fuelled by the transnational network created by the Telugu people living abroad, particularly in the United States of America (Roohi, 2023).

Lastly, the future that Amaravati imagines is produced by the grammar of speed (Nigam 2011, p. 10), an insatiable desire to scale up the global by removing the bottleneck (Datta, 2015), which is inherently embedded in how such abstract notions of futuristic cities are imagined. As Datta argues, the idea of futuring claims centrality to such projects, creating a dialectic relation between the past and the future (Datta, 2019). In the context of smart cities in India, Datta (2019) suggests that smart cities are marked by two parallel mythologies of speed – nationhood and technology. In this, the city, as argued by Nigam (2011), often becomes the space where the "aesthetic of slowness" (p. 88) is either marginalised or made futile and disorderly. In the same tone, Amaravati sets itself for a utopian project reflected in the nine thematic cities – Justice, Media, Knowledge, Electronics, Sports, Tourism, Education, Government and Finance.[16] Amaravati participates in new kinds of urban commons, such as the discourse of "liveability", making competing claims to the quality of life (Government of Andhra Pradesh, 2018, p. 15). These ideas are easily manifested in the real estate scheme and are often achieved by gentrification.

As argued by Datta, one factor that differentiates some of these projects from the earlier experiments of city building in postcolonial India is the "rhetoric of urgency", which further justifies how laws are passed with a sense of urgency to speed up the process (Datta, 2015). The Ease of Doing Business, a ranking system established by the World Bank, is one such example that celebrates and rewards speed that is associated with the projects that streamline the laws and policies to make the implementation of a project easier. The Land Pooling Scheme (LPS) that the AP government implemented to transfer land from farmers to the state for building capital. The difference in the LPS is that unlike the land acquisition done by the state, where there is no right over the land, in LPS, the state promises a partnership between the owner of the land and the developer. However, there have been reports of large-scale co-optation and coercion in the LPS, particularly of the assigned land given to the Dalit and tribal farmers (Kolsto, 2019).

Amaravati exhibits a certain form of "instant urbanism", enforcing unprecedented reordering of the urban space by making large-scale changes in the laws (Murray, 2022; Datta, 2015). In this process, cities largely ignore the existing social inequalities and struggles of urban life and instead "promise to build a new city without any 'annoyances' of everyday urban life" (Datta, 2015). To achieve such grandeur, several legislations and laws are hastily passed. In 2014, one such bill was approved by the AP government, and the power was given to the APCRDA to acquire, sell, transfer, lease or grant licenses for development and redevelopment of land (APCRDA Act, 2014). Similarly, the National Green Tribunal had expressed its concern as the state government failed to complete the mandatory environmental assessment test before deciding on Amaravati as the new capital.

18.3 Conclusion

18.3.1 Voices from Below

In June 2019, the World Bank decided to pull out from the Amaravati project. It was believed non-compliance with environmental policies and farmer concerns were the main reasons.[17] In November, the Singapore consortium also walked away from the project of building the start-up area in Amaravati.[18] As the two major investors pulled out, the urgency of the urban imaginary in which the city was conceived and built was given a rude shock. Since then, Amaravati has gradually turned into a "ghost city" as the key infrastructure projects were either shelved or left in a state of incompletion. What remains of Amaravati today are half-constructed buildings, and roadways leading to shrubs and bushes. The thousand acres of multi-crop land that was given under the LPS also lie largely unused or have become unfarmable. Amaravati today represents what Lucas Pohl (2021) calls "new urban ruins", where abandonment or destruction is an ongoing process; it is a reminder and remainder of a loss that is produced through speculative investment in an urban future (p. 21).

In our field visits, we tried to understand how the idea of a world-class city makes sense to those for whom such cities are planned. One key feature of speculative urbanism in which people are compelled to make sense of and imagine their future by taking risks or looking for highly speculative possibilities is a function of speculative governmentality where the uncertain condition of urban space makes speculation natural and necessary (Goldman, 2023, p. 375).

For instance, Carol Upadhya (2020) shows how the farmers in Amaravati negotiated the speculative logic of land pooling by investing in land and seeing it as an opportunity to accumulate wealth. Further, as they make sense of the uncertainty of their future and the city there is an appropriation of the speculative logic of the world-class city, which is often defined by the caste and so are the narratives of development (Upadhay 2020, 2021).[19] A point that is well documented by Upadhya (2020, 2021) and Ramachandraiah (2016) showing how members of the *Kamma* community benefitted from their political and bureaucratic clout.[20] When we spoke with a woman from the backward caste community about the issue of land pooling, she was hopeful of the risk her family had taken, but her faith was not of absolute certainty.

Therefore, the material and social vision of the future that individuals and communities imagine for themselves are defined by the tangible proximity to the markers of social and economic mobility. The members of the Dalit households we visited were conscious and disappointed with the modest improvement in their lives as compared to others. A young girl that we spoke with had obtained her BTech degree, and she said "one has lost happiness". She further pointed out, "we don't get work opportunities commiserate to our degrees the universities around us develops but not our lives", specifically when the new workspaces accommodated them only as sanitation workers and security guards, despite some people having qualifications for other jobs.

Lastly, we had conversations with the pastoralists who are often discursively constructed as the other, an annoyance to the aesthetics of speed. When we asked members of the pastoralist community in Amaravati, one of them said, "We know that urban spaces are not for us, even before the coming up of the capital".[21] They are conscious of the anxiety that the city and the state confer on them and their ways of living, which is identified with indifference, annoyance and disorder. Pastoralism becomes a symbol of difference further codified in the discursive and built space of the city (Farrar, 2000). To conclude, the postcolonial project of urbanism, such as Amaravati, through the complex imagination of the global city in its built and discursive space, codifies certain practices and ideas that shape subjectivities for the self and others.

Notes

1 During his five-year rule in Andhra Pradesh, Chandra Babu Naidu engaged in a persistent rhetorical comparison of Amaravati and Hyderabad. Naidu often invoked the role he has played in building Hyderabad as a tech city, and this was used as a constant reference point to seek larger legitimacy for building the new capital of Andhra Pradesh from scratch. See, https://www.indiatoday.in/india/story/andhra-capital-amaravati-will-be-bigger-better-than-hyderabad-chandrababu-naidu-at-india-today-conclave-954149-2017-01-10.

2 *Kamma* is a non-Brahmin dominant caste of Andhra Pradesh. Besides, Reddy, Velama and Brahmins, it is one of the prominent landed castes in coastal Andhra Pradesh.

3 The authors' conversation with the women of the Dalit community in Neeru Konda village on 22 March 2023 of the visit.

4 The authors' conversation with the women of the Dalit community in Neeru Konda village on 1 December 2023 of the visit.

5 Jagan Reddy of YSRCP (Yuvajana Sramika Rythu Congress Party).

6 See, Rama Krishna Jagan Puts Amravati on Hold, *The Sunday Guardian*, November 2019. https://sundayguardianlive.com/news/jagan-puts-amaravati-hold.

7 The other two capitals were Visakhapatnam as the executive capital and Kurnool as the judicial capital.

8 See,https://www.hindustantimes.com/india-news/jagans-3-capital-plan-hits-sc-hurdle-101704743770746.html.

9 On 28 March 2014, the Government of India constituted "an expert committee to study various alternatives regarding the location of the new capital for the successor State of Andhra Pradesh and make appropriate recommendations". The five-member expert committee, headed by KC Sivaramakrishnan submitted their final report to the GoI on 27 August 2014.

10 Keng, L. S., & Kumar, T. (2018). From Singapore to Amravati: Developing a Liveable City Together. Singapore: Centre for Liveable Cities. https://www.clc.gov.sg/research-publications/publications/digital-library/view/from-singapore-to-amaravati-developing-a-liveable-city-together (accessed on 14 December 2023).

11 See, Amravati Deep Dive Workshop, 14–15 December 2017, https://crda.ap.gov.in/apcrdaCOMMUNI/media/apcrdadocs/WorkshopPanelPresentations/Amaravati%20Urban%20Design%20Strategy/Urban%20Design%20Strategy.pdf.

12 Government of Andhra Pradesh. *Happy City Blueprint for Amravati: Socio-Economic Mater Plan, April 2018*.
Amaravati,https://crda.ap.gov.in/crda_norifications/NOT04089563/01~Happy%20City%20Blue%20Print%20for%20Amaravati-%20SEMP-compressed.pdf (accessed on 10 December 2023).

13 Amaravati twin tower's design gets Andhra Pradesh CM Naidu nod, *New Indian Express*, 2017, https://www.newindianexpress.com/cities/vijayawada/2017/Aug/29/amaravati-twin-towers-design-gets-andhra-preadesh-cm-naidu-nod-1649448.html.

14 Speaking at the HT Leadership Summit, Chandra Babu Naidu remarked, "Amravati will be bigger and better than Singapore" and "All over the world people will talk about it" (2018: Naidu). See, https://www.hindustantimes.com/singapore-summit/andhra-capital-amaravati-will-be-bigger-better-than-singapore-chandrababu-naidu/story-RD2orApQTnvIsuHGtKYwkO.html.

15 "I will build a bigger, better city than Hyderabad. Amravati, the Andhra Pradesh capital, will be the best city in India". This statement was made by Chandrababu Naidu to the media at the Indian Today Conclave in 2018. See, https://www.indiatoday.in/india/story/andhra-capital-amaravati-will-be-bigger-better-than-hyderabad-chandrababu-naidu-at-india-today-conclave-954149-2017-01-10.

16 Raghavendra, V, Land Allotted to nine thematic cities in Amravati, *The Hindu*, February 2017. https://www.thehindu.com/news/national/andhra-pradesh/land-allotted-to-nine-thematic-cities-in-amaravati/article17327508.ece.

17 World Bank Drops $300 Million Funding for Andhra Pradesh's Amaravati Project, *The Wire*, 2019, https://thewire.in/world/world-bank-amaravati-project-dropped-andhra-pradesh.

18 The Singapore consortium was appointed in 2017 to develop a 6.84-sq. km start-up area including companies such as Ascendas Singbridge Pte Ltd. and Sembcrop Development Ltd.

19 Before land-pooling: Among agricultural labourers men earned an average of 700–2,500 per day and women were able to earn an average of 1,000 rupees minimum per day, working on flexible timing and nature of work was traditional agrarian labour in the village. One woman volunteer at the panchayat office expressed, "Women have lost work because of the loss of agrarian land. Agriculture was one significant livelihood option for women because they could adjust timing as per their domestic work".

20 The assigned land farms were given to landless poor farmers since the 1950s without the right of alienation but were heritable. The compensation package for assigned lands under the LPS was less both in residential and commercial plots as compared to the *patta* landholders (the farmers with ownership rights to alienate the property) who are largely from the upper castes including the *Kammas*. See, Ramachandraiah 2016, p. 6.

21 The authors' conversation with the pastoralist from Kuragallu village.

References

Government of Andhra Pradesh, *Happy City Blueprint for Amaravati: Socio-Economic Master Plan*, April 2018, pp.1–15

Andhra Pradesh Capital Region Development Authority (APCRDA) Act, 2014. Hyderabad: Andhra Pradesh, 2014, pp. 1–24. https://www.indiacode.nic.in/bitstream/123456789/10534/1/crda_act%2C_2014.pdf

Banerjee-Guha, S. (2020). Remaking 'Urban' in twenty-first century neoliberal India. In R. R. Thakur., A. K. Dutt., S. K. Thakur., & G. M. Pomeroy (Eds.), *Urban and Regional Planning and Development* (pp. 83–99). Springer. https://doi.org/10.1007/978-3-030-31776-8_5

Chakrabarty, D. (2000). *Provincializing Europe: Postcolonial Thought and Historical Difference*. New Jersey: Princeton University Press.

Datta, A. (2015). New urban utopias of postcolonial India: Entrepreneurial urbanization in Dholera smart city, Gujarat. *Dialogues in Human Geography*, *5*(1), 3–22. https://doi.org/10.1177/2043820614565748

Datta, A. (2019). Postcolonial urban futures: Imagining and governing India's smart urban age. *Environment and Planning D: Society and Space*, 37(3), 393–410. https://doi.org/10.1177/0263775818800721

Devabhaktuni, S. (2022). Speculation's spatial terms: Imminence and inevitability in amaravati. *Architectural Theory Review*, 26(1), 147–168. https://doi.org/10.1080/13264826.2022.2089185

Farrar, M. E. (2000). Health and beauty in the body politic: Subjectivity and urban space. *Polity*, 33(1), 1–23. https://doi.org/10.2307/3235458

Foucault, M., & Rabinow, P. (1984). *The Foucault Reader*. New York: Pantheon Books.

Ghertner, D. A. (2011). Rule By Aesthetics: World Class City Making in Delhi. In A. Roy, & A. Ong (Eds.), *Worlding Cities: Asian Experiments and the Art of Being Global* (pp. 279–306). Oxford: Wiley-Blackwell.

Goldman, M. (2023). Speculative urbanism and the urban-financial conjuncture: Interrogating the afterlives of the financial crisis. *Environment and Planning A: Economy and Space*, 55(2), 367–387. https://doi.org/10.1177/0308518X211016003

Haines, C. (2011). Cracks in the Façade: Landscapes of Hope and Desire in Dubai. In A. Roy, & A. Ong (Eds.), *Worlding Cities: Asian Experiments and the Art of Being Global* (pp. 160–181). Oxford: Wiley-Blackwell. https://doi.org/10.1002/9781444346800.ch6

Jodhka, S. S. (2002). Nation and village: Images of rural India in Gandhi, Nehru and Ambedkar. *Economic and Political Weekly*, 37(32), 3343–53. https://www.jstor.org/stable/4412466

Khosla, R. (2015). The New Metropolis: Nehru and the Aftermath. *Social Scientist*, 43(3/4), 11–32. https://www.jstor.org/stable/24372933

Kolsto, D. (2019). Amaravati: The making of a disaster capital in Andhra Pradesh? *Economic and Political Weekly*, 54(20), 44–51.

Murray, M. (2022). *Many Urbanisms: Divergent Trajectories of Global City Building* (pp. 166–196). New York Chichester, West Sussex: Columbia University Press. https://doi.org/10.7312/murr20406-0

Nandi, A. (2001). *An Ambiguous Journey to the City: The Village and Other Odd Ruins of the Self in the Indian Imagination*. New Delhi: Oxford University Press.

Narayanan, N. P. (2019). World-class as a provincial construct: Historicizing planning in Colombo and Delhi. *Planning Theory*, 19(3), 268–284. https://doi.org/10.1177/1473095219892999

Nigam, A. (2011). *Desire Named Development*. New Delhi: Penguin Books India.

Ong, A. (2011). Introduction: Worlding Cities, or the art of being global. In A. Roy, & A. Ong (Eds.), *Worlding Cities: Asian Experiments and the Art of Being Global* (pp. 1–26). Oxford: Wiley-Blackwell.

Peck, J., Theodore, N., & Brenner, N. (2009). Neoliberal Urbanism: Models, moments, mutations. *The SAIS Review of International Affairs*, 29(1), 49–66. https://www.jstor.org/stable/27000166

Pohl, L. (2021). Rem(a)inder of Loss: A Lacanian approach to new Urban Ruins. In C. O'Callaghan, & C. Di Feliciantonio (Eds.), *The New Urban Ruins: Vacancy, Urban Politics, and International Experiments in the Post-crisis City* (pp. 21–34). Bristol: Policy Press.

Ramachandraiah, C. (2016). Making of Amaravati: A landscape of speculation and intimidation. *Economic and Political Weekly*, 51(17), 68–75. https://www.jstor.org/stable/44003409

Roohi, S. (2023). No one is self-made: Evolving iterations of giving and shaping of transnational Kamma caste subjectivities. *Ethnography*, 24(3), 352–370. https://doi.org/10.1177/14661381221134442

Roy, A. (2011a). The Blockade of the World-Class City: Dialectical Images of Indian Urbanism. In A. Roy, & A. Ong (Eds.), *Worlding Cities: Asian Experiments and the Art of Being Global* (pp. 259–278). Oxford: Wiley-Blackwell.

Roy, A. (2011b). Conclusion: Postcolonial Urbanism: Speed, Hysteria, Mass Dreams. In A. Roy, & A. Ong (Eds.), *Worlding Cities: Asian Experiments and the Art of Being Global* (pp. 307–335). Oxford: Wiley-Blackwell.

Scott, J. (1998). *Seeing Like a State: How Certain Schemes to Improve Human Conditions Failed*. New Haven and London: Yale University Press.
Shaban, A., & Datta, A. (2019). Towards 'slow' and 'moderated' Urbanism. *Economic and Political Weekly*, 54(48), 36–42.
Sheppard, E., Leitner, H., & Maringanti, A. (2013). Provincializing global Urbanism: A manifesto. *Urban Geography*, 34(7), 893–900.
Sivaramakrishnan, K., & Agrawal, A. (Eds). (2003). *Regional Modernities: The Cultural Politics of Development in India*, Palo Alto, CA: Standford University Press.
Sivaramakrishnan, K. C. et al., (2014). *Report of the Expert Committee, Ministry of Home Affairs, Union of India to Study the Alternatives for a New Capital for the State of Andhra Pradesh*. New Delhi: Government of India. https://www.mha.gov.in/sites/default/files/2023-03/ExpertCommittee_CapitalAP_Final_0%5B1%5D_0%5B1%5D.pdf
Upadhya, C. (2017). Amaravati and the New Andhra: Reterritorialization of a region. *Journal of South Asian Development*, 12(2), 177–202. https://doi.org/10.1177/0973174117712324
Upadhya, C. (2020). Assembling Amaravati: speculative accumulation in a new Indian city. *Economy and Society*, 49(1), 141–169. https://doi.org/10.1080/03085147.2019.1690257
Upadhya, C. (2021). Recasting land: Agrarian Urbanism in Amaravati. *Urbanisation*, 6(1), 82–103. https://doi.org/10.1177/24557471211018304

Index

Pages in *italics* refer to figures and pages in **bold** refer to tables.

For Product Safety Concerns and Information please contact our EU
representative GPSR@taylorandfrancis.com
Taylor & Francis Verlag GmbH, Kaufingerstraße 24, 80331 München, Germany

www.ingramcontent.com/pod-product-compliance
Ingram Content Group UK Ltd.
Pitfield, Milton Keynes, MK11 3LW, UK
UKHW020152200926
475702UK00016B/2666

* 9 7 8 1 0 3 2 6 9 4 3 1 3 *